Contemporary Hinduism

Contemporary Hinduism

Ritual, Culture, and Practice

Edited by

ROBIN RINEHART

A B C ☰ C L I O

Santa Barbara, California   Denver, Colorado   Oxford, England

Library of Congress Cataloging-in-Publication Data
Rinehart, Robin, 1964–
Contemporary Hinduism:
ritual, culture, and practice / Robin Rinehart . . . [et al.].
p. cm.
Includes bibliographical references and index.
ISBN 1-57607-905-8 (hardcover : alk. paper)
ISBN 1-57607-906-6 (e-book)
1. Hinduism. 2. Hinduism—Customs and practices.
3. Hinduism—Social aspects. I. Title.
BL1202.R56 2004
294.5'09'0511—DC22
2003025601

08 07 06 05 04   10 9 8 7 6 5 4 3 2 1

This book is also available on the World Wide Web as an e-book.
Visit abc-clio.com for details.

ABC-CLIO, Inc.
130 Cremona Drive, P.O. Box 1911
Santa Barbara, California 93116-1911

Design by Jane Raese
Text set in New Baskerville

This book is printed on acid-free paper.
Manufactured in the United States of America

Contents

Preface

This book begins by considering the term *Hinduism* and how it came into use. The introductory chapter broadly outlines some of the most important developments in the history of Hinduism. The remaining chapters of this book address specific topics in contemporary Hinduism. Chapter 2, "Hearing and Remembering: Oral and Written Texts in Hinduism," surveys some of the most important oral and written texts used by Hindus today, highlighting how Sanskrit and vernacular texts are used in practice. Chapter 3, "Hindu Devotion," by William Harman, explains how Hindus choose which gods to worship and how they express their devotion. Chapter 4, "The Hindu Ritual Calendar," by A. Whitney Sanford, describes the importance of the lunar calendar in Hindu worship, detailing prayers, vows, festivals, and other religious practices. Chapter 5, "Hindu Ethics," by S. S. Rama Rao Pappu, explains the basis for contemporary Hindu ethics and considers contemporary ethical issues such as family planning. Chapter 6, "Contemporary Hindu Thought," by Brian A. Hatcher, introduces some of the most important Hindu thinkers of recent times. Chapter 7, "Gurus and Groups," by J. E. Llewellyn, highlights the importance of gurus in contemporary Hinduism. Chapter 8, "Caste in Contemporary India," by Eleanor Zelliot, examines how the caste system functions today. Chapter 9, "Voices of Dissent: Gender and Changing Social Values in Hinduism," by Kalpana Kannabiran, focuses on the role of women in Hinduism, highlighting women who have challenged conventional practices. Chapter 10, "Hinduism in Independent India: Fundamentalism and Secularism," by Robert J. Stephens, illustrates the relationship between Hinduism and politics in contemporary India. Chapter 11, "The Environment and Environmental Movements in Hinduism," by George James, considers Hindu attitudes toward the environment and some recent environmental movements in India. Finally, Chapter 12, "Global Hinduism: The

Hindu Diaspora," by Anantanand Rambachan, describes how Hindus have preserved and adapted their traditions as they have migrated to nations around the world.

—Robin Rinehart

Note on Transliteration

Terms from Indian languages that appear frequently in the book are given without italicization. Words from Indian languages appear in the text without diacritic marks. The inherent *−a* in Sanskrit and Sanskrit-derived words is included (except in exclusively Hindi words where it is not pronounced, e.g., *Ramcharitmanas*). The vocalic *r* is transliterated as *ri*. The palatal and retroflex sibilants are transliterated as *sh*.

Proper names of recent figures are typically given with the spelling most commonly used by the person himself or herself. Place names are given with the spelling most commonly used in India at present, with alternate names given when appropriate. Some words in frequent usage in English are spelled as they are best known, e.g., *Swami* rather than *Svami; Brahmin* rather than *Brahman*.

The glossary includes important terms with full diacritical marks and pronunciation.

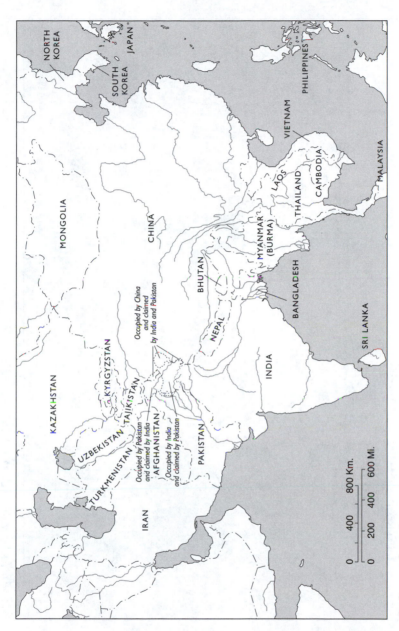

Indian subcontinent

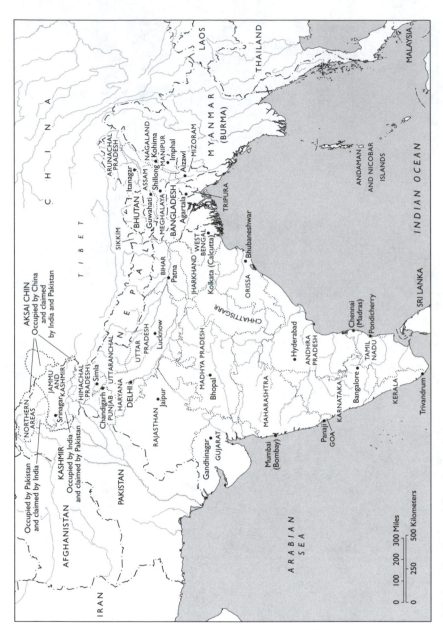

Modern India and Southeast Asia

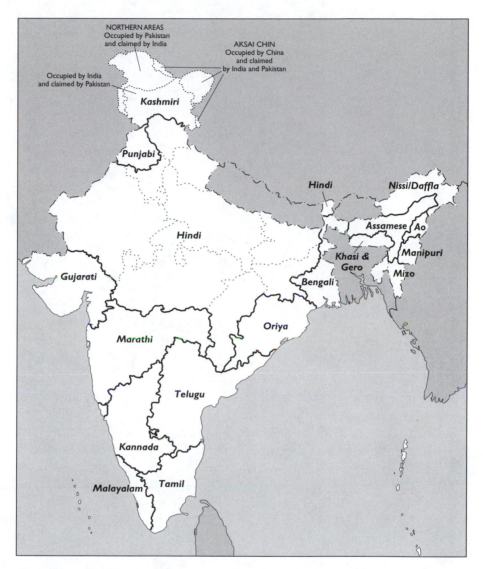

NORTHERN AREAS
Occupied by Pakistan
and claimed by India

AKSAI CHIN
Occupied by China
and claimed
by India and Pakistan

Occupied by India
and claimed by Pakistan

Kashmiri

Punjabi

Hindi

Nissi/Daffla

Assamese Ao

Gujarati

Hindi

Khasi &
Gero

Manipuri

Bengali

Mizo

Oriya

Marathi

Telugu

Kannada

Malayalam   Tamil

Languages of India

Chapter One

Introduction
The Historical Background

ROBIN RINEHART

Hinduism is the name given to the predominant religious tradition in India. In 2001, there were at least eight hundred million Hindus worldwide, making Hinduism the world's third largest religion after Christianity and Islam. *Hindu* was originally a geographic designation Persians used for the people who lived beyond the Sindh River in the northwestern part of the Indian subcontinent, but the term was gradually adopted as a way of distinguishing between practitioners of Islam and others in India. The English term *Hinduism* designating a particular religion did not come into usage until the time that the British ruled India (Hawley 1991). Because the term did not originate among the people who have come to call themselves Hindus, some scholars both in India and the West have argued that it is an artificial label. Even so, millions of people in India and throughout the world identify themselves as Hindus, so it seems reasonable to try to understand what it means to them, keeping in mind that while we may refer to ancient traditions as Hindu, using this name for them is itself a fairly recent practice.

The religion now known as Hinduism encompasses a vast range of practices and beliefs. It has no one founder and no centralized organization. Hindus throughout history have expressed multiple perspectives on the nature of divinity or ultimate reality: monothe-

1

ism, polytheism, monism, even henotheism (belief in one god without denying the existence of others). The richness and diversity of Hinduism mean that we cannot expect to find one list of specific beliefs or practices that would necessarily apply to all Hindus, nor one text that defines all of Hinduism. Generally, Hindus have tended to see diverse views as complementary rather than contradictory. Julius Lipner suggests that we think of Hinduism as being like a banyan tree, which sends out aerial roots that appear to be individual tree trunks even though they are part of the same tree (Lipner 1994, 5–6). In the same way, different aspects of Hinduism may seem to be unconnected or even contradictory, but many Hindus assert that there is an underlying unity amidst the diversity.

In this introductory chapter we will consider the historical origins of Hinduism, focusing on concepts and practices that help us understand the diverse and complex forms of contemporary Hinduism described in later chapters. We will study the surviving texts and archeological evidence, the primary sources of information available. But texts and artifacts can only hint at the human experiences that produced them. Reading a myth about a god in a scholarly translation full of variant readings and footnotes in tiny print is a far cry from listening to a grandmother tell the myth to her grandchildren during the festival celebrating the events of the myth, or hearing the old man in a village who gathers his neighbors in the evenings to tell the tale. Looking at an image of a Hindu god in a photograph or museum exhibit is not the same as seeing it in a temple where devotees prostrate themselves before it, where it is lovingly bathed and decorated by priests, offered sweets and fragrant incense, and praised in chants and songs. We may read about the exploits of the god Krishna as a young child, and ponder the theological implications of his childlike antics, but it is not the same as watching the young boy who proudly acts the part of Krishna in a neighborhood drama. Even the most abstract philosophical speculation on the practice of yoga and meditation has it roots in lived human experience. We may learn from a text the names for different levels of consciousness attained through yoga, but most of us are not likely to experience them firsthand as does the yogi who has abandoned all his possessions to sit in meditation for hours and hours each day as his hair and beard grow long and tangled.

Without firsthand knowledge, however, where do we turn? When trying to understand other religions, many people often want to know what the members of a particular religion "believe." In our quest to learn something about what it means to live as a Hindu in the modern world, we must keep in mind that people typically develop a sense of religious identity through childhood experiences, through families and friends, and through asking questions and seeking explanations during difficult times. Religious allegiance is not simply a matter of choosing to affirm some list of beliefs from a book. Rather, religious faith most commonly develops in the context of sharing traditions as a member of a family and a community. Consider, for example, an American Christian girl celebrating Christmas. She may not know much about the pagan antecedents of Christmas, or its history as a Christian holiday, or debates within biblical scholarship about the circumstances of the birth of Jesus. Although at some point she likely will learn something about the theology of Christmas, her memories of Christmas as an adult will probably center around family memories, special gifts, her favorite decorations and holiday meals, perhaps the first time she questioned whether there really was a Santa Claus. At the heart of every ritual and every belief there lies a set of experiences we cannot fully recover—people comforting one another in times of distress and celebrating occasions of joy, a question, a doubt, a need for reassurance, a treasured family memory. The human experiences that have led to the development of doctrines, myths, and practices are often available to us only in imagination. By the time doctrines and rituals are enshrined in texts, the questions that motivated them may have long since faded, but sometimes the texts are the only evidence we have. But we cannot forget that religious allegiance may sometimes have more to do with treasured childhood and family memories of religious occasions than assent to a specific doctrine or theological treatise. Indeed, much of contemporary Hindu experience revolves around family and community life.

When we turn to the early development of Hinduism, we have to make the best possible use of the evidence we have, even as we acknowledge that we cannot fully recover the experiences that produced that evidence. As we do so, it is important first to examine our own ideas about what a religion is and what areas of life it affects. Many people have argued that Hinduism is not just a religion but a way of life. There is no word in Indian languages that corresponds exactly to the English word *religion*, and the word most commonly used, *dharma*, has a far wider range of meaning. Hindu texts and traditions that examine dharma include ideas about how society should be organized, how kings should rule, even what one should and should not eat and drink and with whom. Furthermore, there has not always been a clear-cut boundary between what we now think of as religion, philosophy, and science, and the purpose of inquiry into these areas was often "religious" in nature. Early Indian mathematics, for example, developed in part out of the need to make precise measurements and calculations in building sites for rituals.

It is also important to remember that religions do not exist in isolation, and that religious thinkers often respond to the ideas of other religions. Hinduism is not the only religion practiced in India, nor indeed the only religion that originated there. Buddhism and Jainism developed in India around the sixth century BCE, and Buddhists, Jains, and Hindus often shared ideas and debated with one another. India has long had contact with other parts of the world through trade by land and sea, by migration, and sometimes by invasion. Islam has been an important feature on the Indian landscape since the eighth century CE. India provided a safe haven for Zoroastrians (known as Parsis in India) when they faced persecution in their native Iran. Sikhism began in the northwestern region of India known as the Punjab in the sixteenth century CE. India is home to both Protestant and Catholic Christian communities, and even had a small Jewish community in the south, though most of India's Jews have now settled in Israel. Thus Hinduism has been in contact with many different religious traditions, and this contact has often inspired reflection, self-definition, and comparison.

Hindu practices and beliefs have not only changed and evolved over the centuries but also vary widely at any given moment in history, whether by region, social status, sectarian group, or simply individual interest. We need only consider the example of contemporary Hinduism in all its diversity to get a sense of how complex a religion is at any given moment, and the role that social, economic, and political issues may play in influencing a religion's development.

The surviving sources of evidence about the early history of Hinduism, however, do not provide as full a view as we have of the contemporary scene. Many of the earliest records of Hinduism are in the Sanskrit ("perfected") language, part of the Indo-European language family. The earliest and most important Sanskrit texts are the Vedas (*Veda* means "knowledge"). Yet the Vedas, like many sources of information on early India, leave many unanswered questions. Although Sanskrit texts are very important, using them to learn about early Hinduism presents challenges. Sanskrit texts were produced throughout the Indian subcontinent, making communication possible across linguistic boundaries, but it is likely that only a small percentage of the population ever actually knew Sanskrit, and only a small number of people had the ability to compose and preserve written texts (whether in Sanskrit or any other language). Sanskrit texts therefore provide only a limited perspective and may at times express an idealized version of belief and practice that might not fully reflect what most people actually thought and did. Nor may everyone agree on what exactly a text means—the Hindu tradition itself has preserved many commentaries on its most important texts that provide multiple and sometimes contradictory interpretations of the same passages.

Even the idea of what a "text" is requires consideration. Modern-day texts typically have a clearly defined content and clearly identified authors. To most modern readers, the term *text* suggests a printed book, which we read silently. Yet much of what we now think of as Hindu texts were first preserved and transmitted as oral traditions meant to be recited and heard, not read from a written or printed page. Each recitation might include variations, elaborations, or explanations of earlier recitations, creating multiple versions of the same traditions with no one clearly identifiable composer or author. When different scribes in different places wrote these traditions in manuscript form, they contributed to the production of multiple versions. When people made new copies of the manuscripts, they introduced even more variations. Most of the printed English translations of Sanskrit texts available today are based on what scholars call "critical editions." Textual scholars compile and compare multiple manuscripts of a text, try to decide which version is the oldest, and then produce a single form of a text. Readers of these critical editions may assume that they are reading the definitive version of the text, but in actual practice the text exists in multiple, variant forms. The variations in some instances may be the most informative parts of the text, because they may reflect the specific interests of a particular time period, or region or group of people. Thus the isolation of an "original" text may prove to be of limited utility. (It is helpful to use the example of a college's publications. Imagine that a college's first catalog, from perhaps a century ago, is used as the most reliable example of the type of courses the college offers, even though a current catalog would obviously better represent the college's current offerings. Both the old catalog and the current catalog are valid examples of the same text—the college's catalog—but represent different times and concerns.)

Although many people are now accustomed to acquiring knowledge through the printed word, for most of human history only small numbers of people have had access to and been able to read the limited number of written manuscripts available. Before the advent of print technology and widespread literacy, most people did not learn about their religious traditions through reading, but through hearing and reciting. Indeed, many of the early Sanskrit texts appear to be written versions of traditions transmitted orally, suggesting that oral tradition was the more important means of communication. Whereas a modern-day reader reads silently, often alone, and may not be able to ask questions, when someone recites or reads aloud to an audience, questions and even debates are possible. Therefore we must be careful not to assume that written materials are necessarily the best or most representative sources of information about Hinduism, or that written materials in ancient India were used in the same way written materials are used today. The earliest Sanskrit texts were the province of a small elite within Indian society, and we have virtually no direct record of the religious experiences of everyone else, particularly women and people considered to be of low social status (who most likely had oral traditions of their own, most of which were never written down). Still, the surviving texts do give us occasional hints about the religious practices of people not of high status, and we will make note of those as we examine the earliest history of Hinduism.

A. L. Basham, an Australian scholar of Indian history and culture, wrote that "the early history of India resembles a jigsaw puzzle with many missing pieces" (Basham 1967, 44) and many others writing about India have used the same image because it so aptly describes the challenge of trying to understand the early development of Hinduism. Texts are an important part of the puzzle, along with archeological and epigraphic evidence, but the interpretation of this evidence is often uncertain or controversial, as we will see when we consider the archeological evidence of the Indus Valley civilization and the textual evidence of the Vedas. As we move closer to our own era, the sources of information increase, with more texts surviving in Sanskrit and India's vernacular languages, as well as outsiders' accounts of Indian culture and religion. But we don't have enough information to form a complete explanation of how Hinduism has evolved over the centuries—there are still many missing pieces of the puzzle, and not everyone agrees about what to do with the pieces we do have. One challenge is that some of the earliest studies of Hinduism, using limited sources, created portrayals of Hinduism that had little to do with actual contemporary practices. Despite their limitations, these portrayals continue to shape attitudes toward Hinduism.

Many early Western scholars of Hinduism studied ancient Sanskrit texts to find Hindu doctrines, hoping this would provide a clear picture of what Hinduism "really" was. This approach rests on the problematic assumptions that the essence of Hinduism lies in some doctrine or set of doctrines, and that the most accurate statement of such doctrines is to be found in the most ancient texts. However, regardless of how much Hindus may respect and revere ancient texts such as the Vedas, the actual content of those texts may have little connection with their beliefs or practices. As we shall see, for many people being Hindu is not so much believing a particular doctrine (though doctrine may be important) as it is engaging in traditional practices. In other words, orthopraxy (following correct practice) is often more important than orthodoxy (following correct doctrine). By assuming that the most ancient text must somehow present the most accurate picture of a religious tradition, early Western studies of Hinduism created a picture of the religion that was very much at odds with Hinduism as Hindus actually practiced it, leading some scholars to criticize the Hinduism of their own era as debased or degenerate because it did not follow the most ancient texts.

Yet another complication is the fact that there is a long history in the Western world of stereotyping and sometimes misrepresenting particular dimensions of Hinduism. Many early Western accounts of Hinduism emphasized aspects of practice that struck westerners as bizarre and exotic, such as an ash-smeared yogi lying on a bed of nails or contorted into a strange position, rather than describing more typical practices. Westerners have also sometimes highlighted what they considered to be negative dimensions of Hinduism, hoping to demonstrate the superiority of their own religious perspective. While the British ruled India, many Western writers highlighted the practice of sati, in which a widow immolates herself on her husband's funeral pyre. However, sati was not a widespread practice in India. Many Hindus themselves were opposed to it and sought to stop it altogether. Thus a relatively infrequent practice, which many Hindus rejected, was taken by some outsiders as representative of Hinduism.

Even ordinary everyday activities such as worshiping images of gods and goddesses have been portrayed as strange and fantastic, focusing on the appearance of images unfamiliar to westerners without making much effort to understand what lies behind the use of such images or comparing their use to practices and beliefs more familiar to non-Hindus. Some westerners tend to characterize India as part of a mythical, "mystic East" and assume that people in India practice a kind of other-worldly spirituality with little regard for mundane matters, but in fact there is a wide range of interest in spiritual matters among Indian people, just as there is virtually anywhere else in the world. Some people are more interested and more involved than others, some people may be deeply faithful, others may have doubts, and some may be heavily involved at certain periods in their lives and less involved at others. As with any religion, it is important to avoid stereotypes and be very cautious about overgeneralizing.

This is especially important for the Indian subcontinent, a region of great political, linguistic, and geographic diversity. For most of its history, India has been divided into a variety of kingdoms and territories, each with its own traditions. The area in which Hinduism developed stretches beyond the boundaries of the current nation of India to include Pakistan, Bangladesh, Sikkim, Nepal, and Bhutan. Through trade, travel, and immigration, Hindu traditions have reached into Southeast Asia and are now found worldwide with immigration and the growth of the Hindu diaspora. Adding to the complexity is the great number of languages used in the Indian subcontinent: Indo-Aryan languages, spoken primarily in the north (such as Hindi, Punjabi, and Bengali); Dravidian languages, spoken primarily in the south (Tamil, Telugu, Malayalam, Kannada); and Austro-Asiatic languages, spoken by tribal peoples in northeast and central India. Today, India's Constitution lists eighteen different languages in use in the country.

The Indus Valley Civilization and the Vedas

One of the most important and most controversial sources of information about the early development of Indian civilization and Hinduism is the archeological remains of the Indus Valley (or Harappan) civilization located in the northwest of the subcontinent in the area around the Indus River and beyond. The Indus Valley civilization was at its peak from about 2300–2000 BCE, then went into decline and essentially disappeared by 1500 BCE. The archeological evidence reveals a well-developed, primarily urban society. The two main early excavation sites, Harappa and Mohenjo Daro, were planned cities with water and sewer systems. British and Indian archeologists first began to excavate Indus Valley sites after they were discovered in the 1920s. Archeologists continue to identify additional sites beyond the immediate area of the Indus Valley, both in Pakistan and India, and many of these have yet to be fully excavated.

The first analyses of this civilization and its people proposed by archeologists have been called into question in recent years, and a number of debates continue on both technical and political grounds. The major points of controversy concern who the people of the Indus Valley were and what relation they had to a group of people who called themselves Aryans. When archeologists first began to explore the Indus Valley sites, scholars already knew a fair amount about the Aryans. Scholars had established through studying the Vedas that Sanskrit was part of the Indo-European language family, suggesting that the Aryans (who preserved the Vedas) had connections with people of central Asia and the Middle East (some of whom migrated into Europe) who also spoke Indo-European languages. (The traditions of the Vedas, for example, bear many similarities to the ancient Iranian religion of Zoroastrianism.) Some passages in the Vedas mention conflict with another group, and many people took this group to be the people of the Indus Valley, though the conflict may have been between rival groups of Aryans.

The greatest mystery, however, concerns the connections between the Indus Valley people and the Aryans. Initially scholars argued that the Aryans were nomadic people from somewhere in central Asia who invaded the Indus Valley and contributed to the eventual decline and disappearance of the earlier civilization. More recently, this invasion theory has been discredited. Many scholars now believe it more likely that the Aryans gradually migrated into the area of the Indus Valley at the time the civilization was already in decline (ca. 1900–1200 BCE). However, others, often called "indigenous Aryanists," have argued that the Aryans themselves were the inhabitants of the Indus Valley sites and did not come from outside India. The indigenous Aryanists have not yet produced a great deal of evidence to support their claim, and critics of this position suggest that it is based less on solid archeological evidence than it is on political concerns, such as the desire to demonstrate that all Indian traditions originated within India and not outside. Nonetheless, it has become clear that the original interpretation of the relation between the Indus Valley culture and Aryan culture is more complex than originally thought, and not yet fully understood.

The Indus Valley people used a script that has been preserved on seals and copper plates, but because the script has not yet been deciphered, it is unclear what type of language the Indus Valley people spoke. One widely held theory is that they spoke an early form of the Dravidian languages and that they gradually migrated to the southern portion of the Indian subcontinent, where Dravid-

Bathing tank at Mohenjo Daro, Indus Valley.
ROBIN RINEHART

ian languages are spoken today. The indigenous Aryanist argument, however, is that the Indus Valley people spoke some form of Sanskrit. As these debates continue, the most intriguing dimension of the Indus Valley civilization for the history of Hinduism remains the connection between particular structures and images found there and subsequent practices in Hinduism. For example, seals, figurines, and other artifacts found throughout the Indus Valley include images of humans and animals that resemble representations of gods and goddesses who are important later in Hinduism. The major towns and cities of the Indus Valley had water and sewer systems, suggesting a concern with purity and cleanliness, a feature of later Hinduism. There were also centrally located bathing tanks, very similar to those found outside Hindu temples in south India. Although it is not yet possible to reach definite answers about the people of the Indus Valley and their fate, it does seem clear that their civilization played an important role in the development of Hinduism.

The Vedas and Cosmic Sound

There are many unanswered questions about the religion of the Indus Valley, but we know far more about the Aryans from the Vedas, a set of four compositions preserved orally. Although printed editions of the Vedas are now available in the original Sanskrit as well as in translation, it is essential to remember that the Aryans memorized the Vedas and passed them down orally from generation to generation. The Aryans used the verses of the Vedas as part of a system of ritual sacrifice understood to guarantee the proper functioning of the world.

There are four *samhitas* (collections) of hymns that include the term *Veda* in their titles: the Rig Veda, Yajur Veda, Sama Veda, and Atharva Veda. (The term *Veda* is often used to refer specifically to these four samhitas or collections, but it may also refer to these four samhitas along with the texts that were appended to them: the Brahmanas, the Aranyakas, and the Upanishads, which are discussed later.) The Yajur Veda and Sama Veda contain much material from the Rig Veda, though organized differently. The fourth, the Atharva Veda, is focused more on rites for health, financial success, and children. As with many other religious texts throughout the world, there are different views about the origins of the Vedas. Within the Hindu tradition itself the view is that the Vedas are not the product of human composition. Some Hindu sources describe them as the linguistic representation of the sounds that create and sustain the cosmos; other Hindu sources describe them as the creation of a god. Textual scholars, however, have generally assumed that they were composed by humans, and they look at the language and other details of the Vedas to try to determine when and where they might have been composed. Most agree that the earliest and most important of the four Vedas, the Rig Veda, was probably composed sometime between 1500 and 1200 BCE in the northwestern region of the subcontinent.

The primary use of the hymns of the Vedas is in rituals that involve offering various substances into a sacrificial fire. Because the verses themselves are understood to represent sounds that create and sustain the cosmos, they are considered to be enormously powerful, and those who know and recite these hymns can harness that creative power through the precise performance of various sacrifices. Thus the Aryans placed enormous emphasis on exact memorization and transmission of the Vedas, and although there are variant versions of some passages in the Vedas, for the most part they were preserved with very little of the change typically associated with orally transmitted traditions. Even so, the Vedic hymns do not provide a complete picture of the mythology of the Aryans; many hymns refer to what are clearly longer and more detailed myths that though they are now lost must have been familiar to the Aryans, and were transmitted orally. Many of the Vedic hymns praise various gods (and a few goddesses), describing their exploits and their association with particular dimensions of the functioning of the cosmos. Recitation of these hymns in the proper ritual context was meant to help one be in harmony with or gain power over the forces the particular god controlled.

A number of hymns of the Rig Veda are addressed to Indra, a powerful god who reigns over the region between the earth and sky, slaying enemies with his thunderbolt. Indra is a heroic figure celebrated for overcoming a serpent-demon who had captured the waters of life, as well as for his fondness for the exhilarating juice made from the soma plant. The plant soma, too, is invoked as a god in Vedic hymns, and preparation and consumption of soma extract was an important part of some Vedic rituals. (The identity of the soma plant remains uncertain; it may have had intoxicating or hallucinogenic properties and is described in the Vedas as conferring immortality.) Agni, the god of fire, is another important figure in Vedic mythology. Vedic rituals center on making offerings of various substances (such as grains, dairy products, and soma) into a fire while chanting the appropriate Vedic hymns. Agni is understood to be present in the sacrificial fire itself, carrying the offerings to their destination and bringing the gods to the sacrifice. Aryan families who performed Vedic rituals needed to maintain at least one sacrificial fire.

In addition to gods and a few goddesses associated with particular dimensions of the functioning of the cosmos, the Vedic hymns express a cosmic principle known as *rita,* which is governed by the kingly god Varuna. Rita is law, rule, the proper order of the cosmos, the idea that things fit together. Vedic ritual, then, is a means of keeping one's actions in line with rita and making sure the world functions smoothly in the way it was meant to when it was created. There is a wide range of rituals, from those performed daily and seasonally by individuals for the well-being of family and business, to much more elaborate undertakings stretching several days or more and requiring a number of specialists. The Vedic system emphasizes the regular, correct performance of particular ritual practices.

Vedic ritual needed no fixed place of worship, although some of the more complex rituals involved construction of a temporary altar. Most important was the proper recitation of the Vedic hymns used in the ritual, which required years of training to memorize the verses and the correct means of reciting them. Different families or clans would focus on one or more specific Vedas. Over time it seems that this ritual system became so complex that specialist priests were required to ensure the proper performance of the more elaborate rituals. This also led to the development, beginning around the eighth century BCE, of a set of texts known as the Brahmanas, which provide detailed instruction on preparing and performing rituals. Particular Brahmanas are appended to particular Veda samhitas. Around the same time, a third class of texts known as Aranyakas came about as well, largely concerned with further discussions of ritual and esoteric speculation, and these too were appended to particular Veda samhitas.

The more elaborate Vedic rituals required that a husband and wife sponsor and participate in them. Whereas the benefit of the ritual was understood to come to the married couple, the major responsibility for the ritual's correct performance fell on the male specialist priests hired to conduct the rite. Most scholars believe that women had a somewhat important role in the rituals of the early Vedic period, but that as Vedic ritual became more complex, the importance of women's role diminished. During this period there likely were other ritual traditions in which women participated but of which we have no surviving record.

When the Brahmanas and Aranyakas were composed, major changes were taking place within the society of northern India. As urban centers developed along the Ganges River through northern India, different groups intermingled and shared social and religious practices, creating a more complex society. The Vedas refer to various groups of people with whom the Aryans came into contact and conflict, and some of these people's traditions became a part of Aryan culture as the groups intermingled. There are conflicting views about whether these were rival groups of Aryans who had perhaps migrated into the subcontinent at different times, the surviving people of the Indus Valley, other indigenous groups, or some combination. This point aside, it seems clear that the Aryans were not the only people on the scene and that they were interested in explaining the complexity of their society in a way that fit into the worldview of the Vedas.

One of the most commonly noted characteristics of Hindu society is the caste system, and there is evidence for some early (and perhaps idealized) forms of this system of social organization in the Rig Veda itself. A hymn from the tenth chapter describes the gods' sacrifice of a primeval man. The sacrifice of the man's body produced a variety of things, including the Vedas themselves, the moon and sun, Indra and Agni, heaven, earth, and the sky. Different classes of people, divided into four classes, or *varnas,* were created out of this sacrifice as well. From the primeval man's mouth were made Brahmins, from his shoulders Kshatriyas, from his thighs Vaishyas, and from his feet, Shudras. Though this particular hymn does not describe the role of each of these classes, we know from other sources that each varna was in theory associated with particular occupations that the males of that varna were to perform. Brahmins were priests, experts in the performance of Vedic ritual, and Kshatriyas were noblemen—kings and soldiers. Vaishyas were merchants and traders, and Shudras were servants. The first three groups could study the Vedas, but the fourth group, Shudras, could not. This hymn thus describes differences among people and their capabilities and responsibilities as a fundamental feature of the creation of the world, an idea that would develop more fully in subsequent Indian culture. How exactly these early ideas of social organization relate to the caste system as it later developed is not fully clear; the scheme of social organization may have come from Indo-European culture, Indus Valley culture, or perhaps the traditions of another indigenous group (Bryant 2001, 164–165).

As the society of northern India grew more complex, people began to ask a variety of questions about the efficacy of the intricate

Vedic rituals, and larger questions about the origin, nature, and purpose of the universe and life itself. A very famous hymn from the Rig Veda's tenth chapter illustrates the growing speculative trend, asking how creation first came about and whether the gods themselves even know because they were born after the creation of the universe. The closing lines read, "No one knows whence this creation has come into being. Perhaps it formed itself. Perhaps not. Only he who looks down from the highest heaven truly knows. Or maybe he does not know" (Mahony 1998, 57). Hindu tradition preserves a number of different accounts of creation, and this particular hymn shows a willingness to acknowledge that it may not be possible to know precisely how the universe came into existence.

The Upanishads

The idea that proper ritual technique allows an individual to tap into the powers that govern the universe was fundamental to the Vedic worldview. Thus the rituals allow participants to establish a connection between themselves and the larger world beyond them. Many Vedic hymns draw connections among humans, gods, and the universe beyond. The hymn about the sacrifice of the primeval man, for example, declares that animals, people, the Vedic hymns, even the gods, are all made from the same substance and thus have something in common. The Vedas also developed the concept of a universal power, *brahman,* which manifested itself in ritual recitation of Vedic hymns (Mahony 1998, 115). (Be careful not to confuse brahman with Brahmin, the varna, or Brahmana, the texts). Brahman, the source of being itself, connected or perhaps even constituted the different elements of the universe. In this respect it was thus quite similar to the idea of rita, but over time brahman became the more dominant concept (Mahony 1998, 118–119). The idea that all things share a common foundation and some common substance, and are therefore connected, was central to Vedic thought.

The concept of the fundamental interconnectedness of all things was further elaborated in yet another group of texts appended to the Vedas, the Upanishads (the exact meaning of the word *Upan-*

ishad is disputed, but it may mean "correspondences," or refer to the act of sitting before a teacher). Like the four Vedas, the Upanishads circulated orally before being written down. There is no fixed list of Upanishads, and new Upanishads continue to be composed. The principal Upanishads, however, were compiled from about the seventh century BCE until the first century BCE and, like the Brahmanas and Aranyakas, are appended to particular Vedas. The Upanishads express a diverse range of ideas but share a general concern with gaining knowledge about the self and the universe through contemplation rather than rote performance of the rituals of the Vedas.

In the Upanishads we find ideas that remain central in many strands of Hindu thought to the present. The Upanishads developed at a time of social, political, and religious change when north Indian society was becoming increasingly urbanized and larger portions of territory came under unified political control. Patrick Olivelle, a scholar who has done extensive study and translation of the Upanishads, points out that with relatively stable states ruled by kings and increased agricultural production, trade and travel became much easier (Olivelle 1992, 31). In this environment, a new form of religious practice known as renunciation began to flourish. There were people (nearly all men) who chose to renounce the increasingly complex society in which they lived, retire to the forests, and devote themselves to acquiring spiritual knowledge. The Upanishads are in part a record of their efforts—their questions, conversations, and debates, the techniques and concepts they developed, and their discussions of these matters with people who were not renouncers. Over time, the practice of renunciation, which involved formally severing one's ties to family, caste, and possessions, living a celibate life totally dependent on others for food and other basic necessities, became an important component of Indian culture, playing a role not only in the Upanishads but also contributing to the development of Buddhism and Jainism.

Whereas the Vedas were predominantly the province of the Brahmin class, the Upanishads include contributions from Kshatriyas (the noble/warrior class) and quite likely incorporate ideas from non-Aryan sources as well. A common theme through the Upanishads is a shift from the focus on external acts of sacrifice as described in the Vedas to notions of internal sacrifice performed through control of various bodily functions. This internalized sacrifice was thought to lead to knowledge of ultimate reality, or brahman. The earlier Vedic idea of the common source and interconnectedness of all things was maintained, but with an increasing emphasis on the correlations or correspondences between an individual's body parts and functions and natural forces. The teachers of the Upanishads saw correspondences, for example, between the organs of speech, breath, sight, hearing, and thought, and fire, wind, the sun, the directions, and the moon. Perhaps the most important correspondence or correlation drawn in the Upanishads, however, is that between the individual self, or *atman*, and brahman.

The concepts of atman and brahman are illustrated in a discussion between a father, Uddalaka Aruni, and his son, Shvetaketu, recorded in the Chandogya Upanishad. When Shvetaketu returned home after twelve years of study of the Vedas, his father found him arrogant and began questioning him to see if he had really understood anything he had learned. Perhaps worried that his son's studies went no further than rote memorization, Uddalaka Aruni asked his son if he had learned about how one hears and thinks that which has not been heard or thought before. Shvetaketu had no answer, so Uddalaka responded with many examples, the first of which involved a lump of clay. According to Uddalaka, a person needs only to see one lump of clay in order to grasp the general concept of clay, and that concept allows the person to identify everything made of clay. The idea or concept of clay itself thus enables a person to think about something not thought about before—namely, other things made of clay besides the lump one has seen. Uddalaka's teaching illustrates a concern with identifying specific things and recognizing their particularity through naming them, but also remembering the common origins and substances of different things that may be obscured by their specific names and features. This contrast between the name of a thing and its essence (e.g., a specific lump of clay and the concept of clay itself) serves as an introduction to Uddalaka's teaching on the essence of the person—the atman—and the other characteristics of people that obscure this essence.

In a very famous episode, Uddalaka instructed his son to take a piece of salt, put it in water, and bring it to him the next day. Uddalaka then told Shvetaketu to bring him the piece of salt, but of course he couldn't because it had dissolved. Yet when Shvetaketu sipped the water, it all tasted salty. That, Uddalaka told his son, is like the atman within a person—it cannot necessarily be specifically identified, yet it is there, and it is what you are in essence (Olivelle 1996, 148–155). To know oneself, then, is to discover one's atman. The goal of religious practice in the Upanishads thus involves uncovering one's true identity, the atman. To do so requires that one give up the more typical sense of identity people have based upon their physical form and mental functions. As part of the foundation of being itself, or brahman, the atman is eternal even though it is confined within a physical form subject to death. Because the atman is a part of brahman itself, recognizing the atman within also opens a person to knowledge about the entire universe.

Behind all this speculation about the atman and brahman and everything in between lies the desire not simply to know about but to apprehend directly the atman as one's true identity. Whereas Vedic ritual was primarily geared toward making one's life on earth run smoothly, with occasional references to the desire to live in the heavens with the gods after death, perhaps becoming immortal, the Upanishads show an increasing interest in determining exactly what happens when one dies and how one's actions affect the afterlife. The atman, as part of brahman, the very foundation of being, is eternal and indestructible. How then does it come to be contained within an impermanent body, and what happens to it when the body dies? It was in the context of answering these questions that the teachers of the Upanishads introduced the ideas of karma and rebirth, which would remain central to Hindu thought thereafter.

Karma and Samsara

In the Brihadaranyaka Upanishad, a sage named Yajnavalkya taught that as a person is dying and the senses gradually cease to function, the atman leaves the body and moves on to a new one, just as a caterpillar moves from one blade of grass to another (Olivelle

1996, 64). The moral quality of a person's actions determine where the atman will go—good actions lead to a better rebirth, bad actions to a worse one. Yajnavalkya linked action to desire, because desire motivates people to act to satisfy their desires. Their actions then lead to rebirth in either this world or some other world. But a person who does not have desires instead returns to brahman.

These ideas in the Upanishads are the basis of the doctrine of karma, which later Indian thinkers elaborated more fully. The word *karma* literally refers to an act, and by extension it implies the effects or "fruits" of that action. The particular nature of an action, whether good or bad, determines whether the "fruits" of the action will ripen, or achieve fruition, in this or another lifetime. What happens to the atman at death is determined by whatever actions have not yet ripened or had an effect. From one lifetime to the next, the atman is confined within particular bodies—animal, human, even divine—each rebirth determined by karma. In some Upanishads, this cycle of death and rebirth is called *samsara*. A person's movement through samsara is governed by karma, and escape from samsara, known as *moksha*, is possible through direct knowledge of the atman. Once a person recognizes the atman as his or her true identity, desires cease, and the atman merges back into brahman rather than being born again.

The idea that people tend to maintain a false sense of self and therefore remain ignorant of their true identity runs through the Upanishads and much later Hindu thought. People identify themselves by name, family status, family, occupation, and social class rather than by the eternal atman. They allow their actions to be dictated by various desires generated by this false and ultimately impermanent sense of identity. Yajnavalkya taught that knowledge of the atman comes to the person who has no desires. But how is it possible to rid oneself of desires? People, after all, desire the most basic things—food, water, clothing, shelter, the welfare of their family, the company of others. If simply pursuing the most basic needs binds a person to samsara or the cycle of death and rebirth, how can one live? The answer lies in a variety of techniques that came to be known as yoga. In its most basic sense *yoga* means joining, harnessing, or yoking things together; yoga and the English word "yoke" have the same origin.

Yoga

Although to many westerners the word *yoga* may evoke images of stretches and poses for relaxation and stress reduction, yoga in its original sense is a spiritual practice whose primary goal is self-knowledge. Breathing exercises, particular physical postures, maintaining celibacy, and meditative exercises to control the senses and still the mind may all be a part of yogic practice, the goal of which is to control desire. One of the later Upanishads, the Shvetashvatara, teaches that practitioners of yoga should seek a clean, sheltered, secluded spot, learn to control their breath, and keep their minds under control. The practice of yoga is likened to a fire that tempers the body and frees people from sickness, old age, and suffering (Olivelle 1996, 256). Yogic practice in a sense parallels Vedic ritual; Vedic ritual involved offering objects into a fire, whereas yogic practice means creating a fire within that burns away one's false sense of identity to reveal the true identity of atman. Extending the fire imagery, Hindu tradition explains that the practice of yoga generates heat. Indeed, one of the words for meditative practice and physical austerities is *tapas,* or "heat." Anyone may take up the practice of yoga, but renouncers are best suited to it because they have given up ties to family and occupation and may devote all their energies to discovering the atman within.

The person who comes to know atman is freed from samsara, but there are different views in the Upanishads about the experience of moksha. The earlier Upanishads generally portray moksha as an impersonal experience in which the atman, freed from the body and mind, simply merges back into the larger, impersonal reality of brahman. But some of the later Upanishads characterize brahman in more theistic or godlike terms, suggesting that moksha is union with a particular god. Hindu thinkers continued to debate the question of what moksha is like in the following centuries, with some arguing that the atman merges completely and indistinguishably into brahman, and others arguing that the atman retains some kind of distinct identity even while merged in brahman, allowing it to recognize that it has achieved release from samsara.

Dharma

By the time that the principal Upanishads had been composed, as the first millennium BCE came to a close, Hindu tradition had already developed a wide range of ideas about human potential and responsibilities in this life and lives beyond. There were the ideals of Vedic society, emphasizing the importance of marriage, family, and performing Vedic rituals properly. But there was also the ideal of renunciation, which on the surface, at least, appears to be a direct challenge to Vedic norms because one of the things a renouncer gives up is the performance of Vedic ritual. In fact, many scholars of Hinduism point to a tension between the ideal figure of the male householder who marries, has children, and performs the proper Vedic rituals, and the male renouncer, who severs all his ties to family and possessions and stops performing Vedic rituals in favor of yogic practice. It became increasingly common for Hindu thinkers to propose models that accommodated the whole range of ideals more or less comfortably rather than seeing them as conflicting. One means of doing so was through the concept of *dharma.* Dharma, from a verbal root meaning "to hold" or "to bear," broadly encompasses duty, responsibility, morality, law, and religion. Like the earlier concept of rita found in the Vedas, it implies the way things ought to be, a universal order or principle. Indeed, some Hindus use the term *sanatana dharma,* or "eternal" dharma, to refer to their religion.

A vast body of Sanskrit literature was compiled around this time, known as the Dharmasutras and Dharmashastras (*sutras* are a series of short sentences; *shastras* are more detailed treatises), explaining dharma and the responsibilities it entails. One of the most important and well-known dharma texts is the Laws of Manu (known in Sanskrit as the *Manavadharmashastra* or the *Manusmriti*), probably fully compiled by about 100 or 200 CE. The Laws of Manu and other dharma texts link the idea of karma not only to the yoga practice of the renouncers but also to the actions of people living within society. The concerns of the dharma literature reveal how the relatively abstract concepts of karma and rebirth as illustrated in the Upanishads came to have broader social implications when applied to Hindu society as a whole.

If everyone is in samsara, the cycle of death and rebirth, and not everyone is destined to escape samsara and attain moksha at the end of this lifetime, how can people know how their actions will affect their rebirth? The dharma literature explains that dharma dictates what a person should do according to certain basic moral and ethical principles, and to specific factors such as stage of life, sex, and social status or one's position within the caste system. Thus there are general principles of dharma that apply to everyone, as well as specific principles of dharma depending on one's place in society. By performing actions in accordance with one's dharma, a person's "unripened" karma at death leads to rebirth in a better state. Conversely, a person who did not act in accord with dharma would create a store of unripened karma that would lead to rebirth in a worse state.

The Laws of Manu ease the tension between the ideal of being a householder living within society and that of the renouncer who rejects society by relegating the two ideals to different stages of life under the dictates of the concept of *varnashramadharma*. Varnashramadharma is a compound of three words: varna, *ashrama* (one's stage in this life), and dharma. According to this concept, individuals have duties according to caste, stage of life, and the more general ethical edicts of dharma. The four varnas—Brahmin, Kshatriya, Vaishya, and Shudra—had been described centuries earlier in the Vedas, and the Laws of Manu enumerate the duties of men of each of the four varnas. The top three, Brahmin, Kshatriya, and Vaishya, are known as the "twice-born" because they are allowed to study the Vedas and are initiated into Vedic study through a ritual involving a symbolic second birth (hence the name "twice-born"). It is the responsibility of Brahmins to teach and recite the Vedas and to perform Vedic rituals for themselves and others. Brahmins are to be given great respect, and killing a Brahmin is one of the greatest offenses against dharma possible. It should come as no surprise that the authors and compilers of the dharma literature were themselves Brahmins. Kshatriya men are to rule and serve as soldiers, Vaishya men are to engage in trade and farming, and men of the fourth varna, the Shudras, are to serve everyone else. In actual practice not everyone could follow the prescribed occupation for their varna, and the Laws of Manu acknowledge this reality by detailing situations in which men may follow an occupation outside that mandated for one's varna, with Brahmins being accorded the greatest flexibility.

Although women have caste identity just as men do, their responsibilities are not as clearly distinguished by varna as are men's, and many Hindu texts equate women with Shudras, meaning that their primary responsibility is to serve. The Laws of Manu state that women are due great respect and that men must provide for them, but also that women must be obedient to their fathers, husbands, and their sons. The stages of life, or ashramas, are different for women and men. For women, the stages are determined by relationships to males: daughter, then wife and mother, and widow should a woman's husband die before she does.

For twice-born men, the dharma literature prescribes four ashramas. First, a young man should live as a celibate student; then he should marry, produce children, and live as a householder; when his children are old enough to start their own families, he should retire to the forest and devote more time to spiritual pursuits (a wife may accompany her husband during this stage); finally, he should sever all ties to his family and become a renouncer. The ashrama system for twice-born men thus suggests that the householder stage is the appropriate time for performing Vedic rituals, and the two later stages allow one to move away from performance of ritual and focus on the ideas and practices advocated in the Upanishads. Here we must remember that religious texts often present ideals that were not necessarily adopted in practice. The vast majority of men chose to remain householders for their entire lives, with only a few opting for renunciation, and some men who chose to become renouncers did so well before the age recommended in the dharma texts. Still, the ashrama system provided one means of structuring a wide range of lived experience, if more in theory than in practice.

The rules of dharma also govern marriage and male/female relationships. Generally men were to marry within their own varna, though they could choose a wife from a lower varna. The dharma texts, composed by Brahmin men, reveal an ambivalence about women. Men are enjoined to respect and honor women, but they are also to guard them, in part to make sure that they remain faithful (Doniger 1991, 197–210). A wife's primary duty is to bear children, especially sons. Sons are highly valued because they inherit property, continue to contribute to the family economy even after they are married (whereas daughters go to their husbands' homes), and perform funerary rituals for their parents. Women themselves often preferred sons to daughters, in part because having a son improved a woman's status with her husband's family. Many Hindus today still express a preference for sons over daughters.

Generally the dharma texts express the principle that women are to be honored and revered in situations in which their sexuality is under control, especially as mothers. Women are considered dangerous when not guarded by a male because, according to the dharma texts, they are easily corruptible and inclined toward lust and malice. In a patrilineal society where property and inheritance are passed down through male lines, knowing the identity of a child's father is critical, further cementing ideas about the importance of men keeping women under control.

Stephanie Jamison, in a study of portrayals of women in Sanskrit literature, suggests that the ambivalence about women expressed in Sanskrit texts may in part derive from the tension between the householder and renouncer ideals for men. On the one hand, men must marry and produce sons. But Hindu tradition also values the renouncer who, as part of his quest to forsake desires entirely, must remain celibate. As in many cultures, Hindu tradition linked loss of semen with loss of power in general; in yogic practice, retention of semen is thought to increase one's spiritual and intellectual capacity. Acting upon sexual desire, of course, has karmic consequences that may further bind a person to the cycle of death and rebirth. The ashrama or life-stage system was an idealized solution to the problem of these conflicting ideals; Jamison suggests that another component to the solution is to attribute active sexuality to women and place men in a more detached, passive role. According to this view, women are lustful and sexually aggressive; men may succumb to them and fulfill their responsibility to bear sons, but by modeling themselves as the passive figures, they may still work toward the goals of asceticism and renunciation even while in the householder stage of life (Jamison 1996, 16–17). With this model of women as aggressors, the karmic consequences of desire fall more heavily on women than men. Of course the dharma texts provide us with only the limited viewpoint of Brahmin males, and how men and women chose to put these ideals into practice likely varied dramatically. Nonetheless, the idea that female sexuality is a positive force only when under male control remained important in later Hindu thought, and this religious expression of male superiority provided justification for the patriarchal character of Indian society.

In addition to dictates about how men and women should interact with one another, the dharma texts also provide instructions on what kinds of food to eat, who should prepare it, and with whom one may eat. One's diet, therefore, has karmic consequences. To what extent people may have followed these rules is difficult to determine; the Laws of Manu, for example, state that twice-born men should not eat garlic, onions, or fish, among other things, yet those are key ingredients in the typical diets of many regions of India. The dharma literature does not advocate a strictly vegetarian diet but includes detailed instructions about what kinds of meat are permissible and how they should be prepared (Doniger 1991, 99–104). The extent to which the dharma text regulations on diet reflect actual practice at the time is uncertain; the regulations may have been most important for people of high caste status. If we take the range of dietary traditions throughout India today as a guide, it is likely that there was a great deal of variety in dietary practices across regional and caste lines. One very well-known feature of Hindu dietary regulations is the prohibition against eating beef, which is connected with the reverence shown to the cow. Recent research by D. N. Jha suggests that beef was, in fact, part of the Indian diet in earlier times, but Jha's work has met with great opposition from some conservative Hindu leaders (Jha 2002).

Rules about food reflect a larger concern about the relative state of purity or pollution of the individual. The dharma texts devote much space to defining activities that allow the twice-born man to maintain purity, activities that are polluting, and the means of removing pollution. Bodily functions are a common source of pollution; the Laws of Manu provide detailed explanations on how to bathe, how to clean one's mouth before and after eating, and even how to urinate and defecate. There are also rules governing when a husband and wife may engage in sexual intercourse. Female bodily functions are particularly polluting; a twice-born man is not to eat with or lie on the same bed as his wife when she is menstruating. Childbirth, too, creates pollution, and women must undergo a period of purification after giving birth. Even though producing children was highly valued, women of childbearing age thus were often in a state of pollution. The death of a family member or coming into contact with a corpse are also sources of pollution. For people of higher varna status, contact with people of lower status may also be polluting. Having someone of lower status prepare food, or simply eating with someone of lower status, is a source of pollution.

The Laws of Manu and other dharma texts clearly indicate that the varna system had already become much more complex than the four-fold division described in the Vedas, illustrating the gulf between ideals recorded in texts and the realities of everyday life. The dharma literature identifies numerous subcategories within the varna system and explains them as the result of different groups of people from both inside and outside India being incorporated into the society and of members of different varnas intermarrying. While most caste groups today recognize their inclusion within one of the four varnas, many people are more likely to identify their caste as one of the many hundreds of *jatis,* or "birth" groups. These groups vary from region to region in India, and the particular grouping and relationships among the jatis (including different jatis that are part of the same varna) in a given region are likely to be more important in everyday life than categorization on the basis of the four varnas alone.

A number of jatis or subcastes are described as having originated with the offspring of marriages between members of different varnas, and there are "out-caste" groups who are enjoined to live outside villages and performs tasks considered polluting to the twice-born (Doniger 1991, 241–243). It is these groups that later came to be known as Untouchables, people whose very presence was thought polluting by those of higher caste status. Members of these groups, along with the Shudras, or servants, were prohibited from participating in Vedic ritual. The surviving records from this period in Indian history provide us primarily with the perspective of upper-caste males. It is not until somewhat later in Indian history that we find any direct record of the religious practices of women and people of low-caste status, as well as their views on a system that defined them as polluting. The fact that the dharma texts list so many subgroups created through intercaste marriages indicates that marriages did not only occur between members of the same varna—in other words, the rules of dharma were often different in theory from actual practice. Nonetheless, the dharma texts do highlight issues that remain important for many Hindus: diet and food preparation, marital responsibilities, and interactions among different castes.

The Epics

At roughly the same time Brahmins were codifying the dharma literature, two major epics were being compiled, the Mahabharata and the Ramayana. Whereas the dharma literature primarily treats dharma in theory, the epics illustrate dharma in practice and show some of the difficulties that arise when people do their best to follow all the dictates of dharma. The epics are collections of both secular and mythological material that developed over a period of centuries (roughly 400 BCE to 200 CE). They largely reflect the concerns and traditions of the Kshatriya or warrior class, though Brahmins eventually became involved in the transmission of the narratives. Both the Mahabharata and the Ramayana indicate a gradual shift away from devotion to the gods of the Vedas to a greater emphasis on the gods Shiva and Vishnu and other deities associated with them. The epics exemplify very important dimensions of Hinduism—its love of elaborate and entertaining tales and complex characters, and its rich appreciation of the complexities of human relationships.

The Mahabharata contains such a vast range of material that it is difficult to summarize, but at its heart is the tale of a great battle between the Pandavas and Kauravas, two branches of an extended family who quarreled over control of the family kingdom. Many scholars believe that the core of the Mahabharata records an actual battle, dating to perhaps 1000 BCE in northwestern India. Hindu tradition attributes the compilation of the Mahabharata to the sage Vyasa, who is also said to have arranged the Vedas.

The Bhagavad Gita

One of the most famous portions of the Mahabharata is the Bhagavad Gita ("Song of the Lord"), which relates a dialogue between one of the Pandava brothers, Arjuna, and his charioteer, Krishna, as they prepare to wage battle against the Kauravas. Arjuna, an expert archer, looks across the battlefield and realizes that he will have to kill his own relatives, whom he loves and respects. Despondent, he tells Krishna that he will not fight because he believes that harming his family would violate his dharmic obligation to honor and respect family members. In the conversation that follows, Krishna instructs Arjuna on how best to fulfill his dharma. Krishna gradually reveals that he is not just a charioteer, but in fact the ultimate power behind the functioning of the cosmos, the one who creates and destroys everything. At one point, he gives Arjuna special sight to see him in his true form as lord of the universe.

Krishna explains to Arjuna that he must fight because it is his dharma as a Kshatriya to fight in a righteous battle. The consequences of Arjuna not participating in the battle with his relatives would be far worse for the proper maintenance of the overall dharma of the cosmos. Even if Arjuna does end his relatives' lives, their atmans are eternal and imperishable, so they have not really died but will move on to another birth. Krishna teaches Arjuna that the proper way to act according to his dharma is by renouncing the fruits, or results, of his actions. Acting according to one's dharma thus becomes a sacrifice; one should act according to dharma simply because it is the proper thing to do rather than acting out of the desire for good results. Krishna teaches that this renunciation of the fruits of one's actions is the best form of renunciation, superior to the ritual sacrifices of the Vedas. Rather than becoming a renouncer who retires from the world, one continues to act in the world; instead of being motivated by desire, one is motivated by dharma; by renouncing the fruits of one's actions, one is not attached to them. This, Krishna teaches, is karma-yoga. If one acts without being attached to the fruits of action and offers the fruits to Krishna, no karma is produced. Arjuna eventually chooses to fight, and the battle begins.

Subsequent Hindu tradition most frequently describes Krishna as an *avatara* (descent or incarnation) of the god Vishnu. An avatara, literally a "crossing down," is a form that a god takes to address a specific dharmic crisis on earth. In the fourth chapter of the Bhagavad Gita, for example, Krishna tells Arjuna that whenever dharma is in decline, he incarnates himself on earth in whatever form necessary to deal with the problem. The final portion of the Mahabharata, the *Harivamsha* ("lineage of Hari," i.e., Krishna) is a relatively late addition to the text that describes the entire life of Krishna, indicating the coalescence of a variety of tales about this increasingly important deity.

The Ramayana

Rama, the hero of the other major Hindu epic in Sanskrit, the Ramayana, also comes to be known as an avatara of Vishnu. The Ramayana is traditionally attributed to the sage Valmiki, and like the Bhagavad Gita, it explores fundamental concerns about how to balance dharmic responsibilities to family, varna, and the cosmos. A talented, handsome prince named Rama has married a beautiful princess named Sita and is poised to take over the family kingdom. Rama's father, Dasharatha, has several wives, and one of them, Kaikeyi, hopes to further her own interests by convincing Dasharatha to make their son Bharata king rather than Rama (who is the son of Dasharatha's wife Kausalya). Invoking a promise Rama's father had earlier made to her, Kaikeyi forces Dasharatha to name their son Bharata the new king. He consents because dharma requires that one honor promises. Virtually everyone involved, including Bharata, believes that Rama is entitled to the throne. Still, Rama insists that it is his dharma as a son to help his father keep his word, and rather than become king, he decides to go into exile in the forest and allow his stepbrother to rule the kingdom. Sita, a princess accustomed to great luxury, has the option of staying at the family palace while her husband is in exile; however, she insists that it is her dharma to serve her husband wherever he goes, so she accompanies Rama in exile. Rama's younger brother Lakshmana also

Arjuna is driven into battle by Lord Krishna.
ART DIRECTORS

Rama and Sita, Pahari style, c. 1740.
VICTORIA AND ALBERT MUSEUM, LONDON/ART RESOURCE, NY

believes that he must honor his older brother and serve him during his exile, so the three set off for the forest. Events there conspire to test their allegiance to dharma.

The Ramayana's plot includes many elements typical of Hindu mythology as a whole, which describes a universe of many different worlds populated not just by gods, goddesses, and humans but various classes of semi-divine beings including demons. Throughout Hindu mythology, demons do their best to interfere in the proper maintenance of dharma and gain power over the gods. Boons and curses figure prominently as well. Whereas renouncers typically perform tapas to gain spiritual knowledge, others may use it to gain worldly power. The gods monitor this closely lest anyone, particularly demons, generate enough power to challenge their authority. When they see that someone has gained a great deal of power through yoga, they often grant that person a favor, or boon. People who have gained such power may also invoke curses against others who have disturbed or irritated them in some way. Those absorbed in deep meditation are particularly likely to curse anyone who disturbs them. The consequences of such boons and curses are frequently central to the plots of Hindu myths.

While Rama, Sita, and Lakshmana are in forest exile, a demon named Ravana hears about Sita's stunning beauty and schemes to kidnap her. One day while Rama and Lakshmana are away, Ravana assumes the disguise of a hermit so that Sita will let him into their hut. He remembers that he had once been cursed that he would die if he touched a woman without her consent, so he digs up the earth around Sita, lifts it up, and spirits her away to his kingdom in Lanka. Rama and Lakshmana then set out to rescue her, aided by a monkey named Hanuman and his monkey-army. Eventually they locate Sita, fight a fierce battle against Ravana and his allies, and recover Sita. Sita's troubles, however, are far from over.

Valmiki's version of the Ramayana records that Rama was very worried about what had happened to Sita while she was in Ravana's custody, and he feared that he could not accept her back as his wife if she had been defiled by the demon. Sita insisted on her purity and faithfulness to her husband and underwent a test of fire to prove it. Later, however, when Rama's period of exile is over and he returns to rule his family kingdom, his subjects question Sita's faithfulness, and she eventually begs the earth to swallow her if indeed she had remained pure. The earth proves her wifely virtue by swallowing her on the spot. Some later retellings of the Ramayana in India's vernacular languages end with Rama and Sita living happily ever after, but in Valmiki's Ramayana, Sita paid a heavy price for having been kidnapped against her will, illustrating the great emphasis on maintaining purity as a critical part of women's dharma.

Both the Mahabharata and Ramayana explore the challenge of following one's dharma in the face of apparent conflicts (such as family versus varna obligations). The characters in the Ramayana subsequently became exemplars of dharma: Rama as the righteous king and loyal son, Lakshmana as the loyal younger brother, Hanuman as the faithful devotee, and Sita as the loyal wife. The two epics are retold again and again in following centuries in India's vernacular languages, with new versions often expressing alternative interpretations of dharma through intriguing variations in plot. Theatrical performances as well as television serials and films depicting the epics have been enormously popular throughout India.

The Puranas

While many of the gods of the Vedas, such as Indra, became less prominent as the centuries passed, the epics narrate the lives of figures who became increasingly important for Hindus. Krishna and Rama, for example, are still two of the most beloved deities in the Hindu pantheon. Alongside the epics there is another body of literature, the Puranas, which elaborates even more of the mythology that remains significant for the practice of contemporary Hinduism. Virtually everyone in India knows some of the stories of the Puranas and recognizes the visual representations of the various gods and goddesses. Typically there are said to be eighteen great Puranas, though in fact there are many more, and even the lists of the eighteen great Puranas vary. The major Puranas date from roughly 100 CE to 1000 CE, though additional Puranas were composed over several more centuries. The Puranas in their written form are in Sanskrit, but the stories they tell most likely also circulated orally in the vernacular languages of different regions of India. The Puranas seem to have originated in different regions of India, although it is not always possible to determine where a particular Purana was composed.

A Sanskrit lexicon defines a Purana as a text that covers five topics: the creation of the universe; its dissolution and re-creation; genealogies of gods, sages, and kings; cosmic cycles; and histories of particular royal dynasties. Despite this definition, the vast majority of the Puranas is not focused on these topics but on a wide range of other matters. One of the most important dimensions of the Puranas is their description of the many gods and goddesses who make up the classical Hindu pantheon. Although the most prominent gods and goddesses from the Vedas do make appearances in the Purana accounts, they are overshadowed by other deities (some of whom are mentioned briefly in the Vedas) who had become more important by this time, suggesting the coalescence of many traditions beyond those of the Aryans.

Many Puranas explain that a trio of gods, Brahma, Vishnu, and Shiva, are responsible for the creation of the cosmos, its preservation, and destruction. Of the three, Vishnu and Shiva and other deities associated with them came to be the most widely worshiped, but as a group Brahma, Vishnu, and Shiva are important for understanding the conception of time in Hindu thought. Whereas the major Western religions typically conceive of time as linear, moving from creation to some ultimate day of judgment, the Puranas view time as passing through an endless series of cycles of creation and dissolution.

The god Brahma, often called "grandfather," is responsible for the creation of the cosmos, which then passes through a series of four *yugas*, or eras. With each passing yuga, the cosmos degenerates more and more from its original pristine state, and it becomes more difficult to maintain dharma. Vishnu, often called the "preserver," presides over this phase after creation, and whenever he sees that dharma is in decline, he manifests himself as an avatara in order to solve the problem. Finally, when the cosmos has degenerated so much that it is beyond repair, the god Shiva steps in to destroy everything in a fiery dance. Brahma then starts the cycle over again, building a new cosmos out of the remains of the old. Each cycle of four yugas lasts roughly four million years, though the precise numbers vary in different Puranas.

Individual Puranas tend to focus on particular gods, though any number of gods, goddesses, semi-divine beings, demons, and humans may appear in any one Purana. The Puranas explain how certain gods were born, the heavenly worlds in which they live, their relationships with other gods and goddesses, and pivotal events in their lives, such as marriages and battles with demons. Most gods have a consort or spouse, and many have children as well. In the Puranas we also find the elements of classical Hindu iconography. The gods are described as having particular characteristics that make them easily identifiable, such as the jewels they wear, weapons they carry, and the vehicle or mount they use to travel. When these gods and goddesses are represented in paintings and sculpture, these characteristics make them easily recognizable.

Vishnu, the preserver, who incarnates in time of need to bring righteousness back to earth.

Vishnu

Vishnu, for example, lies on an ocean of milk, his bed a coiled serpent. He wears a distinctive crown and jewels, has a unique whorl of hair on his chest, and bears four items: a discus, a conch, a lotus, and a mace. His vehicle is the heavenly eagle Garuda, and his spouse is the goddess Lakshmi (also known as Shri). Lakshmi, too, is easily identified by the lotus she holds and the coins she showers down in her role as a bestower of wealth and good fortune. Vishnu watches closely over the affairs of the cosmos and often incarnates himself in animal or human form to solve dharmic problems as they arise during the four yugas. Different Puranic sources list anywhere from ten to twenty-four avataras of Vishnu. Rama and Krishna are the most famous, and the stories of their exploits are lovingly recounted not only in the epics and Puranas but also in many other vernacular sources. It is worth noting that Krishna's role in the Puranas is markedly different from that in the Bhagavad Gita.

The Puranas emphasize Krishna's role as an avatara of Vishnu, sent to earth to battle a wicked king named Kamsa who ruled the north Indian city of Mathura. Vishnu descended as Krishna by plucking a black hair from his head and placing it in the womb of a woman named Devaki. Kamsa had already heard that a son of this woman would challenge him, so he had her sons killed and kept her and her husband in prison. When Krishna was born, to avoid being killed, he managed to help Devaki's husband take him to a nearby village, where he was raised by a cowherding family. Krishna was a mischievous little boy who stole milk and butter from the homes in his village. But he also performed deeds that made it clear he was no ordinary child. For instance, Kamsa sent a demon to kill him by feeding him poisoned milk, but Krishna sucked all the poison out of her with no harm to himself while she shriveled up and died. When a snake poisoned the river where the village cows drank, Krishna subdued him and made the waters safe again. Yet his family and neighbors didn't know his true identity as a god. Once, when his mother caught him eating dirt, Krishna opened his mouth to reveal not just dirt but the entire universe within. Krishna made sure his mother didn't remember the experience afterward.

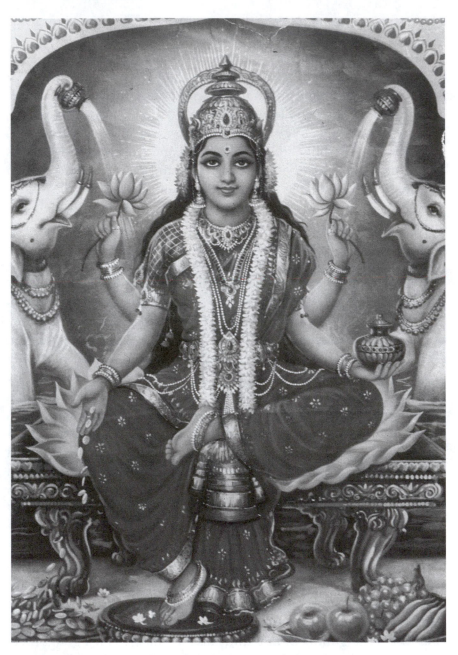

Lakshmi appears as Gajalakshmi, goddess with the elephants, giver of all that is good and bountiful in life.
ART DIRECTORS

Krishna playing his flute.
ART DIRECTORS

As he grew older, Krishna's mischief turned to matters of the heart. A beguilingly handsome young man, he roamed around at night playing the flute so entrancingly that women, married and single, would leave their homes to be with him. As they danced in the woods, Krishna multiplied himself over and over so that he could be with each woman. His favorite was a young woman named Radha, and the two of them would steal away to be together. Their passionate love would become a metaphor for the experience of intense devotion to god, as well as the pain of separation, for eventually Krishna would have to leave to fulfill his task of killing Kamsa. Radha and the other village women's heartbreak and longing after his departure was to become a frequent theme in later devotional literature.

The Puranas also tell of Krishna's successful battle against the wicked king Kamsa, his marriages (at least sixteen thousand and three), ongoing battles with demons (which he always won), and finally his death after a hunter accidentally shot him in the foot. While at one level Krishna's life is richly entertaining and sometimes comic, his relationships—with his mother, brother, friends, Radha, and the village women—became a way of understanding and expressing devotion to god. How can one imagine what god is like, or bridge the distance between this world and the worlds of the gods beyond? The mythology of Krishna gives his devotees the chance to know him in terms of relationships most people readily understand—the love of a mother for her child, the love between brothers, friends, and lovers—and this may be one reason for Krishna's great popularity throughout India.

Shiva

The Puranic mythology of Shiva is equally rich and entertaining, relating not only how Shiva destroys the cosmos at the end of each cycle of yugas but also how he occupies himself during the vast expanses of time between periods of creation and destruction. Spending eons meditating atop Mt. Kailasha in the Himalayas, Shiva is recognizable by the animal skins on which he sits, his ash-smeared skin, the snakes around his neck, the third eye in his forehead, the crescent moon and Ganges River in his matted hair, and his vehicle, the bull Nandi. His weapons are a trident and a club, and he sometimes carries a skull and a drum. His personality is complex, for he is both a practitioner of yoga, performing solitary meditation, and a husband and father. He thus exemplifies the fundamental tension between householder and renouncer (O'Flaherty 1981).

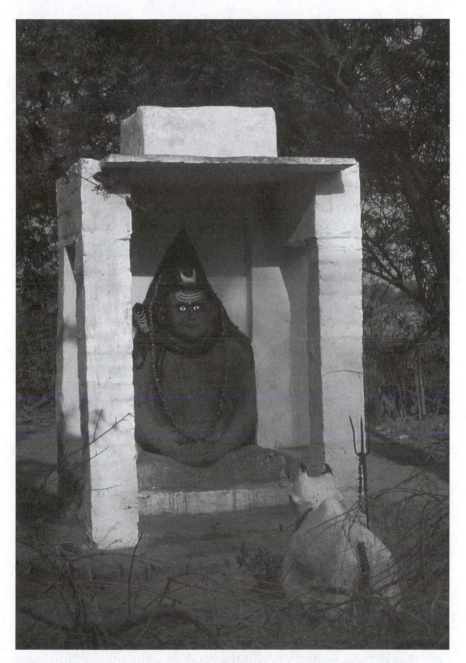

Roadside image of the god Shiva.
ROBIN RINEHART

As a solitary practitioner of yoga, Shiva often remains aloof from the ongoing intrigues of many of the other gods and goddesses. Sometimes he is not invited to events that other gods and goddesses attend regularly because they find his appearance and unpredictable behavior troubling. But his tapas, or ascetic practice, builds incomparable power, and the gods and goddesses must sometimes resort to that power to take care of problems they are having difficulty solving. Many Puranas, for example, tell the tale of a demon named Taraka who had gained so much power through tapas that the god Brahma granted him the boon that he could not be killed by any god or goddess except one born from Shiva's seed.

Taraka meanwhile became so powerful that he threatened the gods' control over the cosmos, and the gods were faced with the challenge of figuring out how to get Shiva to produce a child who could defeat Taraka. A yogi, after all, remains celibate. So the gods recruited Kama, the god of love, to pierce Shiva with an arrow from his flower-bow that would make Shiva fall in love. But Shiva saw Kama coming and reduced him to ashes just by looking at him. (Shiva did eventually restore Kama to life, but without a body, thereby allowing him to sneak up on people from then on.) Still, Kama's power had its effect, and Shiva agreed to wed Parvati, the daughter of the Himalayas. Parvati had performed tapas to win Shiva's favor. Producing a child, however, was no easy task, for though the gods had accomplished their goal of getting Shiva married, they didn't realize what would happen when Shiva and Parvati began to make love. The earth simply couldn't bear the brunt of their activity. Nervously, the gods chose to interrupt Shiva and Parvati, and Shiva ended up spilling his seed on the ground.

According to the Shiva Purana, Agni swallowed Shiva's seed, and because the other gods ate food offered via Agni in a sacrifice, they all became pregnant. The gods found that Shiva's seed burned them from within, so Shiva told them to expel it from their bodies. This left the problem of what to do with the burning seed, for no one seemed able to bear its heat. Eventually the Ganges River, a goddess herself, wound up with the seed, and she flung it into some reeds. There it suddenly transformed into a boy named Skanda, the son of Shiva and Parvati who would slay the demon Taraka (O'Flaherty 1975, 162–168).

Shiva and Parvati.
ART DIRECTORS

Ganesha, the god of wisdom and remover of obstacles, is represented in a batik painting.

ROMAN SOURNAR/CORBIS

According to most Puranic accounts, Shiva and Parvati's relationship was stormy, for Shiva was far more interested in pursuing yoga than married life. Parvati eventually decided to create her own child, a little boy she fashioned from the sweat and dirt of her body. Shiva and the boy wound up fighting, and the boy was beheaded in the battle. Parvati angrily demanded that Shiva bring the boy back to life, and he did so, replacing the boy's head with that of an elephant. The elephant-headed child of Parvati is known as Ganesha, one of the most beloved Hindu gods.

Goddesses

Followers of Hinduism whose primary devotion is to the god Shiva and the gods and goddesses associated with him are known as Shaivas. Followers focused on Vishnu, his spouse Lakshmi, his avataras, and other figures related to him are known as Vaishnavas. There is yet a third important group, known as Shaktas, which includes traditions focused on a variety of goddesses. These are not hard and fast categories—being Vaishnava does not preclude participating in Shaiva activities or vice versa, and both Vaishnavas and Shaivas may express their regard for some of the goddesses of the Shakta tradition. Although the background and history of the Shakta category is less clearly understood than that of the Vaishnavas and Shaivas, archeological evidence suggests that goddess worship may be traced at least to the time of the Indus Valley civilization and may have been widespread throughout the Indian subcontinent. Indeed, for many years both Western and Indian scholars have argued that the origins of the goddess traditions are predominantly non-Aryan. In light of controversies over the identity of the Aryans and the people with whom they came into contact, we cannot reach a definite conclusion on the specific origins of each strand of goddess mythology, but it does seem that these traditions reflect the interaction of different groups within India.

One of the earliest and most important Sanskrit textual sources on the goddess tradition is the *Devi Mahatmya* ("greatness of the goddess"), a portion of the Markandeya Purana, which dates from about the fifth or sixth century CE (Coburn 1984, 1). Like many Puranic passages, the Devi Mahatmya is the recounting of a dialogue—one person telling others the story of the goddess, reflecting the fundamentally oral nature of these traditions. The Devi Mahatmya describes a great goddess who takes many different forms. She is praised as the *shakti,* or creative power, of the gods, and often performs tasks that the gods cannot. In one episode, when the gods were threatened by a demon they could not defeat, the great goddess emerged from the bodies of Vishnu, Brahma, Shiva, and other gods, each of whom gave her a weapon and ornaments. Assuming a ferocious form, she mounted her vehicle—a lion—and decimated the demon's army before slaying the demon himself, cutting his head off with a sword. Then she offered the grateful gods a boon. They asked that she be willing to solve their problems whenever they called upon her.

Not surprisingly, when yet another demon force threatened the gods, they remembered the boon from the goddess. This time she emerged from the body of Parvati, Shiva's wife, and was known as Kalika ("dark, black") because of her dark color. The demon leader heard of her great beauty and decided to seize her as his own. But Kalika informed him that she had vowed she would only marry someone who could defeat her in battle. This led to another battle between the goddess and a demon and his armies. During the battle Kalika created another form out of her forehead, the goddess Kali. A truly fearsome figure, Kali wore a garland of severed human heads, was clothed in a tiger skin, and shrieked loudly at the demons. She devoured them and their weapons, twirled them around by their hair and dashed them to the ground, dicing some with her sword—no demon was safe from Kali's wrath. Still, the battle wore on, and in order to assist Kali, the gods sent forth shaktis, or powers from their bodies. The battle was intensified by the entrance of a demon named Raktabija ("blood-seed") whose unique talent was that every drop of blood spilled from his body immediately transformed into yet another Raktabija, making him very hard to kill. Each of the gods' shaktis fought him, creating more and more Raktabijas as they drew his blood. It was left to Kali to devour each and every drop of his blood so he could recreate himself no more. When the struggle between the various forms of the goddess and the demons finally came to an end, the demons vanquished, the great goddess drew her many forms back into herself.

The narrative of the Devi Mahatmya indicates the fluid, ever-changing nature of the goddess within Hinduism. In this Purana, she creates new forms of herself and reabsorbs them into her supreme form. Other Puranas, however, focus on particular manifestations of the goddess. Thus in some instances the goddess is a single figure incorporating all goddesses, including the gods' spouses; in other cases goddesses maintain distinct identities. Shakta mythology emphasizes the concept of shakti, the feminine creative power wielded by the goddesses. Some commentators distinguish between the spouse goddesses, such as Lakshmi (spouse of Vishnu) and Parvati (spouse of Shiva), who tend to be relatively benign, and the more ferocious goddesses such as Kali who are not always directly associated with a god. Just as the dharma literature stresses that women who are not under the protection and guidance of men may cause trouble, so too the Puranas suggest that a goddess not under the control of a god is potentially dangerous. Some Puranas, for example, report that when the goddess Kali indulges her fondness for blood, she runs the risk of terrorizing the world unless Shiva steps in to subdue her.

At the end of the Devi Mahatmya, the goddess proclaims that anyone who recites these hymns about her conquest of demons will receive her protection and be successful, especially if they do so on certain days of the lunar calendar. Reciting or hearing the Devi Mahatmya serves as an antidote to bad dreams, ill omens, evil spirits, troubled friendships, and myriad other problems. In Vedic sacrifice, the proper recitation of hymns as a part of a sacrificial ritual brought about well-being; now there is the idea that the recitation and hearing of the Puranas also brings about well-being. A major difference, however, is that anyone can hear the Puranas, whereas access to the Vedas is restricted to the twice-born. The emphasis on hearing and reciting also indicates that oral transmission of tradition was still very much the norm.

The account of the goddess in the Devi Mahatmya is but one of many in the Puranas and other literature, and it exemplifies the diversity and complexity of Hindu mythology. Other Puranas portray the goddesses and their manifestations differently. Similarly, there are varying versions of events in the life of Shiva and his family and Vishnu and his avataras in different Puranas. Gods and goddesses are known by multiple names, some of which describe their relationship to other gods, or their appearance (Shiva, for example, is sometimes called the "blue-throated one" because his throat turned blue when he drank poison in order to protect the world from it). The Puranas also express different perspectives on how the gods and goddesses relate to one another. Some may proclaim Shiva the greatest of the gods, others Vishnu, still others the goddesses. Although individual Puranas usually don't indicate the region of India in which they originated, it is quite likely that the variations among the different Puranas reflect the assimilation of local and regional traditions into a larger, pan-Indian Sanskritic tradition. Though relatively few people knew Sanskrit, it had the advantage of being considered prestigious and functioning as a lingua franca throughout regions of India where the vernaculars differed. The sociologist M. N. Srinivas proposed the term *Sanskritization* for the process whereby local vernacular traditions were cast into Sanskrit, and also used the term to refer to the phenomenon of low-caste groups "Sanskritizing" their traditions and practices to give themselves greater legitimacy and prestige (Srinivas 1952).

The gods and goddesses of the Puranas and the practices associated with them are for the most part quite different from those of the Vedic period, but even so the Puranas describe a number of Vedic rituals and accord great respect to the Vedas. Although as the centuries passed there were fewer people who could claim expertise in Vedic knowledge, and Vedic ritual was not the predominant form of religious practice for most, the Vedas maintained a position of high prestige throughout Hindu culture, a situation that continues to the present. Though their content and concerns were substantially different from the Vedas, some Puranas declared themselves to be the "fifth Veda," thereby both acknowledging the significance of the Vedas and according legitimacy to their own perspective (Smith 1994). Many thinkers asserted that the Vedas contained all knowledge, but that as the world passed through the fourth and final yuga in the cosmic cycle, people's spiritual capabilities diminished, requiring the availability of less demanding forms of practice such as those supported by the Puranas.

One way that Hindu thinkers eventually acknowledged the increasing diversity of the tradition was by dividing texts into two categories, *shruti* ("that which is heard or revealed") and *smriti* ("that which is remembered"). The Vedas constituted shruti; revealed, infallible knowledge, accessible only to the twice-born and ideally to be preserved only through oral transmission. Other texts such as the Laws of Manu and the Puranas fell under the category of smriti, traditions remembered and transmitted both orally and in writing. (Some Hindu commentators argued that smriti texts ultimately derive their authority from Vedic texts, although the original Vedic text may be lost.) The law of karma is another way to explain the need for a wide range of religious practices. If people are at different stages in samsara or the cycle of death and rebirth, their intellectual and spiritual capacities will differ, thereby requiring practices tailor-made to differing capabilities.

Bhakti:
The Rise of Devotional Hinduism

Many of the practices associated with devotion to the gods and goddesses of the Puranas do not have their origins in the Vedas but appear to reflect other traditions of the subcontinent. Vedic ritual did not involve images of gods and goddesses and did not require a fixed location. In contrast, archeological evidence from the Indus Valley area and other sites throughout India shows that images of gods and goddesses had long been an important part of people's lives. With the rise of theistic Hinduism in the early centuries of the Common Era, gods were sometimes represented aniconically (e.g., Vishnu by the naturally occurring shalagrama stone) and sometimes iconically in sculptures and paintings depicting their ornaments, weapons, and other distinguishing features. Shiva is frequently represented by the linga, a cylindrical column. Much Western scholarship has highlighted the phallic nature of the linga, whereas some Hindus today object to that characterization. During this period, temples housing images of gods also became increasingly important places of worship, and people built shrines in their homes to house the images of the deities they worshiped. Hindu

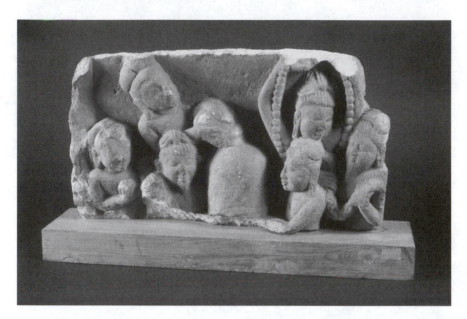

An eighth-century sandstone relief sculpture taken from an Uttar Pradesh temple depicts the worship of the Shiva Linga.
ANGELO HORNAK/CORBIS

thinkers developed a variety of doctrines about how an image represented the deity, who could be said to be always being present in the image, or who might be thought temporarily to descend into the image when devotees offered worship.

Images, whether they are understood as representations of a deity or literal manifestations of a deity, became an important focus of worship. The ritual use of images allows devotees to establish contact with the deity. This contact is explained in part by the concept of *darshana,* or sight. Hindus speak of taking darshana of an image of a god or goddess, explaining that when they look at an image, the god represented by the image looks back at them as well. Darshana is thus an exchange, and as such it forms a central part of many Hindu rituals (Eck 1998).

Just as images could help devotees recall the events in the lives of gods and goddesses, particular locations throughout India associated with those events became places of pilgrimage. The region around Mathura, for example, where Krishna grew up and frolicked with the cowherd girls, remains an important pilgrimage place for Vaishnava Hindus. The Ganges River, which flows through northern India, became especially sacred to Hindus, and the city of Varanasi (also known as Benares) on its banks holds sacred status and is in particular associated with the god Shiva. The myths of the Puranas, therefore, are represented not just in texts but in actual locations people can visit as part of their religious practice. Indeed, from the Himalayas in the north to the southern tip of the subcontinent at Kanyakumari, the whole of India is crisscrossed with pilgrimage routes linking major sites of its sacred geography.

The Devi Mahatmya extolled the virtues of reciting its verses, and indeed there is an increasing amount of information about religious practices from the period during which the Puranic traditions developed. Especially significant was the *bhakti,* or devotion, movement, which developed in south India and gradually spread to the rest of the subcontinent. The bhakti movement advocated an intense, personal relationship with the gods and goddesses. Bhakti is mentioned in earlier sources such as the Bhagavad Gita, where Krishna advocates bhakti yoga as one way of worshiping him. Bhakti became a powerful force in south India beginning about the sixth century CE. In some later Puranas, in fact, a personified bhakti proclaims that she was born in the Dravida country of the south and gradually moved northward. The records of the bhakti movement acquaint us with a far wider range of people than earlier Sanskrit sources, for the bhakti leaders were not just Brahmin males but members of high and low castes, both male and female, and they composed their poetry and songs in the vernacular languages and not just Sanskrit. The bhakti poets told and retold mythological events and analyzed, questioned, and sometimes challenged the gods' actions. The poems of the bhakti leaders illustrate the role of mythology in religious practice and the dynamic relationships between the gods and goddesses and their devotees.

In southeastern India, where the Dravidian language Tamil is spoken, bhakti poets composed verses dedicated to both Shiva and Vishnu. The poets themselves became so popular that people revered them as saints, remembered and told the stories of their lives, and placed images of them in their temples. Tamil tradition recalls sixty-three saints who worshiped Shiva, called the Nayan-mars, and twelve saints who worshiped Vishnu, known as the Alvars. Their poetry details the joys and sorrows of living a life of devotion and recounts the intimate relationships the poet-saints sought to establish with their beloved gods.

The close relationship that the poet-saints sought meant that they not only approached Shiva or Vishnu with reverence and awe but sometimes addressed them mockingly or even angrily. Manik-kavachakar, one of the most important Nayanmar saints, made fun of Shiva's appearance and called him a madman. One of his poems is a conversation between two young girls about Shiva, one of whom asks about Shiva's strange attire of ashes and snakes. Her friend replies, "Why look at his ashes or fear his serpent or heed his elusive Vedic talk? All you need to know is this, he is the essence, the god of all that lives and moves" (Dehejia 1988, 6). The girl's reply illustrates the centrality of knowing that Shiva is the supreme god; she acknowledges that he may be involved in "Vedic talk" but recognizes that his devotees need not.

As with the Puranas, this is an example of paying one's respects to the Vedas without necessarily making Vedic practice the focus of one's religious life. Many other poems of both the Nayanmar and Alvar saints assert that learning of dharma, performing tapas, and engaging in Vedic ritual are futile if one doesn't first and foremost love god. A persistent theme throughout bhakti poetry is the importance of sincere, direct devotion, and its superiority to rigid rules and the rote performance of ritual.

The Tamil saints included many men and women of low caste, even Untouchables, and stories from the lives of these saints show that people questioned and challenged conventional caste practices. Tiruppan, one of the Alvar saints, is said to have stood for years a mile away from a temple dedicated to his beloved Vishnu, because as an Untouchable he was not allowed to enter the temple. One day Tiruppan was so absorbed in his devotion to Vishnu that he failed to move out of the path of a Brahmin priest preparing to worship in the temple. The priest angrily threw a rock at Tiruppan's forehead, but when he reached the temple, he found that Vishnu's image was bleeding in exactly the same spot the rock had hit Tiruppan. Horrified that he had offended Vishnu, the priest frantically sought others to help him salve the wound through prayers to Vishnu, but nothing worked. Finally Vishnu himself appeared to the Brahmin and told him that he must carry Tiruppan into the temple. Only then, when an Untouchable was allowed into a temple from which he was normally excluded, did the wound on the image heal (Dehejia 1988, 89–91). Whereas the Brahmin thought he was showing devotion by following strict rules of caste purity, Vishnu's intervention showed that a sincere love for him could transcend such rules.

The life story of Karaikkal Ammaiyar, one of the Nayanmar saints, shows that bhakti also allowed women to challenge their conventional social roles. A beautiful young woman, Karaikkal dutifully served her husband. One morning he sent home two mangoes for her to serve him later that day, but before he came home, she gave one of them away to a sage who came to the door asking for food. When her husband later asked for the second mango, she prayed to Shiva for help, and a mango miraculously appeared in her hand. But her husband knew that it wasn't the mango he had sent home, and he was so alarmed by her ability to materialize mangoes that he left home and eventually remarried. When her husband returned home many years later, Karaikkal Ammaiyar prayed to Shiva that she be released from her responsibilities as a wife so that she could dedicate herself wholeheartedly to Shiva. She asked him to take away her beauty because she would no longer need it, and then changed into a frightful, emaciated figure who envisioned herself dancing with Shiva in the cremation grounds (Dehejia 1988, 117–138).

The poems of the twelve Alvars and sixty-three Nayanmars are still recited in temples throughout south India, and many Tamil speakers know some of the verses by heart. Beginning in about the tenth century CE, the poets' works were anthologized, and theologians proposed particular systems for understanding the exact nature of Shiva's and Vishnu's relationship to their devotees and the proper means of worshiping them. The work of these theologians led to the development of different sectarian traditions throughout India, often led by a succession of gurus or teachers who traced their lineage back to a particular theologian.

As the devotional movement spread throughout India, other poets added their voices to the growing body of bhakti poetry. In the region of Maharashtra, men and women of high and low caste sang to the gods in the Marathi language, and their followers sang and recited their poetry and recalled the events of their lives. In Rajasthan, a woman named Mirabai, whom legend remembers as a princess, sang of her love for the god Krishna, and many of the stories of her life relate that she had to leave her husband and his family to do so. In Bengal, people recalled Chaitanya's (1486–1533) ecstatic devotion to Krishna, and his followers subsequently established sectarian traditions with complex theologies and devotional practices. Bhakti remains one of the most popular forms of Hindu religious practice.

Islam and Hinduism

The arrival of Islam on the Indian subcontinent was a major development in the latter part of the first millennium CE. Arising during the seventh century in the area that is now Saudi Arabia, Islam reached India quickly through trade and maritime connections. As the first millennium came to a close, Muslim rulers had established small territories in the northwestern region of India, and over the next several centuries they would build larger kingdoms—most notably the Mughal empire, which at its zenith in the fifteenth and sixteenth centuries extended throughout almost the entire subcontinent.

It can be difficult to get a clear or consistent picture of the impact of Islam on India and Hinduism, because accounts of Islam's arrival are often clouded by religious and sometimes political biases. There is a long history of negative depictions of Islam in Western accounts of the religion, and conflicts between Hindus and Muslims both during the period of the Indian nationalist movement and after the creation of the independent states of India and Pakistan have also contributed to stereotyping and misrepresentation. Both Western and Hindu scholars have sometimes portrayed Muslims as violent invaders who converted Hindus and other Indians to Islam on threat of death. In reality, however, the situation was far more complex. To be sure, there were people from central Asia and the Middle East who invaded India, and in some instances they did attack Hindu and Buddhist places of worship. There were some Muslim rulers who imposed heavier taxation and certain restrictions on non-Muslims. But there are also many examples of cooperation and exploration of religious ideas between Hindus and Muslims. It is problematic to make generalizations about Indian Islam, because immigrants and invading forces brought diverse forms of Islam from different regions of central Asia and the Middle East. Over time substantial numbers of Indians converted to Islam—so many that by the twentieth century there were areas of both eastern and western India in which Muslims constituted the majority of the population. Today, India has the second-largest Muslim population of any country in the world, and relations between Hindus and Muslims remain an important issue.

Most scholars agree that one of the most significant forms of Islam in India was the diverse Sufi tradition, which focused on an intense, mystical experience of God. Sufi saints, men (more rarely women) acclaimed for their fervent devotion to God, often attracted devotees and became the focus of great admiration. Some Sufi saints established lineages and orders, and their followers would sometimes build shrines around their tombs. There are many instances of Hindus and Muslims coming together to express their respect and admiration for Sufi saints. Devotion to Sufi saints, however, has sometimes been a point of controversy within Islam itself because some Muslims argue that people should address their worship directly to God without any intermediaries, and because some Sufis have argued that one's love for God is far more important than following the dictates of Islamic law. Such Hindu-Muslim interaction, as well as debates within Islam itself, indicate the complexity and diversity of Indian Islam.

Some Muslim rulers sought a deeper understanding of Hinduism by having Hindu texts translated into the Persian language, and some rulers even provided patronage to Hindu temples and other religious organizations. India's encounter with Islam also found expression in the works of some of the bhakti poets, which scholars often divide into two categories. Those who sang of God's appearance and deeds adopted the *saguna* ("with qualities") approach. Mirabai, who sang passionately of her love for Krishna, is one of the best-known saguna poets. Other bhakti poets, however, believed that God's greatness precluded any description of attributes or appearance, and their approach was called *nirguna* ("without qualities"). It was the nirguna poets in particular who often pondered the ostensible differences between the practices of Hindus and Muslims and asked whether they were meaningful. For example, Kabir, a weaver who lived in the city of Varanasi sometime around the early fifteenth century CE, sharply criticized people who proudly displayed the external signs of their Hindu or Muslim affiliation without seeming to put any of their ideals into actual practice. Kabir attracted both Hindu and Muslim admirers.

Hinduism under British Rule

For centuries, India had extensive contact with central Asia, the Middle East, and Southeast Asia, and Indian traditions spread along trade routes. With the expansion of sea travel in the late fifteenth and early sixteenth centuries, Europeans began to journey to India as well. The Portuguese, French, and British established settlements along India's coasts in the early seventeenth century. Although their initial interest was trade, the British gradually began to assume rule over portions of India. By the middle of the nineteenth century, they controlled much of the Indian subcontinent. Under British rule, India developed an extensive railway system, improved health care, and acquired printing and other communications technology. The British also introduced a Western-style educational system. Soon, graduates of colonial schools formed a new class of Indians with knowledge of both Western and Indian traditions.

Some of the British in India were highly critical of Hinduism and other Indian traditions, and they hoped that Christian missionaries would be successful in winning large numbers of Hindus over to Christianity. However, many Indian intellectual and religious leaders responded by revitalizing and reforming particular aspects of India's religious practices. New movements within Hinduism, Islam, and Sikhism strove to expand and redefine details of doctrine and practice, in the process reforming practices that both Indians and westerners had criticized.

The spread of print technology throughout India allowed Indians to publish newspapers and periodicals, pamphlets, and relatively inexpensive books, making it possible for large numbers of people to communicate quickly across a much greater distance than had been possible when written materials had to be copied by hand. The immediate audience for printed materials was of course fairly limited given that literacy rates were very low, but often people who were literate would read newspapers and other materials aloud so that they reached more people. Virtually every description of life in India's towns and cities during the middle and late nineteenth century highlights the lively debates and discussions taking place both within religious groups and among representatives of different religions. A number of movements, most of them regionally based, arose out of these discussions.

Nineteenth-century religious leaders often focused on issues such as caste practices (especially discrimination against members of lower castes), access to education for both boys and girls, women's roles in Indian society, and Hinduism's relationship with other religions practiced on the Indian subcontinent. In part, religious reformers were trying to address some of the criticisms that the British had of Indian society. But these new movements weren't merely responses to the British; they also considered issues that had been important long before the advent of British rule. Some of the bhakti poets, for example, had challenged caste discrimination. Others had surveyed the enormous range of religious practices in India and proposed that amidst them all there was a unifying core.

During the period of British colonial rule, many religious leaders built upon this precedent by proposing specific definitions of what Hinduism "really" was. British officials, too, had sought to define some essential form of Hinduism in part because they considered it important to understand the customs of the people they were ruling. While the bhakti poets had generally argued that a sincere, humble love for God lay at the core of diverse religious beliefs and practices, both European investigators of Hinduism and many Hindu leaders of the same period assumed that the most accurate representation of Hinduism would be found not in popular customs but in a particular text or set of texts. Texts, in turn, would dictate proper belief and practice. As a result, many reform movements focused on eradicating popular practices deemed to be without textual sanction.

Rammohan Roy (1772–1833), the founder of the first major Hindu reform group, the Brahmo Samaj, was a Brahmin from the eastern state of Bengal who had studied both Hinduism and Christianity. He taught that the Upanishads best captured the spirit of Hinduism and argued that they were superior to other religious teachings because they preached a monotheistic message and were based on reason rather than faith. Any Hindu practices for which there was no basis in the Upanishads, he argued, needed to be eliminated. Thus he opposed the worship of images, something Christian missionaries had sharply criticized. He also fought against the practice of sati (widow-burning), advocated greater educational opportunities for women, was critical of discrimination on the basis of caste, and suggested that Hinduism might borrow ethical precepts from the teachings of Jesus. The Brahmo Samaj never attracted huge numbers of followers, but it did set the stage for a number of other movements throughout India that had similar aims.

The Arya Samaj, established in 1875, was a movement that had greater mass appeal than the Brahmo Samaj. Its founder, Swami Dayanand Saraswati (1824–1883), was a Brahmin from the western state of Gujarat who had a traditional education in Sanskrit. As a young boy, he questioned the efficacy of image worship when he saw a rat scurry across an image of Shiva. If Shiva really were in the image, he pondered, why would he let a rat run across him and steal away with the food devotees had left? He left his family as a young man and, rather than marrying, became a renouncer. He studied with a teacher in north India and promised him that he would reform Hinduism. Whereas the Brahmo Samaj had championed the Upanishads as the essence of Hinduism, Swami Dayanand Saraswati concluded that the Vedas contained the true form of Hinduism. However, he believed that authentic Vedic tradition had been lost and that it was his mission to restore it. He taught that any practice not described in the Vedas was inauthentic. Thus he was opposed to image worship, and he argued that caste should be determined by merit rather than birth. Responding to Western characterizations of Indian culture as backward and superstitious, he proclaimed that the Vedas contained scientific knowledge that the West had only recently discovered. In keeping with his idea that true Hinduism is found in the Vedas, he developed new rituals based upon Vedic fire sacrifices, and he proposed new rituals for important life events such as marriage and death. The Arya Samaj was most popular in the northwestern state of Punjab. Many of its earliest members had been involved with the Brahmo Samaj but thought that it had gone too far in rejecting Indian traditions. The Arya Samaj remains an important part of the Indian religious landscape, and some contemporary Hindu nationalists cite its influence on their thinking.

The Ramakrishna Mission, established in Bengal, became an especially important force in introducing westerners to Hinduism. Swami Vivekananda (1863–1902) founded the mission in memory of his guru, Ramakrishna (1836–1886), a devotee of the goddess Kali who on the basis of his meditation and prayer came to the conclusion that all religions are essentially different paths leading to the same goal. In the western state of Gujarat, Sahajananda Swami (1781–1830) established the Swami Narayan movement, advocating spartan living and developing a complex monotheistic theology. The Swami Narayan movement is still a major force in Gujarat and among Indian diaspora communities throughout the world. In the mid-nineteenth century, branches of the Brahmo Samaj were established in the south Indian city of Madras (now known as Chennai), along with new organizations that accepted some Brahmo Samaj ideals but wished to preserve more traditional practices (Jones 1989, 164–167). A number of the new movements in the south focused on reform of caste practices. For example, the Self-Respect Movement, founded by E. V. Ramasami in 1925, challenged the dominance of Brahmins and north Indian traditions. In the early twentieth century in the southeastern state of Kerala, Sri Narayana Guru, member of an Untouchable group, led a movement that created temples open to Untouchables.

Although there were countless movements advocating changes in traditional practices, some people were concerned that the new movements would challenge traditional ways. In many regions, people organized branches of the Sanatana Dharma Sabha, or "organization for the eternal dharma," dedicated to preserving traditions (such as image worship) that the new movements sought to eliminate.

Hinduism and Indian Nationalism

In the late nineteenth century, increasing numbers of Indians began to challenge British rule over their country, calling first for increased representation in government and later for outright independence. Religious issues came to the forefront as the nationalist movement progressed and leaders questioned how an independent India would govern itself and accommodate its many different religions. Perhaps the best-known of the leaders of the Indian independence movement was Mohandas Karamchand Gandhi (1869–1948), known by the title Mahatma, or "great soul."

Gandhi was born into a Vaishya (the merchant/trader varna) family in Gujarat. He studied law in England and later worked as a barrister in South Africa, where he led agitations against restrictive and discriminatory policies against Indians. He developed a program of noncooperation that he called *satyagraha,* or "truth-grasping." When Gandhi returned to India in 1915, he had already earned a reputation as a powerful leader. Many credit him with expanding the fight for independence to the masses, moving it beyond the relatively small group of Western-educated Indians.

Gandhi believed that Indians could be most effective in opposing the British not by taking up arms in a violent struggle but by resisting the British through noncooperation, demonstrating the moral truth of their position by refusing to cooperate with restrictive and discriminatory policies and laws. Raised in a Vaishnava family, he concluded that truth itself was the best expression of bhakti. He was powerfully drawn to the life of the renouncer, and though he married and had four children, he eventually chose to lead a celibate life.

Gandhi fought for better treatment of Untouchables. However, Untouchable leaders did not always appreciate his efforts, partly because Gandhi believed that the varnashramadharma system could be fair if people actually organized themselves into the four varnas rather than following the more complex practices associated with

Mahatma Gandhi (right), Indian independence leader, consults with future Indian prime minister Jawaharlal Nehru in a 1946 meeting of the Indian Congress.

LIBRARY OF CONGRESS

multiple jatis. Gandhi also hoped that Hindus and Muslims could live together harmoniously in an independent India. That dream faded, however, as tensions and violence between Hindus and Muslims flared up through the 1930s and 1940s.

Gandhi saw his ideas as drawing more upon Indian tradition than having a specifically Hindu origin, but other leaders in the nationalist movement believed that Indians should organize themselves along religious lines. For instance, there were Hindu leaders who believed that because India was the home of Hinduism, it ought to be a Hindu nation. V. D. Savarkar (1883–1966), a Maharashtrian Brahmin, coined the term *Hindutva,* or "Hindu-ness," and his ideas inspired Hindu nationalists for generations to come. Savarkar thought that Hindus should use violence to resist British rule if necessary, and he argued that Muslims were a potential threat to Hindus because their loyalties would lie with a global Islam rather than their native India. Savarkar's Hindutva did not include a specific definition of religious belief and practices but emphasized the territory of India, ethnicity, and Indian culture as its foundations.

Savarkar served as president of an organization called the Hindu Mahasabha from 1937–1942. On January 30, 1948, Nathuram Godse, a former member of this organization, assassinated Gandhi in New Delhi. Savarkar's ideas continued to exert influence on a variety of Hindu nationalist groups, including the Rashtriya Swayamsevak Sangh (RSS, National Volunteer Party), founded in 1925 and still active today. Young men who join the RSS undergo rigorous physical training as well as spiritual instruction so that they might protect the Hindu nation they hope India will one day become.

The Hindu Mahasabha and other Hindu nationalist groups joined calls for an end to discrimination against Untouchables, and like Gandhi, they argued for a reformed varna system. Leaders within Untouchable groups, however, believed that such reforms would not truly eradicate the discrimination faced by Untouchables. B. R. Ambedkar (1891–1956), a remarkable Untouchable leader from Maharashtra, argued that there simply was no place for Untouchables within Hinduism. In 1927 Ambedkar and some of his followers publicly burned a copy of the Laws of Manu, and in 1956 Ambedkar led a mass conversion of Untouchables to Buddhism.

Although Gandhi and other leaders of the nationalist movement hoped that India could become a single independent nation with multiple religious communities, many Muslim leaders concluded that there would never be fair representation of Muslims in a majority Hindu state, and they demanded a separate state for Muslims. When the British officially relinquished rule of India on August 15, 1947, two new nations were born: India and Pakistan. The newly drawn borders between the two countries partitioned the Punjab in the west, and Bengal in the east, creating east and west branches of Pakistan. (East Pakistan broke away to form the nation of Bangladesh in 1971.) The period before and just after the partition of British India in 1947 saw horrific violence and the largest migration in human history as Muslims moved from India to Pakistan, and Hindus and Sikhs moved to India. Conflicts between Hindus

Dr. Bhimrao Ramji Ambedkar, 1891–1956, Dalit leader.

and Muslims in India have persisted, and religious violence has continued to plague many areas of the subcontinent.

We began by considering the term *Hinduism* and how it came into use. This chapter has outlined some of the most important developments in the history of Hinduism. It should be clear by now that Hinduism is enormously diverse, with a range of ideas about divinity and the nature of ultimate reality, about the ultimate goals of human life, about social status and gender roles, and about how to practice one's religion. Hindus themselves have often asked what Hinduism "really" is; groups such as the Arya Samaj and Brahmo Samaj provided possible answers. Perhaps there really is no one answer; instead, there are many varieties of Hinduism, many ways in which people draw upon their heritage to create a faith and practice fitting for their age, social status, region, sex, and personal, family, or community needs.

BIBLIOGRAPHY

Basham, A. L. *The Wonder that Was India*. 3rd rev. ed. London: Sidgwick and Jackson, 1967.
Bryant, Edwin. *The Quest for the Origins of Vedic Culture: The Indo-Aryan Migration Debate*. Oxford: Oxford University Press, 2001.
Coburn, Thomas B. *Devi Mahatmya: The Crystallization of the Goddess Tradition*. Delhi: Motilal Banarsidass, 1984.
Dehejia, Vidya. *Slaves of the Lord: The Path of the Tamil Saints*. New Delhi: Munshiram Manoharlal, 1988.
Doniger, Wendy, trans. with Brian K. Smith. *The Laws of Manu*. New Delhi: Penguin Books, 1991.
Eck, Diana L. *Darsan: Seeing the Divine Image in India*. 3rd ed. New York: Columbia University Press, 1998.
Hawley, John Stratton. "Naming Hinduism." *Wilson Quarterly* (Summer 1991): 20–34.
Jamison, Stephanie W. *Sacrificed Wife/Sacrificer's Wife: Women, Ritual, and Hospitality in Ancient India*. New York: Oxford University Press, 1996.
Jha, D. N. *The Myth of the Holy Cow*. London: Verso, 2002.
Jones, Kenneth W. *Socio-religious Reform Movements in British India*. Cambridge: Cambridge University Press, 1989.
Lipner, Julius. *Hindus: Their Religious Beliefs and Practices*. London: Routledge, 1994.

Mahony, William K. *The Artful Universe: An Introduction to the Vedic Religious Imagination*. Albany: State University of New York Press, 1998.

O'Flaherty, Wendy. *Hindu Myths*. Middlesex: Penguin Books, 1975.

O'Flaherty, Wendy Doniger. *Siva: The Erotic Ascetic*. London: Oxford University Press, 1981.

Olivelle, Patrick. *Samnyasa Upanisads: Hindu Scriptures on Asceticism and Renunciation*. New York: Oxford University Press, 1992.

———. *Upanisads*. Oxford: Oxford University Press, 1996.

Sen, S. P., ed. *Social and Religious Reform Movements in the Nineteenth and Twentieth Centuries*. Calcutta: Institute of Historical Studies, 1979.

Smith, Frederick M. "Puranaveda," in Laurie L. Patton (ed.), *Authority, Anxiety, and Canon: Essays in Vedic Interpretation*. Albany: State University of New York Press, 1994: 97–138.

Srinivas, M. N. *Religion and Society among the Coorgs of South India*. New York: Asia Publishing House, 1952.

Chapter Two

Hearing and Remembering
Oral and Written Texts in Hinduism

R O B I N   R I N E H A R T

Chapter 1 described the historical antecedents of contemporary Hinduism. Drawing from this rich heritage, Hindus have used a vast array of oral and written texts in creating the many varieties of contemporary Hinduism in practice throughout India and Hindu diaspora communities worldwide. In this chapter we will consider how oral and written texts are used by Hindus today. As Chapter 1 notes, it is important to remember that many of the Hindu traditions that are referred to as "texts" are not simply printed books. The Vedas, for example, are first and foremost oral. Many later Hindu traditions, such as the epics and Puranas, also began as oral traditions and even when written down continued to circulate in multiple, varying forms. To understand contemporary Hinduism, therefore, it is helpful to move beyond the notion that a written text defines a religion, and think of a "text" in a broader sense.

When learning about another religion such as Hinduism, westerners will often ask, "What is the Hindu Bible?" This question reveals assumptions that people most familiar with Western religious traditions often make. Judaism, Christianity, and Islam each place great emphasis on the importance of revelation as recorded in sacred texts or scriptures (literally, "writings") such as the Torah, the New Testament, and the Qur'an. For many Jews, Christians, and

Muslims, reading, study, and recitation of sacred texts is a fundamental part of their religious lives. Understood by many as records of God's revelations to human beings, these texts provide critical information about prescribed law, belief, and religious practice. To people most familiar with the Western religions, it therefore makes sense to ask what text defines another religion, because texts or scriptures are so central to defining their own traditions.

Of course Hinduism, too, has its sacred texts, both oral and written, but the role of texts in Hinduism is different from the role of texts in the Western religious traditions. There is no one "Hindu Bible," and no one Hindu text necessarily defines what Hindus practice or believe. The English word *text* literally means "that which is woven," and it is most commonly associated with written or printed words. Upper-caste Hindus, however, have typically placed their sacred traditions into the categories of shruti ("that which is heard") and smriti ("that which is remembered"). Both terms illustrate the primacy of transmission through hearing and remembering over reading and writing. For much of India's history, in fact, writing was considered useful primarily for mundane tasks such as keeping business records, and not worthy of something so powerful as the Vedas.

Even the shruti/smriti distinction, however, may be somewhat misleading if we are trying to understand the full range of Hindu experience. Shruti refers primarily to the Vedas, but not all Hindus have always had access to the Vedas and the rituals of which they are a part. The shruti/smriti distinction seems to have been of greatest significance to those Hindus for whom Vedic study and ritual were important, primarily upper-caste males. It is less directly relevant to people of low-caste status and women, for whom oral traditions outside the realm of shruti have generally been more significant. For a number of reasons, however, the importance of oral traditions in the development of Hinduism until recently has not always received as much emphasis as it deserves. Early scholarship tended to focus on Sanskrit texts, treating them as the defining sources of information on Hinduism. Many nineteenth-century Hindu reformers also sought to define the essence of Hinduism as some text or set of texts. Additionally, oral traditions are much more difficult to study than written or printed texts. Yet another complicating factor is that

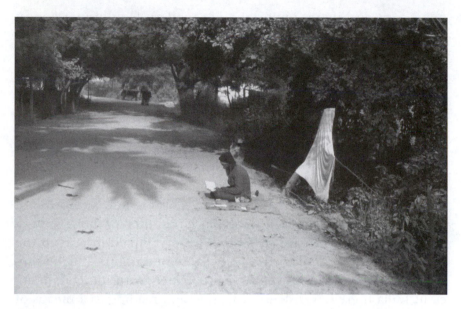

Man reciting a text.
ROBIN RINEHART

women and people of low-caste status have typically had less access
to education and power, meaning that their traditions have not
been as well preserved in written or oral form, and therefore have
not played a central role in the development of historical narratives
about Hinduism. It is important to note, however, that women and
people of low-caste status numerically constitute the vast majority of
Hindus. Recent scholarship has revealed more about their oral and
written texts, giving a more full picture of the range of Hindu experience.

Another important distinction among both written and oral traditions is that of language. The Vedas—shruti—are in an early form
of the Sanskrit language, and the traditions most commonly accepted as smriti, such as the dharma literature, the epics, and the
Puranas, are in Sanskrit as well. Because only a small portion of the
Indian population knows Sanskrit, traditions in India's vernacular
languages, whether oral or written, have been more accessible to
the vast majority of the Hindu population. Thus, categorizing oral
and written Hindu texts in terms of shruti or smriti alone may leave

out a great deal that is important. For modern Hinduism, we must also consider categories organizing oral and written texts according to the language within which they are composed, be it Hindi or Bengali, Tamil or Marathi.

Yet another important issue is the different attitudes people have toward oral and written traditions, and contemporary ideas about literacy. Around the world, many people now associate literacy with being more educated and more civilized. People's ability to read and write is considered one of the primary markers of a society's or nation's development, progress, and modernity. As a result, written sources are commonly treated as more reliable and authoritative than oral sources. The high value placed on literacy, however, is a fairly recent development in human history, linked in part to the spread of print technology. Yet many cultural traditions, such as India's, long valued the spoken over the written word. Indeed, in ancient India there was distrust of writing and reading as a means of learning and making spiritual progress. Instead, ancient Hinduism extolled the virtues of learning from a teacher, considering such study far superior to knowledge gained through the written word. Guy L. Beck highlights ancient Indian ideas about the power of sound and its primacy over the written word and argues that "Hinduism has sacred sound as its heart and soul" (Beck 1993, 6). Even as literacy rates rise in India, reciting, chanting, singing, and reading aloud remain far more important than silent reading and study.

To speak of certain texts as written, for example, may obscure the fact that even though the text may have been composed in writing, and may be available in print, many texts' primary usage is oral as people chant or sing them as part of devotional rituals. And as we have already seen, many written texts such as the Puranas have their roots in oral tradition. Furthermore, oral and written traditions have constantly interacted and influenced one another, and their ongoing dynamic relationship is an important part of contemporary Hinduism. In fact, many scholars now question the usefulness of a fixed distinction between "oral" and "written" traditions, because there are so many areas of overlap between the two (Sears and Flueckiger 1991).

One way we can try to surmount the many difficulties of understanding Hindu oral and written traditions is by using an expanded definition of the word *text*. As noted earlier, *text* literally means "that which is woven" and is most frequently used to refer to printed books. In the field of cultural studies, however, scholars have expanded the concept of text by studying the cultural context of power and symbolism within which a "text" is used. In a wider sense, then, a text becomes not simply a handwritten manuscript, printed book, or oral tradition, but may also extend to the context in which the text is used, its audience, and interpretation. As an example, imagine a teacher or guru instructing his pupils in the practice of yoga, using a standard Sanskrit text on the subject. If we use the term *text* in its expanded sense, the full texts for us to study, to "weave together," would not just be the Sanskrit verses on yoga but also the guru's explication and demonstration of the verses, his illustration of yogic technique, the students' questions and responses, and even the wider cultural context of gender, caste, economic status, and so on within which the guru and pupils operate. Taken together, these different components of the context of teaching and studying the yoga verses may be read as a wider text. If the guru instructs his male pupils that the practice of yoga involved celibacy and avoiding contact with females, for example, this instruction is a kind of "text" about gender. A text, then, in its expanded sense may incorporate both oral and written traditions as well as a community's usage and interpretations of those traditions in a given circumstance.

Using this expanded definition of *text* also helps us understand important issues such as access to texts, how texts are used and transmitted, and how texts may serve different functions at different times in history. If we use the Vedas as an example of a "text," we can think about the different meanings the Vedas as a whole have had over time, from the earliest stages when the Vedas were transmitted only orally among twice-born males, to later stages when the Vedas existed both in written and oral form, to the present day when the Vedas exist as many different "texts," from a Veda committed to memory by a south Indian Brahmin to an English translation of portions of the Rig Veda available in libraries and bookstores in the United States. The Vedas, therefore, in a way become many different texts depending upon the context within which they are recited or studied. A college student who reads excerpts from the Vedas for a class is likely to focus on the meaning and content of the text; a Brahmin who recites those same excerpts as part of a ritual is likely to be more focused on the proper pronunciation and sound of the excerpts. In a ritual, the power of the sound of the Vedic verses remains far more important than the meaning of the words, leading one scholar, Frits Staal, to argue that the Vedic verses are better understood as a kind of music than as meaningful language (Staal 1990; Gardner and Staal 1977). Thus if we read the Vedas in English and focus primarily on trying to understand what the words mean, we are not really reading the full text.

To understand contemporary Hinduism and its expression in oral and written texts, we must take into account the larger context of contemporary Indian culture, its print technology, mass media communications, and educational system. Literacy rates have risen in India—according to the 1991 census, 64 percent of males and 39 percent of females were literate (http://www.censusindia.net/literates1.html). Nonetheless, recitation remains more important than silent reading. Another feature on the landscape of contemporary Hinduism is the Internet, which is creating new Hindu texts and linking Hindus from different communities worldwide. Media reporting on religious issues also creates new texts and new forms of discussion. In the remainder of this chapter we will look at some examples of the many different kinds of Hindu texts and their use in modern India, first considering how some of the texts discussed in Chapter 1 are used today, and then turning to other important traditions.

The Vedas

Vedic ritual long ago ceased to be the primary focus of the religious lives of the majority of Hindus, although there are still situations in which Vedic rituals are performed, and there are still Brahmins, particularly in southern India, who memorize one or more of the Vedas. Some Hindus use Vedic rituals in certain portions of wedding and funeral ceremonies and in other life-cycle rituals. Many high-caste Hindu boys, for example, still undergo the traditional ritual of investiture with the sacred thread, known as *upanayana*, which makes them "twice-born" and thereby eligible for learning the Vedas. It is now common in some parts of India for the sacred thread investiture ceremony to be combined with other life-cycle rituals such as ceremonial tonsure (Prasad 1997). Though they may not undergo extensive formal training in the Vedas, they may at least learn and recite daily the Gayatri mantra, a short hymn from the Rig Veda. Members of the Arya Samaj continue to practice rituals based upon the Vedas as well.

Vedic ritual is not the focal point of most daily Hindu practice, but the notion of "Veda" as a powerful symbol of authority remains in many Hindu communities. As was noted in Chapter 1, some Puranas are identified as a "fifth Veda." Some sectarian groups identify additional texts as Vedas. For example, the Shrivaishnava community of southern India (which focuses devotion primarily on Vishnu and his consort Shri or Lakshmi), highly reveres the *Tiruvaymoli,* a Tamil poem composed by Nammalvar, one of the Vaishnava Alvar saints. Shrivaishnava devotees sing and recite the poem in their homes, and it is recited annually in temple rituals as well. In this tradition, a vernacular poem has attained the status of the Vedas as shruti (Narayanan 1994). The Vedas thus constitute many different "texts" in modern Hinduism depending on the circumstances of their definition and usage.

Hindu Philosophical Texts: Points of View

Religion and philosophy are now commonly considered separate areas of inquiry. But in many of the world's cultures, no such boundaries existed. In India, what we would term "philosophical inquiry" was often conducted for the purpose of spiritual progress or enlightenment. The Sanskritic tradition of Hinduism has traditionally recognized six major philosophical schools or systems, known as *darshanas,* or "points of view." In actual practice, there are far more than six schools, and there are major subdivisions within some of the six, representing a wide range of philosophical positions on issues such as epistemology, the nature of reality, and the efficacy of ritual practices. What the Hindu philosophical schools share, however, is acceptance of the Vedas as authoritative (Radhakrishnan and Moore 1957). The six schools each have their own written Sanskrit texts, as well as voluminous commentarial traditions. As with most Hindu tradition, however, the texts are thought to be best understood when taught by a guru rather than read. These philosophical texts have likely never been widely available to the vast majority of Hindus, but they have received a lot of attention in Western studies of Hinduism.

Given that the vast majority of Hindus likely have little familiarity with the six systems, a detailed discussion of their tenets would be out of place here. In contemporary Hinduism, the philosophical tradition with which Hindus are most likely to be familiar is some form of Vedanta, the sixth darshana. *Vedanta* literally means "the end" or "the culmination" of the Veda, and Vedanta thought has typically focused on the Upanishads. There are three major classical positions within Vedanta. Advaita, or non-dual Vedanta, associated with the ninth-century philosopher Shankara, asserts that the atman is being in and of itself, no different from the fundamental basis of reality, brahman. Vishishtadvaita, or qualified non-dual Vedanta, explicated by the eleventh-century philosopher Ramanuja, instead argues that brahman is personal, not abstract, and that the atman and the material world exist only insofar as they are a part of brahman. Finally, there is Dvaita, or dual Vedanta, taught by Madhva (in the thirteenth century), according to which the atman and the world are dependent on brahman or god. Some sectarian Hindu traditions further elaborate on the ideas of these various forms of Vedanta as part of their theology and devotional practice. Since the nineteenth century, the term *neo-Vedanta* has also become important. Neo-Vedanta thinkers typically assert that Vedanta is the highest form of Hinduism and, in some cases, the highest form of religion as a whole. It is discussed in more detail in Chapter 6, "Contemporary Hindu Thought."

Dharma Texts

The texts about dharma, such as the Laws of Manu (discussed in Chapter 1), were for most of their history preserved and studied by Brahmins, who produced multiple commentaries on the texts providing further explications of various regulations. The dharma literature remains important today because it continues to influence some Hindus' attitudes, and because of its role in shaping Indian law. It became especially important during British colonial rule of India, because British officials sought to use the law texts, particularly the Laws of Manu, as the basis for the Indian legal system. In both colonial law and current Indian law, traditions from the dharma literature have served as part of the basis of personal laws regarding marriage, divorce, inheritance, adoption, and similar matters for Hindus. The role of religious tradition in determining laws remains a matter of great debate in India because personal laws in India differ for each religious group. For example, the government of India's Hindu Marriage Act of 1955 applies to Hindus as well as Jains, Sikhs, and Buddhists, but separate marriage and divorce laws based upon Islamic traditions apply to Muslims in India.

Article 44 of the Indian Constitution calls for the eventual institution of a uniform civil code for all citizens of India, which would eliminate the current system of separate laws for separate religious groups. In 1995, the Supreme Court of India reiterated the call, recommending that the nation adopt a uniform civil code. The recommendation came in the wake of several cases in which Hindu women charged that their husbands had deserted them and converted to Islam in order to take advantage of the Islamic laws allowing a man to have up to four wives. However, given ongoing tensions between religious communities in India, as well as debates among Hindus about whether India should be secular or Hindu, the issue of personal law has been so politically divisive that little progress has been made. Some conservative Hindu politicians, unhappy with India as a secular state, have argued that the Indian Constitution should be a modern version of the Laws of Manu. In contrast, many Dalit ("oppressed"; members of groups formerly considered Untouchable) activists argue that the Laws of Manu are a prime example of high-caste Hindus' oppression of members of lower castes. Ideas about dharma—caste, purity, pollution—thus constitute many different "texts" in modern Hinduism.

Epics and Puranas

As noted already, the epics and Puranas began as oral traditions and even in their written form preserve many of the characteristics of oral compositions. Although most of the early Western scholars of Hinduism treated the Sanskrit versions of the epics and Puranas as the most important, for most Hindus today the vernacular versions of these tales are better known. Children grow up learning the stories of the gods and goddesses, of boons, curses, and the folly of demons, of Sita's kidnapping and Rama's rescue of her, and of Arjuna's dilemma on the battlefield. Mothers and grandmothers, village pandits, traveling storytellers, and musicians may tell these tales, and the epics and Puranas are also depicted in feature-length films and television serials. Indian television productions of the Ramayana and Mahabharata were wildly popular when they first aired in the 1980s.

The Amar Chitra Katha ("Immortal Picture Stories") comic book series, which began in the 1960s, is yet another way young people learn about Hindu tales and Indian legends. The first book in the series was a comic book about the god Krishna. There are now hundreds of titles in the series, and a website, www.amar chitrakatha.com, is being launched as well. The series titles are available in English, Hindi, and some other Indian languages. Some of the tales are based on a particular Purana; others combine stories from different sources. The 1978 *Tales of Shiva,* for example, combines accounts of Shiva's exploits from the Mahabharata, the Tamil text *Tiruvachagam,* and the *Skanda Purana.* In some instances, the Amar Chitra Katha version of Hindu mythology and tradition may be somewhat sanitized or "politically correct," catering to the perceived values of India's growing middle class (Hawley 1997).

Hindu children also learn episodes from the epics and Puranas through the celebration of various festivals commemorating mythological events, such as Dashahara, celebrating Rama's defeat of the demon Ravana. Neighborhoods may organize dramas in which children play the roles of Rama, Ravana, Hanuman, and his monkey-army, as well as other characters, the drama culminating with the explosion and burning of effigies of Ravana and his henchmen. In the north Indian town of Brindavan, where Krishna spent his childhood and adolescence, devotees celebrate the *ras lila* dramas reenacting Krishna's dance with the gopis, with Brahmin boys playing the different roles (Hawley 1991). Every spring, in the south Indian city of Madurai, pilgrims celebrate the Tamil myth of Shiva's wedding to Minakshi, daughter of a local king (Harman 1989). The "texts" of the epics and Puranas may also be read in Indian art, from magnificent temple architecture that depicts mythological episodes in elaborate carvings, to inexpensive posters, stickers, and magnets of gods and goddesses sold on street corners. Even computer screensavers now depict mythological themes. Indian classical dance forms, such as Bharatnatyam, also portray mythological events with a subtle, sophisticated repertoire of movements, gestures, and facial expressions.

There are traditions of exposition and study as well. Many sectarian groups host regular *satsangas* (literally, "company with the good"; a kind of religious service) during which participants recite or sing a particular text. It is common in many Hindu religious communities to study the Bhagavad Gita, and these studies reveal a number of different "readings" or "texts" of the Bhagavad Gita and its interpretation. Some interpret Krishna's exhortation to Arjuna to fight and kill as a justification for violence if one's cause is just (an argument made by some Indian nationalist leaders during the struggle for independence from the British). Others, such as Gandhi, are inclined to interpret the battle as an internal struggle between good and evil impulses, not an actual violent conflict. In yet other situations, the experience of group recitation of the Bhagavad Gita takes precedence over finding a specific meaning or interpretation. For example, the Swami Rama Tirtha Mission in New Delhi (established to preserve and propagate the teachings of the renouncer Swami Rama Tirtha, 1873–1906) includes in each Sunday's *satsanga* the study of several verses of the Bhagavad Gita. Typically, a mission official or renouncer leads the study. Each participant has a copy of the Bhagavad Gita that includes both the Sanskrit text and a Hindi translation. The leader of the study will sing each verse, and members join in, repeating each verse several times. Next, the leader explains the verse in Hindi and may link it to current events of interest.

The Many Texts of the Story of Rama and Sita

Much recent scholarship on Hinduism has explored the relationship between oral and written forms of the epics and Puranas. Here, we will use the example of the Ramayana to explore how a "text" may exist and be used in many different forms. Most early studies of Hinduism treated Valmiki's Sanskrit Ramayana as the primary version of Rama's adventures, but in fact it is probably the least well-known among contemporary Hindus. More important are the many vernacular versions of the stories. There are literally hundreds of different tellings of the Ramayana tale in virtually all the languages of India. Some began as oral poems, others as written poems; some are women's folksongs, some are commentaries on the social and political implications of the story. Two recent books edited by Paula Richman (1991; 2001) illustrate the wide range of Ramayana tellings.

A. K. Ramanujan suggested that these many Rama stories draw from a "pool of signifiers (like a gene pool), signifiers that include plots, characters, names, geography, incidents, and relationships. . . . These various texts not only relate to prior texts directly, to borrow or refute, but they relate to each other through this common code or common pool. Every author, if one may hazard a metaphor, dips into it and brings out a unique crystallization, a new text with a unique texture and a fresh context" (Ramanujan 1991, 46). Thus the basic plot of the story is transformed in different contexts. Some versions of the story even acknowledge that there are multiple Ramayanas; according to some tellings, when Sita was trying to convince Rama to allow her to accompany him into exile in the forest, she argued, "Countless Ramayanas have been composed before this. Do you know of one where Sita doesn't go with Rama to the forest?" (Ramanujan 1991, 33).

When we think of the story of Rama not as a fixed text with set characterizations and plot but as many stories, many texts, or "crystallizations" drawn from a common pool, we discover that the Rama story may reflect many different perspectives on Hindu tradition. For example, whereas many written versions of the story, such as Valmiki's, focus on the character of Rama and issues of male king-

Women singing devotional songs.
A. WHITNEY SANFORD

ship and power, in many regions of India, women's folksongs instead highlight the experiences of Sita and other women in the tale. Velcheru Narayana Rao's study of women's songs in the south Indian language Telugu shows that Brahmin women sing songs about Rama's mother's morning sickness during her pregnancy and her pains in giving birth to him. These songs also explore life in an extended family, and women's strategies for gaining power in family matters. Low-caste women's songs in Telugu envision Ravana's kingdom in Lanka as a place where the gods serve as slaves. In Rao's words, these songs are not "open and confrontational, but subtle and subversive" (Rao 1991).

Usha Nilsson's research on similar songs in the Bhojpuri and Awadhi dialects of north India reveals similar patterns. Women's Ramayana songs there also reveal caste tensions; while all women view themselves as dominated by men, high-caste women are in a dominant position over low-caste women, and some high-caste women's songs criticize low-caste women for singing about Sita.

Low-caste women sing of Lakshmana's sexual desire for his sister-in-law Sita, contrary to written Ramayanas that portray Lakshmana as celibate and so deferential in his treatment of Sita that he looked only at her feet (Nilsson 2001).

Still other interpretations of the Rama story explore the relationship between north and south India. E. V. Ramasami, born into a south Indian trader/cultivator caste, founded the Self-Respect Movement in 1925. He saw the Rama story as an illustration of north Indian, Brahminical culture dominating the more egalitarian Dravidian culture of south India. For Ramasami, Ravana is the true hero of the Ramayana, not a wicked demon but a wise and learned ruler who treated Sita well while holding her in captivity. Ramasami criticized Rama for lusting after power and for being hostile toward women and demeaning in his treatment of lower castes. Sita he decried for being secretly attracted to Ravana, and too attached to her jewelry. Hanuman, leader of the monkey-army, was cruel for setting fire to Lanka and killing innocent people, and a foolish character rather than an exemplary devotee because he is portrayed as performing miracles, which goes against scientific reason (Richman 1991). Ramasami thus turned the Rama story on its head, mocking its heroes and heroines and championing Ravana and his demon cohort as better role models.

Ramasami's critique of the Rama story is but one example. Throughout India, there are longstanding traditions of questioning, doubting, and sometimes criticizing the actions of the characters in the Rama story. Madhu Kishwar interviewed a number of people about their views of the characters. Although many people speak of Rama as a good king, son, and brother, both women and men roundly criticized Rama as a husband because he doubted his wife's chastity even after she had passed a test of fire to prove it. One woman, a college Sanskrit teacher, offered this interpretation of Sita's death: "Sita lives up to the ideal of a wife fully. However, her appealing to Mother Earth to take her back into her bosom should not be interpreted as suicide. It is a statement of protest, that things had gone beyond her endurance limit. It amounted to saying, 'No more of this shit.' I don't think a woman should commit suicide if her husband deserts her. You can't destroy yourself for a man" (Kishwar 2001, 289). The events of the tale of Rama and Sita thus come to life in myriad ways with multiple meanings and nuances, and an occasional dose of irreverence.

One way that people come together to discuss and sometimes challenge these traditions is in the ritual or liturgical uses of the Rama story. Each telling of the Rama story has its own traditions of transmission, performance, and exposition. Philip Lutgendorf has conducted extensive research on the performance and interpretation of the most important Rama story in northern India, Tulsidasa's Hindi *Ramcharitmanas* ("lake of the acts of Rama"), composed sometime during the sixteenth century (Lutgendorf 1991). Tulsidasa, a Brahmin, wrote that Rama's story was first told by Shiva to Parvati. Thus a quintessentially Vaishnava tale (for Rama is revered as one of Vishnu's avataras) is introduced by Shaiva figures and is performed regularly in Varanasi, Shiva's city.

Tulsidasa's text is widely available in printed form, but it is meant to be recited or sung, not read silently. Hindus may treat the book itself reverently, keeping it wrapped in a special cloth and placing it on a special stand when they recite it. Before they recite, devotees bathe and put on clean clothes, and after their recitation, they perform an *arati,* waving a light before the text (Lutgendorf 1991, 68–72). Lutgendorf's title, "The Life of a Text," reminds us that the *Ramcharitmanas* is not just a printed book to read but is best understood in the wider context of its performance and exposition and its place within a community. Reciting, singing, and performing the text are a form of devotional practice, an expression of bhakti. One of the meanings of the Sanskrit verbal root from which the term *bhakti* is derived is "to share," and the performance of the adventures of Rama and Sita and all the other characters is a way of sharing in their experience.

Like the other Rama storytellings discussed above, Tulsi's *Ramcharitmanas* too has its controversial aspects. In a particularly infamous verse, a minor character, the god of the ocean, opines:

> *Drum, rustic, Shudra, beast, and woman—*
> *all these are fit for beating. [5.59.6] (Lutgendorf 1991, 397)*

Lutgendorf notes that some have suggested that Tulsidasa didn't really mean "beating," but instruction; others choose to focus on more positive portions of the text (Lutgendorf 1991, 396–400). Even a single version of the tale spawns multiple interpretations and may be used to support different positions.

For example, the Ramnami Samaj ("society for the name of Rama") is a religious organization in central India comprised of members of former Untouchable castes. Even though Tulsidasa was a Brahmin, and not necessarily a champion of those of low caste status, the Ramnami Samaj considers the *Ramcharitmanas* its official scripture. Many members of the group had the name "Rama" tattooed on their foreheads. In the early twentieth century, group members were sometimes attacked by upper-caste Hindus who objected to Untouchables "defiling" the name of Rama by reciting the *Ramcharitnamas* and inscribing Rama's name on their bodies (Lamb 2002, 64–67).

In contemporary India, the politicization of the story of Rama is also significant. Though the issue is discussed in more detail in Chapter 10, a few points are worth noting here. Like many Hindu mythological traditions, the story of Rama and Sita is associated with a geographical location—in the case of Rama, the town of Ayodhya in India's northern state of Uttar Pradesh. Controversy has raged over a site known to some as "Rama-janma-bhumi," or "the birthplace of Rama." For several centuries, a mosque known as the Babri Masjid stood in Ayodhya. Early in the twentieth century, some people claimed that the site of this mosque was Rama's birthplace and that the mosque had been built on the ruins of a temple dedicated to Rama. In the 1980s, the issue drew more public attention as the Bharatiya Janata Party (BJP) campaigned for a vision of the Indian state its members sometimes termed "Rama-raja," or "the rule of Rama"—a vision of politics based not on India's secular constitution but on Rama's rule as king in Ayodhya. Part of the BJP's platform was the rebuilding of the temple, and in 1992, demonstrators marched to the mosque and tore it down. Whether there really was once a temple on the site remains a subject of intense debate, but the destruction of the mosque in the name of Rama underscores the continuing importance of the story of Rama in Indian life and the diverse, sometimes conflicting interpretations of the story.

Applied Texts:
Worshiping the Goddess

Many of the myths of the Puranas are also strongly associated with particular locations in India, and there are often local legends amplifying Puranic accounts. In the northwestern state of Punjab, goddess worship is especially prevalent, and temples throughout the Punjab are located on sites where particular events in the goddesses' lives are said to have occurred (Erndl 1993). Many goddess temples are linked to the Puranic myths of Shiva's first wife, Sati, who committed suicide after being snubbed by her family. Devastated, Shiva wandered aimlessly, carrying her corpse over his shoulder, disturbing the proper functioning of the world. Finally, Vishnu crept behind him and began snipping off parts of Sati's lifeless body. Where parts of her body are said to have fallen, devotees established temples, such as Naina Devi ("eye-goddess") in Himachal Pradesh, where her eye is said to have fallen. Outside the city of Chandigarh is the Mansa Devi temple, where Sati's mind or forehead fell to earth. Alongside the road leading to the temple, vendors sell materials needed for worship at the temple, as well as posters, small statues, and other representations of the goddess. There are also countless pamphlets and small tracts telling the story of the goddess and how to worship her. A typical pamphlet, in Hindi, is entitled "The Story of Mansa Devi and Her Greatness" (Chaturvedi n.d.). The first page explains that the pamphlet is based on Sanskrit texts such as the Bhagavat Purana and the Mahabharata, and that the pamphlet explains how to worship Mansa Devi, what items are required for her worship, an introduction to the temple, and mantras that one can chant in praise of Mansa Devi. We might think of such pamphlets, found at temples throughout India, as "applied" versions of the Puranas. The Puranic tales are most meaningful when people tell them in a devotional context, as suggested by the fact that the pamphlet begins with a song praising Mansa Devi and only after that tells her story. For many devotees, the myths are the inspiration for pilgrimages to temples and other sites associated with the goddess. A book entitled *Illustrated Call of Nine Goddesses,* available at many of the goddess temples

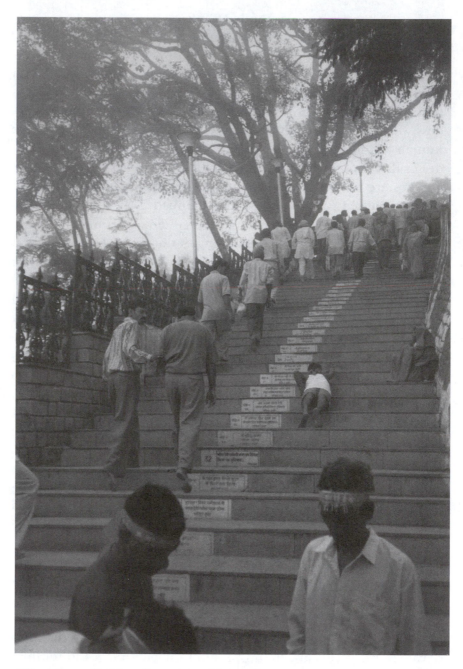

Worshipers climbing the stairs to Naina Devi temple.
ROBIN RINEHART

in the Punjab, bears the subheading "an introduction to the various incarnations of the Great-Goddess, with mythological and historical backgrounds. A complete guide for Pilgrimage to the nine important Shrines of the Goddess, situated in Himalayas, including tourist information and other necessary details of each shrine, illustrated with more than 25 coloured pictures" (Bararoo 1994). As many popular pamphlets and books attest, in contemporary Hinduism the primary relevance of Puranic myths is their usage in a devotional context of prayer and worship.

Storytelling:
The Ongoing Conversations of Hinduism

The dynamic, interactive nature of Hindus' use of the myths of the epics and Puranas is illustrated by the word *katha,* or "story," often used for tellings of the Rama story and Puranic tales. *Katha* comes from a Sanskrit root whose meanings include "to talk" or "to converse." Hindu religious teachings and traditions come not from a static, unchanging text but from ongoing "conversations"—between religious leaders and their followers, between individuals and their families, and among members of particular castes, regions, and sectarian communities.

   A very common form of story, or katha, in contemporary Hinduism is the *vrata katha.* A *vrata* is a religious vow or observance that typically involves fasting, worship, and giving gifts and is connected with a particular story about the origins of the observance and its effectiveness (for examples, see "The Ritual Calendar"). Vratas are discussed throughout the Puranas and dharma literature, indicating that they have long been an important part of Hindu practice. Vrata kathas may be linked to both the Puranas and regional legends. They almost always include a story about someone who performed the vow and how it worked. The vrata kathas themselves illustrate the ongoing relationship between written and oral traditions, and between Brahminical traditions and women's traditions. The roots of many vratas lie in Puranic tradition, and some vrata kathas must be recited by a male pandit. The performance and transmission of vratas, however, is largely in the hands of women, who use both oral and written traditions in keeping vratas. In modern India, women typically perform vratas for the long life of their husbands and the well-being of their families. Some critics have argued that vratas subjugate women by enforcing cultural norms that disempower them and define them only in terms of their husbands and other family members. Anne Mackenzie Pearson, who studied women's vratas in north India, however, explains that vratas are far more complex and often are a source of empowerment for women. The fasting and other forms of self-denial involved in keeping a vrata give women access to the power gained through asceticism (traditionally a male practice in Hinduism). Paradoxically, this self-denial may give women a sense of power and control that their lives otherwise lack.

The complex interaction of oral and written texts is also revealed in Anne Feldhaus's research on rivers and their role in the religion of the western Indian state of Maharashtra. Feldhaus interviewed people about river traditions and observed festivals honoring rivers, and also studied both Sanskrit and Marathi written texts called *Mahatmyas*, verses praising a particular place—in this case, verses praising rivers as providers of wealth, health, and general well-being. Rivers throughout India are commonly associated with goddesses and are revered for the bounty they provide. In her research on the oral and written traditions about rivers, Feldhaus found that river traditions reveal religious values shared by Hindus across sectarian, caste, and gender lines: "wealth, beauty, long life, good health, food, love, and the birth of children" (Feldhaus 1995, 3).

When we consider oral and written traditions and their use in rituals together as a more complex "text" constantly reshaped in new environments, we gain a deeper understanding of the everyday lives and values of contemporary Hindus. From vratas to festivals honoring rivers, much of the practice of Hinduism centers on family well-being and success in this world, expressed in the ongoing interaction between written and oral texts, between new and old versions of the "same" story. In her study of a north Indian religious teacher, his stories, and his audience, Kirin Narayan showed how storytelling in Hinduism serves as an essential component of religious teaching:

Teachings transmitted orally do not encounter the problem of relevance, for they are made contemporaneous with every retelling.
Each time a story is told it can be stretched and moulded to accommodate changing historical circumstances. The value of folk narrative in religious teaching is that oral transmission unselfconsciously
accommodates change even as it plays upon cultural themes familiar
to listeners from other contexts. The act of performance also brings
these themes alive; listeners hear ancient messages coming from a
living source, fleshed out with gestures and shaped around the im-
mediacy of a particular situation. (Narayan 1989, 245)

The persistence of oral tradition is not a sign of weakness or insta-
bility in Hinduism, but rather one of its greatest strengths, allowing
Hindus to apply their traditions to new situations and maintain an
ongoing dialogue with written texts. It is in the telling and retelling
of the stories of Hinduism, through new conversations, that the religion remains alive for its followers.

Hagiography and Devotional Poetry

Many Hindu traditions, such as the myths of the gods and goddesses, are at least partially based upon or informed by Sanskrit
texts. But there are also vernacular traditions, linked to the regions
in which the language is spoken. Here we will consider two very
popular forms of vernacular texts: hagiographies and devotional
poetry.

One of the most popular forms of storytelling in Hinduism, both
orally and in writing, is accounts of the lives of saints, people considered especially holy and spiritually gifted. Unlike Roman
Catholicism, Hinduism has no formal procedure for canonizing
saints, but throughout its history there have been men and women
who have achieved this status among their followers. Saints are most
often renouncers, and they may be known as gurus (teachers), *sadhu*s ("good" or "virtuous"), swamis ("masters"), or other titles. For
some Hindus, devotion to a particular saint is the defining feature
of their religious lives.

As a result, an extremely popular form of both oral and written text in Hinduism is the hagiography, or life of the saint (Rinehart 1999). Because the presence of the saint is so powerful, people seek to reproduce that experience through telling or writing about the saint's life. In a way, hagiographies are like images of deities, a way of focusing attention on something that cannot be seen. Just as people speak of going to a temple for darshana of a deity, they also speak of taking darshana of a saint. The idea is the same—through looking at and being looked at by the saint, through being in his or her presence, people gain spiritual benefit. Just as tellings of the story of Rama and Sita vary according to particular interests and issues of concern, so too do tellings of the lives of the saints vary depending on what is most important to the teller and the audience. This holds true both for hagiographies about saintly figures who lived centuries ago and more recent Hindu saints. We saw earlier that philosophical texts are best understood when taught by a teacher; hagiographies, in a sense, are texts that seek to recreate the saint's presence as a teacher by recounting the spiritually significant aspects of his or her life.

Stories about Swami Rama Tirtha (1873–1906), a saint popular in the Punjab and northern India, show how a saint's followers remember and sometimes reshape the saint's life. Since the swami's death in 1906, his followers have written over twenty-five different accounts of his life in Hindi, Urdu, and English. The varying stories of his life illustrate many of the characteristics of modern Hindu hagiography and are especially interesting when we compare them with the swami's own writings, because his followers saw him very differently than he saw himself. As a result, there is no one set "text" of the life of the swami; rather, there are many "texts" incorporating the swami and his followers' many ideas about what is most significant about him.

Swami Rama Tirtha worked briefly as a mathematics professor before becoming a renouncer and attracting followers who proclaimed him a saint. As a young man, he often wrote letters, essays, and poems about his ardent devotion to Krishna, which was so passionate and intense that he sometimes soaked his pillow with tears. The very first hagiographies of Swami Rama Tirtha, written shortly after his death, report this intense devotion to Krishna and also portray the swami as a man of science who rejected the notion of miracles. The more recent hagiographies, however, have incorporated new stories about the swami that are not reported in the earliest written records at all. A 1989 hagiography of Swami Rama Tirtha tells the tale of a morning when the young mathematics professor was so enraptured by his devotion to Krishna that he forgot to give a lecture at the college where he taught. Later in the day, when he realized what had happened, he rushed to the college, only to learn that not only had he signed the college register that morning but his students were calling that day's lecture the best ever. What had happened? According to the 1989 hagiography, and to followers of the swami who tell the story, Krishna himself had appeared in the swami's guise to give the math lecture for his faithful devotee. And, his followers add, if you doubt this story, you can still go to the college to check the register (Rinehart 1999, 110–112).

The episode of Krishna's math lecture is a good example of how hagiographies develop. The followers of a saint—a saint who never himself told this story about Krishna, who rejected the idea of miracles—are telling miraculous tales about him less than a century after his death, and providing possible proof of the miracle as well. The new written account of Krishna's miraculous math lecture seems to have its origins in oral traditions circulating about Swami Rama Tirtha. Are the swami's followers simply "making up" new stories? After all, there is no verification of this miracle in the earliest hagiographies and other surviving information about the swami. Perhaps it is more helpful to think about hagiography as not a straightforward reporting of verifiable fact but a record of people's memories and imaginations, their "conversation" with the saint's life and their devotion to him. Telling, hearing, reading, or writing the story of a saint's life becomes the closest possible substitute for taking the saint's darshana when the saint is no longer present among his or her followers. Whether Krishna really gave the math lecture is not so important as the fact that this story is plausible and meaningful to the swami's followers—it evokes an image for them. It is like the story of George Washington cutting down a cherry tree and then proclaiming, "I cannot tell a lie," so familiar to American schoolchildren—historians now say that it never really happened, but the story persists because it communicates an important value.

Similar processes have long been at work in the vast hagiographical traditions surrounding the lives of the bhakti poets. As exemplary devotees, the bhakti poets were accorded great authority and respect, themselves becoming viewed as saints. Telling their life stories and transmitting their poems itself became a form of devotion. Particular groups of devotees would tell and retell the story of their favorite poet's life, highlighting those parts of it most meaningful to them. What one group of devotees found most important might differ substantially from what another group would choose to emphasize. For example, some versions of the life of Mirabai, the Rajasthani poet known for her unyielding devotion to Krishna, emphasize her challenge to her husband and family, whereas other versions portray her as a dutiful wife. There is probably no way to know for sure which portrayal is more accurate, but the differences show Mirabai's appeal to diverse audiences, and how a single figure can exemplify conflicting values.

The accounts of the life of Kabir, the sixteenth-century bhakti poet revered as a saint, also help us understand how saints and their compositions are remembered and transmitted after their deaths. There is no one set account of Kabir's life. Scholars have long tried to determine Kabir's exact religious affiliation, for although Kabir is a Muslim name, Kabir's poetry seems to reflect greater knowledge of Hinduism than Islam. Many now believe that Kabir may have been a member of a caste that had recently converted to Islam. The stories of Kabir's life emphasize the regard both Hindus and Muslims had for him, to the point that Hindu and Muslim followers actually fought over his body after his death, the Muslims wanting to bury him and the Hindus wanting to cremate him, each according to their own customs. When they went to his body, however, they found it had transformed into a mound of flowers, and there was nothing to do but divide them among the different followers. This episode illustrates the futility of focusing on outward conventions (including the boundaries between religions), a sentiment Kabir expressed frequently in his poems. Even so, the different ways people chose to remember Kabir led to the formation of different sectarian groups, each of which remembers and reveres a slightly different Kabir (Lorenzen 1991).

The multiple ways in which people remembered the bhakti poets and the variations in the poems that were preserved in different areas and by different groups became a way to bring innovation and diversity into existing traditions. Nowhere is this better illustrated than in the radically varying collections of poems and other writings attributed to many of the bhakti poets. Just as there are many lives of Kabir, so too are there many widely differing collections of poems attributed to him. The poems themselves changed and expanded over time as they were transmitted orally. Many of the bhakti poets' poems were not written down until many decades after their deaths, leaving time for variations and additions to develop. Thus the collections of poetry attributed to the bhakti saints also constitute a shifting set of "texts," shaped not just by the poets themselves but by what their admirers remember as most important.

When we study the lives and works of the bhakti poets, therefore, we cannot assume that the information that survives necessarily always relates to a specific historical figure. Rather, we have poems and life stories associated with people's memories of a poet, which varied in different times and places as particular communities used the poets' personae to express their own needs and concerns. Whether Mirabai really was a dutiful wife, or whether Kabir was a Hindu or a Muslim, may not be as important as the many different ways these poets' followers remember them. The lives and works of the bhakti poets illustrate an ongoing trend of questioning and innovation within Hinduism on a variety of subjects, including caste, gender roles, and relations between religions, recorded in a wide array of "texts."

Hagiographies and devotional poetry are but two of the many forms of vernacular texts in contemporary Hinduism. It would be virtually impossible to describe all the texts that people use. Worth noting, however, are the many songs of Hinduism, such as *bhajans*—devotional songs sung in homes and in temples, often recounting mythological tales (and now often set to the tunes of Indian popular film songs); songs that women sing when a young woman prepares for her wedding (which can be quite humorous, even risqué, in their portrayal of married life); songs about folk heroes and heroines; songs agricultural laborers sing in the fields; and countless other kinds. Some are now found in books, but most songs are passed down from generation to generation.

Hinduism and the Media

Yet another important arena for the creation and discussion of new "texts" in Hinduism is the mass media. The May 2003 dowry case of twenty-one-year-old Nisha Sharma, a Delhi engineering student, is a recent example of how religious issues are discussed in contemporary Indian society. Hindu marriages are most commonly arranged by the parents and families of the bride and groom, and as part of the marriage arrangement, the groom's family may ask for a dowry of cash and other items. Although India's Dowry Prohibition Act makes giving dowry illegal, the act is rarely enforced, and dowry-giving remains very common. Ms. Sharma's parents had arranged a marriage for her and negotiated a dowry with the groom's family. But when the groom's family demanded an additional large sum of cash in order for the wedding to go forward, Ms. Sharma called police, and the groom was arrested. The incident received a flurry of press attention in India and abroad, and it was a hot topic of discussion on a number of Internet discussion boards. Ms. Sharma was interviewed by the BBC, CNN, and other major news organizations, hailed as a heroine for standing up against the dowry demand. Some fear, however, that such sensational press coverage of controversial issues fails to address more deep-seated problems. Shailaja Neelakantan, for example, writing for *Asia Times Online,* points out that most news accounts failed to highlight the fact that Ms. Sharma's family had in fact agreed to provide dowry for their daughter; the controversy arose only when the groom's family made additional demands. When asked why she didn't refuse to have dowry given on her behalf in the first place, Ms. Sharma stated that the appliances and other items her family had given were gifts, not dowry. The effect of Ms. Sharma's actions, and whether it will lead to changes in dowry practices, remains to be seen. Neelakantan, however, worries that the media coverage of the event is superficial and may not lead to substantive change

(http://www.atimes.com/atimes/South_Asia/EF21Df03.html).
Still, others argue that Ms. Sharma's actions may give other young
women the courage to come forward when faced with dowry demands, and indeed since Ms. Sharma called the police other
women have brought similar charges. It is clear that the national
and international media now play an important role in creating
"texts" about Hindu traditions, and they may bring to light issues
that earlier received less attention. In some cases this may be a positive force; less helpful are situations in which the international
media chooses to sensationalize unusual occurrences as if they typ-
ified Hinduism.

Hinduism in Cyberspace

The spread of technology provides the opportunity for the creation
of new kinds of texts. For example, many of the songs mentioned
earlier are available on cassette and compact disc. And now, there is
yet another new form of tradition developing—religion on the Internet. Hundreds of thousands of websites mention topics related
to Hinduism. Chat rooms and list servers dedicated to Hindu topics
create a "virtual" space for devotees around the world to discuss and
debate religious matters. Religious experiences are even available
online through "virtual temples" and sites that allow users to purchase rituals at faraway temples.

For example, the website www.prarthana.com offers "online
Hindu temple worship services." Users of the site may purchase a
puja or worship service online, and the site also offers links to a
website providing information on the Hindu calendar. In 2002,
the founder of the site, K. Ganesan, told a reporter that he had
spent a fortune on the site and not yet made any money, but that
he was sure he would be "showered with divine blessing" for the
service he was providing (Srinivasan 2002). Other sites provide
links to online versions of printed Hindu texts and offer daily astrological predictions, recipes, online shopping for puja items, and
news items related to Hinduism. Some sites allow users to down-
load music files of texts being chanted or recited. Individuals and

religious organizations have developed websites explaining their particular take on Hinduism. The Internet has also created a new forum for arranging marriages. Matrimonial advertisements in newspapers have been common for some time; now there are many Indian matrimonial websites where potential brides and grooms can post photos and information about themselves and their requirements in a mate.

The Internet provides the opportunity to create new, "virtual" communities. It may be an equalizing force in that it allows people to speak out and reach a large audience. After the Nisha Sharma dowry case, for example, there were countless postings on discussion groups by men and women sharing their thoughts about dowry and Hindu marriage practices. Still, it is important to remember that relatively few people in India have Internet access.

The new virtual communities created by the Internet may also include people from outside Hinduism. In some instances, Hindu traditions have been appropriated by individuals who find particular images or ideas compelling. For example, Rachel Fell McDermott's research shows that the goddess Kali has become for some Western feminists an icon of female empowerment and sexual liberation, even though the goddess does not necessarily play this role for her Hindu devotees (McDermott 2003).

Conclusions

Increases in literacy, the availability of printing technology, mass media, and the Internet all play a role in perpetuating and transforming the use of oral and written texts in Hinduism. Some critics have feared that mass production of these texts, whether through television or printed books, may bring about a process of homogenization that will erase the many regional variants of Hindu traditions. Nonetheless, new ways of creating and consuming texts also give voice to people whose voices were not heard as clearly in earlier times. One thing that contemporary Hinduism does make clear is that literacy does not lead to the demise of oral traditions, which remain an essential part of the current Indian landscape.

BIBLIOGRAPHY

Bararoo, Ashok. *Illustrated Call of Nine Goddesses* (adapted from Hindi). Jammu: Pustak Sansar, 1994.

Beck, Guy L. *Sonic Theology: Hinduism and Sacred Sound.* Columbia: University of South Carolina Press, 1993.

Chaturvedi, Jwala Prasad. *Mansa Devi Ki Katha aur Mahatma.* Hardwar: Randhir Prakashan, n.d.

Erndl, Kathleen. *Victory to the Mother: The Hindu Goddess of Northwest India in Myth, Ritual, and Symbol.* Oxford: Oxford University Press, 1993.

Feldhaus, Anne. *Water and Womanhood: Religious Meanings of Rivers in Maharashtra.* New York: Oxford University Press, 1995.

Gardner, Robert, and J. Frits Staal, producers. *Altar of Fire.* Film Study Center, Harvard University, 1977.

Harman, William P. *Sacred Marriage of a Hindu Goddess.* Bloomington: Indiana University Press, 1989.

Hawley, John Stratton. *At Play with Krishna: Pilgrimage Dramas from Brindavan.* Princeton: Princeton University Press, 1991.

———. "The Saints Subdued: Domestic Virtue and National Integration in *Amar Chitra Katha*," in Lawrence A. Babb and Susan S. Wadley (eds.), *Media and the Transformation of Religion in South Asia.* Delhi: Motilal Banarsidass, 1997: 107–134.

Kishwar, Madhu. "Yes to Sita, No to Ram: The Continuing Hold of Sita on Popular Imagination in India," in Paula Richman (ed.), *Questioning Ramayanas: A South Asian Tradition.* Berkeley: University of California Press, 2001: 285–308.

Lamb, Ramdas. *Rapt in the Name: The Ramnamis, Ramnam, and Untouchable Religion in Central India.* Albany: State University of New York Press, 2002.

Lorenzen, David N. *Kabir Legends and Ananta Das's Kabir Parachai.* Albany: State University of New York Press, 1991.

Lutgendorf, Philip. *The Life of a Text: Performing the Ramcaritmanas of Tulsidas.* Berkeley: University of California Press, 1991.

McDermott, Rachel Fell. "Kali's New Frontiers: A Hindu Goddess on the Internet," in Rachel Fell McDermott and Jeffrey J. Kripal (eds.), *Encountering Kali: In the Margins, at the Center, in the West.* Berkeley: University of California Press, 2003: 273–275.

Narayan, Kiran. *Storytellers, Saints, and Scoundrels: Folk Narrative in Hindu Religious Teaching.* Philadelphia: University of Pennsylvania Press, 1989.

Narayanan, Vasudha. *The Vernacular Veda: Revelation, Recitation, and Ritual*. Columbia: University of South Carolina Press, 1994.

Nilsson, Usha. "'Grinding Millet but Singing of Sita': Power and Domination in Awadhi and Bhojpuri Women's Songs," in Paula Richman (ed.), *Questioning Ramayanas: A South Asian Tradition*. Berkeley: University of California Press, 2001: 137–158.

Pearson, Anne Mackenzie. *"Because It Gives Me Peace of Mind": Ritual Fasts in the Religious Lives of Hindu Women*. Albany: State University of New York Press, 1996.

Prasad, R. C. *The Upanayana: The Hindu Ceremonies of the Sacred Thread*. Delhi: Motilal Banarsidass, 1997.

Radhakrishnan, Sarvepalli, and Charles Moore, eds. *A Sourcebook in Indian Philosophy*. Princeton: Princeton University Press, 1957.

Ramanujan, A. K. "Three Hundred Ramayanas: Five Examples and Three Thoughts on Translation," in Paula Richman (ed.), *Many Ramayanas: The Diversity of a Narrative Tradition in South Asia*. Berkeley: University of California Press, 1991: 22–49.

Rao, Velcheru Narayana. "A Ramayana of Their Own: Women's Oral Tradition in Telugu," in Paula Richman (ed.), *Many Ramayanas: The Diversity of a Narrative Tradition in South Asia*. Berkeley: University of California Press, 1991: 114–136.

Richman, Paula. "E. V. Ramasami's Reading of the Ramayana," in Paula Richman (ed.), *Many Ramayanas: The Diversity of a Narrative Tradition in South Asia*. Berkeley: University of California Press, 1991: 175–201.

Richman, Paula, ed. *Many Ramayanas: The Diversity of a Narrative Tradition in South Asia*. Berkeley: University of California Press, 1991.

———. *Questioning Ramayanas: A South Asian Tradition*. Berkeley: University of California Press, 2001.

Rinehart, Robin. *One Lifetime, Many Lives: The Experience of Modern Hindu Hagiography*. New York: Oxford University Press (Scholars Press), 1999.

Rosen, Steven J., ed. *Holy War: Violence and the Bhagavad Gita*. Hampton, VA: Deepak Heritage Books, 2002.

Sears, Laurie J., and Joyce Burkhalter Flueckiger. "Introduction," in Laurie J. Sears and Joyce Burkhalter Flueckiger (eds.), *Boundaries of the Text: Epic Performances in South and Southeast Asia*. Ann Arbor: Center for South and Southeast Asian Studies, University of Michigan, 1991: 1–16.

Srinivasan, S. "Dealing with Deities on the Net." *The Morning Call*, June 25, 2002: B25.

Staal, J. Frits. *Rules without Meaning: Ritual, Mantras and the Human Sciences.* Toronto Studies in Religion, vol. 4. New York: Peter Lang, 1990.

http://www.atimes.com/atimes/South_Asia/EF21Df03.html. Accessed June 25, 2003.

http://www.censusindia.net/literates1.html. Accessed June 24, 2003.

http://www.dalitstan.org/journal/brahman/braooo/manuconst.html. Accessed June 20, 2003.

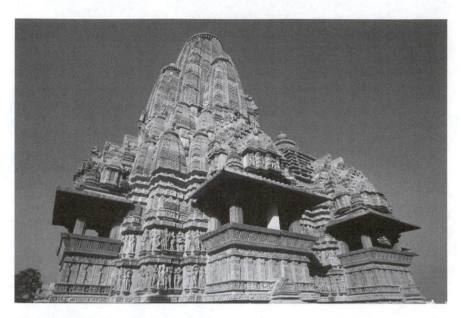

Temple in Madhya Pradesh, India.
TIBOR BOGNAR/CORBIS

Chapter Three

Hindu Devotion

WILLIAM HARMAN

It is a hot, dry summer in a small city near the southern tip of India, a city that lies on a rocky promontory jutting out into the placid waters where the Indian Ocean and the Arabian Sea meet. For most town residents, air conditioning is an unaffordable luxury. In their circumstances, two sources of relief from the heat are available: the evening sea breezes, and a walk into the massive town temple, which is especially crowded during the early afternoon hours. Built in the seventeenth century by a grandiose Nayak king, the temple's floor and walls are constructed of massive, hand-cut granite blocks that remain relatively cool all day long. That coolness pervades the dark hallways that were deliberately constructed to exclude direct sunlight. And it is enhanced by the large manmade, spring-fed, and granite-lined pond of water inside the temple where worshipers bathe before entering the sanctum to visit the image of the local goddess. Simply walking into the cool halls of the stone temple is a physical relief for those who go there to relax, to socialize, and to worship. Typically, that worship involves a brief *puja,* a time when the devotee places himself or herself in the presence of a deity's image so that the deity can "see" that person. Appearing before the image of the goddess, and presenting her with pure, temple-approved offerings purchased in the temple's outer courtyard, is a simple act: Once the "gift" basket (containing, usually, a coconut, cosmetic powders, bananas, and camphor) is purchased, a person

will proceed to the shrine of whichever deity he or she wishes to
worship, and in doing so will usually prepare spiritually by circling
the shrine of that deity clockwise, keeping the right side of the body
toward the deity. The number of circuits will vary, depending on a
worshiper's resolve, time available, or intensity of emotions attached to the reason for worship. But always, the number of circuits
will be odd, indicating incompletion, an unfinished-ness. Temples
will often have images of many different deities, but the shrine areas within each temple, those occupied by the most important
deities, are tended by priests who, at regular intervals, emerge to accept from devotees their baskets of offerings. Generally, half of what
is offered in the basket will be taken by the priest and placed in a
container near the deity, and half will be returned to the devotee,
graciously "left" by the deity as a sign of divine grace and generosity.
Once the gifts are presented, the image of the deity is understood
to accept and to absorb the "subtle essence" of the material, and
then allows the devotee to take back a portion of the gift as that deity's generous "leavings," or *prasada*. In using and consuming these
leftovers at a later time, the devotee participates in an act of "communion," of sharing substances with the deity. During these sessions, termed *arachanai,* as the priest moves from one devotee to
the next, accepting the offerings, he (almost always the priest is
male) will question each worshiper, asking that person's name and
astrological sign, and will generally insert those two pieces of information into a chant directed to the deity. In demonstrably presenting the worshiper's gifts, he thereby makes it clear who the giver is.
It is then up to the worshiper to make private requests, should there
be any, with a barely audible prayer intended only for the super-
sensitive "ears" of the deity.

Every day in this temple hundreds—on Tuesdays and Fridays,
thousands—of people will perform essentially the same act. Some
do it because they desperately want a special boon from the deity, a
boon that ranges from assistance with difficult family dynamics to
winning the lottery to getting a job or healing an illness. Others
come to relax, meet friends, or cool off, and figure they might as
well spend a few minutes of "face time" with the goddess, making
themselves known just in case future circumstances will require divine intervention. And for some young men, doing puja is some-

thing they can tell their mothers they have gone to the temple to do when, in fact, they are far more concerned that the temple is one of the few neutral places in town they know they can go to watch the girls discreetly. Devotion need not always take precedence over other concerns.

"Devotion" in Hinduism has many textures and arises out of a variety of motives. It is not always intense, but neither is it always casual. Still, at nearly every level the term entails involvement and, often, commitment, but a special kind of commitment—the kind that is probably best described as "palpable," "obvious," "physical," and readily observable. On the surface, at least, there seems to be general agreement about what people consider to be a devoted person. Discipline, self-sacrifice, and a life of principled activity based on religious teachings and injunctions would likely qualify someone as "devoted." But we must take care: A devoted person need not necessarily be saintly by the standards of all observers. Dedicated crusaders (such as suicide bombers or airline hijackers) willing to give their own lives (and then some) for their principles may understand themselves to be devoted to a religious cause. For those who share their religious commitments, these devotees will be considered saints, or martyrs, or both. For others of us, those same devotees may be seen as dangerously insane fools. What cannot be denied, though, is that if we wish to so label someone with these pejorative terms, we must at least admit that such a person is dangerously or insanely or foolishly devoted. Devotion, then, can be more than a pattern of activity that reflects an obvious and readily observable dedication: It can sometimes be seen as disturbing, offensive, even destructive. It is not always or necessarily nice, pleasing, or edifying for the rest of us, especially if we have no sympathy or understanding of the motivation underlying it. Devoted commitment from the inside of a religious community can, from outside that community, look like fanatic madness. It will be important to keep this in mind when we consider some of the more extreme forms of devotion found in Hinduism, a tradition in which spectacular forms of asceticism can be common: more about this detail shortly.

We start, then, with the proviso that devotion within a tradition must be evaluated by the standards of that tradition. Hindus, in other words, are more likely to be able to recognize devotion in their own tradition than are non-Hindu observers from the outside. Still, there are no final objective standards for what devotion actually is, except to say that it involves the sort of dedication you can frequently identify because it is backed up not simply by words, or by declarations, or by professions of faith, but rather—and especially—by a consistency of deeds. The *Oxford English Dictionary* traces the Latin origins of the term *devotion* to the act of "being devoted or consecrated by a vow." The vow is a promise to *do* something: sometimes to do something just once, sometimes for a season, and sometimes for a lifetime. Devotion, then, suggests activity, a "doing" of faith, an enactment that takes form and shape in a visible lifestyle: how you eat, how you work, with whom you associate, what you do on each Friday evening, full-moon day, or Sunday morning. Normally, we would expect that a person earnestly devoted to an idea, a deity, or an ideal would be someone willing to act, to put into practice what he or she professes.

For the casual Western observer of Hinduism, devotion in that tradition comes across as forcefully obvious. It is rarely concerned simply with words and ideas, with speculation, theological discussion, or the spinning out of possible theories about abstract notions of how the deities work or the way the world is put together. In Hinduism, orthopraxy—not orthodoxy—seems to take precedence. Before Hindu children are taught doctrine (if indeed they are taught doctrine at all), they learn to "do" their faith. The message tends to be, "Do your faith, and then you will discover in the doing what it is you believe, think, feel." In this way, Hindu devotion is faith that takes form in lifestyle, diet, and everyday ritual activity. So while devotion might ultimately refer to what we observers would consider abstract things, things we cannot immediately see, touch, taste, or hear (such as gods and goddesses), in the immediate here-and-now that devotion must somehow reveal itself and validate itself in visible action and in a distinctive lifestyle. Put another way, devotion as committed activity is, for the faithful, a willingness to "put your body where your mouth is," an inclination to back up what you say is important with acts that affirm the realities you claim to know and to put into practice. Devotion is conviction acted out. To be devoted to your faith is to walk your religious talk. As we shall see in

Hinduism, doing faith is everywhere—and in mind-boggling variety—the norm.

Action, or karma, is basic to understanding the way much of Hinduism works. In this world, we act. We must in order to live: Simply eating (and thus deciding what to eat) is a basic act with long-term consequences for our own lives and futures, and for those with whom we live. Eating certain substances, such as specific meats, for example, will bring unwanted consequences for both physical and spiritual health. When we act, then, we participate in a cosmic process of either purifying or polluting ourselves and the world around us. Acting in reference primarily to our selfish, basic desires is polluting and dangerous, for it is not in accord with the religious and social norms embodied in the rules and expectations called dharma. Acting in reference to supernatural beings tends to generate purifying action, good karma. At least, this is mostly true: There are demons, ghosts (*bhuta*), goblins (*preta*) and such that are impure and are likely to cause impurity and pollution when they are contacted or invoked. The only reason to approach them deliberately would be to placate them because they are suspected of haunting or possessing or simply making miserable certain selected, unfortunate individuals. Dealing with them when they afflict you becomes a necessary evil, a bit like surgery undertaken knowing that the immediate inconvenience and pain are likely to be worth the effort if the procedure is successful.

But the vast majority of supernatural figures in India, the millions of deities that compose the Hindu pantheon, are worthy of human approach and worship because doing so is considered positive, beneficial, and purifying both for humans and for deities. It transforms a worshiper from someone who is in a state of being less pure and less auspicious into someone more likely to live prosperously, happily, and in harmony with the cosmos. In the discussion that follows, I will be addressing how it is that a person might develop a devotion for a particular deity or a particular group of deities. Though the nuances will occupy several pages, the bottom-line explanation for devotion is that devotion develops when people become convinced that it pays off, that it gets results. Again, I want to emphasize the fact that Hindu devotion tends not to be either theoretical or abstract. Religious activity is understood to be very practical, even hard-nosed and pragmatic. It usually develops in its most self-conscious form when a devotee has experienced positive results from prior religious activity. Those results can be quite specific ("I prayed for a job and got one") or diffuse ("praying to this deity brings me peace of mind") (e.g., Moreno-Arcas 1984).

Object of Devotion/Objective of Devotion

In a tradition famous for its polytheism, how does a person decide which deity shall be the object of his or her devotion? No simple answer here is possible, but some generalizations can be offered. First, there are several kinds of deities. And about many deities a devotee simply does not decide. The decision is determined by circumstances of birth. The lineage deities, the *kula devam,* are often localized "family deities" worshiped by the extended family and passed down from one generation to the next through the male line. Frequently, they will be worshiped in the home at a family shrine where their pictures or iconic images are placed. Worship is commonly on a daily basis, in the company of other deities worshiped at the same time. But it also happens that a lineage will sometimes sponsor or adopt a local shrine outside the home where family members assemble on a regular basis to worship and to commemorate lineage solidarity. The event becomes something of a family reunion. The fervor of a worshiper's attachment to the kula devam can vary enormously. For some, the lineage deity is given perfunctory attention and is worshiped only when other deities receive offerings. Such acts of worship might be done simply to placate family elders who demand this occasional expression of allegiance to the clan. Others will take the deity more seriously, regarding worship as an important expression of family and group identity.

For males, the kula devam is inherited through the father's line. For women who marry into the normally patrilocal lineage, it is different. When a woman marries into a family, she usually is expected to adopt a respect and reverence for the lineage deity of her husband's family. Women, at the time of their marriage, will therefore be expected to shift allegiance from the kula devam of their natal family to that of the family into which they marry. But it is important to note that Hindus normally don't pick their lineage deities any more so than they pick their parents. And just as a person's parents are, whether she likes it or not, an important part of who that person is, so the lineage deity that she has inherited is important to who she will become. More often than not, that deity will determine the songs she learns as a child, the stories she knows about the gods, goddesses, and demons, the festivals she learns to celebrate, the texts she hears recited, and the temples she visits on special occasions with her family. The identity of the lineage deity will even determine how she learns to apply her makeup in the morning—those traditional markings that can be found on the forehead. It will determine what kinds of foods—vegetarian or otherwise—she learns to eat and to cook, and it will determine the type of family into which her parents are willing to allow her to marry. Of course, there are renegades and "contrarians" in any tradition, and occasionally people will defy tradition by marrying whom the family believes they should not, or by worshiping in ways the family does not approve. But such acts would be exceptions: Generally speaking, when it comes to basic matters of lifestyle, Hindus are practicing acts of devotion long before they know they are doing so or have even made the choice to do so. Family lifestyles, traditions, and habits reflect and are reflected by the designated lineage deities that embody specific values and orientations. Devotion in this sense is "programmed in" and can often be discerned by the trained observer by noting what a person wears, the way he or she speaks in terms of accent and word choice, one's name, or what holidays the family observes.

A similar dynamic can be found in the worship of the *grama devam*, the "village deity" whose autochthonous identity is rooted in a particular spot, a particular town. Just as we do not choose our parents, from whom we inherit a lineage deity; so, too, we do not choose our place of birth, our village, and the deity that protects and represents it. Often these village deities are goddesses, and people born into a village are likely to understand such deities as responsible for the physical health and welfare of the inhabitants of that area. Devotion to these deities can become fervently intense, and it is often correlated with a sense of attachment to the place of a person's birth or, in some cases, to a person's newly adopted home. Some of the most dramatic forms of devotion can be found in worshiping these village deities. These deities are often designated by the addition of the town or village name to the name of the goddess. Several deities, though having the same generalized name, will be distinguished by the name of the town in which we find their shrines. Mariyamman is a good example: In the Indian town of Aruppurkottai she is known as Aruppurkottai-Mariyamman, and she has a distinctive personality under that name, one quite different from the Mariyamman enshrined in the town of Pandikoyil, Pandikoyil-Mariyamman. This dynamic is limited neither to small towns nor to Indian contexts. The bustling south Indian city of Madurai is famous for its Madurai-Meenakshi, a goddess who has recently expanded her realm of activity by taking multi-form residence in an impressive Hindu temple in Pearland, Texas, in the form of Pearland-Meenakshi. The large Indian community in and around the Houston area takes great pride in the magnificent temple and the goddess under whose care they understand themselves to be living. One variant of a common Indian proverb has it that "Every town must have its temple," and, by implication, its presiding deity. The flurry of construction of Hindu temples in the United States during the latter decades of the twentieth century demonstrates that Hindu immigrants have not forsaken this notion when they left their homeland: Hindu deities from traditional India are "subcontracting" their powers to newer franchises, newer forms of the divine taking shape in Western countries. But the nature of Hindu devotion has changed a bit since its arrival in North America: Groups and castes who would not normally worship together in the same temple find themselves sharing religious space and religious celebrations, and images of deities not normally found sharing architectural space are often installed together in a common temple sanctum.

But there are other deities worthy of devotion who are not worshiped necessarily on the basis of ascribed attributes such as lineage or place of birth. The great pan-Indian gods and goddesses such as Ganesha, Shiva, Murugan, Rama, Krishna, Vishnu, Lakshmi, Sarasvati, Kali, and Durga claim fervent followings among those who have simply made a private, personal choice to become devotees. The choice is often made on the basis of an approving familiarity with the stories about these deities or perhaps due to a residential proximity to one of their temples. Most of the "pan-Indian" deities are associated with colorful, dramatic stories, and each tends to project a certain "personality" as well as commanding certain skills or powers. Different devotees are attracted to different deities on the basis of these distinct characteristics. For example, Ganesha is that beloved elephant-headed deity, the paragon of filial piety, adorably pot-bellied, and uniquely endowed with the power to enable people beginning new ventures to succeed. Ganesha's blessings help to remove obstacles that might thwart a new project's success. Worship may be directed to him only on selective occasions as a task-oriented expression of a devotee's determination to succeed. Other individuals, however, might be more inclined to focus primarily on Ganesha as their "deity of choice." He is approachable, not in the least bit threatening, unknown for fits of anger, and anxiously wills success and prosperity for those who approach him. Ganesha has attained extraordinary popularity in the Marathi-speaking areas around Bombay, where worshipers enthusiastically commemorate his annual festival. Ganesha's father, Shiva, attracts a real variety of devotees, for Shiva embodies many contradictory elements. Because Shiva is often represented as a celibate ascetic, renouncers, sadhus, and sannyasis invoke his symbols, his name, and his austere example in pursuing rigorous ascetic exercises that reach superhuman (divine?) extremes: Lying on a bed of nails is small-time stuff when compared with vows taken, not infrequently, to stand on a single leg for a period of several years (the unused leg often withers and becomes permanently crippled), or to hold one arm above the head, fist clenched, for years as the fingernails grow through the hand and out the back of it. Shiva is more than just an ascetic, however. Often he is praised for his prodigious sexual exploits, and those who worship him may do so with the expectation of internalizing his capacities in that regard by devoting their time and energy to meditating on the powers and virtues of such a deity. The list of Shiva's characteristics could be extended, as could the sorts of devotees who might find him worthy of emulating: He is at times a model of the perfect bridegroom, but just as suddenly he becomes a bawdy, impudent trickster free to flaunt the social norms of a repressed society. The more complex a deity's nature, the more accessible that deity becomes to a wide variety of devotees whose devotional lives will naturally incorporate the emotional conflicts and contradictions we all encounter as we try to make sense of the world. People will choose to worship deities with whom they can identify and often will move toward an active self-identification with the deities they have chosen to worship. Indeed, a disciplined imitation of the deity in Hindu devotion is frequently the sincerest form of flattery and praise. To become like the deity—indeed, to identify with the deity—is one of the more important forms of worship, and that identification is sought through the practices of puja worship (where the deity becomes an equal, a guest), dance (where the dancer, in portraying a deity, "becomes" that deity), song (where supplication and praise enable the singer to create beauty by virtue of intimate communion with the divine source of all beauty), yoga (where the practitioner transcends the limits and capacities of the human body, achieving superhuman/divine status), and the assumption of vows to renounce earthly, human conditions for a temporary period.

Still, it is important to remember that deities and humans have different dharmas, different codes of conduct, different "life scripts." Behavior acceptable for a deity is often not acceptable for human beings. There is not, then, a one-to-one correspondence between how a tradition portrays a deity and what a devotee is expected to do. As usual, Hinduism is far more complicated than that. That said, it is also true that the goal of the devotee is to purify him- or herself, to move toward the perfection or near-perfection the object of devotion represents. To become more and more like the deity is a praiseworthy goal. Certain devotees—renouncers, for example—will judge their spiritual mettle by the extent to which they are able to cast aside the dharmic expectations of society in favor of the model offered by Shiva as a wandering, naked ascetic, oblivious to the basic issues of human survival. Eventually, to become like a deity is to forsake completely the values and ideals of this human world. In the traditional four stages of life a Hindu male devotee should pursue (student, householder, retired recluse, and renouncer), the final stage, that of renouncer, involves giving up everything you have: name, personal attachments, social status, property, and wandering from one holy place to another. Few people actually move beyond the stage of married householder, but the values remain clearly articulated. To become like God, you relinquish the things of this world. Or, in more positive terms, you transcend the limits of this world to which you are in so many ways bound. Attachments to this world become a distraction at best and an obstacle to real devotion.

Though I have implied to this point that people are the self-selecting agents in choosing deities to worship (except in the cases of lineage and village enshrinements), there are many devotees who report having been "called" or "chosen" by a deity, often through dreams or miraculous events taken as signs. Between certain deities and certain humans there is said to be a "compatibility," and deities use these compatible individuals whom they "choose" as their servants, representatives, priests, or priestesses. (We might equally observe that there is a sense in which the devotee uses the deity, for often serving as a priest or priestess for the deity becomes a life's work, and sometimes a very remunerative one.) A deity may develop a "need" to be worshiped in a particular place, for example, and may appear in a dream and command a devotee to build a temple for that purpose. The devotee may, then, become the mouthpiece of that deity, going so far as experiencing regular religious possession trances. During these trances, the devotee is said to embody the deity and may even respond to questions posed by other devotees about what that deity wants, how to avoid ill fortune in the future, or how to exert favorable influence on the world in which we live (Egnore 1984).

Devotion to certain deities, particularly fervent devotion, can mean abandoning basic human values in favor of affirming the notion that the deities are not bound by human conventions or standards. Deities act, it is said, without discernible purpose or meaning. Humans cannot comprehend or understand the logic that underlies the way they operate, and so the activities of the deities are characterized by the term *lila,* or "play." In pure play—not that associated with a game, rules, or competition, but rather free-play, acting for the sheer pleasure of it—there is no extrinsic purpose. It is done for the sake of itself. Deities act with no motives comprehensible to human beings (Schechner 1982). We can only acknowledge our inability to fully understand how the world, under the care of deities, is unfolding. Certain groups of devotees, in their worship and devotion, embody this notion by proudly claiming the epithet of madness. Thus, the Bauls of Bengal and the Cittars of Tamilnadu abandon constructive worldly activity and spend their days in a spiritually intoxicated abandon, wandering usually in groups from one village to the next, reciting poetry and singing to the lord, often eating only what they can beg, bathing rarely, and generally acting in such a way that would qualify them for mental wards in Western societies (Dimock 1966; McDaniel 1989). Surrendering sanity to the deity worshiped becomes one expression of ultimate sacrifice as well as of ultimate freedom from the constraints of the human world. The madman, like the deity, acts unpredictably and with abandon. For such worshipers a preoccupation with devotion should, done properly, drive you crazy. Devotion, at its most serious, involves obsession verging on the freedom of madness: freedom because the madman cares little for the complicated and arbitrary common mores and manners. He is the divine hedgehog and no longer the human fox: The hedgehog knows one big thing, and the fox knows many, many dizzying details.

Before we take this notion of *imitatio dei* too far, additional exceptions should be noted. Some individuals will choose to worship a deity only because that deity has a specific and particular power or influence. In such a case, there is little question of worshiping a deity by imitating or internalizing that deity's characteristics. Rather, the issue is seeking power and influence by offering gifts and worship consonant with the preferences ascribed to that deity. Students hoping to pass their year-end exams will discover near the end of the school year a deepening devotion to Murukan of Palani, for Murukan is said to have special powers to enable superior exam results. The worship is less focused on Murukan's personality and attributes and more focused on his powers, and usually the devotion is limited to a particular time period. Still, to worship a deity, a person needs to know enough about the customs and stories—usually found in texts associated with that particular temple—that narrate what kinds of powers the deity might have and what kinds of offerings he or she prefers. The goddess Mariyamman, as a goddess of fevers, is understood to appreciate blood offerings. She is also a demanding deity in that she is more likely to bestow her gifts on supplicants willing to exert great physical effort during worship as a visible form of sacrificial devotion. At many of her temples we find devotees walking on fire, piercing their bodies with steel hooks, and performing acts of extreme endurance as a public demonstration of devotion to her. In comparison, such acts performed at the more "establishment" urban temples to Vishnu would be strictly forbidden. Indeed, they would be an offense and an affront to Vishnu's worshipers. Worshipers seeking specific boons from a specific deity need, therefore, to know about the deities they are worshiping, and to act in accord with what they know. When practical devotion is concerned, there is simply no substitute for knowing, first of all, what you want and, second, for getting reliable information as to where you can find it. For example, it would make about as much sense worshiping at a Naga (snake) shrine (almost always seen as a source of agricultural or human fertility) in order to get a good job as it would going to a hardware store to buy groceries. There is such a thing as stupid devotion, and, among other things, that would include going to the wrong deity for what you want or offering a deity a gift that would offend.

It can appear at times that the Hindu pantheon is organized in much the same way as the Western medical establishment. On one hand we have the "general practitioners," the deities who deal with a wide array of problems, ranging from chronic pain to winning the lottery to finding a suitable spouse, and much else. These tend to be deities found in the larger temples, often in cities. Because they are capable of a wide range of ministrations, their clientele is large. Usually the pan-Indian deities, such as Shiva and Vishnu, would fit this category. Their capacity for responding to supplicants is great. Then there are "the specialists," the deities associated with specific powers to heal or to assist. These would include, for example, deities said to be especially adept in healing fevers, preventing snakebite, addressing problems of infertility in women, and calming family strife. It almost seems at times as though Hinduism might be able to claim, "You've got a problem? We've got a deity."

By way of summary, the reasons for people to worship deities are many: They include (1) expressions of attachment, fidelity, and commitment to a lineage or to a geographic locale embodied by the deity, (2) a sense of admiration of, attraction to, and affinity for a deity's "personality and power," (3) a hope to derive specific benefits from a deity said to be able to deliver those specific benefits sought, and (4) a compelling perception on the part of a devotee of being singled out, "called" by a deity to render him or her specific service, such as serving as that deity's public interpreter/priest/priestess or building a temple for the deity. Finally, (5) there is a more diffuse but very pervasive reason for devotion, probably best described by the question, "Why not?" The deity is there, available in a local temple, and the shrine is convenient. Because so many other respected acquaintances worship here, there must be something to their devotion; otherwise it would not be sustained. And besides, spending a bit of time in the shrine is not such a bad experience nor is it likely to do harm. In fact, if we are to believe the many satisfied worshipers, it just might render some benefits. This sort of regular worship functions a bit like a health insurance policy. Intermittent visits to the temple may be seen as devoted or as instrumental "payments" in time and energy intended to maintain or keep current a policy/relationship with a deity who is more likely to be of assistance in a crisis if the relationship remains intact. Visits to the temple could be seen as occasional payments of a retainer to legal counsel. On the basis of the "credit" built up, assistance can be expected when the proper time comes. And eventually, this sort of prophylactic devotion can often transmute from something casual and not-so-serious into something more intense, particularly if the devotee experiences positive results from the worship.

Doing Devotion:
How It Works and the Work It Does

Visible worship—the acting out of Hindu religious devotion—takes many forms, but it also has a core of common characteristics. Most notable from the Western perspective is that it tends not to be congregational. Hindu worship in its most observable form occurs in temples that are often public (though some are exclusive, prohibiting the entrance of non-Hindus or of members not from a particular lineage or group of lineages) or in shrines in the home. In both domestic and public contexts, individuals perform acts of worship without participating in such things as unison singing, reading, or listening. Though in the more public temples you may find yourself worshiping amidst a large group of people, what you do during the worship emphasizes your individual relationship with the deity, a relationship that is mediated by the temple priest.

Temples outside the home are usually served by priests, whose responsibility it is to act as "middlemen" (though there are the rare, exceptional temples where women also play the role of priest) between humans and deities. Priests of the Brahmin caste are at times referred to as "deities among humans" as a way of emphasizing their capacity to bridge the gap between divine and human worlds. Not all priests are Brahmin, though generally speaking the priestly task is one of mediation. These priests observe a lifestyle that maintains their relative purity and that therefore permits them to be in close contact with divine images they would otherwise ritually pollute. Strict vegetarianism, assiduous care about the people from whom they will accept vegetarian fare, and caution about contact or relationships with those who deal in polluting substances (death, waste materials), are a part of their daily regimen. They clean and decorate the images of the deities for worship. Because of their purity—as reflected in their avoidance of impure activities, impure people, and impure foods—priests can touch the images, decorate them, and pass on to the deities gifts of fruit, money, and other valuables that devotees wish to offer. Basic to acts of devotion in both domestic and public shrines is an exchange between humans and the deities whose images are worshiped. People bring flowers, money, cosmetics, and other objects a particular deity is known to appreciate. Because each deity is understood to have a distinct "personality" with his or her own unique preferences for kinds of offerings, the variety of gifts can differ substantially. More established deities in urban temples tend to prefer vegetarian food offerings, jewels, money, and even parcels of land. Deities of the village are more likely to accept with gratitude offerings of meat, shed blood from sacrifices, or acts and public demonstrations of devotion that reflect a worshiper's willingness to serve and suffer for the deity. Walking on fire or undergoing arduous acts that include forced marches of hundreds of kilometers would not be unusual. In all of these acts and offerings, a common theme emerges: Entering into an exchange with a deity is good. Worship and devotion take on physical forms, and faith is invested in the exchange of physical objects. The classic tradition of puja becomes a model for how this occurs. As noted earlier, in puja a worshiper presents gifts before the image of a deity. These gifts can include flowers, fruit, money, or the body of an animal sacrificed for the deity. Such worship can occur at a home shrine on a regular basis, usually in the mornings, or at a temple attended by priests. In larger temples, that portion of the gift remaining with the deity and his priestly attendant becomes a part of the temple's holdings, and it is used to prepare food or offerings distributed to pilgrims. In the home the entirety of the offering is usually consumed by the family with some sense of reverence for the gift the deity has returned. Performing puja in public temples on a regular basis is one of the most common forms of active devotion many Hindus will enact.

These simple, straightforward, small-scale acts of puja exchange are for many Hindus a constant reminder and sign of the rhythm and comfort that can become the source of a life of reassuring devotion. Part of the power in these acts is that they place the worshiper squarely in a position to "make deals" with particular deities: to address deities directly, to offer them gifts they are understood to "need," and to derive benefits from this interaction. These are not inconsiderable benefits for the person seeking some sense of relationship with a purer and more powerful source of beneficence. One of the dynamics that provides Hinduism with such remarkably variegated energy and form is the array of exchanges that devotees can initiate, either in the form of simple acts of regular worship or in the form of vows.

The long-term vow, almost always initiated by a single person, illustrates the range of possibilities: Anyone who sincerely wishes to achieve a goal for himself (riches, employment, success in a civil service exam) can perform a brief ritual at the shrine of a deity understood to have the power to effect that goal. What a devotee is willing to offer can be minimal or considerable, and in making this vow (which can be written or simply uttered by the worshiper) the devotee promises to offer the pledged resources once the desired goal is achieved. Vows involve not simply gifts of money or jewelry

Man selling puja materials outside a goddess temple, Punjab.
ROBIN RINEHART

(though many do). They can be offers of service, such as returning regularly to the temple to clean it, or to feed pilgrims. They can include long periods of celibacy or other forms of hardship and self-denial, such as extended months or even years of total silence, a promise always to tell the truth, or, for the local enterprising thief, a pledge to cease stealing for a specified period of time.

Because so many forms of devotion involve a particular discipline, it would not be misleading to interpret those disciplines as forms of a vow. Mentioned earlier was the discipline of the renouncer, or *sannyasi*. The ceremony during which a person becomes a renouncer is tantamount to the public declaration of a vow to live the homeless, ascetic life. Even in the Indian law courts, such a public vow is considered binding: Because a renouncer is understood to "die" to his former life and identity, all his property devolves to his heirs. Even if he changes his mind about wanting to be a renouncer, he no longer has a claim on the worldly possessions he once possessed. Strictly speaking, he no longer exists.

Religious devotion thus becomes serious business: A publicly performed vow can eliminate a person's legal claim to be alive. When
we see—as we often do, especially in villages—people fulfilling
devotional vows by lacerating themselves and offering their own
blood to the goddess, or by crawling two hundred miles on their
hands and knees to a shrine, or by walking across blazing firepots of
red-hot coals, we are forced to realize that here is a very palpable
devotion, and one that is taken seriously.

Important to remember about Indian devotion, then, are several
premises:

(a) *Devotion is based on the notion of mutuality and reciprocity
    between a deity and a worshiper.*

This does not mean that deities and humans are understood to
be equal to each other. But it does mean that the devotee and the
deity mutually interact to change each other, to respond to each
other, and to effect basic transformations in each other. Deities
need devotion; otherwise they would not be deities. They are literally and figuratively fed by this devotion, whether it be their spiritual bodies or their egos that receive offerings from worshipers.
When a deity is understood to be at the service of her or his worshipers, that deity's attendants or priests often understand that the
flow of gifts and blessings cannot always be one-way; that is, they
cannot always expect the deity to give to devotees without receiving
some sort of reinvigorating replenishment. For this reason, worshipers must return the favors with offerings suitable to that deity,
and with lavish praise. Humans recognize, however, that no matter
what gifts they offer, they never really deserve the boons deities offer. What comes from the deities is always better. The exchange is
never equal, but still it is important. A sense of lingering gratitude is
one of the most basic sentiments any devotee must have when a gift
has been bestowed by a deity. Indeed, so important is this gratitude
that a devotee who receives a boon from a deity—and who has
pledged a specified form of "payment" should that gift be
granted—should not immediately pay off that gift. The devotee
should wait some period of time during which he or she must rest
mindful of the fact that there remains an unpaid debt to the deity
to be settled. This period of indebtedness becomes a specially desig-

nated time when obligation and responsibility to the deity is at its highest level. This should be expressed in frequent devotional visits to the shrine, visits that will assure the deity that her gracious delivery of a requested gift is neither forgotten nor subject to calloused ingratitude.

Deities almost always are purer and more salubrious than humans. In seeking to establish a relationship between oneself and a deity, a person seeks to become worthy of the relationship through pure and proper ritual conduct, impeccable intentions, and intense adoration. There are, clearly, times when this attempt fails miserably, when a desired result of a request simply doesn't pan out. This can be attributed to defective intentions, faulty ritual procedures, a failure to consult the right deity, inadequate offerings, or a general state of unworthiness in the worshiper. Steadfastness in a worshiper will sometimes pay off, but not always.

(b) *Devotion has a contractual nature in many cases.*

Devotion to a deity may be based on a clear stipulation regarding what a person wants from a deity or, in some cases, as in appearances in a dream, what a deity wants from a person. Once the designated boon or gift is granted, devotion may legitimately cease, or it may be transferred to another deity. This specificity in terms of time period, goal, and nature of the expected interaction allows devotees to maintain some control in the relationship, though the phenomenon of giving oneself wholeheartedly and without question to one particular deity is quite common, particularly as manifest in the devotional literature and history of bhakti. In bhakti the devotional vow is the dedication of one's life to god.

(c) *Depending on the deities involved, Hindu devotion can be either very public or very private.*

Devotion to clan lineage deities or to village or territorial deities expresses a verifiably public and communal solidarity, and it can include either perfunctory and formulaic ritual performances or intensely felt events that enlist enthusiastic participation. In village festivals celebrating the healing capacities of a local goddess, for example, it is not unusual for an entire family to designate one of its members to serve as its ritual representative during the festival.

One member of the family who practices austerities and makes offerings during the festival is understood to do so on behalf of the health and welfare of the entire family. The family's designated representative will often rotate among the able-bodied members of the group. In representing the family, a person need not be intensely or emotionally tied to the goddess. However, in the eyes of the family, if he or she is intensely devoted, that will likely be an asset and will more likely assure the efficacy of the rituals performed. Perhaps the ultimate call for group devotion to a Hindu deity can be found in the appeal for devotion to "Mother India," the topocosmic goddess tended by priestlike politicians, and to whom all inhabitants of the country are expected to express a patriotically tinged sense of dedication. The temple to Mother India in New Delhi consists of an image of a gigantic map of the country with careful designations of each linguistic and political region. The temple is the subject of frequent and enthusiastic pilgrimages that have tended recently to increase during the tense military confrontations between India and Pakistan.

Personal, private devotion can be directed toward any deity, whether it involves either the lineage-affiliated, the village-based, or the more widely recognized "free floating" deities, as M. N. Srinivas has termed the pan-Indian figures such as Shiva, Vishnu, or Ganesha. In addition to their family- and home-centered devotion, individuals may well choose a personal deity, and in doing so they will generally approach their relationship with that deity as a very private thing. Normally, a vow taken to any deity—but especially to one's "chosen deity," or *ishta devam*—is a vow about which a person must not generally speak with others. Like the wishes North Americans make when birthday cake candles are blown out, vows must remain basically secret in order for them to be effective. The relationship with the ishta devam often involves a respectful, private discretion during the period when a request is being made. It may be uttered as a silent prayer or written on a piece of paper and presented to the temple caretakers in relatively discreet circumstances. The vow sets into operation a relationship, and to do otherwise than keep it secret is to risk exposing the relationship to criticism and public scrutiny should the vow not bring about the desired results. Perceived inadequacies either in a worshiper's faith or even in a deity's powers might characterize an onlooker's estimate of what is happening. Specific vows become public, generally speaking, only when the worshiper feels bound to make a public display of the fact that his or her request has been granted. There are, of course, exceptions, and we know that when earnestly requested vows fail to get results from one deity, the petitioners are free and even likely to look elsewhere for divine assistance. Indeed, one of the most interesting dynamics in this process comes in what Selva Raj calls "ritual dialogue" among Hindus, Muslims, and Christians: The faithful from each of these traditions will occasionally look to sacred figures in another tradition for assistance that their own deities have not or cannot offer. Christians whose devotion to Mary fails to provide healing from fevers will often resort to Hindu goddesses on a case-by-case basis. Hindus seek out Roman Catholic ceremonies for the exorcism of demons. And both Hindus and Christians take vows at the tombs of certain Muslim saints for assistance in matters related to civil government.

It would be tempting to conclude that devotion is a sentiment and an attitude reserved exclusively for theistic entities, that is, for gods and goddesses. But I would want to avoid that notion. Devotion sometimes has rather indistinguishable referents: It isn't always easy or even possible to know to *what*, ultimately, an act of devotion is consecrated. A person, for example, might well be devoted to the ideal of nonviolence, as was Mahatma Gandhi. The ultimate root of that devotion will often be religious, but it need not be a deity. A person may be devoted to the care and service of parents, whom the Hindu tradition enjoins children to respect and serve. Devotion to them, devotion to the principle of respect for the elderly, devotion to the examples provided by deities in the Hindu pantheon (such as Ganesha) who respect divine parents—all of these aspects of devotion come into play, and it would be difficult to distinguish which bears more weight in determining motivation. In this sense, we might want to talk about religious devotion as a form of deeply felt obligation to the world around us. Simply being in this world means we have obligations to fulfill and debts to pay. In fulfilling those obligations by serving society, respecting life, or acting responsibly in relation to families, Hindus understand themselves to be acting with a profound devotion. Indeed, many of these basic obligations and responsibilities are marked by the celebrations of crucial life-cycle ritual events, called *samskaras*. In undergoing a samskara such as marriage or initiation, a person moves into a period of life defined by new expectations and obligations. The process of moving through this series of scheduled ritual events is said to purify a person, to perfect that person in preparation for a new rebirth. Failure to devote oneself to the tasks at hand at each stage will botch the spiritual progress leading toward purity and eventual perfection.

Another disclaimer about Hindu devotion is worth considering, as well. Devotion need not be intense, white-hot, fervent, or even passionate. It may be expressed regularly and consistently on a low-key, plodding, possibly even mindless basis. It can become little more than an obsessive habit, a way of punctuating the day, of providing regularity in a humdrum life or a chaotic schedule. Consider the man who, everyday on the way home from work, stops at a small shrine to a local goddess just to mumble a ten-second mantra his grandmother taught him twenty-five years ago and whose meaning he no longer remembers. He is performing an act of devotion. He need not think intently about the meaning or purpose, but he is acting out of some faith that what he does will be efficacious in some way, some time, somehow. For such people, devotion is a term that describes what they do because they feel they should, they must. Why they must isn't always clear, but the bottom line is simple: better to do it than not to do it. Obligation, responsibility, debt, faith, hope, a desire to take control of the uncontrollable: All these sentiments weigh into the mix when we're trying to answer the question, "Why devotion?" But for most Hindus who find themselves in a world pervaded by temples, ritual activity, and religious language, the more realistic and operative answer to this question is another question: "Why not?"

BIBLIOGRAPHY

Dimock, Edward. *The Place of the Hidden Moon: Erotic Mysticism in the Vaisnava-Sahajiya Cult of Bengal.* Chicago: University of Chicago Press, 1966.

Egnore, Margaret. "The Changed Mother, or What the Smallpox Goddess Did When There Was No More Smallpox," in Vol. 18 of *Contributions to Asian Studies* (1984): 24–45.

McDaniel, June. *The Madness of the Saints.* Chicago: University of Chicago Press, 1989.

Moreno-Arcas, Manuel. "Murugan, a God of Healing Poisons: The Physics of Worship in a South Indian Center for Pilgrimage." Ph.D. diss., University of Chicago, 1984.

Schechner, Richard. "Ramlila of Ramnagar and America's Oberammergau: Two Celebratory Ritual Dramas," in Victor Turner (ed.), *Celebration: Studies in Festivity and Ritual.* Washington: Smithsonian Institution Press, 1982: 89–108.

Chapter Four

The Hindu Ritual Calendar

A. WHITNEY SANFORD

One of the ways Hindus express their devotion to various deities is by performing rituals. Hindu ritual practices vary widely according to region, caste and social status, chosen deity, gender, and stage of life. Three generations living within the same household might each have different patterns of ritual practice. The Hindu tradition reveals an enormous flexibility and adaptability to individual and community circumstances, and thus there is no single authoritative text or body to dictate ritual practice. Although numerous ritual manuals describe and suggest how rituals should be performed, most are not obligatory.

This chapter will present patterns of ritual life as they are structured by the Hindu ritual calendar, exploring the ritual calendar as it establishes daily, weekly, monthly, seasonal, and annual practices. It is helpful to think of these elements as a series of concentric rings, or cycles, each of which determines specific elements of Hindu ritual life. This circular view of time aligns with the Hindu concept of cosmic time and the four *yugas,* or eras. This does not, however, mean that rituals and practices never change. Participation in rituals and festivals changes over time according to social and historical circumstances. Many festivals, such as Durga Puja, provide the opportunity to reflect and comment upon contemporary issues. The variety of Hindu ritual practices is so vast that we cannot discuss each one, but this chapter will present examples from each of the concentric cycles. First, it is important to understand the structure of the ritual calendar.

The Ritual Calendar

Calculating Dates

The Hindu ritual calendar largely follows the lunar calendar, which is based upon the cyclical waxing and waning of the moon. Since India adopted a solar calendar for civil use in 1957, most festival dates are now determined using both the more traditional lunar calendar as well as the solar calendar. Solar calendars reflect the lunar cycle as well; many temples, for example, each year publish pamphlets that provide both lunar and solar dates for festivals and events specific for that temple.

The lunar calendar is divided into twelve months:

Chaitra (March–April)
Vaishakha (April–May)
Jetha (May–June)
Asadha (June–July)
Shravana (July–August)
Bhadrapada (August–September)
Ashvina (September–October)
Kartika (October–November)
Margashirsha (November–December)
Pousha (December–January)
Magha (January–February)
Phalguna (February–March)

The calendar starts with the month Chaitra and ends with Phalguna in February–March. In a standard lunar calendar, the months cycle throughout the year rather than being fixed to a solar date. An intercalary month is inserted every few years to readjust this schedule so that the lunar calendar never shifts more than a week or so within the solar calendar.

Each lunar month is divided into two parts: the light half (*shukla paksha*) when the moon is waxing, and the dark half (*krishna paksha*) when the moon is waning. Typically, the bright half is considered auspicious or favorable, and the dark half of the month is less favorable or inauspicious. The days (*tithi*) of the moon are numbered by the state of the moon in each half. For example, *ekadashi krishna paksha* is the eleventh day of the dark half, when many Vaishnava devotees fast or abstain from foods made with grain. There are fifteen tithis in each stage of the moon's cycle. Unlike the fixed twenty-four-hour day that starts and ends at midnight, a tithi is calculated by the time between successive sunrises. Tithis thus are not fixed in length, and a lunar date can vary between twenty-two and twenty-six hours in length. Thus calculating lunar dates in the context of the solar calendar can be quite complicated at times.

Many days of each month, such as the full moon day (fifteenth day, *purnima*) and new moon day (fifteenth day, *amavasya*), are significant for the ritual calendar as well. Most of these days each month are associated with a festival or ritual observance. Divali, for example, falls upon the *amavasya,* or new moon day of the month Ashvina, the darkest night of the year. On this night, Hindus invite Lakshmi, Vishnu's consort and the goddess of prosperity, into their homes and businesses to gain prosperity in the coming year. Devotees keep rows of candles lit through the night to guide her way.

All dates for rituals, festivals, and life-cycle rituals must be calculated according to a complicated set of criteria. It is important to know these days—or to consult someone who does—because specific times of the day, month, and year are often either auspicious or inauspicious for any given activity. So, for example, the new moon day is inauspicious for marriages (Raheja 1988, 41). Traditionally Brahmins and pandits have relied upon Vedic almanacs, known as *panchanga* (a Sanskrit word that means "five limbs"), to fix important dates, from festivals to weddings. The *panchanga* dates back to approximately 1000 BCE. It divides a solar year of 360 days into twelve lunar months of twenty-seven days (according to the *Taittiriya Samhita,* the book that deals with the study of stars and constellations) or twenty-eight days (based on the Atharva Veda). These almanacs include the five basic elements that are necessary to determine dates: *tithi* (lunar day), *nakshatra* (the constellation of the moon), *karana* (half-day), *yoga* (a specific angle of the sun and moon), and *vara* (solar weekday). The *panchanga* also follows the movements of the sun—the *Uttarayana,* when the sun navigates the northern course from the Tropic of Cancer to the Tropic of Capricorn, and the *Dakshinayana,* when it changes its orbit southwards toward the Tropic of Cancer.

To fix the timing of an event, a Brahmin or pandit would need the following information, here described with an example of each calculation:

Vara: Monday
Sunrise: 07:13:32
Sunset: 17:54:21
Tithi: 10
Tithi Ending: 21:32:09
Paksha: Krishna
Nakshatra Name: Anuradha
Nakshatra Ending: 27:10:10
Yoga Name: Vradhi
Yoga Ending: 21:17:36
Karan Name: Vanij
Karan Ending: 10:22:18

The nakshatra are equivalent to the houses of the lunar zodiac. The moon occupies one of twenty-seven signs of the zodiac each day of a lunar month. In Hindu astrology, the nakshatra of the moon at an individual's birth is important for determining life-events such as marriage. The yoga determines the time and length of the auspicious moment. With the elements mentioned above, Brahmin priests and astrologers can determine auspicious times for events ranging from major festivals to marriages.

Days

The smallest cycle of the ritual calendar is the daily one, and many Hindus perform daily rituals on an individual basis. Some of these rituals are done according to personal motivation and individual proclivities whereas others are prescribed according to one's gender as well as social and caste status. For example, many Hindu families start the day with puja at home, worshiping the family's chosen deities. These pujas may be as simple as offering flowers and incense to the deity, or they may include up to sixteen different offerings, similar to temple puja. Many Hindus also start the day with a ritual bath in a sacred river such as the Yamuna or the Ganges. Water is a substance that absorbs and washes away impurities, and so this bath is believed to wash away one's transgressions. One unifying factor amidst the enormous array of ritual practices within Hinduism is the timing of rituals. Although much is voluntary and flexible about such practices, the timing is usually not. The occasion when any ritual occurs is significant and prescribed according to times of day that are deemed significant within the Hindu tradition. This section will next present two types of daily rituals in which time of day is a critical aspect of the performance of the ritual.

Daily Recitation of the Gayatri Mantra

High-caste males who have undergone the upanayana ceremony of investiture with the sacred thread rise early to recite the Gayatri mantra, a twenty-four-syllable hymn from the Rig Veda (III, 62, 10):

> Om, earth, atmosphere and sky.
> May we contemplate the desirable radiance of the god Savitri;
> May he impel our thoughts. (Flood 1996, 222)

The ritual of reciting this hymn is restricted to those who have been invested with the sacred thread, which essentially limits this practice to Brahmin males. Optimally, the Gayatri mantra should be recited three times daily, during the conjunctions (*sandhya)* of early morning, afternoon, and evening. *Sandhya* is the junction of two stages of time, so dawn is when night turns into day, noon occurs at the conjunction of morning and afternoon, and evening when the day becomes night. This mantra honors the sun as the giver of all things as it passes through the stages of the day. This ritual recapitulates the traditional role of those higher-caste males who undergo the upanayana ceremony to become twice-born. The ceremony marks the young boy's beginning study of the Vedas to acquire knowledge. The daily recitation of this mantra thus directs the individual's thoughts toward attaining wisdom.

Daily Rituals in Service of Krishna

Many devotees follow a daily and seasonal ritual cycle that regulates their worship of the god Krishna. These rituals are practiced in homes and temples and help the devotee live in accord with Krishna's life. Many devotees rise in the morning with Krishna, eat only the foods that Krishna eats, and eat only when (or after) he does—according to ritual patterns of worship. In this way, every aspect of the devotee's life is tied to devotion to Krishna, and mundane aspects of life become invested with sacredness.

The ritual periods are based on patterns of life of sixteenth-century northern India, when this form of devotional Hinduism became popular. This ritual pattern is called *seva,* or service, and devotees serve Krishna in activities such as feeding him or clothing him. Seva is similar to puja except that devotees of Krishna note that all of their activities are in service of Krishna. They see these periods as opportunities to make offerings and to share in his life.

Each day is divided into eight periods, each of which represents the different events of a typical day for the boy Krishna. These daily periods, or *pahars* (watch or guard, about three hours), are specifically calculated according to *muhurtas,* auspicious "moments" lasting forty-eight minutes. (A *muhurta* may also refer to specific periods of the day, such as the *Brahma muhurta* at sunrise, considered particularly auspicious.) The early morning period consists of the first three *muhurtas* after sunrise, approximately two hours and twenty-four minutes (Chatterjee 1998, 60). The eight daily periods are as follows:

1. *Mangala* (early morning)—Devotees wake up in the morning with Krishna.

2. *Shringara* (adornment)—Devotees dress Krishna and adorn him with finery.
3. *Gvala* (cowherding)—Devotees honor that time in which Krishna plays with his mother or takes the cows out for grazing.
4. *Rajabhoga* (midday meal)—Devotees feed Krishna a midday meal.
5. *Utthapana* (after the nap)—Krishna awakes from his mid-afternoon nap.
6. *Bhoga* (meal)—After his nap, Krishna eats a light meal, such as fried foods.
7. *Sandhyaratri*—Devotees feed Krishna dinner.
8. *Shayana*—Krishna is put to bed.

The goal of these rituals is for the devotee to see or take dar-shana of Krishna through participating in his daily activities. These ritual periods help devotees synchronize their lives with Krishna. To help them visualize the scenarios, devotees view the image of the god in a particular tableau in each of the ritual periods. Krishna's dress and his foods in the tableau, for example, reflect the particular darshana period. To help the devotee focus on this period, musicians may sing songs that set the scenario for the devotee and offer details about Krishna's actions at that particular time. In temples, Krishna seva is primarily performed by male Brahmins who trace their lineage to key figures of popular Krishna devotion in the sixteenth century. However, most devotees will also perform seva themselves in their homes.

The recitation of the Gayatri mantra and ritual service for Krishna provide two examples of how some Hindus ritually structure their day, and of how natural phenomena such as the sunrise are integrated into ritual life.

Weeks

Each of the seven days of the week also have specific rituals associated with them, although the weekly cycle is not as predominant as the daily or yearly cycle. The seven-day week was adopted in the Gupta era (ca. 300 CE) and is based upon the planets, similar to the Western system developed in the Greco-Roman world. Each day has a planetary association, reflecting the importance of astrology within Hindu practice. Most days of the week are associated with devotion to at least one Hindu deity as well. Additionally, most days of the week are considered auspicious or inauspicious for any given activity (Chatterjee 1998, 1–25). Though these prohibitions are not specifically "religious," they structure devotees' lives and daily activities in a variety of areas (Raheja 1988, 39).

Certain days are also designated for fasting, depending on individual choices and on one's chosen deity. For example, Hindus may fast on certain days of the month such as Purnima (full moon) and Ekadashi (the eleventh day of the fortnight). This section will describe some of the popular ritual activities associated with the weekly cycle.

Fasts are an important aspect of Hindu ritual life, and there are many different types. In some cases, fasting simply means abstaining from certain types of foods, such as grains. Devotees fast for a variety of reasons. Some fast to honor a particular deity, and others fast to obtain a specific end, such as an end to a child's illness or to gain a child. Many women, in particular, fast to maintain the well-being of their family and to ensure domestic tranquility. The important role of fasting in Hindu ritual life points to two issues: first, fasts are considered efficacious, that is, fasting brings results. The stories noted later will demonstrate this. Second, many of these fasts are undertaken by women, particularly married women, to maintain their family's well-being. In the Hindu tradition, it is a woman's responsibility to maintain her family's health, particularly that of her husband, and she is considered to have the power to do so. Women have a considerable power, or shakti, and, according to the Hindu tradition, this power is auspicious when a woman is married because she can use this power to maintain her family. Her power only becomes inauspicious or threatening when she is not in the state of marriage. A widow is considered inauspicious and is viewed with great suspicion because she did not protect her husband.

Although fasts are a significant part of Hindu devotional life (especially for women), their importance is not reflected in the formal textual tradition of Hinduism. Instead, much of the information about fasts is passed down orally or through pamphlets available at temples and pilgrimage centers.

Sunday: Ravivara (Day of Sun)

Sunday, the first day of the week, is associated with the sun. Sunday is not a particularly significant day, but its connection to the sun— the giver of all things—renders this day auspicious. Some individuals fast, taking food only once before sunset to guard against skin diseases such as ringworm or leprosy (Babb 1975, 109–120).

Monday: Somavara (Day of Moon)

Somavara, associated with the moon, is a day for devotees to honor Shiva. In addition to honoring Shiva, fasting on this day brings prosperity and ensures family harmony, traditionally the responsibility of women. Women may keep a full or partial fast for Shiva on this day. It is common to make a vow to keep a fast on sixteen consecutive Mondays. The rationale for the sixteen-week Monday fast is illustrated in the following story, or vrata katha:

> Lord Shiva and Parvati decided to visit the Shiva temple in the city of Amravati. One day, Parvati suggested a dice game to Shiva. Shiva agreed, and the game began. When the temple priest approached, Parvati asked him to foretell the game's winner. Quickly and without much thought, the Brahmin answered that Shiva would win the game. But Parvati won the game and became angry that the Brahmin had lied. Despite Shiva's attempts to pacify her, Parvati cursed the Brahmin to become a leper.
>
> Some fairies later saw the Brahmin's miserable condition, and after hearing the story, they took pity on him and told him to observe a Monday fast for sixteen consecutive weeks. "On the seventeenth

Monday," they advised, "prepare prasada with flour, ghee [clarified butter] and sugar. Give some to your family and take some for yourself. After that, you will be free of leprosy." He did as they said and regained his health.

When Shiva and Parvati again visited the temple, Parvati inquired about the priest's good health. After hearing his story, Parvati herself decided to undertake the fast. When she broke the fast sixteen weeks later, her son Kartikeya appeared and asked about his mother's new power. Impressed, Kartikeya himself then undertook the fast in order to bring about a reunion with a friend in a foreign country. Next the friend too undertook the fast, and on the seventeenth Monday he went to a city in which the ruler was planning to marry his daughter to the man upon whose neck an elephant placed a garland. Benefiting from the power of the fast, the friend won the daughter's hand in marriage as well as a substantial sum of money. His princess bride asked why the elephant had ignored the waiting princes and chosen this man, and the man attributed his fortune to the sixteen-Monday fast. The bride herself then began the fast, hoping to conceive a beautiful and wise son.

Once again the fast yielded results, and when the beautiful and wise son had grown up, he asked about the miracle of his birth. Then he too undertook the fast to gain a kingdom for his parents. In the meantime, the son married a princess from a nearby kingdom and became king. He had arranged a prayer party for the Monday on which he would break his fast. The queen, however, refused to attend the party. The king's oracle proclaimed that unless he turned out the queen, he would be destroyed. With a heavy heart, the king sent his queen from the palace.

The queen left the palace in old clothes and soon became tired and hungry. She met a old woman heading to the city to sell yarn. The queen offered to help and carried the yarn upon her head. But a strong wind arose and blew the yarn away, and the old woman asked the queen to leave.

An oilman then agreed to shelter the queen in his home, but as soon as she set foot in the house, the pots began to crack. The oilman too turned her out. The queen's bad luck continued when she sought water; a creek dried up as soon as she touched it. A crystal-clear forest water tank muddied at her touch. As soon as she attempted to rest under a tree, its leaves all fell away.

Nearby cowherds witnessed the queen's effect on her surroundings and reported it to a temple priest. The priest summoned the queen. Recognizing her royal features, he provided her with necessities, but her touch continued to render everything impure. The priest asked what she could have done to bring on such misfortune. She told him of her refusal to attend the Monday fast prayer, and the priest immediately diagnosed her problem as Shiva's curse. He advised her to fast for sixteen consecutive Mondays so that she would be absolved of her sins.

On the seventeenth Monday, the priest realized that the queen's condition must be quite desperate, so he sent men to seek her. When they found her, the priest demanded that the king himself come. The king did so and told the priest that he had sent his queen away to avoid Shiva's wrath. The couple returned home and distributed food and money to the needy. From then on, the pair observed the fast and dwelled in Shivapuri, Shiva's city, after their deaths. (Kaushik n.d., 22–29)

This story is told upon the completion of the sixteen-week fast. It demonstrates that those who follow this fast will gain many benefits whereas those who do not will suffer.

Tuesday: Mangalavara (Day of Mars)

Mangalavara is associated with the planet Mars, which is considered astrologically inauspicious. Mars is associated with the color red, bloodshed, and war. Many devotees worship forms of the goddess on Tuesdays, particularly those manifestations that are powerful and malevolent, such as Shitla, the goddess of smallpox (Babb 1975, 112). Devotees of the goddess might attend a special temple *arati* and fast if they have a special request from the deity.

Tuesday is also special for the deity Hanuman, and many devotees observe a special Tuesday fast for him. Upon breaking the fast, they wear red clothes at worship and offer red flowers.

Budhavara: Wednesday (Day of Mercury)

Wednesday is associated with the planet Mercury and is generally considered auspicious. Wednesday would be a good day upon which to start a trip or some kind of project.

Guruvara: Thursday (Day of Jupiter)

Thursday is associated with the planet Jupiter, which has a strong planetary influence, and women often perform vows to protect their husbands on this day. In Uttar Pradesh, women will fast either on Thursdays for an entire year or on Thursdays during the inauspicious months of Kartika, Shravana, and Chaitra if their husbands' illness or afflictions have been caused by the inauspicious influence of Jupiter (Raheja 1988, 72).

Skukravara: Friday (Day of Venus)

Friday is associated with Venus, a benevolent planet. In the Punjab, women perform a vrata in honor of the goddess Santoshi Mata. Devotees make a small offering to Santoshi Mata and partake of prasada and only one meal so that the family will receive the deity's beneficence. Additionally, devotees of Santoshi Mata abstain from eating or drinking anything sour to avoid angering the goddess (Erndl 1993, 142–143).

Shanivara: Saturday (Day of Saturn)

Saturday is associated with the planet Saturn, typically considered inauspicious. Saturn, or Shani, is a malevolent warrior whose inauspiciousness must be balanced or countered with fasts, offerings, or by wearing certain gems. Devotees offer mostly black items, including black sesame seeds. Saturn is linked with darkness and disease, so people are careful not to anger this deity.

Seasons and Years

Most festivals commemorate events from Hinduism's rich mythology, as expressed in oral and written traditions from both Sanskrit and vernacular languages. Hindus follow a yearly cycle and observe a variety of festivals and holidays. This section will describe some of the major festivals as the year cycles through the changing seasons. India was and still is largely based on an agrarian lifestyle and economy. Even in urban regions, festivals reflect their rural roots. India's year contains six seasons, each of which spans approximately two months:

Vasanta (spring), Phalguna and Chaitra; March–April
Grishma (the hot season), Vaisakha and Jetha; May–June
Varsha (the rainy season), Asadha and Shravana;
   July–August
Sharada (autumn), Bhadrapada and Ashvina;
   September–October
Hemanta (late autumn), Kartika and Margashisha;
   November–December
Shishira (end of winter), Pausha and Magha;
   January–February

The seasonal cycle begins with the onset of spring, when winter's cold is abating and the time for spring harvest is approaching. Spring officially begins on a day known as Vasanta Panchami, the fifth day of the bright half of Magha.

Vasanta Panchami

Vasanta Panchami heralds the onset of spring, and Hindus celebrate the day with a ritual bath in the morning, then don yellow clothes, because yellow represents the ripening of the spring harvest. At this time, mustard fields are bright yellow, and the winter's edge is gone. Vasanta Panchami also heralds the beginning of Holi season, and the following six weeks or so are the build-up to the ma-

jor festival of Holi. This day also commemorates Shiva's destruction
of the god Kama. The other gods had sent Kama to distract Shiva
from his intense meditation. Shiva became angry at this interrup-
tion and burnt Kama to ashes.

Though Vasanta Panchami is a pan-Hindu celebration, regional
variations are nonetheless evident. For example, Vasanta Panchami
also highlights devotion to Sarasvati, the goddess of learning and
the wife of Brahma. On this day Bengalis, in particular, perform a
special puja for Sarasvati. In northern India, especially the Punjab,
people welcome the spring with the Festival of Kites. Children fly
kites from the rooftops, often competing to cut down one another's
kites using razor-sharp string.

Holi

By the end of February or early March, most of India is anticipating
the spring festival of Holi. Holi officially occurs on the fifth day of
the dark half of Phalguna, but the season has been building up
since Vasanta Panchami. The actual festivities associated with Holi
take place over approximately a week. Though Holi is now primarily linked with devotion to Radha and Krishna, it is also a spring
harvest festival with obvious links to the agricultural calendar.

On the full moon day of the month of Phalguna, devotees build
an enormous pile of wood that will become a bonfire in the
evening. The Puranas tell the story of a young devotee of Vishnu
named Prahlada. Prahlada's father, the king Hiranyakashipu, however, was a dedicated enemy of Vishnu and was infuriated by his
son's steadfast devotion to Vishnu. Hiranyakashipu made many attempts to sway his son's devotion, but the boy appeared immortal
and immovable. Eventually Hiranyakashipu called upon his sister
Holika to enter a bonfire carrying Prahlada, assuming that she was
impervious to fire. Holika entered the fire holding the boy on her
lap, but to the king's surprise, Prahlada was untouched by the
flames while Holika perished. The Holi bonfire reenacts this story
and commemorates Prahlada's steadfast devotion to Vishnu. Before the fire is lit, a statue of Prahlada is placed in the woodpile. After the fire has been burning for some time, just when it appears

Girls playing Holi in New Delhi.
ROBIN RINEHART

almost too late, a young boy will leap in and rescue Prahlada from the fire.

The celebration of Holi involves "playing Holi." Though Holi is played throughout India, it is most enthusiastically observed in the north of India and has become tied in practice and myth to Krishna devotion. The throwing of color commemorates Krishna's play with his beloved consort Radha and her friends the cowherd girls. On the days leading up to Holi and on the day of Holi itself, devotees exchange color with fellow devotees. Devotees note that exchanging color is a means to renew social bonds (Sanford n.d., 18). This color takes the form of colored powder or colored water, and methods of exchange range from tenderly applying color to another's cheek to dousing crowds with buckets of color. Typically Holi and the days leading up to the festival are times when social norms break down, so for example, women and the poor, respectively, can verbally abuse men and the rich. By the actual day of the Holi festival, the streets become a virtual battleground of color, and anyone not prepared to get doused should stay inside.

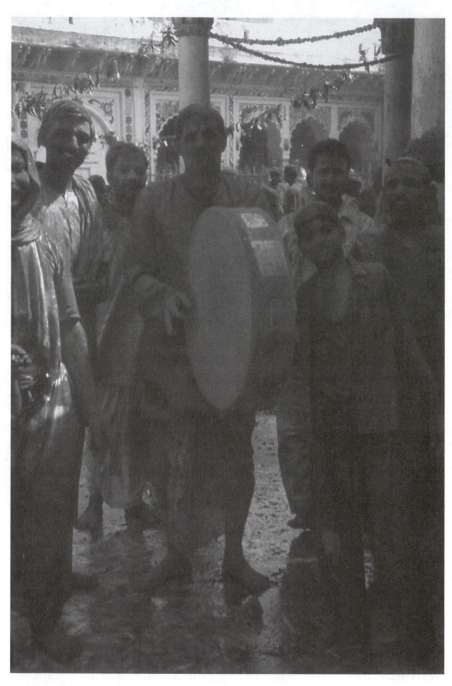

Men playing Holi.
A. WHITNEY SANFORD

Vaisakhi

Vaisakhi (also spelled "Baisakhi") falls in mid-April and marks the beginning of the Hindu solar new year. Vaisakhi occurs when the harvest is ready to sell or just has been sold, so this festival celebrates agricultural bounty. Vaisakhi has special significance for both the Hindu and Sikh traditions. (For Sikhs, Vaisakhi commemorates the day Guru Gobind Singh inaugurated the Khalsa order, establishing the Sikh community.) Hindus celebrate with special pujas to give thanks for renewed prosperity and attend colorful fairs to mark this happy occasion. For Hindus, this day is additionally important because, on this day, the goddess Ganga descended to earth thousands of years ago, and in her honor many Hindus gather along the sacred Ganges River for ritual baths.

Ramanavami, Rama's Birthday

On the ninth day of the bright half of Chaitra, devotees of Rama celebrate the anniversary of Rama's birth on earth. In some parts of India, this celebration is a nine-day festival that coincides with Vasanta Navaratri, the nine days on which the goddess is honored. Some of the ritual practices on Ramanavami include morning ablutions, chanting Vedic mantras dedicated to Vishnu, and pujas for Rama. Devotees fast on this day and break the fast at midnight with fruit. During the day, devotees may gather to recite excerpts from the *Ramacharitmanas,* a Hindi version of the story of the life of Rama. These recitations are particularly popular in the northern states of Uttar Pradesh and Bihar and are attended by all levels of society.

Festivals of the Hot Season

By the onset of the summer months, the weather over much of India has changed from a balmy spring to an intense heat, with temperatures reaching as high as 125 degrees in the deserts of Rajasthan.

Honoring the River Goddess Ganga

During the first ten days of Jetha, devotees honor the Ganges River, also known as Mother Ganga. According to Hindu tradition, the Ganges flows in all three worlds: In heaven she is called Mandakini; on earth, the Ganges; and in the lower region, the Bhagirathi. Hindus thus know the Ganga as the "Three Path River." Devotees travel long distances to pilgrimage centers to bathe in the Ganges in the hope of washing away their sins. The main pilgrimage centers for the Ganges are:

1. Gangotri (the source of the Ganges in the Himalayan mountains)
2. Hardwar (the city where the Ganges meets the plains of northern India)
3. Allahabad (the city in which the confluence of the Ganges and the Yamuna is located)
4. Varanasi (a pilgrimage city for Shiva, famed for its bathing ghats, or stairs, on the Ganges's banks)
5. Sagara Island (where the Ganges merges into the Bay of Bengal)

This period of time commemorates Ganga's descent to the earth from heaven. According to this story (which appears in the Puranas, the Ramayana, and the Mahabharata) a king named Sagara performed the horse sacrifice, in which a horse was sent to wander for a year, its journey marking the boundaries of the king's territory. After much wandering, the king's horse reached the home of the sage Kapila. Thinking that the sage had kidnapped the horse, sixty thousand of the king's sons attacked. They planned to destroy the sage, but instead the enraged sage cursed the men and they were all burnt to ash on the spot.

When neither the king's sons nor the horse returned, King Sagara sent his grandson Anshuman to search for them. When the sage Kapila told Anshuman the whole story, Anshuman asked him how the men's sins could be erased. The sage replied that their sins would be destroyed if the waters of the Ganges would flow over the land where the ashes lay. Both Anshuman and his son Dilip unsuccessfully tried to coax the Ganges down to earth. Finally the sage Bhagiratha underwent severe austerities to gain the mercy of the Ganges. She was pleased with Bhagiratha's austerities, but asked him to obtain Shiva's favor. Shiva agreed to assume the burden of bringing the Ganges to earth, and, on the tenth day of the bright half of Jetha, the Ganges descended from heaven to Shiva's matted hair. Then, its mighty flow tamed by Shiva's matted locks, the Ganges reached the earth and washed away the sins of King Sagara's sons. For this reason, the Ganges is also known as the Bhagirathi.

Festivals of the Rainy Season

The heat builds during the months of the hot season, and people long for the cooling rains of the rainy season. The monsoon first reaches southern India in early June, arriving in Delhi and northern India by mid- to late June. The rains are welcomed because they provide significant relief from the fiery temperatures of the hot season. The rains, however, render travel extremely difficult, and the rainy season is typically a time to remain in place. During this time, wandering ascetics traditionally remained in monasteries. The risk of snakebites as well as diseases related to poor sanitation and unsafe drinking water is particularly high during the rainy season.

Maha-Ekadashi

For many Hindus the eleventh tithi (*ekadashi*) of each half of the lunar month is important. For example, many Vaishnavas fast, abstaining from grains and cereals, on each ekadashi because ekadashi is considered a boon from Vishnu to alleviate the world's suffering. The ekadashi of Asadha's bright half is known as the Great Ekadashi, or Maha-Ekadashi, and its celebration is linked to a tale from Hindu mythology.

According to the Puranas, the demon Mura and his seven thousand sons were harassing the gods. The gods asked Vishnu for protection against Mura, so Vishnu sent Yogamaya (the embodiment of

Vishnu's creative powers) to destroy the demon and his sons. Vishnu offered Yogamaya a boon. He proclaimed that those who observe ekadashi would be freed from sin and that Yogamaya would be known as Ekadashi. However, because Mura was created from the sweat that dropped from Brahma's head, he had assumed the form of a demon and demanded a place to dwell. Brahma responded, "Demon, go live in the rice and cereal bits in the stomachs of those who have eaten. Become worms in their stomachs." Mura was sentenced to dwell among the consumed rice particles, whereas Yogamaya received the boon of being known as Ekadashi.

Devotees in the state of Maharashtra go on pilgrimage to worship the deity Vithoba (associated with Vishnu) of Pandharpur, a town in south Maharashtra. Hundreds of thousands go in procession from different parts of Maharashtra, some carrying palanquins with the images of the great saints of Maharashtra. After the procession, devotees partake in the ekadashi feast at Pandharpur (Flood 1996, 142).

This ekadashi is also known as Shayani (Sleeping) Ekadashi, because on this day Vishnu falls asleep and will awaken four months later on Prabodhini Ekadashi in the Kartika (October) month. This four month period is known as Chaturmas (four months), and most of it coincides with the rainy season.

Tija

There are several variations of Tija. One form of Tija celebrates the arrival of the monsoon during the month of Shravana and takes place amidst the new verdancy brought on by the monsoon rains. It occurs on the third day of the bright half of Shravana. This festival is particularly important to girls and women because it marks the day that Parvati left her parent's home as Shiva's bride. Tija is particularly important to women of northern India. Married women return to their natal home to celebrate this festival. Women sing in praise of Parvati's devotion to her husband Shiva. Special swings are hung on tree branches, and the women swing on them. After performing puja for Parvati at home, a red-and-gold–clad image of Parvati is carried in a palanquin in a procession representing her marriage procession. Often camels, dancers, and elephants accompany this procession. Because women are responsible for their family's health and well-being, Tija is an occasion for women to fast for their families and pray to Parvati for marital bliss.

Another form of Tija (Haritalika) occurs in the following month of Bhadrapada and highlights the efforts of young girls to gain a husband like Shiva. This fast is one of the most important fasts kept by women in Varanasi, and the story of Shiva and Parvati—recited to the fasting women—demonstrates that perseverance will result in the attainment of their goals (Pearson 1996, 158). For the three days of the festival, unmarried girls pray to Parvati to gain a husband like Shiva, and married women pray to maintain their auspicious state as married women. Girls hope to emulate Parvati's success in marriage. As the story goes, young Parvati was in love with Shiva, but Shiva, deep in meditation, failed to notice her. Parvati performed exhausting penance in the Himalayas for many years until Shiva finally noticed her. Parvati's great love and devotion impressed him so much that he married her.

Naga Panchami

On Naga Panchami, the fifth day of the bright half of Shravana, many Hindus visit temples specially dedicated to snakes and worship the snake, or naga. The most important ritual event is to offer crystallized sugar and milk to a cobra (Alter 1992, 137). The festival occurs during the rainy season, when the risk of snakebite is especially high. Shiva is associated with snakes, so many devotees venerate snakes at Shiva temples. In south India, Hindus build images of snakes out of cow dung on either side of the entrance to the house to welcome the snake god. Some go to anthills, a place where snakes reside, to worship the snake. Others build a five-hooded snake out of substances including turmeric powder, sandalwood, and saffron. The following story describes why the snake is worshiped:

A farmer plowing his field inadvertently destroyed an anthill and killed the young snakes living inside. When the mother snake returned to find her children cut to pieces, she vowed to take revenge on the farmer who killed her children. Late one night, the vengeful mother snake came to the farmer's house and began to bite the feet of the sleeping farmer as well as his wife and children's feet. The snake then realized that the eldest daughter was not there. She was soon to be married and had gone to her father-in-law's home. The snake resolved to bite her as well and headed toward a nearby village.

The snake recognized the eldest daughter but paused when she saw the girl worshiping a snake she had made. The girl was praying to the snake god to forgive her family for any faults committed inadvertently. She pleaded with the snake god to protect her family from snakebite. Pleased by the girl's devotion and feeling remorse at her own actions, the mother snake appeared before her, but the girl became frightened. The mother snake told her not to be afraid, told the girl what had happened to her family, and gave her nectar to sprinkle over her family, which brought them back to life (Alter 1992, 137; Vogel 1995, 277).

Raksha Bandhana

Brothers and sisters celebrate Raksha Bandhana, or Rakhi, on the full-moon day in the month of Shravana. Sisters tie an amulet, the Rakhi, around their brothers' right wrist to ensure long life and happiness. The word *raksha* means protection, and this holiday represents a mutual protection. Girls and women have a responsibility to protect their brothers by engaging in practices such as Raksha Bandhana and fasts. The brother plays an important role in his sister's life. Practically, he acts as a safeguard for her protection, particularly after she joins her husband's family. The brother is also responsible for bringing his sister back and forth to her natal family during home visits. By custom, her father cannot accept hospitality from his daughter's in-laws, but the brother can do so. Raksha Bandhana thus illustrates the importance of maintaining strong ties between siblings.

The celebration of Raksha Bandhana is based on a story about a battle between the gods and the demons. Indra's wife tied a piece of silk around her husband's wrist to ward off the demons. Although this story represents the important role a wife plays in protecting her husband, this festival emphasizes the sister's protection of her brother. Now Hindu girls give their brothers (or special stand-ins) red-and-gold silk wrist amulets that symbolize the sibling bond. Sisters may also give their brothers candy along with the bracelets, and the brothers offer their sisters small gifts.

Krishna Janmashtami

Krishna Janmashtami marks the birth of Krishna. According to tradition, Krishna was born on the eighth day of the dark half of Bhadrapada. Vishnu had agreed to take birth as Krishna to destroy his tyrannical uncle Kamsa, who ruled Mathura. Kamsa had been warned of Krishna's impending birth and imprisoned Krishna's parents. Immediately after Krishna was born, he was spirited away across the Yamuna River by his foster father, Nanda. He and his elder brother Balarama remained with Nanda and foster mother Yashoda throughout an idyllic cowherding childhood. When they reached young adulthood, they returned to Mathura to kill Kamsa.

Janmashtami is celebrated most intensely in northern India. Devotees of Krishna visit temples in Gokul and Vrindavan, the sites of Krishna's childhood years. Many temples host "Krishna-Lilas," musical dramas in which male child actors reenact scenes from Krishna's lives, and devotees crowd into temples to watch these performances and sing devotional songs about Krishna. While in these roles, these child-actors represent the actual deity Krishna, so devotees watching the drama enjoy the merits of "taking darshana" of Krishna.

Ganesha Chaturthi

Hindus celebrate the birthday of the elephant-headed deity Ganesha (or Ganapati) on the fourth day of the bright half of Bhadrapada. Ganesha is one of the most popular deities in the Hindu pantheon and is honored by almost all Hindus regardless of affiliation. Considered the patron of learning as well as the "Remover of Obstacles," Ganesha's invocation at the start of any venture is considered critical to its success. Many homes have an image of Ganesha near the entrance, and his image graces virtually every wedding invitation.

On Ganesha's birthday, devotees buy images of Ganesha, which they keep as a guest in their homes for up to ten days. On Ananta Chaturdashi, the fourteenth day of the bright half of Bhadrapada, the images are carried in a procession to a nearby river or body of water and ceremonially immersed. Devotees then invite Ganesha to come again next year.

Vamana Dvadashi/Onam

Onam falls on the twelfth day of the dark half of Bhadrapada, and it is the main festival of the southwestern state of Kerala. Onam honors Vamana, the fifth avatara of Vishnu, and marks the annual visit of the benevolent demon king Bali. Bali visits Kerala annually because of a boon given by Vamana. Bali had conquered all the gods with his heroic deeds and enslaved Vishnu's wife, Lakshmi. Despite being the king of the demons, Bali was also a devotee of Vishnu and a just ruler. Still, while Bali ruled heaven and earth, the gods were in exile and had no place to go. They sought out Vishnu and complained that Bali had taken their freedom. They admitted, however, that he was a good and just king and his subjects liked him. Vishnu said he would take care of this problem.

Vishnu did not want to fight with his devotee, so he had to find another solution. He assumed the form of a dwarf, Vamana. Just as Bali was about to perform a sacrifice that would render him the most powerful king in the three worlds, he saw the dwarf approaching him. Realizing immediately that this was no ordinary person, Bali asked him to name one boon. Vamana asked for as much space as he could cover in three paces. Thinking that a dwarf could cover very little territory, Bali offered him to ask for more, but the dwarf insisted. Vamana took one step and then assumed his full form as Vishnu. His second step covered all three worlds. Vishnu then again assumed the form of Vamana and asked where the third step should go. Bali told Vamana to step on his head so the touch of Vishnu's feet would bestow a blessing on him. Bali then asked for one boon: the opportunity to visit his people once a year. Vamana granted this boon, so Bali visits once a year on Onam. On this day, Keralites clean their houses and light lamps to welcome King Bali. At Alapuzha, a city in Kerala, boaters race long snake-shaped boats with almost one hundred men paddling in each boat.

Early Fall Season

The fall season brings many festivals. The monsoon is slowly ending, and temperatures are pleasant.

Navaratri/Durga Puja

The festivals of Navaratri and Durga Puja, honoring the goddess, begin on the first day of Ashvina and last for nine days. The goddess is known by many names, including Kali, Lakshmi, and Durga. This festival particularly celebrates her power, or shakti, with which she vanquishes evil. The Puranas describe the goddess sitting astride a lion, clutching her weapons, including an axe, wheel, and sword. They also tell of her long, fierce battle against the buffalo demon, and her victory on the ninth day. In the south, the festival is celebrated as Navaratri. Friends and relatives visit each other's homes to exchange greetings, and young girls build elaborate tableaus with dolls and trinkets.

Durga Puja is celebrated with the greatest enthusiasm in the eastern state of Bengal. During these nine days, devotees of Durga build *pandals,* or tents, that show Durga in her different guises. Communities compete among themselves to create the best pandals, and these pandals show off the creativities of numerous artisans. The images display magnificent clothing and jewelry as well as artistic skill. Each evening, devotees gather to view the pandals and see which is the best. Each day of the nine days brings different pujas and events. On the final day, which coincides with Dusshehra, the images are taken to a body of water for immersion.

Effigies of Ravana and his henchmen burn in New Delhi.
ROBIN RINEHART

Dashahara

Dashahara (also known as Dussehra), the tenth day of the bright half of Ashvina, honors Rama's victory over the demon Ravana. This day is marked by large-scale dramas known as Rama-Lila, which enact the hero god Rama's life. The highlight of the day is when devotees explode effigies of the demon Ravana and his brother and son that have been stuffed with firecrackers. Thousands of spectators cheer the demise of the demons.

Karva Chautha

Karva Chautha occurs on the fourth day of the dark half of Kartika, about nine days prior to Divali. It is a fast kept by married Hindu women of northern India to seek the health and longevity of their husbands. This fast lasts from sunrise to sunset, and no food or water is allowed. Traditionally the newlywed bride performing her first Karva Chautha receives a new sari.

Late Fall Festivals

The highlight of the fall season is Divali, a festival that heralds the approach of winter and the onset of the sowing season.

Divali

Divali (also known as Dipavali), the festival of lamps, is a highlight of the fall season, with celebrations lasting for five days. Divali is truly a festival of the home, and most pujas and festivities occur within the home and family. Families and friends exchange gifts and sweets, and firecrackers explode continuously for the duration of the festival. Everyone wears new clothes. Divali itself falls on the amavasya (new moon day) of Ashvina. Like many festivals, the Divali period celebrates events significant to different parts of India and different deities. For example, Divali commemorates Rama's return to Ayodhya after slaying the demon Ravana and his coronation as king as well as honoring Lakshmi, the goddess of wealth.

Divali preparations begin on a day known as Dhana Teras, when people clean and whitewash their homes and purchase new utensils. Women clean the areas just in front of their homes and create designs on the ground known as *rangoli*. This is a traditional art in which people adorn walls and courtyards with a powder of white stone, rice flour, and other similar materials. These designs can be geometric, include figures of deities, or can be based on animals such as cows, elephants, and birds. Hindus create rangoli designs on many occasions other than Divali. Some create their own designs whereas others base their work on books of rangoli designs.

The markets bustle with shoppers collecting Divali material, including firecrackers, earthen *diyas* (oil lamps), and *hatris* (a small houselike structure made of mud) for Lakshmi. Additionally each household will purchase a pair of images of Ganesha and Lakshmi. Because much of this festival focuses on prosperity, Lakshmi and

Ganesha are essential. Lakshmi is said to visit each household the night of Divali and bless each household with prosperity.

The night just prior to Divali itself is called Chhoti Divali, or "little Divali." In each house there is a small platform decorated with small toys and geometric designs. The small house and the images of Ganesha and Lakshmi are placed on this platform along with small lamps. The family performs puja for these deities this night.

Much of the Divali preparations are in anticipation of Lakshmi's visit on the new moon night, or *amavasya,* of Ashvina, the night that commemorates Lakshmi's freedom from enslavement at King Bali's hands. Vamana, the dwarf, freed Lakshmi from King Bali. So, on this night, the darkest night, Hindus hope Lakshmi will visit their homes, and they light rows of candles that lead the goddess to their homes. These lamps must be kept lit all night to guide Lakshmi. Shopkeepers, accountants, and merchants worship their account books and their merchandise in honor of Lakshmi's prosperity. The following day, the first day of Kartika, is the New Year's Day for merchants.

The fifth and last day of Divali is known as Bhai Duja, the second day after the new moon, and it commemorates the bond between sisters and brothers. On this day, Yama, the god of the underworld, goes to visit his sister Yami, and his sister places a small mark (*tilaka*) on his forehead to protect him. To honor this day, sisters give their brothers a protective *tilak,* and brothers offer their sisters gifts.

End of Winter Festivals

Makara Samkranti/Lohri/Pongal

This festival is one of the few to occur according to the solar calendar. It falls on January 14 and marks the beginning of the end of winter. On this day, the sun is farthest from the earth, and from this day on, the earth moves back toward the sun in its orbit. Makara indicates the zodiac sign Capricorn, and Samkranti, an auspicious day in any month, signifies the day when the sun passes from one sign of the zodiac to the next. This change is celebrated in the north as Lohri, in central India as Makara Samkranti, and as Pongal in the south.

Mahashivaratri

On the fourteenth day of the dark half of Magha, the great night of Shiva is celebrated. Devotees of Shiva observe a fast to honor Shiva's marriage to Parvati. They go to Shiva temples and make offerings, and many devotees stay up the entire night to commemorate Shiva's marriage. The story behind this festival appears in the Mahabharata and goes like this:

Once King Chitrabhanu was observing a fast with his wife on the day of Mahashivaratri. The sage Ashtavakra came to visit, and he asked the king why he was fasting on that day. Able to remember events from previous lives, the king explained that he had once been a hunter. One night, darkness had fallen quickly, so he sought shelter in a bel tree, sacred to Shiva, for the night. The hunter had shot a deer that day but was unable to take it home, so he tied it to a tree branch. He remained in the tree all night and, by circumstance, maintained a fast. His torment of hunger and missing his family evoked tears of misery. While he sat in the tree, he plucked and dropped bel leaves onto the ground.

The following morning he returned home, sold the deer, and bought food. Just as he was about to break his fast, a stranger appeared and asked for food. The hunter first fed the beggar, then took some food for himself. When the hunter died, he saw two messengers who had been sent to escort his soul to Shiva's heaven. He learned then that he had fulfilled the conditions for the Shivaratri fast that night in the tree. Unknowingly, he had been offering bel leaves to the Shivalingam at the base of the tree, and his tears had bathed the image. The hunter remained for some time in Shiva's heaven and was eventually reborn as the King Chitrabhanu.

Conclusion

It would be hard to overestimate the importance of the ritual calendar in determining the patterns and cycles of Hindu life. The Hindu ritual calendar provides a guide as one goes through the days, weeks, and years of one's life. Each moment is significant and, depending on whether it is considered auspicious or inauspicious, guides the devotee in what activities are appropriate for any given time. This calendar informs Hindu ritual life from the public temple-based festivals such as Janmashtami, observed by scores of devotees, to the private home- and family-based rituals and vows primarily observed by women. The rituals and festivals discussed in this chapter are not casually observed events but are intrinsic to every aspect of Hindu life. For example, many practices involve fundamental aspects of life such as what and when one eats, and these activities are considered efficacious—that is, they are seen to have real power. For women in particular, there is little that is more important than preserving the auspicious state of marriage. Fasting provides the power (shakti) to protect husbands and children. These rituals have the power to affect the most basic and important conditions of life. It would be a momentous task to provide an exhaustive account of each and every Hindu ritual and festival. Our goal in this chapter therefore has been to illustrate how the ritual calendar shapes and structures Hindu ritual life.

BIBLIOGRAPHY

Alter, Joseph S. *The Wrestler's Body Identity and Ideology in North India.* Berkeley: University of California Press, 1992.

Babb, Lawrence A. *The Divine Hierarchy.* New York: Columbia University Press, 1975.

Bahadur, Om Lata. *The Book of Hindu Festivals and Ceremonies.* 2nd rev. ed. New Delhi: UBS Publishers' Distributors Ltd., 1997.

Chatterjee, S. K. *Indian Calendrical System.* New Delhi: Ministry of Information and Broadcasting, Government of India, 1998.

Erndl, Kathleen M. *Victory to the Mother: The Hindu Goddess of Northwest India in Myth, Ritual, and Symbol.* New York: Oxford University Press, 1993.

Flood, Gavin. *An Introduction to Hinduism.* Cambridge: Cambridge University Press, 1996.

Harlan, Lindsey. *Religion and Rajput Women: The Ethics of Protection in Contemporary Narratives.* Delhi: Munshiram Manoharlal, 1992.

Kaushik, J. N. *Fasts of the Hindus around the Week.* Delhi: Books for All, n.d.

Merrey, Karen L. "The Hindu Festival Calendar," in Guy R. Welbon and

Glenn E. Yocum (eds.), *Religious Festivals in South India and Sri Lanka*. Delhi: Manohar, 1982: 1–25.

Pearson, Anne Mackenzie. *"Because It Gives Me Peace of Mind": Ritual Fasts in the Religious Lives of Hindu Women*. Albany: State University of New York Press, 1996.

Raheja, Gloria Goodwin. *The Poison in the Gift: Ritual, Prestation, and the Dominant Caste in a North Indian Village*. Chicago: University of Chicago Press, 1988.

Sanford, A. Whitney. "Holi through Dauji's Eyes: Alternate Views of Krishna and Balarama in Dauji," in Guy Beck (ed.), *Alternative Krishnas*. Albany: State University of New York Press. Forthcoming.

Voegel, J. P. H. *Indian Serpent-Lore or the Nagas in Hindu Art and Legend*. New Delhi: Asian Educational Services, 1995.

Wadley, Susan S. "Hindu Women's Family and Household Rites," in Nancy Auer Falk and Rita M. Gross (eds.), *Unspoken Worlds: Women's Religious Lives*. Belmont: Wadsworth Publishing Company, 1989: 72–81.

Crowds of Hindus gather at the Procession of the Elephants of Shiva in Kerala, India.

CHARLES AND JOSETTE LENARS/CORBIS

Chapter Five

Hindu Ethics

S. S. Rama Rao Pappu

In addition to age-old questions about right and wrong, religions in the modern age are confronted with difficult questions raised by advances in science and medical technology. In this chapter we will consider the principles upon which Hindu thinkers have traditionally based ethical principles and guidelines. Because Hinduism has no one founder and no centralized organization or authority, Hindu ethicists draw upon a wide range of tradition. The chapter concludes with an exploration of ethical issues related to family life and reproduction. Given that India now has over one billion people— roughly 16 percent of the world's population, living on 2.4 percent of the world's land area—matters of family planning and population growth are of vital importance (http://www.unescap.org/pop/database/law_india/india1.htm).

Can Ethics Be Hindu?

The expression *Hindu ethics* poses a problem and needs clarification. If ethics is conceived as a set of universal norms applicable to all rational beings, then ethics cannot be uniquely Hindu, because "Hindu" refers to a religious group that is a subset, and not the whole, of all rational beings. However, if we mean by "Hindu ethics" a set of moral norms that are prescriptive for Hindus and Hindus alone, then ethics will be relativistic, without universal validity.

Hindu ethicists long ago raised and resolved this problem by distinguishing between (1) *sadharana* dharmas, or duties pertaining to persons-qua-persons, without reference to their station in life or their particular circumstances, and (2) *vishesha* dharmas or relative duties, that is, duties pertaining to one's station in life and life stages. For example, the Laws of Manu include patience, not stealing, and truth-telling as sadharana dharmas, or universal moral norms, but define duties pertaining to the four varnas (varna dharmas) and the four stages of life (*ashrama* dharmas) as vishesha dharmas or relative duties. Other Hindu ethicists have included in the list of sadharana dharmas duties such as nonviolence (*ahimsa*) and concern for the welfare of all creatures.

The Laws of Manu and other dharma texts illustrate basic principles of Hindu ethics; the philosophical schools, or darshanas, of Hinduism address ethical matters as well. For example, the Mimamsa school, which is particularly concerned with Vedic exegesis, distinguishes between secular and scriptural duties, creating a distinction similar to the Laws of Manu between universal duties and relative duties. Secular dharmas, according to the Mimamsa school, are experiential and therefore universal, but the scriptural commands are those that are relative to the Hindus. According to the Mimamsa teachers, actions are good if they benefit people and bad if they bring bad consequences. In contemporary idiom, the Mimamsa school's secular ethics is universal and utilitarian. Scriptural commands (*shastric* dharmas), in contrast, prescribe and prohibit actions unconditionally and are thus deontological. Because they are founded on the Vedas, they only apply to the followers of Vedic dharma or the Hindus. In short, for the Mimamsa school, secular duties are universal, but scriptural duties are particular and relative.

The universality of ethics is also implied in the doctrine of *purusharthas,* or "human aims," around which the Hindu system of values revolves. *Purushartha* literally means *"human* aim" or *"human* ideal," not *"Hindu* aim" or *"Hindu* ideal." Hindu thinkers have recognized four purusharthas: artha, or wealth and power; kama, or desire, especially sexual desire; dharma, or morality and virtue; and moksha, or liberation. These four human aims are universal aims, common to all human beings, and thus they exclude aims and ideals of persons relative to their station in life or positions they hold. For example, the duties of kings and carpenters are relative to their respective positions, but in so far as they are human beings, their purusharthas, or human aims, are the same. Thus, by "Hindu ethics" we should understand a set of norms, ideals, and a way of life developed by the Hindus. Some of these norms are universal and applicable to all human beings, but other norms are applicable only to followers of Hinduism.

Sources of Hindu Ethics

The sources of Hindu ethics are (1) shruti (sacred scripture, i.e., Vedas) and (2) smriti (remembered tradition), (3) sadachara, standards laid down by virtuous persons, and (4) individual conscience. The sacred literature of Hinduism is classifed into shruti (that which is "heard"), and smriti (that which is "remembered"). The shruti literature is believed to be eternal, infallible, and authorless, the eternal, infallible truth heard by the ancient sages. Smriti literature includes the dharma literature, *itihasas* (history texts), and the Ramayana and the Mahabharata (which includes the most important ethical work, the Bhagavad Gita). Smriti also includes the Puranas as well as economic and political literature such as the Artha Shastra. Smriti literature is understood to have been composed in time by human authors—it is essentially a human tradition passed on from generation to generation. Whereas shruti literature is understood to survive each cycle of world dissolution and creation, smriti literature becomes extinct at the end of the world dissolution. Though smriti and shruti are recognized as authoritative for moral guidance, in case of conflict, shruti overrides smriti, because smriti texts, having human authorship, are fallible.

In addition to shruti and smriti, Hindu ethicists have recognized two additional sources of morality (dharma): *sadachara,* moral standards laid down by the examples of great sages, saints, and morally virtuous persons; and *atmasantosha,* enlightened conscience or self-satisfaction. Despite the fact that Hindu ethics has multiple sources, each source containing a large number of texts and moral examples that have evolved over thousands of years, purusharthas remain the central concepts of Hindu ethics, which are accepted by everyone. As we noted above, dharma or morality itself is considered one of the four purusharthas. By understanding the purusharthas, therefore, we will understand the essence of Hindu ethics.

The Purusharthas

The central questions of ethics are "What is good?" and "What is right?" Hindu ethics, like Greek ethics, examines the "moral good" as an aspect of "the good," and "moral life" as an aspect of "the good life." For example, when we ask "What sorts of things are good?" we generally reply, "wealth is good," "courage is good," "virtue is good," and so on, meaning that morality is one of the goods. In the Hindu and Greek view, the good life is not identical with the moral life. Hence, conceptions of moral good and right should be discussed in Hinduism in the context of their conception of the good life, because good life is wider than morally good life. Therefore, purusharthas enunciated in the Hindu ethics examine "the good" and the "good life," of which dharma is the moral good and moral rightness.

The Hindu theory of purusharthas ("human aims") recognizes four goods: artha (wealth, power), kama (desire, sexual desire), dharma (morality, virtue), and moksha (liberation). Among these, dharma is both the right and the good. Artha, kama, and dharma are empirical goods, and moksha is the transcendental good. Sometimes the purusharthas are classified into instrumental and intrinsic goods. Artha and kama are considered instrumental goods, whereas dharma is an intrinsic good, and moksha is both an intrinsic good and the supreme good.

To repeat, *purushartha* means "human aims" or "what is sought by humans." Both the words "human" and "aim" are important here. Purusharthas are "human" in that they take into account what human beings are like and what they, as humans, ought to aim at. Likewise the word *aim* implies an objective that is neither too utopian nor too easy. It also suggests the possibility that one may not be able to attain those aims. Therefore purusharthas may be understood as those desires that any rational and reflective person who understands his or her nature, station in society, and place in the universe aims at naturally. A rational and reflective person aims at the four purusharthas because they contribute to his or her well-being. Purusharthas are not a set of prescriptions or ideals that direct the individual to act in a particular way. They are the reasons for which reflective individuals act in the way they do. Hindu ethicists have arrived at these four goods because they are the most general goods all human beings seek. All humans aim at economic prosperity, political power, satisfaction of sexual instincts, and desire to live in a society governed by moral rules and ideals.

What is, however, distinctive in the Hindu classification of goods is the inclusion of moksha, or liberation, as a good—in fact, moksha in Hindu ethics is the supreme good. Moksha has both a transcendental and an empirical dimension. As a transcendental good, moksha is variously conceived as merging oneself with brahman (the absolute), realizing one's self, attaining heaven, and so on. In its empirical dimension, moksha implies *liberation from* the very desires for wealth and power that human beings seek. We not only desire wealth but also want to renounce it; we not only desire power but also to move to a state where we want to relinquish power; we not only desire a well-ordered moral society but also seek to get out of the society and the obligations society imposes on us. In the fourfold system of purusharthas, therefore, it is envisioned that there is a time to seek wealth and there is a time to renounce it; there is a time to seek power and there is a time to give it up. According to the Isha Upanishad, we should "enjoy by renunciation." Let us now briefly discuss each of the fourfold purusharthas.

Artha

Artha is a polymorphous concept. It literally means "thing, object, substance." In the context of the purusharthas, artha connotes profit, worldly advantage, and political, business, and professional success of all sorts. A study of Indian thought since Vedic times bears ample evidence that artha is sometimes glorified, at other times given a lower importance, but never neglected. Vedic, Brahminical, and Mimamsa thought gave artha the utmost importance, because without wealth one cannot perform rituals and sacrifices and discharge one's obligations to the gods, forefathers, and society. Upanishadic and Vedantic thought, however, relegated it to a lower position. The smriti literature (e.g., the epics and the dharma literature) gave artha equal importance along with kama and dharma. The Laws of Manu state that dharma, artha, and kama have equal value and that one should aim at all of them without neglecting any one of them. Artha is considered a purushartha not only because humans naturally *want* to acquire wealth but because, in the absence of artha, a Hindu cannot perform his religious duties such as the performance of rites and rituals, feeding renouncers, and engaging in charitable activities, which are all obligations for people in the householder stage of life.

Kama

Like artha, kama is difficult to define. In the broadest sense, kama refers to desire as well as the object of desire. In a narrow sense, however, kama denotes erotic or sexual love, a desire for carnal gratification. In the Mahabharata, kama is defined as pleasure derived from both sensuous and intellectual/emotional exercise. Vatsyayana, the author of the Kama Sutra, defines kama as the "enjoyment of appropriate objects by the five senses of hearing, feeling, seeing, tasting, [and] smelling assisted by the mind together with the soul. The ingredient in this is a peculiar contact between the organ of sense and its object, and consciousness of pleasure that arises from the contact is called kama." In the dharma literature, kama is recognized as the motivating force behind all actions. According to the Laws of Manu, dharma, artha, and kama are all important ends, and the chief good consists in the pursuit of all three.

Moksha

Moksha is variously translated as immortality, salvation, liberation, freedom, spiritual realization, self-realization, and God-realization.

There is wide disagreement among Hindu thinkers concerning the exact nature of the liberated state and the means by which liberation can be obtained. Some Hindu thinkers, such as the Advaita Vedanta philosophers, maintain that moksha is a state of positive bliss (ananda), and others conceive of it in neutral terms as a state of absence of pain and suffering. Some say that in the state of moksha one merges with brahman whereas others assert that it consists of an individual's remaining nearer to God. However, there is wide agreement that moksha is not a state of affairs that arises only after death, and that one can in fact attain moksha while living (jivanmukti).

There are various positions concerning the means for attaining moksha. Some have emphasized jnana, or knowledge, as the path to liberation; others said that it is bhakti, or devotion; and still others emphasized karma, or moral action, in this world. In the Ramayana and the Mahabharata, it is said that one who lives a life of dharma attains moksha. No special effort is needed to attain moksha. In the theistic bhakti traditions, and in common religious practice, it is believed that one can attain moksha by bathing in the holy rivers, by visiting holy places, by receiving the blessings of holy men, and even by "merit transference" and "proxy" by one's relatives and well-wishers. According to the Bhagavad Gita, all the above are equally valid means of attaining moksha, and one should adopt the means best suited to one's nature (svabhava). Despite these differences, it is generally agreed that moksha is something intrinsically desirable and that it is a state of liberation from the empirical world and from the transmigratory cycle of births and deaths. In the context of purusharthas, moksha is understood not as the culmination of dharma but as the transcendence of dharma. That is, moksha is conceived here as beyond dharma (good) and adharma (evil).

Dharma: Morality, Duty, and Virtue

Hindu ethics revolves around purusharthas, of which dharma is the most important "human aim." In the fourfold scheme of purusharthas discussed above, though dharma is only one of the four, it is generally given a much higher status than the rest. Sometimes the other three purusharthas are subsumed under dharma; for example, artha and moksha are also called dharmas. There is thus artha-dharma and moksha-dharma, implying that dharma is the most important one.

Dharma is a rich and complex concept. The word *dharma* comes from a Sanskrit root meaning "to hold" or "to sustain." Dharma holds together the universe and its laws, inanimate and living beings, and human beings and the society in which they live. Therefore dharma may signify religion, law, morality, equity, usage, tradition, merit, virtue, righteousness, justice, propriety, disposition, essential property or attribute, resemblance, devotion, duty, and so on. To use Gilbert Ryle's expression, dharma is a "polymorphous concept," like "work" or "thinking." In what follows, important meanings of dharma will be explained.

Dharma as a Cosmic Impersonal Law

As a cosmic impersonal law, dharma was the successor to the Rig Vedic concept *rita*. Rita means "the course of things." The Vedic Hindus understood rita as the principle of harmony and orderliness of the universe, and gave it moral status. Rita is the first principle of the world, which is both physical and moral. Using the language of rita, an empirical fact such as "water flows downstream" is explained as "It is because of rita that water flows downstream." Water flowing downstream is not only a particular law of nature, it is in the cosmic order of things that water must flow downstream. Rita is the cosmic order of things. When we add the moral component of rita to the empirical fact of "water flows downstream," we get the conclusion "it is (morally) right that water flows downstream." Dharma as a conceptual successor to rita not only retained the full meaning of rita as explained above but also acquired additional meanings in the course of its long history, as we shall next discuss.

Dharma as Laws of Nature

Dharma also connotes what scientists ordinarily call "laws of nature." It is the dharma of the sun to rise in the east; it is the dharma of water to flow downstream. Hindus thus use the language of dharma where the scientists use the language of natural laws. However, dharma language goes beyond the language of laws of nature. Whereas the scientific conception of laws of nature include only "what *necessarily* happens" and "what *regularly* happens," the language of dharma also includes "what *ought* to happen," where the word *ought* means a "moral ought."

Dharma as Essential Property/Disposition

Dharma also means "the nature of a thing." By "the nature of a thing" it means (1) essential property, and also (2) a disposition (svabhava). Thus when we say that the dharma of the river is to flow downstream, we are attributing an essential property to the river. However, when we say that the Kshatriya dharma (the dharma of kings and warriors) is to protect and fight for the people, it is meant that the Kshatriyas are by nature (svabhava) disposed to and temperamentally suited to fight and protect. In the dharma literature, we find a great emphasis on the essential connection between one's nature (svabhava) and one's duty (svadharma). Thus, for example, a Kshatriya has a duty to protect his subjects and fight for his kingdom because by nature and disposition he has the qualities of a warrior and a protector.

Dharma as Social/Moral Norms

Dharma connotes all the social norms and moral norms that govern an individual's life in society. These include moral, legal, customary, traditional, religious, etiquette, and proprietary rules. It is, for example, one's dharma to tell the truth (a moral rule), to obey the sovereign (a legal rule), to perform morning ablutions (a rule of religion), and to greet a friend (a rule of etiquette). Dharma includes all these social rules because historically Hindus never compartmentalized social norms and social life into legal, moral, customary, and so on. When we say that the dharma of a king (Kshatriya dharma) is to protect his subjects, the dharma of a king is not merely legal, it is also customary, moral, religious, and fitting the office he holds. In passing, we may also state here that social/moral norms are both prescriptive and descriptive in the Hindu tradition.

Dharma as Duty/Obligation

The word *dharma* is most commonly used in the context of duty or obligation. Duties and obligations arise out of the rules of the society and roles people play. Dharma includes rules, roles, and relations. We have a duty (dharma) to keep our promises because there is a moral rule (dharma) that "everyone ought to keep his/her promise." In other words, dharma connotes not only rules but also the duties that arise from rules. Rules create duties, sometimes directly and sometimes indirectly. Indirectly, rules create duties via roles. Duties arising out of positions of trust (such as that of a judge) or out of recognized social roles (such as that of a father or a mother) are of this nature. In other words, social rules are creations of dharma, and social roles and relations are also creations of dharma. It should be noted here that rules, roles, and relations are creations of dharma, not human creations. Human beings only discover dharma; they are not its creators. We are all born with a bundle of duties, and there is no escape from it except by becoming a renouncer.

By conceiving the world as ruled by dharma, Hindu ethics has subordinated rights in favor of duties. In Hindu ethics, duties are what we always have, and rights are acquired by the proper discharge of our obligations. The Upanishads state that we are all born with three debts or obligations: the debts or obligations we owe to the ancient seers and sages, the debts we owe to our ancestors, and the debts we owe to the gods. In the smriti literature, no one talks about rights. Everyone either asserts or denies that he or she has duties. As a matter of fact, the notion of rights did not enter Hindu ethics until about a hundred years ago, as an importation of Western liberalism.

Dharma as Virtue

Dharma is more than moral obligations and moral "oughtness," because it includes a naturalistic element. As a naturalistic ethic, dharma joins hands with virtue ethics of the West. Like the Greek texts, Hindu texts list a number of virtues to be cultivated by humans. As early as the Taittiriya Upanishad (sixth century BCE), we find a guru who gives a sort of "commencement address" to his students after he has taught them the Vedas and exhorts them: "Speak the Truth, follow Dharma, be one to whom mother and father are gods. . . . One should give with faith, one should give with sympathy" (Taittiriya Upanishad, I.11.2). This exhortation to be truthful, to respect elders, and to live a life of modesty, humility, and sympathy is not about duties or obligations, but virtues. Similarly, in the Ramayana, a list of virtues (dharmas) is attributed to the hero Rama, namely that he embodies "truth, righteousness, prowess, kindness to creatures, smart speech, worshiping the twice-born, gods and guests." Hindu ethical literature abounds with long lists of virtues that one ought to cultivate. It also gives innumerable examples of paradigmatic individuals who are virtuous.

Dharma and Karma

By the performance or nonperformance of duties and obligations, an individual not only produces consequences in the world for which he is held accountable but also gets an appropriate amount of moral merit or demerit for which he or she will receive a fitting happiness or unhappiness in a future life. According to the doctrine of karma, my present status in society—and therefore the kind of dharmas I have to perform now—is determined by what I did in my previous life, and the consequences of my acting according to dharma in this life will determine my dharmas in the next life. It is karma that binds together an individual's dharma in the past, present, and future. Thus karma not only provides the acceptance of one's way of life in this present life but also provides an incentive to act according to dharma and reap its results in the future. Because of its close association with karma, dharma ceases to be a rigid system of rules. It is rigid insofar as one's dharmas in this present life are concerned, but flexible in planning one's future ways of life.

Manifestations of Dharma

There is no strict separation between "is" and "ought" in Hindu ethics. What is implied in the doctrine of purusharthas and the concept of dharma is not merely the Kantian dictum of "ought" implies "can." In Hindu ethics, moral oughts (dharma) are founded upon what the Hindus consider to be one's nature (svabhava). One's nature (svabhava) determines one's dharma (svadharma), and one's dharma (svadharma) is dependent upon one's nature (svabhava). It is the nature (svabhava) of the sun to rise in the east, and therefore it is also its dharma (svadharma). It is the dharma (svadharma) of the Kshatriya (king, warrior) to fight and protect his subjects, because it is his nature (svabhava).

Everything in this world shares the common *gunas* (qualities, properties) of *sattva* (transparency, lightness), *rajas* (activity), and *tamas* (lethargy); therefore all inanimate and animate beings have in common the three gunas. In addition to these common qualities, humans, nonhumans, and inanimate objects have their own natures (svabhava) and therefore their own dharma. In matters of dharma, what distinguishes the humans from the nonhumans is the fact that nonhumans, whether living or inanimate, never violate their dharma. Does the sun ever violate its dharma to rise in the east? Does the cow ever violate its dharma to be gentle? Never, the Hindu ethicists argue. It is only the human beings who, because of their free will, sometimes choose to violate their dharma. Hindu ethicists seem to believe that "the nature of things" is fixed and unchangeable, and therefore dharma grounded in the nature of things is eternal. Dharma, in other words, is natural and conventional. It may be pointed out that in Hinduism even God is not the author of dharma, nor can God change it. As early as the Rig Veda, the moral god Varuna was only given the function of *protector* of rita (morality). God only "preserves, protects, and defends" dharma and occasionally pardons transgressors of dharma.

Dharma, which is eternal, manifests itself in this world as "laws of nature" and in nonhuman life as "the nature of a species." Dharma as manifested in human beings is more complex. What distinguishes human beings from nonhuman beings is the existence of social institutions, and it is said that social institutions in Hinduism are also manifestations of dharma, and therefore they are eternal, not conventional and artificial. We find in Hinduism a complex set of social institutions, divided into varnas (loosely translated as "castes"), ashramas (stages of social life), bio-social life stages, and so on.

Let us first consider the bio-social life stages. Hinduism divides human life into four bio-social life stages: childhood, adulthood, parenthood, and old age. By calling them bio-social life stages, Hindu thinkers did not separate the biological from the social aspect of one's life. For example, to call someone a "child" implies not only the child's chronological age but also the values we attach to the age, such as innocence and nonaccountability. By calling someone an "old person," we attribute to that person values such as maturity, respectability, and wisdom. Hindu thinkers also maintained that each bio-social life stage, with its attendant values, has an equal value. Adulthood and its attendant values are no more important than childhood and old age. Childhood is no more important because of its potentiality to reach adulthood, nor is old age considered a fall from childhood and therefore less important.

Hindu ethicists have also divided the life of an individual into four ashramas, or "stages of life," wherein each ashrama has its own dharmas except for the fourth stage, in which one renounces all dharmas. The word *ashrama* means a "resting or halting place" where the individual halts in the course of his journey through life, the end of the journey being attaining brahman. The four ashramas, or life stages, recognized for upper-caste males are the student stage, where one receives education; the householder stage, where one marries and begets children; the forest-dweller stage, to begin when a man's hair turns gray and his skin becomes wrinkled, where he lives the simplest life devoting himself totally to the study of scriptures and meditating on God; and, finally, the renouncer stage, where he abandons all worldly desires and objects and detaches himself from the society and social values. As noted earlier, for women the life stages are typically daughter, wife and mother, and widow, should a woman's husband die before she does.

The most well-known Hindu social institution is the division of society into four varnas, or castes, of Brahmin, Kshatriya, Vaishya, and Shudra. Some historians have argued that in ancient India "caste by worth" was the norm—that is, one entered into one of the fourfold castes based upon one's nature and aptitude—but that this later gave way to "caste by birth." "Open castes," in other words, became "closed castes." "Caste citizenship" was then possible only by birth into a particular caste. Each varna has specific dharmas that are enumerated in the dharma literature. These dharmas are, as stated already, the vishesha-dharmas, or duties relative to each caste.

If we combine caste by birth with an autonomous system of dharmas or rules and obligations that bind members of that caste, we get in the caste system a rudimentary notion of a modern state. In a modern state, citizenship is primarily through birth in that state, and the citizens' primary obligations are to the state of which they are members. In passing, we may also note that each caste in practice is divided into a number of subcastes (jatis). A jati is typically a kin group that is linguistically and geographically limited with its own norms of behavior, distinctive dress, and food habits. Each jati has its own dharmas, or rules of conduct. The relationship between jati (subcaste) and varna (caste) may be compared with that of states and a federation in a nation with a federal constitution. The jatis have their own dharmas, but these dharmas may sometimes be overridden by the varna-dharmas, just as a federal constitution overrides state constitutions.

The Hindu caste system should not be confused with Karl Marx's notion of a class system. In Marxism, class is essentially an economic phenomenon where in the very process of producing wealth, one class exploits the other. This exploitation leads to class conflict. The Hindu caste system is not divided according to the economic production of the population. The castes in theory are associated with different traditional occupations, and each caste is dependent on the others for specialized services. All the traditional occupations are considered important for the smooth running of the society. Moreover, each of the four castes is governed by the eternal dharma. The Hindu caste system and the traditional occupations associated with each caste may be compared to the "division of powers" in modern democracies, wherein the ecclesiastical authority was given to the Brahmins, the political power and ruling authority was given to the Kshatriyas, the economic power was given to the Vaishyas, and so on.

Dharma in Practice

One of the central questions in ethics is "What ought I to do?" or "What makes actions right actions?" In Christian ethics, for example, one ought always to obey God's commands, because right actions are those actions commanded by God. The Ten Commandments, for example, are typically what the Christians ought to obey. What is commanded by God is contained in the Bible. What if one is faced with a moral problem—for example, the problem of abortion, or the problem of war—for which there is no explicit answer in the Bible? If we use the example of the Roman Catholic Church, at this point the role of the church or the Pope becomes more important. It is assumed that there is a right conduct commanded in the Bible for every moral problem, and the church has the insight and final authority to interpret the scripture and provide the solution to the problem. Therefore, in Roman Catholicism, what one ought to do is what the church says one ought to do, because the church has deeper insights and is vested the authority to interpret and promulgate the commands of God on each and every problem.

The answer to "What ought I to do?" is more complex in Hindu ethics than in the Western religious ethics like Christianity. Of course, a simple but formal answer to this question is: "Do what dharma dictates," or "Do whatever your dharma is." This answer, however, is empty of content. It is like the captain of a team advising his or her players, "Do your best," which cannot guide the players' conduct. We saw earlier that there are multiple sources of Hindu ethics, namely shruti (Vedic revelation), smriti (remembered tradition), sadachara (conduct of the virtuous), and individual conscience, each of which tells us what is dharma. Unlike a single scripture such as the Bible, which is the primary authority in moral matters for Christianity, there is no single book or a single authoritative church in Hinduism to interpret what one's dharma is. Moreover, Hinduism is a pluralistic religion and has no central authority to say conclusively what one ought or ought not to do in moral matters. Each individual is therefore responsible to find out what one's dharma is and act accordingly.

Most of the moral matters we encounter in our day-to-day life, such as telling the truth or keeping our promises, are not at all problematic in Hindu ethics. Likewise, in the Hindu way of life, everyone knows his or her varna-dharma or caste obligations. But moral problems do arise when there are conflicting dharmas or when one has violated one's dharma due to ignorance, weakness of will, or some similar fault and would like to salvage one's dharma and do some "damage control" of the consequences without further deterioration. In the Hindu tradition, moral reasoning in problematic cases generally proceeds in two directions. First, Hindus typically appeal to precedents in the smriti literature to resolve those problems.

Take the example of teenage pregnancy, wherein a teenage unmarried girl—let us call her Sheila—who out of ignorance or irresistible temptation fell in love with a man and becomes pregnant. Sheila has, no doubt, violated her dharma and wants to "salvage" the situation to the best of her ability. She faces several decisions, including: Should she reveal the matter to her parents and community, or should she keep it secret? Should she resort to abortion, or should she secretly deliver the baby and give the child up for adoption? A philosophical reasoning using moral theories like utilitarianism may help Sheila arrive at a moral decision.

A common Hindu way of resolving such moral problems is by using what we may call "reasoning from precedent." The smriti literature in part consists of quasi-historical narratives, mythic histories of gods, and so on, wherein the characters in these stories narrate all kinds of problems the heroes and heroines face and how they have solved them. The case of Sheila, the teenage unwed mother-to-be in our example, is similar to the situation of Princess Kunti, who when she was young and unmarried fell in love with the sun god, secretly delivered their son, Karna, and left the infant in a small boat in a nearby river to be picked up downstream and adopted by childless parents. She kept her premarital pregnancy a secret, letting it be known to her legitimate children only when her pre-wed son and her own married children were about to fight in the battlefield. When Sheila remembers the story of Kunti, her dharma becomes obvious.

Sheila's reasoning in this case goes something like this: "Kunti, who was a princess and a heroine in our tradition, was faced with a situation similar to mine. Kunti did X. Therefore I ought to follow her example and do the same that Kunti did." The important thing to note here is that the smriti literature, which includes the epics and the Puranas, is taught to children at home and at schools, so everyone knows these stories. They are not merely stories, but stories accompanied by a didactic moral teaching. Thus when someone is facing a moral problem, he or she already knows that he or she is not alone and that someone else in the tradition has already faced a similar problem; therefore everyone has an insight into a possible solution to the moral problem. Likewise, children routinely are taught animal fables with human values, which help them to appeal to precedents in the tradition when they face moral problems as adults.

Now suppose our example of a mother-to-be is not a teenager but a mature adult who is also a learned person. By reason of her maturity and learning, she does not just resort to doing what someone in the tradition did. She contemplates her problem "to abort or not to abort" rationally and may argue as follows. Abortion is the intentional termination of the life of a fetus. As she is a Hindu she would like to find an answer within her own religious tradition. She will first contemplate what shruti and smriti have to say on the matter. She will find that as early as the Rig Veda it is said that it is not the mother but the god Vishnu who is the protector of the unborn, and therefore she may conclude that she will be encroaching on Vishnu's territory by aborting the fetus. She may now turn to the smriti literature, where she will find that killing the unborn is likened to the killing of a pious person (for example a Brahmin), and therefore doing so is not just wrong but doubly wrong. She may then turn to the Hindu dharma literature, where it is said that one who resorts to abortion loses one's caste status and becomes an outcast. Does she really want to lose her caste? But the wrongness of abortion comes into her reasoning only if the fetus is a human person and not a mere tissue in her body. What does the Hindu tradition say about it? She will find that Hindu tradition is emphatic that a fetus is a combination of a body and a soul (atman, purusha) and therefore it is a human person. As the killing of a human person is wrong, and as the fetus is a human person, causing the death of the fetus is morally wrong. In addition, she believes that in the Hindu tradition all birth is indeed rebirth, and one is reborn in order to

enjoy and suffer the fruits of one's past karmas. By aborting the fetus she, as a mother, is not only interfering in the law of karma but
is also acquiring some bad karma for which there will be negative
consequences for her either in this life or in the next. In Hindu
thought, the man and the woman are not really the causes of conception, they are only instruments, facilitators to fulfill the karma of
some person who "chose" to be born to this woman, to these parents. Given all these reasons, she will conclude that "abortion is
morally wrong." From here it is a short step to decide "therefore let
me not abort my fetus." From this example, it is clear that moral decisionmaking in Hinduism is more complex than in religious traditions that rely on the Divine Command Theory of Ethics, whereby
the only question that is asked is: "Did God, in fact, prohibit abortion?" If He did, it is wrong; if not, what God does not prohibit, He
permits; therefore abortion is permissible.

Although the majority of Hindu leaders agree that abortion is
wrong according to the dictates of dharma, abortion has been legal
in India since the passage of the 1971 Medical Termination of Pregnancy Act. The cultural preference for sons over daughters—because
sons traditionally care for their parents in their old age, because sons
perform funeral and death anniversary rites, and also because of the
great expense of dowry in marrying a daughter—has also had an impact on attitudes about abortion. There is currently a serious sex imbalance in the Indian population—with only about 927 girls for every
1,000 boys (http://www.ippfwhr.org/publications/serial_issue_e.
asp?PubID=33&SerialIssuesID=127). Many attribute this imbalance
to people's preference for sons, leading to female infanticide and
sex-selection abortion. To address this problem, India has instituted
laws against the use of ultrasound and other means for determining
the sex of a fetus, but the laws have not been strictly enforced.

Population growth is also a major issue in India. In 1952, India
became the first country in the world to launch a family planning
program. There is no single view on birth control within Hinduism
(Mahatma Gandhi, for example, advocated birth control through
abstinence, whereas other leaders have advocated artificial means),
but generally Hindus consider it to be acceptable. One argument in
favor of birth control is that dharma dictates that one should con-

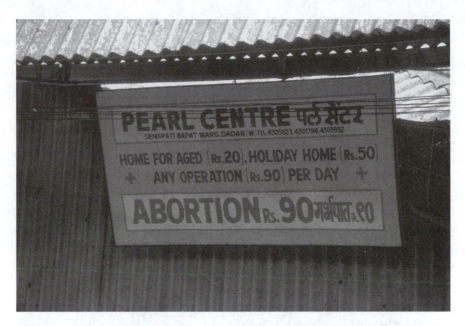

A sign advertises prices for temporary lodging for the aged, as well as for various surgeries in Mumbai Bombay, India, ca. 1990.
ARVIND GARG/CORBIS

sider the good of the world. If a family produces more children than it or the community and environment can support, then it is a violation of dharma (http://www.religiousconsultation.org/summary_of_sacred_choices.htm).

On some issues, it is possible to reach different views using the various sources of dharma. For example, with respect to euthanasia and the use of life-support machines, one could argue that it is good to help a person end a painful life, or one could argue that ending a life interferes with the cycle of death and rebirth and is thus opposed to dharma. One could argue that using life-support machines to keep a person alive artificially is bad, or, alternatively, that it is good as part of an attempt at healing (http://www.bbc.co.uk/religion/ethics/sanctity_life/euthhindu.shtml). Most Hindus accept the latter position and may note that Hindu tradition places great emphasis on respecting the elderly.

Dharma, Moral Reasoning, and War

The problem of abortion was never philosophically discussed in Hindu ethics exactly as we have discussed it above. But discussions of moral problems using philosophical reasoning have been part of Hindu ethics, providing a model for moral reasoning and making moral decisions. The best example of a philosophical discussion of a great moral problem occurs in the Bhagavad Gita, where Krishna advises Arjuna whether or not to fight in a just war. In the Mahabharata, the Pandava princes were unjustly deprived of their kingdom by their cousins, the Kaurava princes. After all negotiation for a peaceful settlement of the dispute had failed, the Pandava brothers declared a war against the Kauravas. Arjuna was the commander-in-chief of the Pandava army, and his charioteer was Krishna. Arjuna was fully aware that he was fighting a just war. When the lines in the battlefield were drawn, however, Arjuna was overcome by dejection and refused to fight.

Arjuna gave Krishna the following reasons why he was not morally obliged to fight: (1) Arjuna will incur sin by killing, and, after all, we all have a dharma not to kill rather than to kill; (2) the people whom he will be killing are his own cousins, teachers, and other relatives, which makes his sin more reprehensible; (3) in the four stages of life, renunciation is held to be the highest stage of life, and Arjuna argues there is no reason why he should not renounce life right away instead of waiting for it later; and (4) even if Arjuna wins the war, he cannot be happy because he will have killed so many people in war, and this will haunt him throughout his life.

Krishna advises Arjuna to fight the war, arguing that Arjuna's reasons do not have merit. To summarize Krishna's reasons: (1) Arjuna as a king and as the commander-in-chief is duty-bound to fight in the war, and by abandoning the war, he is guilty of dereliction of his dharma. (2) If a petty soldier were to run away from the war, it would be excusable, but the same action performed by the commander-in-chief is inexcusable, because the commander-in-chief sets the standards others will follow and also sets a precedent for conducting wars for future generations. (3) If Arjuna kills his enemies as a matter of duty, he will not incur sin. (We know everywhere in the world soldiers are never thought of as "paid murderers" be-

Illustration of the Mahabharata: Combat with archers and swords with four people. India, Paithan school, nineteenth century.
RICHARD LAMBERT/MUSEE DES ARTS ASIATIQUES-GUIMET, PARIS/
ART RESOURCE

cause they were only discharging their duty.) (4) Arjuna's nature (svabhava), by virtue of his being a Kshatriya (warrior), is to fight, and by renouncing the fight, Arjuna is going against his own nature. (5) Arjuna's dejection and refusal to fight does not come out of rational considerations but out of weakness of will; his reasons therefore are not rational but rationalizations. And finally, (6) Arjuna is ignorant of the metaphysics of the atman, or self. He has not distinguished between the eternal atman and the temporal self (jiva). If Arjuna thinks that in killing his enemies he is killing their atmans, he is grossly mistaken.

In the Hindu worldview, death and birth are two sides of the same coin. Just as one changes one's clothes when they become old, so also do people change their bodies when they die. Arjuna is worried about a "what if" reason, that is, what if he loses the war?

Krishna says that if Arjuna wins the war he will enjoy the happiness on this earth, the happiness that comes out of his rulership of the kingdom; if he loses it, because he has done his duty, he will be rewarded with happiness in heaven. Fighting the war for Arjuna is therefore a "win-win situation." Last but not least, Arjuna is dejected because he is attached to the consequences of his actions. Krishna's classic solution to Arjuna's problem is that he should fight with a spirit of detachment. Also, Arjuna is likely to incur sins of commission and omission if he identifies himself as the actor and enjoyer of his actions. Instead, if he performs his actions as an "agent of God," he will not be held accountable for his actions, and therefore he will get neither credit nor blame for his actions. When Arjuna considered all of Krishna's reasons, he became enlightened and decided to fight.

It is said in the Mahabharata that "the secret of dharma is hidden." The more complex the moral problem one faces, the more reflection and meditation on dharma is needed to resolve the problem. In Hindu ethics, moral decisions are not made as obedience to commands like "Do this" or "Don't do this." As we have seen in the Bhagavad Gita, though Krishna is God, he does not *command* Arjuna that he should fight. God in the Hindu tradition is believed to be a guru, or a teacher, the First Teacher (*adi guru*). Hindu tradition has developed a string of teachers, not preachers. Gurus as teachers educate and guide those who seek their advice. In the Bhagavad Gita, Krishna engages in a *dialogue* with Arjuna, enumerating all the reasons, pro and con, and when Arjuna *weighs* them carefully, he realizes that he ought to fight because he ought to perform that action that has the greatest rational weight. Hindu ethics and moral values are based upon these principles of reasoning and careful consideration of the examples provided by both shruti and smriti.

BIBLIOGRAPHY

Crawford, Cromwell S. *The Evolution of Hindu Ethical Ideals*. Honolulu: University of Hawaii Press, 1982.
Creel, Austin B. *Dharma in Hindu Ethics*. Calcutta: Firma KLM, 1977.

Hiriyanna, Mysore. *Indian Conception of Values*. Mysore: Kavalaya
    Publications, 1975.

Hopkins, E. Washburn. *Ethics of India*. New Haven: Yale University Press,
    1924.

Maitra, Susheel Kumar. *The Ethics of the Hindus*. Calcutta: University of
    Calcutta, 1956.

Potter, Karl H. *Presuppositions of India's Philosophies*. Englewood Cliffs,
    N.J.: Prentice-Hall, 1963.

http://www.bbc.co.uk/religion/ethics/sanctity_life/euthhindu.shtml.
    Accessed July 23, 2003.

http://www.ippfwhr.org/publications/serial_issue_e.asp?PubID=
    33&SerialIssuesID=127. Accessed July 23, 3003.

http://www.religiousconsultation.org/summary_of_sacred_choices.htm.
    Accessed July 23, 2003.

http://www.unescap.org/pop/database/law_india/india1.htm. Accessed
    July 23, 2003.

Sir Sarvepalli Radhakrishnan, Indian philosopher, statesman, and president 1962–1967.
BETTMANN/CORBIS

Chapter Six

Contemporary Hindu Thought

Brian A. Hatcher

The many new Hindu movements prominent during the colonial period in India presented a variety of interpretations of what Hinduism really is or should be. Hindu thinkers advocated changes in traditional practices and often compared Hindu traditions to Western religions, especially Christianity. This chapter explores some of the most important trends in Hindu thought of the past two centuries, focusing especially on the concept of neo-Vedanta and its role in contemporary India.

It has been suggested that what passes for contemporary Hindu thought (or more broadly, modern Hindu thought) is a species of "Western-influenced neo-Vedanta" propagated worldwide by the likes of Rammohan Roy, Mahatma Gandhi, and Sarvepalli Radhakrishnan (King 1999, 69). It is a fair assertion, but it bears some careful consideration. Is modern Hindu thought really (principally? only? essentially?) represented by what some call neo-Vedanta? What is Vedanta, anyway? How does neo-Vedanta relate to Vedanta, and what exactly happened to produce neo-Vedanta? Does the difference between the two have to do with Western influence? These are not trivial questions. Perhaps by using them to interrogate the category of "Western-influenced neo-Vedanta" we can form some idea of what makes up contemporary Hindu thought. This is our goal in this chapter.

Insofar as ours is an age grown wary of essentialisms, it makes good sense to begin by asking whether there is, in fact, one essential form of modern Hindu thought. Without a doubt, this has been the claim made by modern intellectuals from Rammohan Roy to Sarvepalli Radhakrishnan, who see contemporary thought as the expression of a perennial Hindu philosophy. For his part, Rammohan Roy tells us that belief in the unity of God is what constitutes "real Hindooism" and that this belief is shared by ancient and modern Hindus alike (Roy 1906, 90). Radhakrishnan makes a similar claim, assuring his readers that from the "seers . . . of the Upanishads down to Tagore and Gandhi," Hindus have affirmed a consistent belief in the manifestation of divine unity under the "vestures of many colours" (Radhakrishnan 1980, 27). The question is, To what extent are we prepared to agree with these claims? As indicated at the outset, Rammohan and Radhakrishnan could certainly be ranked as leading proponents of a neo-Vedantic vision of Hinduism. However, it is also worth noting that these men lived in quite different time periods, as well as in different linguistic and cultural regions of India. As a result, their experiences of the modern world were vastly different, spanning the earliest phases of colonial rule in Rammohan Roy's case to the freedom movement and the travails of post-independence India in Radhakrishnan's. These differences are significant; they remind us that, perennialist claims notwithstanding, modern Hindu thought is a product of history. Therefore, whatever similarities we may discern among the ideas of different modern spokespersons, we should also bear in mind that contemporary Hindu thought has been worked out and expressed in a variety of historical contexts over the preceding two hundred years. To understand this thought, we must explore both its diverse modern manifestations and its complex genealogy. We might begin by looking briefly at its manifestations.

The Range of Contemporary Hindu Thought

It is certainly tempting to think that if we could inventory the movements that account for modern Hindu life, we might be able to speak comprehensively about the nature of modern Hinduism. As tempting as this thought is, the task is no easy one. Such an attempt was made over one hundred years ago by John Nicol Farquhar, whose *Modern Religious Movements in India* (1915) sought to provide a handy scheme of categories for understanding the range of religious thought and activity in the India of his day. According to Farquhar, when surveying religious change in nineteenth-century India one was confronted with (1) movements that favored "serious reform," such as the Brahmo Samaj in Bengal and the Prarthana Samaj in Bombay; (2) movements in which reform was "checked by defense of the old faiths," such as the Arya Samaj in the Punjab and the Radhasoami Satsang in northern India; and (3) movements that depended upon a "full defence of the old religions," among which Farquhar placed not only older sectarian movements (such as Gaudiya Vaisnavism and Saiva Siddhanta) but also the figure of Ramakrishna Paramahamsa, a mystic from colonial Bengal.

Unfortunately, Farquhar was not prepared to acknowledge the degree to which his system of classification was unable to contain the movements he surveyed. Given more space than we have in the present context, we could work our way down Farquhar's list of movements and demonstrate its many limitations. Two examples will have to suffice.

As a first case consider the Arya Samaj, which Farquhar viewed as a movement in which reform was offset by a consistent appeal to what he called an "old faith." In this case the old faith was Vedism, the religion enshrined in the ancient Vedas, texts that the movement's founder, Swami Dayanand Saraswati, considered to represent the true form of Hinduism. However, Dayanand was himself both the benefactor and co-creator of a particular construction of Vedism. His view of the religion of the ancient Vedas was itself the legacy both of recent European research into what was taken to be the glory of ancient Indian civilization and of the teachings of Rammohan Roy regarding Vedic monotheism (to which we shall turn presently). His "old faith" (to use Farquhar's phrase) was thus rather more of a new thing. Even Farquhar had to admit that Dayanand's concept of an ancient monotheism was unprecedented in Indian history. As Farquhar put it, "though he claims to have restored the ancient interpretation, in reality he departs from it" (Farquhar 1967, 116). Nevertheless, this awareness didn't stop Farquhar from promoting the category of "appeal to an old faith" as a useful tool for understanding modern Hindu thought.

As a second example, consider Farquhar's decision to place Ramakrishna Paramahamsa in the category of a movement offering a "full defence" of the older faith. Here we note a similar breakdown in Farquhar's very system of classification. Though Ramakrishna was certainly one of the more spontaneous of religious leaders—insofar as he was without any formal education in the colonial curriculum—it is difficult for this very reason to view him as motivated by the logic of defending or reviving an embattled faith. His profound mystical experiences were in keeping with long-standing patterns of both devotional and tantric Hinduism, but the context for these experiences was decidedly structured by the dynamics of life in colonial Bengal. Ramakrishna was not isolated in a Himalayan cave but lived in a Kali temple just north of Calcutta, then the capital of British rule in India.

It was the highly educated young men of Calcutta who effectively discovered Ramakrishna and made him known to the larger world. Indeed, Ramakrishna's religious vision was lived out and recorded in dialogue with these young men, who for a variety of emotional and spiritual reasons found meaning in the idiosyncratic teachings of the saint. The man Ramakrishna would ultimately designate as his spiritual heir, Narendranath Datta, would in fact go on, under the monastic name of Swami Vivekananda, to radically reshape Hindu thought. It therefore makes little sense to speak of the Ramakrishna-Vivekananda movement as a defense of Hinduism. It is far more profitable to jettison the dichotomy of reform-versus-revival and situate Ramakrishna and his followers in a vortex of cultural change—one in which competing Hindu teachings (Vedanta versus Tantra, for instance) converged with bourgeois socioeconomic norms, utilitarianism, positivism, and enlightenment rationality—not to mention Orientalist tropes about the nature and essence of Hindu culture.

Indeed, one of the most pervasive and significant Orientalist tropes to shape constructions of modern Hindu thought is the very idea of a golden age of Hindu culture, after which the tradition had fallen into decay and rampant error. It was the British Orientalists

Ramakrishna, 1836–1886.
CORBIS

active in the earliest decades of colonial rule who promulgated the notion that contemporary India—which they viewed as suffering from the abuses of caste prejudice, polytheism, image worship, and renunciatory other-worldliness—was in fact merely the corrupted descendant of a once-pristine Hindu culture (Kopf 1969). According to such thinking, India could boast the highest attainments of civilization in its classical traditions of literature, philosophy, and architecture. It was a handy trope upon which to establish an empire, insofar as it justified both the colonizer's interest in India and the colonizer's project of restoring civilization in India. Indeed, it would seem that this classicist trope was developed by the Orientalists less to educate the Indian population than it was to garner support for the colonizer's agenda back home. How could one bring the British people on board the colonial project unless it could be shown that India once boasted enormous cultural riches?

As it turned out, the British Orientalists could scarcely have imagined that "the admiration for Indian culture . . . that they sought to inspire in the British public would influence the perception Indians had of their own culture" (Rocher 1993, 241). But it did. As we shall see below, the myth of a golden age of Hinduism was appropriated by indigenous intellectuals in rather short order, beginning with Rammohan Roy, who used the same invocation of long-lost classical glories to legitimate his reformation of Hinduism in terms of the metaphysics of classical Vedanta. By appealing to Vedanta, Rammohan Roy set in motion an intellectual project that would constitute the basis for one major trend in modern Hindu thought. Subsequently the glories and virtues of Vedanta would be rearticulated by Swami Vivekananda at the turn of the twentieth century and further canonized by the likes of philosophers such as Sarvepalli Radhakrishnan, in addition to gurus such as Swami Shivananda of the Divine Life Society. Shivananda speaks for all such thinkers when he claims that "Vedanta reveals the majesty of man in his essential nature" and that "Vedanta is the basic culture of India" (quoted in Tejomayananda 1999, x). We shall explore the genesis and repercussions of such a claim later in this chapter. For now it is enough to note that during the twentieth century, Vedanta-based visions of Hinduism were immensely influential in India and worldwide, perhaps none more than the Ramakrishna Math and Mission, known outside of India as the Vedanta Society.

However, whereas Vedanta renders the path to liberation into a problem of right knowledge (*jnana*), there are many Hindu movements in which devotion (*bhakti*) to God or service (*seva*) to the guru—as well as more esoteric practices of yogic alchemy—are seen to be the most efficacious means to salvation. On this matter, as in prior centuries, Hindu movements and teachers today continue to disagree over some of the most basic questions of theology and practice. Thus if we were to attempt, like Farquhar, to survey the scene over the past twenty-five years, we would soon discover that Vedanta-based thought represents only one dimension of current Hindu life. Our survey would lead us to Tantric yoga-based traditions, such as Swami Muktananda's Siddha Yoga, and other guru-based movements, such as those centered on the miracle-working Sathya Sai Baba and the holy mother, Anandamayi Ma. We would, in addition, have to reckon with those figures who achieved enormous international success, such as Swami Prabhupada, the founder of the International Society for Krishna Consciousness (ISKCON), Maharishi Mahesh Yogi, or the former Bhagwan Shree Rajneesh (currently known as Osho).

Some of these movements, with their ashrams, publishing houses, and colleges in Europe and North America, look decidedly like the products of today's transnational culture. At the same time, there are equally modern—and modernist—movements, such as the Radhasoami Satsang and Swami Narayan Hinduism, that might strike the casual observer as more authentically or traditionally Indian. Surprisingly, though, these latter movements are just as decidedly "new," even if they appear to carry forward older traditions. Indeed, in their combination of eclectic teachings, traditional ritual trappings, appeal to middle-class urbanites, and astute use of modern forms of organization and communication, some of these movements suggest important parallels with other so-called new religious movements around the world (Wilson 1988).

If one of the new platforms adopted by members of the Vedanta-based movements has been the promotion of religious tolerance—seen by many contemporary Hindus to be the only way to promote the dream of a secular Indian republic—it is nevertheless not the case that all modern Hindus have concurred on this point. Indeed, some individuals view their primary goal to be bolstering the supremacy of Hindu identity. An early forerunner in this regard would be Swami Dayanand Saraswati, who founded the Arya Samaj in Bombay in 1875. Unlike the prophets of Vedanta, Dayanand self-consciously promoted opposition to the inroads made in Indian culture by Islam and Christianity. Indeed, the Arya Samaj strategy of reconversion (*shuddhi,* or "purification") is a notable example of an aggressive program of Hindu self-assertion. From such a program it is but a short step to more overtly communal and nationalist Hindu movements, such as the Hindu Mahasabha, founded in 1909, or the Rashtriya Swayamsevak Sangh (RSS), founded in 1925. These, and more recent organizations, such as the World Hindu Council, or Vishva Hindu Parishad (VHP; est. 1965), all promote the ideal of Hinduness (i.e., Hindutva) as the ultimate litmus test for Indianness. At first glance it seems as if the spokespersons for these so-called Hindutva movements could share but little with the prophets of Vedantic tolerance. However, first impressions can be misleading.

To treat movements like the Vedanta Society and the VHP as arising from diametrically opposed visions of Hinduism—tolerant versus intolerant—would be to miss their genesis within a common discursive field (van der Veer 1993, 40). It takes but little effort to see how the aggressive promotion of a muscular Hindu spirituality by the likes of Swami Vivekananda could serve as the inspiration both for the Vedanta Society and for the very different platform of a figure like Swami Chinmayananda, founder of the VHP. This may be an unsettling thought, both for those Hindus who would reject the claims of a Chinmayananda and for scholars, but it suggests that the proper task for both groups is to take a hard look at the genesis of this common heritage.

Here we may pause in our survey of the range of modern Hindu thought. It should be clear by now that the task of characterizing the worldview of contemporary Hinduism is fraught with problems—historical, epistemological, and political. For the time being, it seems that rather than attempting to define *a priori* what modern Hinduism is—and being frustrated by the obvious competition among the divergent constituencies one encounters—we do better to explore the factors that worked to promote the overall discursive field that has given shape to the various Hindu leaders and movements of the modern period. Even a quick survey of the major factors—the growth in India of British colonial rule; Christian missions; Orientalism; social, educational, and legal reform; urbanization and economic upheaval; the decline of Islamicate knowledge-systems; and the transformation of shastric and popular

Hindu norms—is enough to suggest that all such factors cannot be addressed in this short chapter. The best we can do is provide a general framework for pursuing more in-depth research.

For the purposes of this chapter, we shall limit our historical gaze to the past two centuries. While any such periodization is open to question, we follow long-standing scholarly convention in dating the birth of Hindu modernity to the lifetime of Rammohan Roy (1772–1833), the Bengali Brahmin polymath and founder of the reformist Brahmo Samaj. In so doing, we call attention to the fact that the conditions of economic, social, and intellectual life that Rammohan Roy encountered in Calcutta in the first decades of the nineteenth century played a profound role in shaping the way he understood and communicated the meaning of Hinduism.

We have already had occasion to note the signficance of Rammohan Roy's decision to focus his attention upon Vedanta. We need now to consider the ramifications of this decision in more detail. Though he was born a high-caste Hindu intellectual, his choice of Vedanta was by no means obvious. As a system of philosophy, Vedanta was accorded little attention in Rammohan's Bengal; other schools of Hindu thought and worship could have claimed a far greater following (for instance, among devotees of Krishna or the mother goddess, Kali). Furthermore, Rammohan was well educated within the Islamic cultural matrix, as evident from his early study of Persian and Arabic and his facility with trends in Muslim theology. In itself this would hardly have been surprising for an elite intellectual of Rammohan Roy's day, given the dominance of Islamic cultural values in the late Mughal era. What should surprise us, then, is not the fact that he was a Brahmin trained in Muslim thought, but that he chose to abandon this intellectual framework in order to promote his particular vision of Vedantic Hinduism. The singularity of this choice is a powerful illustration of the changes that were taking place in early British India. For all that there are strong continuities between Rammohan's thought and the intellectual life of precolonial India, it nevertheless seems as if with his advent we enter into a new era.

One distinguishing feature of that new era would be the prominence of Vedanta. What precisely is the meaning of this term and how does it relate to its latter-day cousin, neo-Vedanta? And how did Vedanta achieve such hegemony in the modern Hindu worldview?

The Origins of Neo-Vedanta

Early in the nineteenth century, Rammohan Roy identified his personal creed as the "Holy Vedanta" (Sharma 2002, 54). With this phrase he directed his readers to a school of Hindu thought rooted in the ancient Upanishads (ca. seventh century BCE–first century BCE). *Vedanta* is, in fact, a collective designation for the Upanishads meaning "end of the Veda." The word *end* may be understood in at least two senses. First, because the Upanishads constitute the last layer of revealed literature to be included in the Vedic canon (understood to be comprised of the fourfold collection of Samhita, Brahmana, Aryanaka, and Upanishad), they are said to mark an end to the Veda. However, at the same time, because the teachings of the Upanishads contain esoteric knowledge regarding the ultimate meaning of the language and rituals employed in the cult of Vedic sacrifice, they can also be said to be the philosophical culmination of the Vedas, the quintessence of Vedic knowledge.

Over subsequent centuries the relatively unsystematic teachings of the Upanishads were to become the basis for a number of competing philosophies, all of which claimed to be schools of Vedanta. Among these schools, that associated with the teachings of the philosophers Gaudapada (ca. sixth century CE) and Shankara (ca. ninth century CE) eventually attained a wide following. Shankara's school of Vedanta is known as Advaita Vedanta, a name that expresses its fundamental belief in the nonduality (*advaita*) of ultimate reality. Rammohan Roy's teachings are most closely related to Shankara's.

However, Rammohan was no mere transmitter of an earlier teaching. Instead, his was a creative intellectual project. Not only did his presentation of Vedanta draw directly upon both ancient source texts and classical commentators, it was enriched by direct dialogue with contemporary native scholars and Christian missionaries, and further inflected by his study of Islam and his awareness of the work of early Orientalists such as William Jones and Henry

Thomas Colebrooke. The central aspect of Rammohan's work involved translating several important Upanishads into Bengali and English. Working from these translations and his own rephrasing of classical summaries of Advaita Vedanta, he endeavored to present Vedanta as the doctrine of belief in the "One True God." In this his goal was neither scholarly nor antiquarian; instead, he sought to demonstrate that in Vedanta Indians possessed a religious heritage that inculcated monotheism and rejected the worship of images. His project to define the essence of Vedanta set perhaps the most important hermeneutical precedent for subsequent modern Hindu thinkers. Just as the mystical teachings of the Upanishads purport to transcend the lower-order theology of Vedic sacrifice and polytheism in the name of one supreme reality (brahman or *sat,* "being"), Rammohan's representation of Vedanta offered a theology more fundamental than the polytheism and image worship that were taken to be the hallmarks of Hinduism in his day.

If we consider Rammohan Roy to have been engaged in a two-pronged campaign of representing Hindu thought to its European critics (rationalists and missionaries alike) and defining it anew for his co-religionists, we can appreciate why Vedanta was so important to him. On the one hand, Rammohan felt compelled to address Christian charges that Hinduism was not only a polytheistic faith but also one irrevocably enslaved to blind ritual and erroneous, even degenerate, mythology. On the other hand, he earnestly sought to deliver into the hands of his fellow Hindus a theology in which they could take pride. Because European Christianity claimed to be the benchmark of true and valid religion, and furthermore because Rammohan's urban contemporaries were already beginning to internalize metropolitan norms of reason, morality, and respectability, a restored sense of Hindu pride could only be won by proving Hinduism to be everything one found in modern European Christianity—a rational, monotheistic faith that served as the bedrock for ethical rectitude and public civility. Vedanta was the key he would use to demonstrate that Hinduism possessed these same qualities. For Rammohan Roy, Vedanta could be shown to teach a kind of ancient monotheism that rejected polytheism and idolatry while inculcating a fundamental respect for the dignity of all human beings.

The Brahmo Samaj, which Rammohan Roy founded in 1828, set as its goal the propagation of the teachings of Vedanta with respect to the unity of God and the equality of humanity (two concepts Rammohan seems likely to have imbibed from the Islamic culture of his day). The Brahmo Samaj had in Rammohan Roy a leader of uncanny abilities. Here was a Brahmin intellectual who could read Arabic, Hebrew, Greek, Sanskrit, Bengali, French, and English; here was a polemicist who had no compunctions about waging open battles with the Christian missionaries of his day. Well versed in the political developments of early modern Europe and the classics of Hindu culture, Rammohan Roy could also quote the Bible with the best of missionaries; indeed, he even undertook the audacious task of editing the Gospels in light of his own unitarian and rationalist creed. At the same time, he took on representatives of popular Hindu religion who advocated the validity of image worship and the meaningfulness of Hindu myths as found in the Epics and Puranas. For his part, Rammohan Roy could countenance no irrational myth, whether framed in terms of the Christian trinity or the incarnations of Vishnu. Following the Upanishads, he held firmly that reality was one; between the Vedanta and our own reason, we had all the tools we needed for grasping this most basic of truths.

The motto of the early Brahmo Samaj, which carried on Rammohan's work after he left on a trip to England in 1830 (from which he never returned), was *ekamevadvitiyam,* "one only without a second," a phrase culled from the Upanishads. This message of unity, though theologically quite simple, was to be of profound significance for the development of modern Hindu thought. Unity referred at once to the proper relationship between humans and God and to the proper relationship among human beings on earth. It spoke of the need to transcend all limited views of self and world in the name of the "higher knowledge" (*para vidya*) praised in the opening verses of the Mundaka Upanishad (Radhakrishnan and Moore 1957, 51–55). It reminded the Brahmo that no single image or concept of God could be considered supreme because in its absolute transcendence, ultimate reality, or brahman, was beyond all imagery and imagining. Therefore, not just the sectarian Vaishnava and sectarian Shaiva but Jews, Christians, and Muslims could all meet on a common ground of reverence for that which was "one only without a second."

We have already noted that Rammohan Roy's appeal to the Vedanta amounted to a kind of strategic classicism equivalent to that deployed by his Orientalist counterparts. Having identified in the Upanishads the essential and timeless truth of Hinduism, he and his followers in the Brahmo Samaj were able to explain away those aspects of contemporary Hinduism that so troubled both his European interlocutors and many of his progressively educated contemporaries. Idolatry, caste exclusivity, and sectarian strife could all be dismissed as departures from the "one true religion" of the ancient Hindus. If this appeal to a universal, rational religion as the cure for religious discord seems to echo concerns of the European enlightenment, it is no coincidence, because as we have seen, Rammohan and the early Brahmos were well versed in the intellectual history of modern Europe.

Indeed, much like the Enlightenment *philosophes,* the Brahmos saw in their teachings a cosmopolitan philosophy that promised to promote democratic social change and international understanding. The sheer durability of this melioristic hope in the universalism of the Vedanta is everywhere evident in the literature of modern Hinduism. So characteristic of modern Hindu thought has this doctrine become that one finds it presented as the guiding principle of Indian thought in general. A recent summary of contemporary Indian philosophy sings the praises of Vedantic thought as both universal and perennial: "The man in India is the man in England, America, Europe, Asia and every other corner of the world. Indian philosophy today recasts the ancient ideas of *saccidananda* . . . meaning pure existence, consciousness and bliss, in the contemporary socio-political and economic contexts of the country" (Roy 1997, 282–283).

With this claim, we jump from the inaugural teachings of Rammohan Roy to the seasoned truths of any number of latter-day Hindu "masterminds" (Bakhle 1991). This is not to ignore the fact that there is an enormous historical, social, and political gap between Rammohan and twentieth-century figures like Gandhi. Indeed, within the realm of Brahmo thought alone there is a complex history to tell of theological battles and organizational schisms. Rammohan

Roy's work was carried forward by a series of gifted, but varied, individuals—men like Debendranath Tagore, Rajnarain Bose, Keshub Chunder Sen, and Sibnath Shastri. The decades of the 1830s and 1840s alone are rich with Brahmo experimentation in achieving the proper balance between reason and revelation, intuition and empirical knowledge.

It is during this period, in fact, that the term *neo-Vedanta* was first coined by Christian commentators, some of whom were firsthand observers of developments in Brahmo theology. Missionaries such as James Mullens and Alexander Duff, as well as native converts like Krishnamohan Banerjee, engaged in open, sometimes acrimonious debates with the Brahmos, whom they partly admired for their courage in abandoning traditions of polytheism and image worship but whom they also scorned for having proffered to other Hindus a viable alternative to conversion. To such commentators, Brahmo theism was a kind of halfway measure, one that prevented reasonable and inquisitive Hindus from taking the final necessary step toward Christian belief (Hatcher 1999, 102). These commentators began to look upon the Brahmos' invocation of Vedanta, therefore, as something suspect—certainly it wasn't what the missionaries claimed to see in the Vedanta of classical authors.

What classical Vedanta taught, if one listened to someone like Duff, was a form of cosmic self-infatuation and ethical nihilism. The desire to experience one's unity with brahman amounted only to an escapist and other-worldly philosophy that denied the fundamental fact of human sinfulness. Much to Duff's chagrin, Brahmo leaders such as Rajnarain Bose were more than ready to respond to such attacks, in the process refining Brahmo theology while redefining standard Hindu notions of the path to liberation. Where once the path to brahman was the sole prerogative of the male Brahmin renouncer, who left home and family to seek liberation in the solitude of the yogi's cave, in the skillful hands of the Brahmos the religious path was opened up to seekers of either gender and any caste. Following Rammohan Roy's lead, later Brahmos reconstrued Hinduism as a householder religion. According to the Brahmos, complete understanding of the unity of God did not lead to other-worldly navel-gazing but to the commitment to treat one's fellow humans as the embodiment of the divine. On this Vedantic platform, Hindus began to indigenize notions of democracy and worldly improvement—again, much to the missionaries' consternation. It is in this sense that the "neo" in neo-Vedanta must be read. As used by missionary commentators, it connoted something new-fangled, contrived, and therefore dubious.

Neo-Vedanta proved to be no passing fad, however. Educated, urban Hindus in cities like Calcutta, Bombay, and Madras gravitated to it as a creed that allowed them to reconcile their Western education with their sense of indigenous religious commitments. The impulse of Brahmo reform that began so markedly with Rammohan Roy in Calcutta grew with the increased entrenchment of colonial institutions in the Indian social and cultural world. Elsewhere new reform movements arose in greater or lesser degrees of similarity to the Brahmo Samaj. Central to many was Rammohan's tactic of construing religious reform as a project of recovering long-lost Hindu legitimacy. In the middle decades of the nineteenth century neo-Vedanta grew in both sophistication and appeal, especially as it came to be allied with nascent nationalist sentiment. The supposedly newfangled creed dismissed by the missionaries soon became one powerful emblem of Hindu pride. Nowhere do we see the efflorescence of this pride more clearly than in the speeches and writings of Swami Vivekananda from around the turn of the twentieth century.

Under the rubric of his "Practical Vedanta," Vivekananda put the finishing touches on Rammohan Roy's effort to redefine Vedanta as a rational and socially responsible theology. Like Rammohan, Vivekananda appealed to the classical authority of Advaita Vedanta as promulgated in the writings of Shankara. However, whereas Rammohan emphasized democratizing access to Shankara's liberating knowledge of brahman, Vivekananda emphasized Advaita Vedanta as an ethical code of action. "Vivekananda . . . argued as follows. If a man realizes his identity with Brahman, which is the all-powerful Absolute, then he must feel that the compass of his potentialities is just as unlimited as Brahman itself. This will give him boundless self-confidence and irresistible power. He will thus become capable of working efficiently for the spiritual recovery of India, and this will bring about a national reconstruction" (Hacker 1978, 594).

Vivekananda's Practical Vedanta at once furthered Rammohan's democratizing vision while yoking Vedanta to the task of energizing the Indian people to face the tasks of social uplift and national integration. In his own words, Vivekananda found in Vedanta a "man-making religion." This energetic creed would not only eradicate such errors as the "don't touch me-ism" of caste prejudice but also work to strengthen India in its quest for national self-definition. According to some scholars, this is what sets Vivekananda apart as a key representative of neo-Hinduism, because the neo-Hindu's "primary concern is nationalism" (Hacker 1978, 594). Alongside Vivekananda, Gandhi, Aurobindo, and Radhakrishnan rank among the masterminds of neo-Hinduism.

The significance of the prefix "neo" should not be lost on us. Just as nineteenth-century missionaries questioned the authenticity of what they called neo-Vedanta, twentieth-century scholars have been prone to doubt the authenticity of what they call neo-Hinduism. Indeed, it is the very newness of the teaching that has made it seem suspect. As one influential scholar put it, "Vivekananda derived from the monistic dogma [of Advaita Vedanta] a practical consequence which every Advaitist of the old school must consider a fatal deviation from the road that alone leads to the goal." In other words, "by making the religious heritage subservient to the tackling of modern national problems," Vivekananda had mortally wounded true Advaitic Hinduism (Hacker 1978, 594). One further concern with neo-Hinduism was its apparent indebtedness to Euro-American thought. Though thinkers such as Vivekananda claimed to preserve and transmit ancient norms and philosophies, their teachings—emphasizing such ideals as social service, positivism, and humanistic individualism—seemed to be suspiciously Western. And if neo-Hinduism bore the marks of Western influence, it could scarcely be called Hinduism any longer. This is a concern to which we shall return. First, though, we must continue to follow the genealogy of neo-Hinduism through to its present-day denouement.

Vivekananda's unofficial successor as torch-bearer of neo-Hinduism was Sarvepalli Radhakrishnan (1888–1975), who as a school boy in Madras (now known as Chennai) found in Vivekananda's fiery lectures an ennobling vision of truth and harmony as well as a message of Indian pride. As Radhakrishnan once put it, "It is that kind of humanistic, man-making religion which gave us courage in the days when we were young" (quoted in Minor

1987, 13). Educated by missionaries, and therefore well versed in the standard Christian critique of Hinduism, Radhakrishnan began his career with a master's thesis that "defended Vedanta against the charge that it lacked ethics" (Sharma 2002, 337). After this, Radhakrishnan quickly established himself as a top-notch philosopher, publishing studies of the Upanishads and what we would today call the philosophy of religion. Over the course of his career he would succeed in ways Rammohan and Vivekananda could scarcely have imagined, all the while building upon their Vedantic legacy both as a scholar and a statesman. He was a for a time Spalding Professor of Religion and Ethics at Oxford University and served terms as both vice-president and president of the Republic of India. In his erudite and compelling writing, Vedanta truly came home as the religious discourse of an awakened and independent India.

One of Radhakrishnan's most enduring works is a short volume with a telling title: *The Hindu View of Life*. Delivered originally as a series of lectures at Oxford in 1926, this little book was immensely successful at equating Vedanta and Hinduism. It is worth noting that Radhakrishnan did not offer his audience merely *one* view of Hinduism but rather (as the title announces) *the* view. Needless to say, Radhakrishnan's perspective was through and through informed by classical Vedantic metaphysics and neo-Vedantic ethics.

Central to Radhakrishnan's presentation of Hinduism was the claim (first effectively explored by Vivekananda) that religion is fundamentally a kind of experience. Building on (though never explicitly invoking) his mastery of European philosophical thought from Plotinus to William James, Radhakrishnan reduced religion to the core experience of reality in its fundamental unity. In phrases that might have been taken from Friedrich Schleiermacher's *On Religion,* he wrote that "Religion is not the acceptance of academic abstractions or the celebration of ceremonies, but a kind of life or experience. It is insight into the nature of reality" (Radhakrishnan 1980, 13). Such experience was taken to be self-validating; no further authority (textual or ecclesiastical) was needed to certify its validity. And for Radhakrishnan, it was precisely the genius of Vedanta to have identified the self-validating essence of religious experience. Thus he would go on to assert that Vedanta taught the core of what can be found in other sacred scriptures. "The Vedanta," he claimed, "is not a religion, but religion itself in its most universal and deepest significance" (Radhakrishnan 1980, 18).

With only a bit of extrapolation it becomes clear that not only has Radhakrishnan found in Vedanta the key to uniting and harmonizing the diversity of Hindu thought, but he has also proposed Vedanta as the very bedrock of religion. As he says, Vedanta is religion itself. The power of this assertion is hard to overestimate. On the one hand, for Hindus living under British rule and subject to Christian claims of superiority, this was the ultimate assertion of independence. Hinduism is not simply one valid religious path, as Rammohan Roy worked so hard to convey; it is in fact the very core of religion. If Christianity has any claim to truth, in other words, that claim must first acknowledge the fundamental truth of Vedantic experience, which lies at the root of Christian experience (as Radhakrishnan attempts to show through reference to mystics like Jacob Boehme). Put simply, Vedanta counters Christian exclusivism with a higher species of inclusivism. On the other hand, Vedantic inclusivism was praised by Radhakrishnan and others as the surest path to promoting tolerance among religions. In a volatile era of communal misunderstanding and violence that often witnessed Christians, Hindus, and Muslims (as well as members of India's many other faiths) battling over truth-claims and special rights, the search for religious harmony was a paramount concern. Indeed, the second chapter of *The Hindu View of Life* is dedicated to presenting the Vedantic solution to the "conflict of religions." Perhaps, said Radhakrishnan, as India moves toward becoming an independent, multireligious democracy, Vedanta will provide the key to ensuring the secular dream of harmony and tolerance.

In Vedantic inclusivism, neo-Hinduism reaches its zenith; but it is an ascent that is marred by what has had to be suppressed along the way. Put simply, "If . . . the hidden goal or centre or essence of all religions is the Vedanta which primarily constitutes the spiritual unity of Hinduism, then all religions are in a way included in Hinduism" (Hacker 1978, 601). Though neo-Hindu authors prefer the idiom of tolerance to that of inclusivism, it is clear that what is advocated is less a secular view of toleration than a theological scheme for subsuming religious difference under the aegis of Vedantic truth. Thus Radhakrishnan's view of experience as the core of religious truth effectively leads to harmony only when and if other religions are willing to assume a position under the umbrella of Vedanta. We might even say that the theme of neo-Hindu tolerance provided the Hindu not simply with a means for claiming the right to stand alongside the other world religions, but with a strategy for promoting Hinduism as the ultimate form of religion itself. Viewed in these terms, the darker side of neo-Hindu tolerance is not hard to see. What becomes of Muslim beliefs, Christian creeds, or Buddhist visions of truth when these are reduced to a core experience identified in terms of Vedanta?

To pursue the genealogy of neo-Hindu thought to its conclusion, logically and historically, is thus to run head on into the problem of the hidden communal agenda at the heart of modern Hinduism's message of tolerance. Scholars have long noted the degree to which the nationalist movement became increasingly inflected by the tones of Hindu religiosity after the advent of such figures as Mahatma Gandhi (one of Hacker's representative neo-Hindus). Although no one would accuse the polymorphously religious Gandhi of being an agent of Hindu self-assertion, what we encounter in neo-Hindu discourse is the unintended consequence of the initial moves made by thinkers like Rammohan Roy and Vivekananda. For all of the efforts made by the post-independence government of India to promote the ideal of equality toward all religions (*sarva-dharma samabhava*), including the intentional use of the varied religious symbolisms of the subcontinent—to those non-Hindus outside the corridors of power, it remains difficult to ignore modern India's Hindu veneer. The hegemony of Vedanta, its obvious leadership role in modern Indian culture, cannot be denied. And it is this hegemony that recent nationalist groups such as the RSS and the VHP are eager to steer into ever more strident pleas for equating India with Hinduism.

In the current Hindutva movements, we encounter the unfortunate political ramifications of Radhakrishnan's mystical reduction of Hinduism to Vedanta. Though Radhakrishnan would never have made the claim, it is now being made: You are welcome in India, provided you're prepared to affirm your Hinduness. And here is where the theme of hegemony once again becomes relevant: Those advancing the politicized agenda of Hindutva are those who have gained leadership power in today's India—the middle-class, urban-ized, free-market Hindus who are the force behind movements to promote Hinduism as the national religion of India. To identify this group and its socioeconomic profile is to remind ourselves that there are factors other than theology and philosophy at work in the "saffron wave" of militant Hinduism today (Hansen 1999). More detailed discussion of the genealogy of Hindutva would re-quire a careful consideration of such issues as the implementation and legacy of colonial policies, the history of modern Indian poli-tics, and India's struggle to achieve civil society in the post-colonial context.

This said, it also becomes clear that there isn't a neat line of cau-sation that leads from the philosophies of Rammohan Roy, Vivekananda, and Radhakrishnan to the agenda of those militant Hindus who demolished the Babri mosque in Ayodhya in 1992. Rather, what we witness is the potential within a single field of dis-course for alternative figurations of Hinduism to emerge. The po-tential for harm can often be found in the most well-intentioned of formulas. Recall Swami Shivananda's paean to Vedanta as "the basic culture of India." Or consider the following statement, taken from an authoritative essay on contemporary Indian philosophy: "Con-temporary Indian thought in India seems to be grounded in the metaphysics of Vedanta" (Roy 1997, 282). In both these claims we can see very clearly the tendency to equate the heart of Indian thought and culture with Vedanta. Though we recognize that such authors may have intended to suggest nothing more than the pro-fundity and enduring appeal of ancient Indian thought, this is scarcely enough to allay our anxieties. After all, it is precisely in con-temporary discourse that claims about the legacy of ancient Indian thought have become the fuel for Hindu nationalist self-assertion. In other words, the issue of the legacy is not something we should accept as inevitable. The legacy itself is something that needs care-ful scrutiny. How did Vedanta come to stand in such seemingly self-evident fashion for Indian thought? To raise this question is to fore-ground a problem that the promoters and defenders of Vedanta from Rammohan to the present were perhaps unable to foresee: Given the hegemony of Vedanta in the modern context, the creed of tolerance arrogates to itself the right to speak for all that is best and most true about Indian religious thought—and in so doing, to ignore many other points of view.

Speaking of Vedanta as one form of ancient Indian thought is entirely acceptable, but to equate Vedanta with modern Indian thought is to elide huge portions of South Asian intellectual history and culture. Is the philosophy of contemporary Indian Islam (assuming there is only *one* such philosophy!) grounded in Vedanta? What about modern Buddhist movements or trends in recent Indian Christian theology? What about the worldviews of Sikhs, Jains, Dalits, and tribals—not to mention those other Hinduisms we surveyed at the outset of this chapter? That these other voices do not register in the popular mind as representative of Indian thought is precisely due to the hegemony of Vedantic discourse, which has sent down roots and implanted itself in modern India as if it were organically one with the people. Thanks to the persuasive writing of men like Rammohan Roy and Radhakrishnan, the charisma of Vivekananda and Sri Aurobindo, the imprimatur of Western Romantic fascination from Arthur Schopenhauer through Paul Deussen, the energetic agency of movements like the Ramakrishna Math and Mission, and the quasi-official status granted by government patronage and the continual publication of books on Hindu spirituality, Vedanta rules unchallenged as the "essential" worldview of Hinduism.

The hegemony of neo-Vedanta was achieved by a long, circuitous, and ultimately international pathway. That pathway featured local attempts by colonized intellectuals to defend Hindu culture from Eurocentric and Christian denunciation; with time it featured the attempt to transform the previously embattled worldview of Vedanta into a kind of aggressive missionary message. In figures such as Vivekananda and Radhakrishnan we witness Vedanta traveling to the West, where it nourished the spiritual hunger of Europeans and Americans in the early decades of the twentieth century (a hunger with its own fascinating history). During its sojourn in the West, Vedanta was in turn nourished with both financial support and the increased intellectual prestige that came from being associated with the likes of Aldous Huxley and Christopher Isherwood. Some would argue that it was, in fact, this refashioning of Vedanta in the West that allowed it to assume a veneer of genuine

"Indianness" that it might not otherwise have had. Returning to India under the banner of India's spiritual wisdom, Vedanta could be compared to pizza—an "authentic" Italian meal created in America (Bharati 1970). Thus Vedanta's international prestige helped further cement its position of cultural leadership in India.

All of this returns us to the inescapable question: Is Vedanta—or should we speak of neo-Vedanta or neo-Hinduism—an indigenous philosophy? Does it arise orthogenetically, or is it the somewhat artificial outcome of a cultural graft from West to East? Is it merely a transplant, as Hacker at times seems to suggest of Radhakrishnan's philosophy? These are important and much-debated questions. Answering them must play some part in any attempt to answer the question, What is contemporary Hindu thought?

Western Influence or Creative Convergence?

That the creation of modern Hinduism stands in some relationship to the history of India's encounter with the West is clear. However, just how we care to construe the nature of this encounter and its impact on Hindu thought is open to debate. It would be possible, for instance, to assert that modern Hinduism owes no appreciable debt to the changes that were set in motion by the establishment of British rule in India. To take such a view would be to argue for the strict continuity of modern Hinduism with what was thought and practiced in premodern India. This seems to be the logic behind the frequently voiced claim that Hinduism is the *sanatana dharma,* or "eternal religion." And yet this rubric serves an obvious legitimating purpose in its promotion of the hallowed antiquity and unbroken continuity of Hindu thought. Indeed, such assertions of historical continuity have to be reckoned as more ideological than empirical. In this respect neo-Vedantin claims regarding the validity of the transtemporal experience of brahman as the root of religion may also be viewed as a powerful tool for legitimating Hindu thought by linking it to a changeless sacred order. The problem is, religions—when viewed as an aspect of human culture rather than a timeless experience—are subject to constant change. As such, it is impossible to acknowledge the widespread changes wrought by colonial rule in the areas of social, economic, and political life without also acknowledging profound changes in thought, belief, and worship.

Granting, then, that modern Hindu thought differs in important ways from the thought of previous eras of South Asian history, we are left with the question of how to account for the changes we notice. There are those observers of colonial India who have advocated what amounts to a billiard-ball theory of change: Modern Hindu thought is the direct result of the "impact" of Western thought—where "Western" may be taken to mean European Protestantism. To adopt a somewhat different metaphor, the ingredients of modern Hindu thought were imported into India along with the printing press and the steam engine. An inventory of the essential ingredients might include such concepts and values as monotheism, rationalism, humanism, and liberalism.

This model of change is not without its problems. The most basic of these is that though such "impact-response" models attempt to account for religious change, they assume that both the efficient cause and the material form of that change may ultimately be attributed to what is sometimes only vaguely identified as "Western influence." Because of this, these sorts of models are ill-suited to explore either the part played by actual Indian agents in the creation or modification of Hindu thought or the role that preexisting forms of South Asian thought and culture played in constraining or promoting religious change.

There is another way we might look at the problem: We could choose to speak of convergence instead of impact. Behind this way of speaking lies the basic premise that any number of previously existing ideas, values, and practices from precolonial India converged in the modern period with those ideas, values, and practices that made their way into India as a result of colonial rule. To speak of convergence is to recognize the role that Indian intellectuals, Indian concepts and values, even Indian languages themselves played in shaping the discourse of modern Hinduism. To speak of convergence is to acknowledge that in the colonial arena, indigenous norms worked to inflect Western norms just as surely as Western norms transvalued South Asian norms; it is to acknowledge that under such circumstances preexisting concepts and values (indige-

nous and Western) were routinely thrown into entirely new relationships with one another. We will never understand the uniqueness or the originality of a Rammohan Roy or a Mahatma Gandhi if
we view them as transplanted Enlightenment critics or Protestant
reformers clad in *dhotis* and sandals. We must view them, instead, as
skillful manipulators of indigenous fields of knowledge and shrewd
creators within their native linguistic realms. That such thinkers
also engaged in extensive dialogue with European philosophy and
theology is but one (albeit highly significant) component of their
messages.

No simple model of cultural impact can account for the distinctive (and sometimes surprising) ways in which modern Hindu
thinkers have endeavored to define what it means to be a Hindu.
The spokespersons for modern Hindu thought have neither been
parrots nor patsies. If anything, they have been poets. They have endeavored to work with the bits and pieces of a rapidly expanding
and increasingly cosmopolitan intellectual world to create what
might be for them and others meaningful expressions of Hindu belief. As Gandhi put it, "while we adhere to our own faith, we have
every right to adopt acceptable features from any other faith"
(Gandhi 1962, 3). Gandhi and the other poets of modern Hinduism have not shied away from borrowing what they needed—be it
from the many religious traditions of South Asia, the knowledge
bank of Orientalist scholarship, the European intellectual tradition,
Judaism, Unitarianism, or Christianity. Indeed, under the conditions of colonial life, it was virtually a necessity for any creative Indian intellectual to become such a borrower. Nor is such a claim
meant to trivialize the endeavor of the borrower. Gandhi was clear
in saying that such borrowing did not entail trading in his faith for a
new one, because only a fanatic would claim "you cannot accept
anything from other faiths" (Gandhi 1962, 3).

Modern Hinduism is thus best viewed as the product of a rich
and extended conversation between India and the West. This is not
a fact to be lamented, but it is one that needs to be recognized and
confronted. Bharati's "pizza effect," which we noted earlier, in fact
suggests that we must pay close attention to the ways European
colonialism, missionary rhetoric, Orientalist scholarship, and even

the spiritual longings of the modern West converged with indigenous intellectual forces to support the emergence of distinctively modern modes of Hindu thought; it also suggests we need to view this process as continuing into the present in the on-going transnational construction of Hinduism.

In the end, it is a complex history to narrate, with many perspectives and numerous encounters to explore. To name but a few: Rammohan Roy's discourse with Christians, Unitarians, and Brahmins; Keshub Chunder Sen's lectures in England; Swami Vivekananda's wanderings through India and his presentation of Vedanta to the West; Gandhi's encounter with Hindu thought in London and his exploration of nonviolent resistance in South Africa; Rabindranath Tagore's 1913 Nobel Prize for the English-language mysticism of *Gitanjali;* Sri Aurobindo's early experiences of the colonial educational bureaucracy, his foray into nationalist agitation, and eventual evolution into the mystic philosopher of Pondicherry; and the emigration of countless Hindus to Africa, Europe, North America, and the Caribbean, right down to the propagation of transnational Hinduism in the worldwide diaspora today.

Indeed, when thinking of the Hindu diaspora, we must acknowledge the degree to which the transnational character of modern Hinduism has only intensified in the postcolonial world, where people of South Asian descent have added an important dimension to religious life in countries like the United Kingdom, Canada, and the United States. Understandably, in such diaspora communities, it is not uncommon to hear a child ask, "Daddy, am I a Hindu?" (Viswanathan 1988). For Hindus living outside of India, the task of constructing a sense of identity has proven to be a matter of great importance. "They need a Hinduism that can be explained to outsiders as a respectable religion, that can be taught to their children in religious education, and that can form the basis for collective action" (van der Veer 1993, 42). In the middle of the twentieth century this role was largely played by various neo-Vedanta organizations (such as the Vedanta Society); today, as we have seen, newer forms of Hindu discourse are emerging, most notably that of the VHP. Transnational movements such as the VHP take deliberate advantage of the sentiments and bank accounts of nonresident Indians to support forms of Hindu nationalism within India, often embodied in the platform of political organizations like the Bharatiya Janata Party (BJP).

As we survey the genesis of modern Hindu thought with this global awareness, we are certainly entitled to look skeptically at some of the products of this complex convergence of ideas, norms, and practices. Indeed, we may need to state quite directly that certain of the strategies developed and deployed by modernizing Hindus have proven problematic and even dangerous. Destruction of Muslim holy places in the name of "rebuilding" Hindu temples, and the murder of Christian missionaries in the name of protecting Hinduism, are but two instances of the bad faith of some forms of modern Hinduism. And though we cannot hold a Rammohan Roy or a Radhakrishnan guilty for what later generations may have made of their messages, we ignore the genealogy of modern Hindu discourse at our peril. It is only by understanding, for instance, how Radhakrishnan's tolerant vision of Vedanta could transmogrify into platforms of violent Hindu inclusivism that we can begin to fathom the ideology of today's politicized Hinduism.

Conclusion: Dispensing with the Dichotomies

It should by now be clear how much our understanding of contemporary Hindu thought depends upon the framework within which we conceptualize its origins. Even if we agree to move beyond a simplistic model of impact-response, we need to recognize the degree to which our thinking remains dependent upon an array of related conceptual schemes. Too often these schemes rely on sets of binary oppositions that appear to neatly capture the complexity of Hindu thought but that in fact foster continued misconceptions. Two such schemes bear identifying as we conclude, so that they may be laid to rest: (1) apology and polemic; (2) conservative and progressive.

One of the most pervasive conceptual schemes, often unelaborated by scholars but operational nonetheless, is that which construes modern Hindu thought as the apologetic response to Christian polemic. Although it makes perfect sense to speak of modern Hindu apologetics, we do well to move cautiously as we attempt to sketch out the relationship between such a "defense" of Hinduism and the "attacks" that called it forth. If we are not careful, picturing a Rammohan Roy or a Mahatma Gandhi as merely an apologist for Hinduism will lead us right back into the bind of thinking of such men as merely responding to the overwhelming impact of Western thought.

To be sure, polemic and apologetic are at the heart of modern Hindu discourse. However, these represent nothing more than the oscillating modes of such discourse. From the time of Rammohan Roy, individual spokespersons for modern Hinduism have moved fluidly between staving off the dismissal of their religion and actively attacking the errors of other religious systems. To be sure, Rammohan wrote important tracts bearing the words "Defense" and "Apology" in the title. However, these very works—and several others—reveal him to have been a sophisticated polemicist who skillfully employed not just the tools of historical analysis and philology but also those of satire, irony, and pseudonymous authorship. And his presentation of Hinduism in light of Christian attacks on polytheism, image worship, and world renunciation was not dictated by the terms of his attackers. Rather, he created his own polemical assault on Christianity in an attempt to throw the missionaries' very assumptions into doubt. Why would a Hindu want to read the New Testament? he asked. They can get enough myth and mystery from their own Puranas. Wouldn't it be a good thing to edit the Gospels and attempt to remove the miracles and mysteries? And when it came to the hermeneutical key that guided Rammohan's interpretation of Christianity, it was forged not just from Enlightenment rationality but also from Islamic monotheism and Hindu/Tantric philosophy. In other words, we return to the image of convergence—a concept that captures the dynamics of encounter far better than dichotomous notions such as "impact" or "defense."

As another illustration, consider what has become a basic component of modern Hindu thought: tolerance. The modern Hindu invocation of tolerance is far more than a desperate appeal for mercy in the court of the world's religions. In fact, we fail to appreciate the ramifications of modern Hindu tolerance if we see this tenet as somehow only the quietistic response of a beleaguered faith to the aggressive posturing of Christian missionaries. As we have seen, in the rhetoric of neo-Hinduism, tolerance is a potent weapon. It represents the cutting edge of a forceful critique of other religions. Only consider the argument: Tolerance is something Hindus have by virtue of the Vedantic roots of their religious experience; it is a virtue they practice as a matter of course. Furthermore, wherever one finds genuine tolerance in the world, it serves to validate the very truth of Hindu thought. To view the world otherwise, to fail to accept the basic metaphysical truth of Hindu tolerance, is an error. Religions that foreground confession of faith and conversion are by definition misguided. In other words, as we noted earlier, modern Hindu tolerance can become but another name for intolerant chauvinism. Is tolerance, then, an apologetic device or a polemical weapon?

For precisely the same reasons, we do well to consider jettisoning another standard conceptual tool in the study of modern Hinduism: the distinction between "conservative" and "progressive" thinkers, which can assume a variety of related forms—traditionalist versus modernist, revivalist versus reformer, orthodox versus liberal. The inadequacy of such dichotomies was noted decades ago by scholars exploring the dynamics of modernization in India; as soon as simplistic notions of unilinear development are abandoned, it becomes possible to see that oftentimes it is tradition that provides the key to reaching modernity's goals. One notable study in this respect is Lloyd and Suzanne Rudolph's *The Modernity of Tradition* (1967), with its influential interpretation of Gandhi. Furthermore, once scholars recognized that tradition itself is often something invented to suit new circumstances, the apparent clarity of the tradition/modernity distinction had to be questioned. As a result, today we realize that being Hindu in modern South Asia (or elsewhere in the world) is not as simple as making a choice between following one's traditions or abandoning those ways for the new ways of the so-called modern world.

Was Rammohan Roy modern? Well, certainly, if we mean to say that his attempt to articulate the truth of his religion in a rational debate with Christian sources and Enlightenment values was unprecedented within his Brahmin social and intellectual milieu. And yet one can quite easily make the case for the importance of tradition both in Rammohan's general educational background (with his study of Islamic culture and Tantric philosophy) and in his particular attempt to revive and propagate the ancient wisdom of the Upanishads. Needless to say, much the same may be said of all the great proponents of contemporary Hindu thought, from Rammohan through Gandhi and Radhakrishnan, down to the many swamis of today's Vedanta Society.

A case in point demonstrating the limitations of the traditional-modern dichotomy can be found in Paul Hacker's influential 1978 essay contrasting what he called neo-Hinduism (or alternately, modernist Hinduism) with "surviving traditional Hinduism." By the former, Hacker had in mind the likes of Vivekananda and Radhakrishnan. As an illustration of the latter, he chose the publications of the influential north Indian publishing house, Gita Press, along with its journal *Kalyan*. His choice at first seems to make prima facie sense, because the agenda of the Gita Press is wholeheartedly aimed at promoting what might be called the lineaments of popular Hindi-belt religion, complete with image worship and Puranic mythology, respect for the ideals of Vedic authority, and the ethos of Vaisnava devotionalism. However, the frailty of Hacker's scheme is revealed in his own essay, when he is compelled to admit that even the Gita Press betrayed the "assimilation of foreign elements," such as Christian-style "sermons" and "edifying essays." More important still, the lexicon of devotion employed in the Gita Press publications was by Hacker's own admission something rather different than that found in "older Hindu literature" (Hacker 1978, 587). Consequently, by reading against the grain of Hacker's own essay we find convincing evidence of the inadequacy of the tradition-modernity dichotomy for capturing what is at stake in the development of modern Hindu thought. Hacker's neo-Hindus and his Gita Press are both implicated in the processes of convergence associated with colonial and postcolonial South Asia.

Such reflections make it easier to call into question other supposed dichotomies, such as that between the liberal and the conservative or the reformer and the revivalist. On the latter point, there has been no shortage of attempts to spell out the difference between reform and revival in modern India (Sen 1993). However, what is rarely questioned is the assumption that these categories can, in fact, be neatly distinguished. Do they really represent—as some would argue—discrete moments within the history of modern Hinduism (reform preceding revival preceding nationalism, for instance)? Or might it be more profitable to explore the ways in which concepts such as revival and reform function discursively within an enormous field of reflection (indigenous and Western) on socioreligious change in India, a field that includes other important idioms such as renaissance, awakening, resurrection, enlightenment, dawn, and new age?

Rather than invoking such idioms as descriptive categories, it may be far more profitable to think about their role as ideological markers, used by both Hindus and others to propagate specific claims about how the meaning of modern Hinduism should be understood. Why, for instance, have commentators thought it best to refer to Rammohan Roy as a *reformer* while reserving the word *revivalist* for someone like Vivekananda? Would it not be just as legitimate to reverse the labels? If we don't see it this way, is it because the earliest Western commentators who applied such rubrics to modern Hindus did so with a tacit understanding that *reform* meant rational progress whereas *revival* meant blind fundamentalism? And if this is so, do we wish to continue enshrining these tacit meanings in our scholarly categories?

It is the basic premise of this chapter that our understanding of contemporary Hindu thought will be deepened to the degree we are able to move past some of the blanket claims and neat categorizations that have been made about it in the past. In this sense, the phrase we invoked at the outset to define modern Hinduism— "Western-influenced neo-Vedanta"—should now appear to be fraught with ambiguity. All those questions we raised in getting started need to be answered in light of a sophisticated understanding of the complex dynamics of cultural convergence that make up the genealogy of modern Hinduism. How did it come about that modern Hinduism could be described as the same as neo-Vedanta? Is neo-Vedanta just another name for neo-Hinduism? And if so, is neo-Hinduism just another name for Hinduism? If not, then is the difference a matter of Western influence? All good questions, well worth exploring!

BIBLIOGRAPHY

Babb, Lawrence. *Redemptive Encounters: Three Modern Styles in the Hindu Tradition*. Delhi: Oxford University Press, 1987.

Bakhle, S. W. *Hinduism: Nature and Development*. New Delhi: Sterling, 1991.

Bharati, Agehananda. "The Hindu Renaissance and Its Apologetic Patterns," in *Journal of Asian Studies* 39, 2 (1970): 267–287.

Chakravarti, Sitansu S. *Hinduism: A Way of Life*. Delhi: Motilal Banarsidass, 1992.

Farquhar, John Nicol. *Modern Religious Movements in India*. Delhi: Munshiram Manoharlal, 1967.

Gandhi, Mahatma. *All Religions Are True*. Edited by Anand T. Hingorani. Bombay: Bharatiya Vidya Bhavan, 1962.

Ghosh, Aurobindo. *Sri Aurobindo Birth Centenary Library*. 29 vols. Pondicherry: Sri Aurobindo Ashram, 1971–1973.

Hacker, Paul. "Aspects of Neo-Hinduism as Contrasted with Surviving Traditional Hinduism," in Lambert Schmithausen (ed.), *Kleine Schriften*. Wiesbaden: Harrassowitz, 1978: 580–608.

———. *Inklusivismus: Eine indische Denkform*. Edited by G. Oberhammer. Vienna: University of Vienna, 1983.

Halbfass, Wilhelm. *India and Europe: An Essay in Understanding*. Albany: State University of New York Press, 1988.

Hansen, Thomas Blom. *The Saffron Wave: Democracy and Hindu Nationalism in Modern India*. Princeton: Princeton University Press, 1999.

Hatcher, Brian A. *Idioms of Improvement: Vidyasagar and Cultural Encounter in Bengal*. New Delhi: Oxford University Press, 1996.

———. *Eclecticism and Modern Hindu Discourse*. New York: Oxford University Press, 1999.

———. "Great Men Waking: Paradigms in the Historiography of the Bengal Renaissance," in Sekhar Bandyopadhyay (ed.), *Bengal: Rethinking History; Essays in Historiography*. New Delhi: Manohar, 2001: 135–163.

Inden, Ronald. *Imagining India*. Cambridge, Mass.: Basil Blackwell, 1990.

Jones, Kenneth. *Socio-Religious Reform Movements in British India*. Vol. III, 1 in the New Cambridge History of India series. New York: Cambridge University Press, 1989.

Juergensmeyer, Mark. *Radhasoami Reality: The Logic of a Modern Faith*. Princeton: Princeton University Press, 1991.

King, Richard. *Orientalism and Religion: Postcolonial Theory, India, and the Mystic East*. New York: Routledge, 1999.

Kopf, David. *British Orientalism and the Bengal Renaissance: The Dynamics of Indian Modernization, 1773–1835.* Berkeley: University of California, 1969.

Minor, Robert. *Radhakrishnan: A Religious Biography.* Albany: State University of New York Press, 1987.

Nikhilananda, Swami. *The Essence of Hinduism.* New York: Ramakrishna-Vivekananda Center, 1946.

Prabhavananda, Swami. *The Sermon on the Mount According to Vedanta.* London: George Allen and Unwin, 1964.

Radhakrishnan, Sarvepalli. *The Hindu View of Life.* London: Unwin Paperbacks, 1980.

Radhakrishnan, Sarvepalli, and Charles A. Moore, eds. *Sourcebook in Indian Philosophy.* Princeton: Princeton University Press, 1980.

Rocher, Rosane. "British Orientalism in the Eighteenth Century: The Dialectics of Knowledge and Government," in Carol A. Breckenridge and Peter van der Veer (eds.), *Orientalism and the Postcolonial Predicament: Perspectives on South Asia.* Philadelphia: University of Pennsylvania Press, 1993: 215–249.

Roy, Archana. "Contemporary Indian Philosophy," in Brian Carr and Indira Mahalingam (eds.), *Companion Encyclopedia of Asian Philosophy.* New York: Routledge, 1997: 281–299.

Roy, Rammohan. *The English Works of Raja Rammohun Roy.* Allahabad: Panini Office, 1906.

Rudolph, Lloyd, and Susanne Rudolph. *The Modernity of Tradition: Political Development in India.* Chicago: University of Chicago Press, 1967.

Said, Edward. *Orientalism.* New York: Vintage, 1978.

Sarkar, Sumit. *A Critique of Colonial India.* Calcutta: Papyrus, 2000.

Sen, Amiya. *Hindu Revivalism in Bengal, 1872–1905: Some Essays in Interpretation.* New Delhi: Oxford University Press, 1993.

Sharma, Arvind. *Modern Hindu Thought: The Essential Texts.* New Delhi: Oxford University Press, 2002.

Smith, Brian K. "Re-envisioning Hinduism and the Hindutva Movement," in *Religion* 26 (1996): 119–128.

Tagore, Rabindranath. *Gitanjali: Song Offerings.* London: Macmillan, 1971.

Tejomayananda, Swami. *An Introduction to Advaita Vedanta Philosophy.* Shivanandanagar: The Divine Life Society, 1999.

Van der Veer, Peter. "The Foreign Hand: Orientalist Discourse in Sociology and Communalism," in Carol A. Breckenridge and Peter van der Veer (eds.), *Orientalism and the Postcolonial Predicament: Perspectives on South Asia.* Philadelphia: University of Pennsylvania Press, 1993: 23–44.

Visvanathan, Ed. *Daddy, Am I a Hindu?* Bombay: Bharatiya Vidya Bhavan, 1988.

Vivekananda, Swami. *The Complete Works of Swami Vivekananda.* 8 vols. Calcutta: Advaita Ashrama, 1985.

Williams, Raymond. *A New Face of Hinduism: The Swaminarayan Religion.* New York: Cambridge University Press, 1984.

Wilson, Bryan. *Religion in Sociological Perspective.* New York: Oxford University Press, 1988.

Chapter Seven

Gurus and Groups

J. E. LLEWELLYN

The Maharishi Mahesh Yogi sat on a stage festooned with flowers in his 1975 appearance on *The Merv Griffin Show,* beaming blissfully while Merv and celebrity guests testified to the benefits they had derived from practicing his Transcendental Meditation technique. A more sober picture of another guru appeared in *Newsweek* in 1985, of the Bhagwan Shree Rajneesh accompanied by a marshal with a shotgun. Rajneesh was arrested for alleged immigration violations, but the article also reported on rumors of everything from illicit sex to conspiracy to commit murder among his followers (Karlen 1985, 26, 31–32). For better or worse, these are the kinds of images that are liable to come to the mind of someone in the United States when Hinduism is mentioned; images of gurus—in these cases contrasting images—one of a saintly purveyor of enlightenment, and the other of a felonious fraud. This chapter will introduce the reader to these two gurus and seven others, along with the movements they founded. Following a guru or teacher is a central part of religious life for many Hindus, a tradition dating back at least as far as Vedic times, when twice-born boys would study the Vedas with a teacher.

One recent important guru is Swaminarayan. In *An Introduction to Swaminarayan Hinduism,* Raymond Williams argues that "The best approach to Hinduism is through acquaintance with a particular sampradaya in its contemporary settings." He defines a *sampradaya* as "a tradition which has been handed down from a founder through successive religious teachers and which shapes the followers into a distinct fellowship with institutional forms." The sampradaya is the place to start in the study of Hinduism, Williams maintains, because it is with this kind of "Hinduism in particular" that most people identify, rather than with any overarching "Hinduism in general" (Williams 2001, 3–4). From the beginning of this book, the Swaminarayan movement is called a "sect." But this usage is dubious on the basis of Williams's own characterization of Hinduism. In the parlance of the sociology of religion, a *sect* is a group of dissenters. What sectarians dissent from is a church, which in this context is a dominant social institution that has the power to impose its will upon its members. The problem with calling the Swaminarayan movement a sect is that there is not now and probably never has been a Hindu church. In other words, all that we have in contemporary Hinduism are sects, groups with competing theologies and social forms.

By this logic, this chapter should cover all Hinduism, but that is obviously too large a task. Instead I will concentrate on groups founded by gurus. In the history of South Asian culture, a guru is just a teacher, but in contemporary India, as in the West, the term *guru* has come to be applied more and more to charismatic leaders. Though this term is often used for powerful men, and sometimes women, in politics or business, the focus here will be on the heads of religious groups. The reader will find that these charismatic leaders of religious groups are very different in background and in the way that they relate to their disciples. I have made some effort in this chapter to spell out the teaching of these leaders, but the reader should note that the focus of disciples is often on personal devotion to the guru regardless of his or her teaching. This chapter will begin with an introduction to nine different gurus, followed by some comparisons between them; it will conclude with an analysis of the role of gurus in modern Hinduism.

Nine Gurus and Their Movements

Swaminarayan

The man who would eventually be known as Swaminarayan was born in 1781 in a village near Ayodhya in what is now the state of

Uttar Pradesh in India. After the death of his parents when he was eleven, Swaminarayan began a life of wandering. Eventually settling in the western Indian state of Gujarat, Swaminarayan became a renouncer and a disciple of Ramananda Swami. Swaminarayan thus was a teacher in a lineage that traced its origins to the great eleventh-century philosopher Ramanuja. Consistent with this, Swaminarayan advocated the worship of Vishnu, especially in his human incarnation as Krishna. Yet as early as 1804 a work was written by one of his followers claiming that Swaminarayan himself was an incarnation of God (the name Swaminarayan could be translated as "Lord Narayan," Narayan being one of the forms of the god Vishnu). Swaminarayan clearly had a very profound effect on his disciples, with testimony that contact with him could produce "a trance state called *samadhi*" (Williams 2001, 21). Raymond Williams has estimated that Swaminarayan may have had as many as 1.8 million followers by the time of his death in 1830 (Williams 2001, 20).

It is probably at least partially a reflection of the times in which he lived that Swaminarayan advocated a program of religious and social reform, criticizing widow immolation, eliminating animal sacrifice from Vedic rituals, providing food for the destitute in times of famine and plague, and holding renouncers to a strict code of conduct. Swaminarayan was also an advocate of caste reform, but ironically this was not in the direction of loosening caste exclusiveness but of holding more firmly to caste rules. It is evidence of Swaminarayan's practicality that he established a regular structure of leadership for his movement, dividing his followers into two dioceses, each of which was headed by a member of his family. These dioceses have continued to exist down to the present, though not without internal conflict and institutional innovation. The greatest change in the Swaminarayan movement came with the establishment of the Akshar Purushottam Sanstha by Yagnapurushdas, a renouncer who lived from 1865 to 1951. "He taught that Swaminarayan promised that he would always be manifest in the world with his devotees in the person of his chief devotee, who is, in fact, *akshar* [that is, eternal], as the manifestation of an eternal principle and an abode of god" (Williams 2001, 55). The theological difference between more traditional Swaminarayan Hindus and the Akshar Purushottam Sanstha is obvious in their temples. Whereas the temples of the former are focused on images of Krishna, the latter are centered on images of Swaminarayan himself and include representations of later leaders of the movement who, like him, are regarded as manifestations of God and therefore worthy of worship.

A noteworthy feature of the Swaminarayan movement is its international scope. There are now Swaminarayan temples not only in India but also in East Africa, the United Kingdom, the United States, and Canada. In fact, Williams claims that "The Akshar Purushottam Sanstha was the fastest-growing Hindu group in Britain in the last quarter of the twentieth century" (Williams 2001, 218). The pattern of the spread of the Swaminarayan movement was established by the flow of Gujarati immigrants from India to East Africa and then to England and North America. The growth in the number of adherents of the Swaminarayan religion outside India has been almost exclusively through the conversion of Gujaratis and, to a lesser extent, other Indian emigres. "Swaminarayan Hinduism in East Africa formed a vital part of the Gujarati Indian culture. No attempt has been made to attract Europeans or Africans as members. The Gujarati language, rituals, and theology remain inaccessible" (Williams 2001, 210). For the members of the group outside India, the temples are not only a place to celebrate Swaminarayan theology, they are also an oasis of Gujarati culture.

Soamiji Maharaj and the Radhasoami Movement

Known as Soamiji Maharaj, the founder of the Radhasoami movement was born in Agra, which is now in the state of Uttar Pradesh, in 1818. Soamiji Maharaj's interest in spiritual matters was so great that even at a young age he had difficulty dedicating himself to a job, though he did marry. For most of his life Soamiji Maharaj was supported financially by his brother, who was employed in the British Indian postal service. Soamiji Maharaj's teaching included a rather elaborate cosmological system, but the heart of the matter is that each of us is really a soul that must escape from the material world to return to its true spiritual home. This message was preached publicly by Soamiji Maharaj in *satsangs* (literally, gatherings of the saints) beginning in 1861, and it is estimated that the founder may have initiated as many as ten thousand devotees by the time of his death in 1878 (Babb 2000, 21).

The sermons of Soamiji Maharaj emphasized the importance of the living guru for the disciple's salvation. For example, he wrote: "Such is the greatness of the *Sant Sat Guru* [the saint true guru] that those who have His *Darshan* [seeing and being seen by Him] receive some spiritual uplift and escape *Chaurasi* [literally eighty-four, referring here to all the possible species into which one might be reborn, which are traditionally said to number eighty-four *lakhs,* or 8,400,000]; they are protected from much suffering and affliction, and, by his grace, the road to ultimate emancipation is opened. Therefore, for their own good and happiness, all *Jivas* [souls] should go to a *Sant Sat Guru,* wherever He manifests Himself, and add to their *Bhag* [earn merit] by *Darshan* and *Seva* [service of the guru]" (Soamiji Maharaj 1974, 129–130). Because of this teaching, great reverence was shown to Soamiji Maharaj by his followers. Given the importance of the living guru, it is perhaps no surprise that there has been some conflict in the Radhasoami movement concerning succession. The first split took place soon after Soamiji Maharaj's death, between one group centered in Agra and another in Beas in Punjab. The Beas Radhasoamis claimed that Soamiji Maharaj himself had deputized their leader, Jaimal Singh, to spread his religion in Punjab, thereby designating him as his successor. In Agra, leadership was assumed by a man who came to be known as Huzur Maharaj.

From the beginning there was a substantial theological difference between the Radhasoamis in Punjab and those in Agra. The Punjabi group regarded Soamiji Maharaj as part of a lineage of gurus going back at least to Guru Nanak (1469–1538), the founder of Sikhism. For the disciples in Agra, Soamiji Maharaj was a *svatah sant,* an independent saint who did not need a guru. In fact, they regard the founder as a manifestation of the Supreme Being, a status shared by his successors as guru. It is within this context that Radhasoamis read passages in Soamiji Maharaj's writings that characterize great religious figures from the past as having attained only a limited knowledge of the Supreme Being, in contrast to the true saint who *is* the Supreme Being in some sense. Thus in the Radhasoami movement, as in Swaminarayan history, there was a split over the status of the founder, which also involved the status of later leaders. Given the exaltation of the living guru in the Agra Radhasoami branch, it is particularly problematic that the official list of gurus ended in 1949. There have been pretenders to the office of guru since that time, but none has been successful in winning over most of the group. Despite the internal conflicts, the Radhasoami movement has built up a substantial following in India, particularly in the areas where the Hindi and Punjabi languages are spoken, and to a certain extent outside India among emigrants.

Swami Dayanand and the Arya Samaj

The Arya Samaj was founded in 1875 in Mumbai, on the western coast of India, but had its greatest success early on in Punjab—the center of the movement was in Lahore, which is now a part of Pakistan. The founder was born in a village in Gujarat in 1824. Discontented with worldly life, he ran away from home as a young man and took the name Dayanand Saraswati upon initiation as a renouncer. Swami Dayanand traveled for many years, studying with various teachers, until he met Virajanand, a blind renouncer who instilled in Dayanand a revulsion for contemporary Hinduism, but also a burning desire to revive the glorious religion of India's most ancient texts, the Vedas. After unsuccessful attempts to found Sanskrit schools, Dayanand and his followers formed the Arya Samaj to realize his vision of the revitalization of Vedic Hinduism. Though there is some evidence of personal devotion to Dayanand in contemporary Arya Samaj practice (for example, almost all Arya Samaj temples display a picture of him), from the start the group was governed by a constitution and leaders elected by the membership, with little formal role for the founder. In fact, Dayanand and later Arya Samajists criticized the "gurudom" of other Hindu movements, which advocate slavish devotion to a spiritual master. The Arya Samaj proved popular with social groups just coming to prominence in the late-nineteenth century under British rule, and the movement had a significant following by the time of Dayanand's death in 1883.

In many ways Dayanand's understanding of the history of the religions of India, an ancient golden age followed by centuries of decline, was similar to the opinions of the British Orientalists of his time. Like the Orientalists, Dayanand condemned the idolatry and priestcraft of contemporary Hinduism. He rejected widow immolation and criticized restrictions on widow remarriage. He advocated education for girls as well as boys, though primarily to prepare them for their domestic responsibilities. About caste Dayanand accepted in principle this division of society but maintained that caste identity should be determined on the basis of the qualities of the individual and not by birth. The history of the Arya Samaj has seen a kind of oscillation on the issue of caste, with radical caste-breaking fervor sliding back into acquiescence to the status quo. Concerning caste, one important innovation that is often attributed to the Arya Samaj is the invention of rituals to alter one's caste status. Originally intended to reclaim individuals who had temporarily fallen from caste, these rituals were eventually used to "reconvert" large social groups, from Islam especially, that were understood to have formerly been Hindu. In general, over the course of the twentieth century Arya Samajists were often involved in communal conflict, especially with Muslims (Llewellyn 1993, 97–108).

The most substantial impact of the Arya Samaj on Indian society came in the area of education. In 1886 the Dayanand Anglo-Vedic (or D.A.V.) High School was established in Lahore as a memorial to the recently deceased founder of the Arya Samaj. This initiative appealed to progressive families in India looking for a Hindu alternative to Christian mission schools, and eventually hundreds of D.A.V. schools were established across north India, including some of the earliest schools for girls (Llewellyn 1998, 32–45). Soon a split developed in the Arya Samaj over education and other issues as well, and an alternative system of schools was founded in 1902; it trained students in a more narrow version of the teachings of the Arya Samaj than did the D.A.V. schools. Despite this conflict, missionaries traveled to Indian emigrant communities overseas, and for a time in the first quarter of the twentieth century the Arya Samaj made a fair bid to be *the* arbiter of what was "Hindu" for emigres in places such as Trinidad and Fiji. Though this move was eventually countered by other Hindu groups, the Arya Samaj did establish centers in eastern and southern Africa and more recently in the United Kingdom and North America, though they have largely appealed only to immigrants who came from Arya Samaj families in India in the past few decades.

The Arya Samaj has never been a particularly large group. Kenneth Jones estimated that the total membership was only around 1.5 to 2 million in 1947, when India became independent of British rule (Jones 1995, 37). Still, Arya Samajists played an important role in the emergence of the Independence movement, contributing political leaders such as Lala Lajpat Rai and Swami Shraddhanand.

Ramakrishna, Swami Vivekananda, and the Ramakrishna Math and Mission

The Ramakrishna Mission is named for its founder, who was born in a village in Bengal in eastern India in 1836. Qualified by his Brahmin birth and some study of Sanskrit, as a young man Ramakrishna went to work as a priest at the Dakshineshwar temple on the northern outskirts of Calcutta. Alarmed at reports that he would frequently fall into a trance, Ramakrishna's family arranged for his marriage to a young girl, Saradamani, hoping to tie him to worldly life. But this proved unavailing in the end. Eventually Saradamani went to live with her husband at Dakshineshwar, but his followers believe that their marriage was never consummated. Ramakrishna's approach to religion was eclectic but always oriented to practice. He experimented with various forms of Hinduism, particularly devotion to the goddess Kali, but also including everything from Tantra to nondualism. Ramakrishna also tried out Christianity and Islam by practicing Christian and Muslim prayers. Eventually some of the educated elite from the cosmopolitan city of Calcutta were attracted by Ramakrishna's reputation for saintliness; he evidently had a profound effect on many. Vivekananda, who would become Ramakrishna's most important disciple, recalled being himself driven into trance by the master's touch (Isherwood 1980, 197). By the time of his death in 1886, Ramakrishna was surrounded by a small but dedicated group of disciples.

This group was cast into disarray by Ramakrishna's death, only to be reformed upon Swami Vivekananda's triumphant return from the West. Vivekananda was born in Calcutta in 1863. The son of an urbane attorney, Vivekananda seemed destined for the law himself when he was derailed by the spiritual search that led him to Ramakrishna. After his guru's death, Vivekananda spent several years traversing India, eventually winning support to travel to the United States to represent Hinduism at the World's Parliament of Religions at the Chicago World's Fair in 1893. Here Vivekananda caused something of a sensation, and he stayed to travel and lecture in the United States and later in England and France. Vivekananda returned to a hero's welcome in India in 1897, and he soon asserted leadership over the disciples of Ramakrishna before his death in 1902.

It was under Vivekananda that Advaita (nondualism) was established as the official teaching of the Ramakrishna movement, though there has been some tension between this rarified pantheism and Ramakrishna's own seemingly theistic devotion to the goddess Kali, as well as the later devotion to Ramakrishna himself as an avatara, or incarnation of God. Another important innovation of Vivekananda was that he organized the followers of Ramakrishna into a community of monks, but monks with a regular commitment to social service; for example, the Ramakrishna movement has been particularly active in medicine, overseeing thirteen hospitals and seventy-seven outdoor dispensaries in 1978–1979 (Ramakrishna Mission 1981, 3). Though the Ramakrishna Math, which is dedicated to training of the monks (a *math* is a renouncers' center), is formally separate from the Ramakrishna Mission, which organizes the social service work, the hospitals and schools are generally managed by monks.

The number of Ramakrishna devotees is relatively small. In a court case in the mid-1980s the Ramakrishna Math and Mission claimed the allegiance of fourteen hundred monks and one hundred thousand lay followers (Williams 1995, 79). But the movement has been influential in creating a new kind of this-worldly Hindu renouncer. Ramakrishna monks played an important role in introducing westerners to Hinduism, maintaining centers in the United States and elsewhere that had originally been established by Vivekananda at the end of the nineteenth century. Publication has been an important part of this missionary work, with the Ramakrishna movement making good English translations of Hindu texts available in the West, some for the first time.

Bhaktivedanta and the International Society for Krishna Consciousness

A rather different movement that like the Ramakrishna Mission had its origins in Bengal in eastern India is the International Society for Krishna Consciousness (ISKCON). The founder, A. C. Bhaktivedanta Swami Prabhupada, was born in a suburb of Calcutta in 1896. Married while in college, after graduating, Bhaktivedanta began a career in pharmaceutical sales and other business ventures in Calcutta, but also in other cities across north India, including Allahabad and Lucknow. During this time, Bhaktivedanta's interest in religious matters grew, and in 1932 he was initiated as the disciple of Bhaktisiddhanta Saraswati, a renouncer in the Gaudiya Vaishnava tradition. Popular in Bengal, the Gaudiya movement can be traced back to the medieval saint Chaitanya (1485–1533), who advocated passionate devotion to the god Krishna. After decades of trying to balance his business and religious pursuits, Bhaktivedanta finally decided at the age of fifty-eight to dedicate himself full-time to the spread of Krishna-consciousness. This was what led Bhaktivedanta to travel to New York in 1965. By then sixty-nine years old, he would have seemed an unlikely missionary, but ISKCON boasted 108 centers around the world by the time of Bhaktivedanta's death in 1977 (Mitchiner 1991, 75).

It was probably the very exoticism of ISKCON that appealed to many young American adults in the late 1960s and early 1970s. From Bhaktivedanta they learned about not only Indian religious literature but also Indian vegetarian cooking, and some of his disciples were initiated as renouncers, donning orange robes and shaving their heads except for a top-knot. In the early period of its history ISKCON developed a reputation for aggressive proselytizing in airports and other public places, but there was no denying the zeal of the young converts, who committed themselves to a disciplined life of religious practice abjuring intoxicants and casual sex. The group was labeled from its public devotional singing of the names of God, "Hare Krishna." ISKCON has since lost some of its counter-cultural edge. After Bhaktivedanta's death, leadership in ISKCON passed to the Governing Body Commission, which was dominated by the founder's Western disciples, but in the 1980s Asian Indian immigrants began to play an ever larger role in ISKCON affairs (Williams 1998, 130–137). Despite the rather unusual demograph-ics of the ISKCON, it is worth emphasizing again that Bhak-tivedanta's teaching was firmly rooted in the Hindu tradition. He worked tirelessly, writing and publishing commentaries on the great Krishna classics such as the Bhagavad Gita and the Bhagavata Pu-rana, and the emphasis in the movement was more on devotion to Krishna than on devotion to the guru.

The Maharishi and Transcendental Meditation

Maharishi Mahesh Yogi was born in what is now the Indian state of Uttar Pradesh in 1918. After studying physics at Allahabad University, he lived in the Himalayas for more than a decade with Brahmananda Saraswati. As the shankaracharya of the Jyotir Math, Brahmananda was heir to one of Hinduism's most influential spiritual lineages, said to have been founded by the great philosopher Shankara. Initiated as a renouncer by Brahmananda, the Maharishi began to travel India af-ter his teacher's death, first propounding Transcendental Meditation in 1957. The heart of the Maharishi's approach is the nondualist phi-losophy he inherited from Shankara, that is, that we are all ultimately brahman, the spiritual substratum of the phenomenal world. The ge-nius of the Maharishi was in packaging this tradition in a simple tech-nique in Transcendental Meditation. The Maharishi began to make preaching tours outside India in the late 1950s, and his fame jumped in the West in 1967 when the Beatles declared themselves his disci-ples, visiting his ashrama in Rishikesh in India the next year. The Ma-harishi's movement was marked by continuing institutional expan-sion through the last decades of the twentieth century, from the establishment of Maharishi International University in Fairfield, Iowa, in 1971, to the Maharishi World Centre for Ayurveda in India in 1976 (to develop and market India's traditional medicines), to the Natural Law Party in 1992 with branches in the United States, the United Kingdom, and other countries.

Sathya Sai Baba

Sathya Sai Baba was born in a village in what is now the state of Andhra Pradesh in 1926. At the age of fourteen he is said to have proclaimed, "I am Sai Baba," which his followers take as evidence that he is a reincarnation of an earlier saint, Sai Baba of Shirdi in Maharasthra, who died in 1918 (Babb 2000, 163). In his teaching, there are times when Sathya Sai Baba has sounded like a nondualist, preaching a kind of pantheistic omnipresence of God. For example, he once said, "The sages have laid down three categories which comprise the knowable world. God, Nature and the I (Iswara, Prakrthi, and Jiva). God seen through the mirror of Nature appears as I. Remove the mirror; there is only God; the image merges in the Original. Man is but the image of God. Even nature is but an appearance of God; the reality is He alone" (Sathya Sai Baba 1978, 64).

Yet the emphasis in the movement is on Sathya Sai Baba himself as an incarnation of God, and devotion to him is understood to be crucial to spiritual progress. For his disciples, powerful evidence of Sathya Sai Baba's divine status is provided by the miracles that he regularly performs, most characteristically the materialization of *vibhuti*, sacred ash, which he gives out as a physical token of his grace. Sathya Sai Baba has encouraged his followers to do social service work, and the movement sponsors an extensive network of Sathya Sai schools that impart a purportedly nonsectarian spiritual education, but with clearly Hindu leanings (Babb 2000, 169). The Sathya Sai movement has had some success in attracting followers outside India, including Indian immigrants. Smriti Srinivas has argued that devotion to Sathya Sai Baba has proven ironically appropriate to Asian Indians in the United States because their belief in miraculous encounters with the guru seems to overcome the distance from home (Srinivas 2001).

Sathya Sai Baba.
CORBIS/SYGMA

Bhagwan Shree Rajneesh

Born in 1931 in a village in what is now the Indian state of Madhya Pradesh, Bhagwan Shree Rajneesh studied philosophy, earning an M.A. and teaching the subject in college for nine years. Rajneesh gave up his job in 1966 to dedicate himself to giving lectures and holding meditation camps. He established a center in Mumbai and later shifted to Pune in the state of Maharashtra. From 1970 Rajneesh began to initiate disciples, primarily westerners, as renouncers, though it does not appear that he was ever formally initiated himself. About the guru's teaching, John Mitchiner has written, "Rajneesh's goal, the experience at the end of the road, was Monistic: it was the unitary goal of Advaita Vedanta, the goal of '*Tat tvam asi*': 'I am Brahman'" (Mitchiner 1991, 126). Yet Rajneesh was a thinker who resisted confinement in any narrow dogmatism, and at his center in Pune various therapeutic techniques flourished—everything from massage to Rolfing.

In 1981 Rajneesh moved to eastern Oregon, where his large community of five thousand permanent residents and twenty thousand visitors for summer festivals was none too popular in its rural setting. During his first four years in the United States, Rajneesh maintained a vow of silence, and his community was directed by an increasingly dictatorial female renouncer disciple from India named Sheela; she later fled following rumors of everything from embezzlement to attempted murder. Rajneesh himself was deported in 1985 after pleading guilty to immigration fraud. He and a core group of his followers spent some months on the road, looking for a country that would grant admission to the whole group, before Rajneesh returned to India. Though the American media depicted him as a broken man, Rajneesh returned to his ashram in Pune and had begun to undertake new initiatives before his death in 1990. In addition to his colorful career as a guru, Rajneesh was also a remarkably prolific author—over 650 books have been published by him, many under the name Osho (a form of address for a Japanese Buddhist or Shinto priest, because of Rajneesh's frequent references to Zen Buddhism) (Mitchiner 1991, 128).

Bhagwan Shree Rajneesh.
JP LAFFONT/SYGMA/CORBIS

Chidvilasananda and Siddha Yoga

Gurumayi Chidvilasananda was born around 1959. At a young age she became a follower of Swami Muktananda (1908–1982), who was himself a disciple of Bhagwan Nityananda (d. 1961). Muktananda claimed that his guru was a *janma siddha,* that is, that he was spiritually perfected from birth, so that he never actually required a guru to introduce him to the spiritual life (www.siddhayoga.org/guru/nityananda/nityananda.html). However, Nityananda's teaching was in the Kashmir Shaiva tradition, whose origins stretch back at least as far as the ninth century. The Siddha Yoga website explains: "According to the philosophy of Kashmir Shaivism, the whole universe is a manifestation of *Shiva,* or the Lord. To live with the awareness that Shiva is in all things is a powerful spiritual practice that leads to unity-awareness" (www.siddhayoga.org/teachings/essential/essential.html). Muktananda himself was given a kind of initiation by Nityananda called *shaktipat,* which is said to awaken the *kundalini* spiritual energy, and within nine years the disciple became a "perfected one," or a *siddha.* Chidvilasananda was in turn given the *shaktipat* initiation by Muktananda and is regarded as a *siddha* by the adherents of the Siddha Yoga movement.

During Muktananda's time the base of the Siddha Yoga movement was in Ganeshpuri in Maharasthra, but he began regular tours of the United States, establishing a center in South Fallsburg, New York. Before his death in 1982, Muktananda deputized Chidvilasananda and her brother Nityananda, but the latter eventually resigned as guru, and Chidvilasananda became the sole leader of a movement with over six hundred centers in fifty-two countries (Johnsen 1994, 74). Siddha Yoga activity is concentrated on intensive retreats in which new disciples receive the *shaktipat* initiation, but the movement has also supported social service work, especially free medical care, in Maharashtra since the 1970s, and more recently in Mexico and even in rural New York.

Plotting the Gurus and Their Movements

If I were to compare the aforementioned gurus by plotting them on a graph, one of the axes would surely have to be theological, on a scale from monism to theism. In the history of the religious thought of South Asia, the extreme monist position was classically expressed by the philosopher Shankara, whose advaita (nondualist) teaching was that the single ultimate reality of the seemingly variegated world is brahman. After Shankara, and even within his own school of Vedanta, the progress of Indian thought was marked by a number of attempts to reestablish theism, devotion to a more or less personal God. With abstruse names like "qualified nondualistic" (associated with Ramanuja) and "dualistic-cum-nondualistic" (associated with Nimbarka) these efforts often represented not a simple repudiation of Shankara's nondualism but rather an attempt to incorporate advaita within an overarching system that is theistic.

Given the attempts to mix theism and monism in various ways over the course of the history of Indian philosophy, it should come as no surprise that it can be difficult to categorize the teachings of these modern gurus. For example, it would seem a simple matter to assign the Ramakrishna movement to the monist camp because it explicitly identifies itself with advaita. Yet, as noted above, Ramakrishna himself was a passionate devotee of the goddess Kali. In Christopher Isherwood's biography of Ramakrishna, one of Ramakrishna's many teachers is an adherent of advaita, whose practice Ramakrishna does master, but their association ends with the advaitin guru attaining a vision of the goddess who was the object of the disciple's devotion (Isherwood 1980, 122–123). On the other end of the spectrum should come Bhaktivedanta, who advocated devotion to Krishna, but even he argued that his theology was consistent with texts like the Upanishads, which seem to advocate monism at least in some parts.

To make a long story short, in the teachings of most of these gurus some ideas concerning an impersonal absolute can be found alongside ideas about a personal God, even one who has manifested himself in human incarnations. The odd man out of this generalization is Swami Dayanand, the founder of the Arya Samaj, who held to a rigorous theism, rejecting the monistic idea that God is immanent in the world, but at the same time rejecting the idea that this God has taken on human incarnations. Overall, I would call Swaminarayan, Soamiji Maharaj, Dayanand, and Bhaktivedanta fairly clear theists, whereas the Ramakrishna movement (if not Ramakrishna himself), the Maharishi, Sathya Sai Baba, Rajneesh, and Chidvilasananda probably belong more or less in the monist category.

A second axis along which these gurus might be compared concerns the basis of their authority. At one end of the spectrum is a teacher, whose authority derives from his study of and commentary upon earlier writings. At the other end of the spectrum is a god-man (or god-woman), who has or, probably better, *is* a new revelation and who needs no book to confirm it (Gold 2001). Like our first theological axis, it can be difficult to know where to place some of these gurus on the axis of authority. The most obvious problems are with Swaminarayan and with Soamiji Maharaj, whose own disciples disagreed so violently on this issue that there was a schism among them. Let's take Soamiji Maharaj as an example. In his case, and for the other gurus as well, a crucial question would be if he had a teacher himself; in other words, whether he was a part of an ongoing lineage or tradition or a self-made guru. But this is precisely the point on which the Punjabi and the Agra branches of the movement disagreed, with the former claiming he had a guru in the Sikh tradition and the latter denying it. And there is evidence that could be used to support either position in Soamiji Maharaj's own writings. On the one hand, he argued that the key to salvation is the living guru, rather than any old book. On the other hand, he did mention earlier saints whom he believed had attained the highest spiritual level, and his teaching was more or less consistent with theirs, so he might have been taken as continuing their lineage. Even if we grant Soamiji Maharaj's argument that the living guru has more authority than the tradition, his disciples would have been unlikely to follow him if his life and teachings did not fit into some idea of saintliness prevailing at the time.

Sometimes in South Asia stories of miraculous events in childhood are seen as proof that a religious figure is not self-made but born divine. Such stories are told about Swaminarayan, Ramakrishna, and Sathya Sai Baba. But this by itself is not sufficient to place a guru in the god-man category, because these kinds of stories are part of the general hagiographic practice in South Asia and are liable to attach themselves to any religious figure.

Perhaps the clearest example of a teacher-guru, rather than a god-man, in this chapter is Swami Dayanand, who consistently maintained that his religion was based upon the ancient and inerrant Vedas. Yet it is significant that Arya Samajists often call their founder "Maharishi." Given that the *rishis* were the sages to whom the Vedas were revealed by God, to label Dayanand *maharishi* (literally great, *maha-*, *rishi*) would seem to place his writings on a par with, or even above, the Vedas, though Dayanand certainly never claimed that himself.

Finally, the very reverence with which a guru is treated might be taken as evidence that he is regarded as a god-man rather than just a teacher. Against this argument, it should be noted that teachers traditionally are treated with great respect in South Asian culture. Bhaktivedanta is another obvious teacher-guru, but he once said that "the Guru should be offered the same respect that one would offer to God," although this is only because "The Guru is God's representative" (Mitchiner 1991, 77). Though there may be a difference in theory here, as a practical matter it might be difficult to distinguish the homage accorded a guru who *represents* God and the homage accorded a guru who *is* God. Even with all of these caveats, I would still hazard that Dayanand, Bhaktivedanta, the Maharishi Mahesh Yogi, and Chidvilasananda belong in the guru-as-teacher camp, and that Ramakrishna, Sathya Sai Baba, and Rajneesh were god-men, with Swaminarayan and Soamiji Maharaj in either category because of the disagreement on this among their own followers.

An argument could be made that there is a certain degree of covariance here, with theists tending to be teachers and monists tending to be god-men. To the extent that the theists see that there is a strong difference between the divine and the human, it might be expected that they would not pretend to divinity themselves, but only claim to be the students of those who had received divine revelation. The monists, in contrast, believe that the Absolute is present everywhere. By this argument the guru could logically be expected to say, "I am the Absolute." Then again, the guru could also acknowledge that we are all one with the Absolute, downplaying her or his own significance.

Gurus in Modern Hinduism

For the purposes of this book, the most important axis upon which these gurus should be plotted concerns how modern or traditional each is. If we are to borrow the chronology of European history, then all of these movements are modern, starting near the beginning of the nineteenth century at the earliest. There are some obvious ways in which all of these movements are modern, for example, in utilizing recent technology to convey their message. Take Swami Dayanand, the founder of the Arya Samaj. He propagated his revitalized Vedic religion in the nineteenth century through a commentary on the Vedas that he mailed to his followers on a regular basis, after printing that commentary on a press he owned. The Arya Samaj and the other movements surveyed in this chapter have continued to communicate via everything from printing and the postal system to e-mail and the World Wide Web. And I would argue that the use of these media has had some impact on the message being conveyed.

In premodern Indian culture, the word *guru* most often referred to a teacher. One model for the classical educational system is described by the Laws of Manu, a legal code written in the early centuries of the Common Era. Here twice-born males, that is, males from one of the three higher castes (priests, warriors, and merchants), would leave home to study with a guru in childhood, beginning as young as five for a boy of the priest caste. The Laws of Manu (3.1) sets out a period of study of thirty-six years but then permits a lesser commitment, down to "whenever the undertaking comes to an end" (Doniger 1991, 43). The primary occupation of the student was to learn the Vedas, the ancient Hindu scripture, but he had to endure otherwise a life of fairly stern self-control, including celibacy. Reverence to the guru was a regular feature of the student's routine. For example, he was required to touch the guru's feet before and after studying the Vedas with him. In fact, the Laws of Manu holds that for the student, "The teacher is the physical form of ultimate reality," presumably because he gives the student access to ultimate reality through teaching him the scriptures (Doniger 1991, 40). In contemporary India very few boys go off to study with a guru as they would have done in times past. Most attend school and live at home. And although *guru* is still used to refer to this kind of teacher, or to any kind of teacher, it now often specifically refers to the charismatic leader of a religious group. Unlike the regular intimate contact of the child-disciple with the traditional guru who was a teacher, the interaction of disciples with the modern guru who is the head of a large movement tends to be of a much less immediate variety, mediated by modern technology.

In addition to technological modernity, there are also institutional ways in which these movements are clearly modern, from the dioceses into which Swaminarayanan divided his followers, to the legal registration of the Arya Samaj soon after its founding, to the 1980s court case by the Ramakrishna Math and Mission claiming that it was a religious minority under the provisions of the Indian Constitution. And these examples of institutional modernity are also not trivial in their effects.

However, the most significant question is the extent to which these gurus and their followers are substantively modern, incorporating modern ideas into their teaching. A classic description of modern Hinduism can be found in J. N. Farquhar's *Modern Religious Movements in India,* which was first published in 1914. In his conclusion Farquhar identified ten traits that he understood to be increasingly characteristic of religious movements in India in his time. They are: (1) monotheism; (2) rejection of *"polytheism, mythology, idolatry and man-worship";* (3) acceptance that "all men are brothers" and an attendant rejection of casteism; (4) advocacy of moral reform; (5) an insistence that *"the worship of God must be spiritual,"* and an attendant rejection of rites that Farquhar saw as insufficiently spiritual, such as "animal and vegetable sacrifices, ceremonial bathing, pilgrimage and self-torture"; (6) advocacy of devotion to a personal God; (7) a rejection of the doctrines of transmigration and karma (which Farquhar condemned as inimical to social reform); (8) an advocacy of training for religious teachers; (9) support for the *"Social Reform Movement"*; and (10) an organization copied from the Christian missionary groups, which Farquhar deemed more "efficient" than the medieval practice in which new religious ideas were propagated by wandering ecstatic singers (Farquhar 1977, 434–444). For the sake of simplicity, most of these traits can be grouped under two headings: (a) social reform, including especially caste reform (Farquhar's items 3, 7, and 9), and (b) theological reform (Farquhar's 1, 2, 5, and 6).

If social reform is defined very broadly as being involved in some kind of social service work, then that is at least a part of several of the movements described here, including those founded or led by Swaminarayan, Dayanand, Ramakrishna (though Ramakrishna himself was not a social activist), Sathya Sai Baba, Rajneesh, and Chidvilasananda. On caste particularly there have been a range of responses in these movements. Though he supported relief work that helped people without regard to caste, in general Swaminarayan himself advocated a kind of reformism that increased the scrupulousness of observance of caste rules. However, it is noteworthy that his followers have since relaxed some caste strictures, for example, by allowing members of lower-caste groups to become renouncers (Williams 2001, 171). At the other extreme are public demonstrations of caste breaking that have sometimes taken place in the history of the Arya Samaj, though these demonstrations have only been occasional. On the issue of caste, it is interesting to note the prominence of the priestly caste among the gurus described here, including Swaminarayan, Dayanand, and Ramakrishna (though Vivekananda was not a Brahmin), but it should also be noted that many movements have emerged in modern Hinduism led by members of lower-caste groups. Whatever their stand on caste, none of these movements repudiates the ideas of karma and rebirth, despite Farquhar's claim.

If anything, Farquhar's platform of theological reform is even less in evidence in the movements surveyed in this chapter. The Arya Samaj is really the only one that has advocated monotheism, for instance, and repudiated polytheism. On this latter point the position of Soamiji Maharaj is interesting. On the one hand, he wrote as if there is only one God, whom he sometimes called the *sat purush* (the true person). And he also disparaged other gods and their messengers. For example, he wrote: "It has been mentioned previously that all incarnations, *Yogishwar-Gyanis*, prophets, *Yogi-Gyanis* and others came either from *Daswan Dwar*, or *Trikuti*, or *Sahasdal Kamal* and that the four *Vedas* were revealed at *Trikuti* by *Nad* or *Pranav*—and that the gods such as Brahma, Vishnu and Maha Dev originated from below *Sahasdal Kamal*. Their status is, therefore, much lower than that of the Saints and of Sat Purush, Who are superior to all of them" (Soami Maharaj 1974, 70). The argument in this quote reflects Soamiji Maharaj's cosmology, and I don't want to take a detour through that rather abstruse system here. Suffice it to say that the Daswan Dwar, Trikuti, and Sahasdal Kamal are all spiritual levels below the highest realm in which God resides, so that the beings that emanate from them, including Brahma, Vishnu, and Shiva (who is called Maha Dev in this quote) and their incarnations are ranked below God. It should be noted that this is not a simple monotheism of the Western variety, in which all gods but the one God are denied any existence. Rather, these other gods do exist, though they are ranked below the one God. This is a rhetorical strategy that is relatively common in the movements surveyed in this chapter, where it is even sometimes used to exalt the guru himself above other gods, as in the case of Sathya Sai Baba and Rajneesh. Still, it is not clear to me that this is proof of the impact of Christianity in India, as Farquhar argued, because this rhetorical strategy is quite old in South Asia. It can be found in devotional works such as the Bhagavad Gita and elsewhere.

J. N. Farquhar allowed that a number of factors contributed to the development of his modern Hinduism. He listed "the British Government, English education and literature, Christianity, Oriental research, European science and philosophy, and the material elements of Western civilization." But, in the end, Farquhar assigned the greatest importance to his own religion, because he concluded that "Christianity has ruled the development throughout" (Farquhar 1977, 433). Perhaps it is not surprising that he came to this conclusion, because on the title page of *Modern Religious Movements in India* he is identified as "Literary Secretary, National Council of Young Men's Christian Associations, India and Ceylon." There is certainly a kind of theological slant in the book that other analysts of the same period in the history of South Asia have not shared. Even so, it is common to look upon India's encounter with colonizing cultures of Europe, especially the British, as crucial for the modern history of Hinduism. An example of this is Kenneth W. Jones's book *Socio-Religious Reform Movements in British India,* in which religious groups are categorized by their relationship to the colonial encounter, being divided into transitional or acculturative movements (Jones 1989). For that reason, in India, as in other parts of the developing world, "the modern" has often been identified with "the colonial."

If that understanding of history is accepted, then India should have entered a kind of postcolonial, and therefore postmodern, period in 1947 when the country threw off the yoke of British rule. It would be difficult to make an argument about the nature of postcolonial guru-centered movements on the basis of this chapter, because most of the groups surveyed here were founded in the colonial period—that is, those associated with Swaminarayan, Soamiji Maharaj, Dayanand, Ramakrishna, and Sathya Sai Baba. Three other groups were founded after 1947, but by gurus who themselves were raised in the colonial period. The Maharishi Mahesh Yogi first taught Transcendental Meditation in 1957, but he was born in 1918. Bhaktivedanta founded ISKCON in the 1960s, and this was the decade when Rajneesh began to attract a following, but they were born in 1896 and 1931, respectively. Of the gurus introduced here, only Chidvilasananda has lived her entire life in the postcolonial period, and even she is the head of a movement with colonial roots. These chronological complications suggest a more basic point. There is much in contemporary Indian culture with roots in the colonial era, everything from the structures of political organization, to the basic framework of business practice, to the English language itself. Under these circumstances, it would be a mistake to assume that religious movements in independent India are wholly different from those that came before because of a simple accident of chronology.

All that being said, there is one interesting difference between our one postcolonial guru and all of the others analyzed here, and that is that she is a woman. There were occasionally outstanding women in the premodern history of the religions of South Asia, of course, but those with institutional power have been very rare indeed (see Young 1987, 59–103). The emergence of women gurus in recent decades thus is genuinely new, a consequence in part of a gradual rise in the status of women in South Asian culture over the course of at least two centuries.

The cultural trend of the past couple of decades in India that is commented upon most frequently is *globalization*. Strictly speaking, globalization refers to the worldwide expansion of multinational corporations, particularly into developing countries. This change is viewed as sanguine by U.S. president George W. Bush, because it opens up new markets and creates new opportunities for profit for American business interests. But there are many in India and around the world for whom "globalization" is a bad word, signaling the deepening immiserization of workers in poor countries along with the destruction of their cultures. Regardless of the how this process is judged, there can be no doubt that the Indian economy was opened up to foreign business in the 1990s in a way that is unprecedented in the history of independent India (with some foreign corporations banned earlier), something which may have a substantial effect over time on the religions of India.

Globalization is also used more loosely to describe the emergence of a contemporary scene in which cultures from around the world rub elbows in a kind of transnational metropolitan space. There can be no doubt that several of the groups in this chapter have gone global in recent decades. Yet Raymond Williams has issued a clarification about the international reach of the Swaminarayan movement that could very well be applied to others. "Such emigrations are best viewed as transnational movements—not as a generalized globalization—because related immigrants are found in several distinct locations where economic, political, and even religious forces have created space for particular types of immigrants. They participate in chain migrations that follow established networks to specific locations" (Williams 2001, 197). In general, two patterns are discernible in the international growth of the groups in this chapter. One is the spread of Hindu movements by the emigration of their adherents from India to other parts of the world. This is the model for the rather spectacular expansion of Swaminarayan Hinduism, but the same might well be said for the much more modest growth of the Arya Samaj as well. The other pattern of international spread is when a movement attracts westerners as adherents. The clearest example of this here is ISKCON, but the same pattern to a certain extent can be found in the Transcendental Meditation movement and among the followers of Sathya Sai Baba.

There is a chance that the distinction between these two transnational patterns in guru-centered movements will be blurred as immigrants from South Asia grow in numbers and social prominence in North America and in Europe, especially the United Kingdom. In fact, such a blurring has already taken place to a degree in ISKCON. Yet to the present, these two patterns have been based on rather dissimilar social practices in different movements. Raymond Williams notes that Swaminarayan temples have provided a kind of home away from home for Indian emigres to East Africa, Europe, and North America, where they can worship a Hindu God and also speak the language, eat the food, and even wear the clothing of their native Gujarat. But this experience is only possible in a place where Gujaratis predominate, not Western converts to the Swaminarayan religion. And the Swaminarayan movement has not yet made a substantial effort to win Western converts. It is not as if elements of Indian culture are entirely absent from groups that appeal to westerners. On the contrary, I suggested earlier that its exoticism is one of the things that appealed to the first Hare Krishnas, and many came to study the Sanskrit language, to wear the orange robes of a Hindu renouncer, and to cook Indian vegetarian food. Still, the relatively superficial veneer of Indian culture in groups like ISKCON is rather different from the Swaminarayan case.

For Hindu movements that do attract Western followers, a significant problem is what is sometimes called "bliss-hopping," with a substantial number of people who appear interested in a group soon moving on to other gurus to try novel spiritual practices. This may be a particular problem for Hindu groups in the West, because there is a certain pressure to find a guru who is "authentic." Once a guru has established him- or herself, he or she begins to look more like a part of an institution and less like a kind of religious virtuoso, and so later seekers gravitate to a guru who is new. To a certain extent it appears that a kind of consumerism is operative here, with even spiritual seekers chasing the latest fashion, casting aside the outmoded.

For groups that cater to immigrants, the problem with being more or less culturally Indian was brought home to me when I did research on the Arya Samaj in North America in the late 1990s. In interviews many expressed concern that young people did not seem to be interested in the movement. Some said there was an inherent conflict between the old and the young. First-generation immigrants came to Arya Samaj gatherings in part because they wanted to celebrate their culture, by speaking the Hindi language, for example. But most second-generation Arya Samajists, raised in Canada or the United States, did not speak Hindi well and felt left out of meetings in which that was the dominant medium of communication. It is possible that the Arya Samaj in North America will remain a kind of cultural halfway house in which the membership is always made up largely of relatively recent immigrants, while the second generation continually drifts away.

In his *Introduction to Swaminarayan Hinduism,* Raymond Williams makes a distinction between what he calls that movement's "manifest" and "latent" functions. On a superficial level, "The goal is to spread the teachings of Swaminarayan and to lead the followers along the spiritual path to salvation." But particularly outside Gujarat the latent function of the movement is to provide a context in which to enjoy Gujarati culture. Then Williams comments, with some sagacity, but in diplomatic language, "any attempt to universalize the religion may cause the two [functions] to be in some tension" (Williams 2001, 198–199). In other words, there would seem to be a contradiction between the regional profile of the movement and its stated commitment to a universalist theology. If it is true that Swaminarayan Hindus know the ultimate truth about God, then it would seem to be incumbent upon them to communicate that truth to the world, not just to those who speak Gujarati.

This is an issue not only for Swaminarayan but for all movements that have a regional base but that make universalist claims. This brings us back to an issue that opened this chapter. With the spread of mass media communication in India, the relationship of the various regional expressions of Hinduism to each other and to "Hinduism" as a whole is bound to become a problem of greater urgency. This may have been one factor that contributed to the rise of Hindu nationalist politics in India in the last two decades of the twentieth century. In the future, as new gurus emerge in India, they will have to reckon with what Hinduism is and how their preaching and practice relate to it.

BIBLIOGRAPHY

Babb, Lawrence A. *Redemptive Encounters: Three Modern Styles in the Hindu Tradition*. Prospect Heights, Ill.: Waveland Press, 1986; reprinted 2000.

Doniger, Wendy, translator, with Brian K. Smith. *The Laws of Manu*. London: Penguin Books, 1991.

Farquhar, J. N. *Modern Religious Movements in India*. 1914. Repr., Delhi: Munshiram Manoharlal, 1977.

Gold, Daniel R. Response to panel "Mahagurus and Their Movements in a Global Context," American Academy of Religion, Denver, November 20, 2001.

Isherwood, Christopher. *Ramakrishna and His Disciples*, 4th Indian ed. Calcutta: Advaita Ashram, 1980.

Johnsen, Linda. "Gurumayi Chidvilasananda: Beauty and Grace," in *Daughters of the Goddess: The Women Saints of India*. St. Paul: Yes International Publishers, 1994.

Jones, Kenneth W. *Socio-Religious Reform Movements in British India*. Vol. III, 1 in the New Cambridge History of India series. Cambridge: Cambridge University Press, 1989.

———. "The Arya Samaj in British India, 1875–1947," in Robert D. Baird (ed.), *Religion in Modern India*, 3rd ed. Delhi: Manohar, 1995: 27–54.

Karlen, Neal, et al. "Busting the Bhagwan: The 'Swami of Sex' Is Arrested in North Carolina." *Newsweek* 26 (November 1, 1985): 31–32.

Llewellyn, J. E. *The Arya Samaj as a Fundamentalist Movement: A Study in Comparative Fundamentalism*. Delhi: Manohar, 1993.

———. *The Legacy of Women's Uplift in India: Contemporary Women Leaders in the Arya Samaj*. Delhi: Sage Publications, 1998.

Mitchiner, John. "Bhaktivedanta and Krishna Consciousness," in *Guru: The Search for Enlightenment*. Delhi: Viking, 1991.

Ramakrishna Mission. *Report 1980–1981*. New Delhi: Ramakrishna Mission, 1981.

Sathya Sai Baba. *Sadhana: The Inward Path; Quotations from the Divine Discourses of Bhagavan Sri Sathya Sai Baba*, rev. ed. Bangalore: Sri Sathya Sai Education and Publication Foundation, 1978.

Soamiji, Maharaj. *The Sar Bachan*, 6th ed. Translated by Sardar Sewa Singh. Beas: Radha Soami Satsang, 1974.

Srinivas, Smriti. "Mahagurus and Their Movements in a Global Context." Panel at American Academy of Religion, Denver, November 20, 2001.

Williams, George M. "The Ramakrishna Movement: A Study in Religious Change," in Robert D. Baird (ed.), *Religion in Modern India*, 3rd ed. Delhi: Manohar, 1995: 55–79.

Williams, Raymond Brady. "International Society for Krishna Consciousness," in *Religions of Immigrants from India and Pakistan: New Threads in the American Tapestry*. Cambridge: Cambridge University Press, 1988: 130–137.

———. *An Introduction to Swaminarayan Hinduism*. Cambridge: Cambridge University Press, 2001.

Young, Katherine K. "Hinduism," in Arvind Sharma (ed.), *Women in World Religions*. Albany: State University of New York Press, 1987: 59–103.

http://www.siddhayoga.org/guru/nityananda/nityananda.html. Accessed May 30, 2002.

http://www.siddhayoga.org/teachings/essential/essential.html. Accessed May 30, 2002.

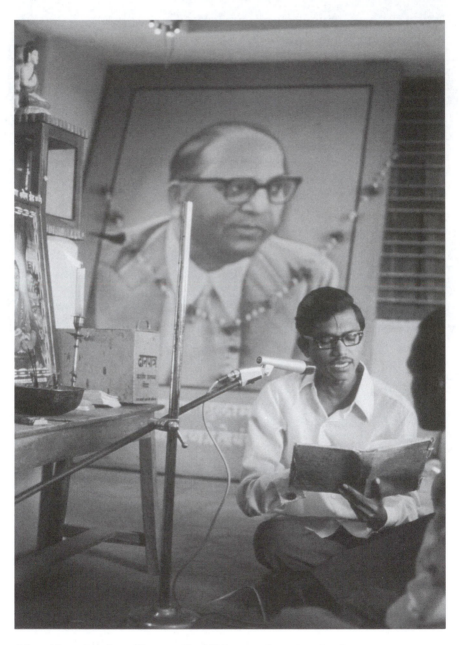

*Man chanting in a Nagpur Buddhist temple; portrait of
Dr. B. R. Ambedkar in background.*
ELEANOR ZELLIOT

Chapter Eight

Caste in Contemporary India

ELEANOR ZELLIOT

Caste is one of the most pervasive and controversial aspects of life in India. It is found in all religions in India, including—although not sanctioned by scripture—Christianity and Sikhism. Only tribal peoples are totally outside the system. It is a form of graded inequality with a varied but distinct hierarchy wherever it exists. In some form, it has been a factor in Indian society for at least 2,500 years.

The origin of caste in terms of the classic texts has been described in the introduction of this volume in terms of the picturesque image of the primeval man creating by sacrifice the four varnas: Brahmins from his mouth, Kshatriya from his arms, Vaishya from his thighs, and Shudras from his feet. The word *varna* itself means "color" or "covering," and this has led to a racial theory of caste that has become one of the most controversial of the many theories surrounding caste. The system is an integral part of the concept of varnashramadharma, and the three upper varnas were given an initiation ritual, which made them the "twice-born." Numerically, the twice-born have always comprised only a small percentage of castes as a whole.

The law books that were created in the first centuries of the common era vastly complicated the whole notion of caste. Privileges, punishments, and obligations were specific to each varna to control behavior, to deal with caste relations, and to make clear the scale of purity and pollution on which the hierarchy was based. Women were generally assigned a totally subordinate role. There are many such law books, but the best known, the symbolic book of Brahmin authority, is the Laws of Manu, the book of the "first man," Manu, created some 2,000 years ago.

Manu is particularly harsh and strict on the character and the ideal behavior of Shudras and often of women as well. He writes much advice like this: "the Lord assigned only one activity to a Shudra, serving the higher varnas" (I:91). The Shudras (and women) were not allowed to recite the Vedas. This restriction removed Shudras and women from what was seen as the heart of Hindu orthodoxy and from the priesthood. The most horrendous punishments are found in the *Medhatithi*, a commentary on Manu, probably dating from the early years of the Common Era. If a Shudra intentionally listens so that he may commit the Veda to memory, his ears should be filled with molten lead and lac. If he utters a word of the Veda, his tongue should be cut in two. If he masters the Veda, his body should be cut to pieces (Dutt 1968, 178). The restrictions were also applied to the performance of austerities for a religious purpose, as we will see later in the story of the Ramayana.

The classic texts also offered an explanation for one's birth in a certain caste. The doctrine of karma, so satisfying to some castes, is explained in the Gautama Sutra this way: "People belonging to the different classes and orders of life who are steadfastly devoted to the Laws proper to them enjoy the fruits of their deeds after death; and they, with the residue of those fruits, take birth again in a prosperous region, a high caste, and a distinguished family, with a handsome body, long life, deep Vedic learning, and virtuous conduct, and with great wealth, happiness, and intelligence" (Olivelle 1999, 97). And, of course, the "Laws proper to them" are different for each varna or caste. Duty is a strong and loaded word in India, but it must be added that belief in karma is not totally universal. And though the privileges for Shudras are nonexistent, Shudras are allowed more freedom than are the Brahmins. It must be said that the requirements of Brahminhood are many and detailed. The male Brahmin is the sacrificer, and sacrifice and ritual are essential, it is believed, for the maintenance of the order of the universe. To do this, the Brahmin must be pure, and he must protect his purity with great thoroughness and also safeguard the purity of his wife.

The duties of a Shudra are given in one source as these: "He should make ancestral offerings; support his dependents; be faithful to his wife; serve the upper classes; seek his livelihood from them; use their discarded shoes, umbrellas, clothes and mats and the like; and eat their leftovers." But Chapter 10 of the Gautama Sutra ends with the surprising statement, "If Aryans do the jobs of non-Aryans and vice versa, they become equal" (Olivelle 1999, 56). "Aryans" here refers to the word the Vedic upper classes called themselves; it means "pure" or "noble" and indicates the three "twice-born" varnas.

The classical law codes of ancient India often seem humorous in their pedantry about the punishment of sin. For instance, there are various penances for misdeeds, and this one involves the Shudra: "Crow, chameleon, peacock, Cakravaka goose, Hamsa goose, Bhasa vulture, frog, common mongoose, Derika rat and dog—the penance for killing any of these is the same as for killing a Sudra" (Olivelle 1999, 36). And the times in which impurity does not exist are varied: in battle, when the country is invaded or when the town or village is on fire, or on public roads that are purified "by the rays of the sun and the moon and by the wind."

In these law books, which probably were never the code of any specific kingdom, the formation of new groups is explained by unequal sexual alliances, the worst being the progeny of a lower-caste man and a higher-caste woman. The name that stands for the lowest of the low, *chandala,* means the product of a Shudra man and a Brahmin woman. The basis for all this is the idea of purity and pollution, the Brahmin being the purest, the Shudra the carrier of pollution. The idea of an Untouchable caste even less pure than the Shudra is not in the Vedas or the law books, which list only four varnas.

What are we to make of these ancient texts? They clearly were never more than fictional law, ideas that were an ideal for some orthodox Brahmin-dominated society, but they do have echoes in the modern period. One of the Hindu holy men said recently that the life of a cow was more important than the life of an Untouchable, a statement roundly criticized all over India.

There is no historic evidence that such punishments as decreed for the Shudra pursuing religious privilege were carried out. However, Valmiki's Sanskrit Ramayana, which dates roughly from the same period as the Laws of Manu, tells the basic story of Rama and includes this passage about the punishment of a Shudra who practiced disciplines that were the domain of the Brahmin:

> One day Rama saw an ascetic performing austerities beside a tank, with his head downwards and his legs upward. Rama asked him why he was performing such rites, and to which caste he belonged. The ascetic, whose name was Shambuka, said that he was a Shudra, and went through such austerities that he might reach the celestials with his body. On hearing this, Rama cut off his head, upon which Indra, Agni and the other celestials, showered down flowers, and praised him for having "performed this god-like work." (Valmiki 1896, 132)

The episode, however, is *not* in the most popular version of the Ramayana, the *Ramcharitmanas* (the lake of the story of Rama), by Tulsidas, which is in Hindi and is the basis for the enactment of the story in the popular *Ram Lila* dramas. But the Shambuka story is well known to low castes, who identify with the mistreated Shambuka. It must also be added that the villain of the northern versions of Rama's story, Ravana, who was a Brahmin and an evil man, practiced austerities to gain power. It was his abduction of Sita, Rama's wife, however, that brought Rama to war against him, and Rama's killing of this Brahmin was not a sin. In the popular mind there is another story, that of a tribal woman who tasted berries to see if they were sweet before offering them to Rama, who ate them willingly in spite of pollution rules!

The varna system itself is still an image of human organization that is the subject of belief, disbelief, and much comment. It received sanction in the Bhagavad Gita. Krishna, speaking to Arjuna as his charioteer on the verge of battle, tells him that he created the four varnas according to mankind's various qualities (IV:13) and that each varna should do its duty, Arjuna's duty as a Kshatriya being to fight. Gandhi's devotion to the Gita may be the reason for his belief in the varna system, which he saw as similar to the four fingers of a hand—all equal and necessary. The varna system is also reflected today in the ceremony of initiation for Brahmins, Kshatriyas, and Vaishyas that enables them, as the twice-born, to begin the study of the Vedas and often symbolizes superior status. But, in general, varna is not nearly as important as jati, the smaller endogamous unit that may for the most part be fitted into the varna system but that seems to have had a different origin and certainly has greater relevance to society today. There are perhaps 4,000 jatis, and they form the basic unit of the caste system.

Varna and Jati

The varna system does not work even as a rough outline of caste all over India today. True, everywhere there are Brahmins and Untouchables (a group not mentioned in the classic texts), soldiers and rulers, merchants, farmers, artisans and laborers. But the Shudras, probably even as the law books were being compiled, were far more than servants. As the Vaishyas began to specialize in trading and business, the land came into the hands of Shudras, and land is the wealth of those who live in India's villages. The "twice-born castes" are probably no more than 15 percent of the population, and the great majority of people are Shudras, Untouchables, Tribals, Muslims, Sikhs, Jains, Christians, and Buddhists, with the Shudras by far the largest group among these. Moreover, in the west central and southern parts of India, there are no Kshatriyas or Vaishyas; although soldiers and merchants do exist, they are classed as Shudras by those for whom varna is meaningful. The division in the south and Maharashtra is Brahmin, Shudra, and Untouchable. In the northern part of India, the Vaishyas have become not "the people," as the original Sanskrit word indicated, but merchants; and the Shudras are peasants, farmers, artisans, musicians, painters, ironmongers, tailors, goldsmiths—that is, anyone who works with his or her hands. The Shudra today has the advantage of numbers as well as the possibility of wealth from land and in today's India often holds political power.

The real unit of caste is the jati, and the some 4,000 jatis in India may be grouped roughly, very roughly, into the varna scheme, at least in the north. A jati is usually found in one language area and is defined by endogamy (marriage within the group), food practices and dining together, common myths and customs, and somewhat by occupation. It is the basic form of social organization, and larger castes are divided into many jatis in each area. It is well to observe that the word *caste,* which covers both varna and jati, is from the writings of the Portuguese, who entered the west coast of India in 1492. They described the groups they observed as *castas,* meaning species or breeds, tribes, races, clans, or lineages (Marriott and Inden 1985, 348). There is no word in the Indian languages as inclusive as "caste." *Varna* and *jati* are the words used for the English word *caste.*

The division of humanity into jatis in India will be clearer if we look at the caste structure of one language area before we consider the theories of origin and the contemporary nature of the system.

The Jatis of Maharashtra

In the west central state of Maharashtra, the threefold division of caste holds: Brahmins, Shudras, Untouchables. The dominant Brahmin caste (but only in the modern period) is the Chitpavan Brahmins. The name *Chitpavan* can mean "pure from the pyre" or "pure in heart." An alternate name is Konkanastha, which means they came from the Konkan coast on the Arabian Sea, an area just below the modern city of Bombay or Mumbai. Their myth is that the god Parashurama created the caste from the bodies of shipwrecked sailors, purified on the pyre, restored to life and taught Brahmin rites. The physical appearance of many of the caste invites speculation. Were they originally Turks, Iranians, Egyptians, Greeks, Jews, Berbers, from further north in India, or what? Many have aquiline noses and/or blue, green, or gray eyes.

The Chitpavans began their migration from the coastal area in the late seventeenth century at the invitation of King Shahu, who asked Balaji Vishvanath Bhat (a Chitpavan Brahmin) to serve as prime minister of the Maratha empire. That post within a few years allowed the Brahmin to become the chief ruler of the empire, a Brahmin doing Kshatriya work! The Chitpavans never served as priests but did flock to Varanasi to become Sanskrit scholars. They also early on took advantage of the British need for English speakers and became clerks, administrators, lawyers, scholars, and teachers, and in the nineteenth century they entered the political world. The best-known names of Maratha history after the British took over the area in 1818 are Chitpavan: among them, Mahadeo Govind Ranade, Gopal Krishna Gokhale, and Bal Ganghadar Tilak. Recently Chitpavans have entered high-tech business; many have migrated to England, the United States, or to international organizations in Switzerland (Marriott and Inden 1985, 348–356; Zelliot 1992, 68–71).

The priestly Brahmins in the Marathi-speaking area were and are Deshastha Brahmins, whose name means they come from the Desh, or the inland portion of the modern state of Maharashtra, but they also are found in contemporary Karnataka, the state just to the south. They served as village accountants as well as performing the priestly duties of a Brahmin. Their division into Rigvedi and Yajurvedi Brahmins who eat together but do not intermarry, and the further division of the Rigvedis into followers of the god Shiva and followers of the god Vishnu, indicates something of the complication of a single jati branch. There are a number of other smaller Brahmin jatis, but the total percentage of Brahmins in the Marathi-speaking area is no more than 4 percent.

The largest grouping of castes in the state are the Marathas, who form about 50 percent of the population in Maharashtra and have lent their name to the huge territory that was centered in the area in the seventeenth and eighteenth centuries, the Maratha empire. The previously allied but separate caste, the Kunbis, are now grouped as Marathas. They are landowners, farmers, cultivators, and soldiers, and because India is still largely rural, they have great political power in the Indian democracy. After a Maharashtrian Brahmin assassinated Mahatma Gandhi in 1948, Brahmin power declined, and Marathas dominated politics in the state until very recently, when political groups supporting the idea of Hindutva allowed some Brahmins to reenter politics. Throughout premodern and modern history, the Marathas have been chieftains and warriors. In the seventeenth century, a Maratha prince, Shivaji, was able to create a unified territory out of a number of chieftains' fiefs. His Maratha state, which rebelled successfully against Mughal power, is still seen as a golden age, and Shivaji, who died in 1680, as the ideal warrior and ruler, still a Maratha hero known to every school-child. Certain Maratha families claim to be Kshatriya, related to the warriors of Rajasthan. The development of sugar cooperatives in the modern period has given Marathas in the southern part of the Desh considerable wealth.

The artisan and service castes—Telis (oil pressers), Malis (gardeners), Sutars (carpenters), and the like—are grouped with Marathas in any classification of the varnas in Maharashtra, but except for Brahmins and Untouchables, little attention is paid to castes as part of the varna system, and no one says he or she is a Shudra.

Outside the varna system but very much in the caste hierarchy are the Untouchable castes of Maharashtra. The largest group are the Mahars, who form about 9 percent of the state's population. Their position in society was as village servants who brought firewood to the cremation ground, carried the village treasure to the central court, hauled off the dead cattle, carried death messages, and took care of the horses of the traveling government officials—a variety of responsibilities, few of which were polluting, none of which involved a craft. The modern period found them forced to find new occupations, which they did in the British army until the late nineteenth century, and then in the mills of Bombay and the railroads of the British raj. They also developed a spirit of rebellion against their low status and in the twentieth century produced an all-India leader, Dr. B. R. Ambedkar, who won for all Untouchables in India certain rights of representation in government matters (Keer 1992; Zelliot 2001). Most Mahars followed Ambedkar into the Buddhist religion and now call themselves Buddhists. The word *dalit* ("oppressed") is used in general for aspects of their movement. The Dalit literary movement begun in Maharashtra in the early 1970s is now spreading across India as more Untouchable castes find their voices (Dangle 1992).

The two other important Untouchable castes in the Marathi area are the Chambhars, leather workers, who rank above the Mahars when the castes are assigned hierarchical places, and the Mangs, rope makers and musicians, who rank below others. There is no Marathi-speaking Bhangi caste, so the removers of human waste and scavengers are generally migrants from Gujarat, Rajasthan, or the Hindi-speaking areas. Although lower castes now do not generally claim a higher varna status, there is an effort to use a respectable name. Chambhars now prefer to call themselves by the Sanskritized name *Chamarkars* and have succeeded fairly well in the modern world because of their business base in leather. Mangs, who now call themselves by the Sanskritic word *Matangs,* have not managed to turn their traditional work into a modern economic benefit and are only now beginning an awakening of self-respect and ambition. The great majority of Untouchable castes are landless agricultural laborers.

The complexity of the Maharashtrian scene can be duplicated in every area in India, often with greater numbers of castes involved. Many villages in the north contain as many as twenty castes. Some states have dominant agricultural castes similar to the Maratha caste, such as the Jats in the Punjab and Haryana. Andhra Pradesh has a caste that resembles the Mahars, the Malas, but most states do not. Chamars dominate the Untouchable groups in the north, and leather-working castes are found everywhere. Bhangis, many of whom prefer to be called *Valmikis,* are omnipresent in the north. The structure of caste in each language area must be considered separately if one is to understand the caste movements in that area. The rise of the Bahujan Samaj Party (Party of the Majority; BSP) in Uttar Pradesh, for instance, must be seen as possible due to the large base of the party in the Chamar caste. In Gujarat, the merchant castes, both Hindu and Jain, dominate rather than the Brahmins. In Tamil Nadu, the Chettiyars are merchants par excellence but are considered Shudras in the caste hierarchy.

This sketch of jatis in Maharashtra and elsewhere leaves one with many questions about the varna theory of caste. Clearly the Marathas are not "servants of all," and just as clearly not all Brahmin castes are priestly. And how do the Untouchables fit into the fourfold varna theory? Clearly they do not. Perhaps the Aryan tribes brought with them into India a loose class system of Brahmin priests, Kshatriya warriors and kings, and common citizens,

Vaishyas, a system of three groups found in classical Greece. Shudras may have emerged out of either unsuccessful Aryans or native inhabitants who could not adjust to Aryan domination. There were also tribal groups outside the system. It would also seem that India in the first millennium BCE possessed some sort of exclusion theory that made endogamous groups prevalent, and those groups were fit into the varna scheme, however awkwardly, by the Brahmin lawgivers, whose theoretical works indicate a rigid system that probably never existed.

The Theories of Caste

There are many theories of the origin of caste, none of which are totally satisfactory. One is the race theory, which differentiates a race of "Aryans" from that of the people who lived in India when the Aryans entered (Risley 1908). This theory now sets Aryan against Dravidian, a name used for the languages and peoples of the four states of south India. Another is a purity and pollution theory, with the necessity of the priestly caste to maintain absolute purity and the creation of a group at the bottom who absorbed all pollution. This theory was best elaborated by Dumont in his *Homo Hierarchicus* but also in a strange way has been presented by the Untouchable leader and scholar B. R. Ambedkar, who held that the Brahmin pollution and purity ideas, which insisted on marriage within the group, were then copied by other castes, each forming an endogamous group that was then ranked hierarchically according to degrees of pollution (Ambedkar 1979). Some scholars hold that castes were formed when tribal groups entered mainstream society, clan becoming class or caste based on access to economic resources. Others see it as an elaboration of certain ideas of taboo. Recently, caste development has been linked to patriarchy (Jaiswal 1998).

Early scholars tended to adopt a racial theory of caste. The Aryans were seen as a fair Indo-European people coming into conflict with dark-skinned inhabitants of the land they "conquered." This theory was in part based on the fact, discovered by William Jones in the eighteenth century, that Sanskrit, the language of the

Vedas, was related closely to Greek and Latin, forming part of a huge Indo-European language family. Subsequent research and careful reading of the texts, however, indicate that the race theory does not hold up. The Aryans (remember, the word simply means "pure" or "noble") did not come as an invading force but probably trickled into India over a period of years in the second millennium BCE, adapting their language and their ways to fit in with the inhabitants with whom they mixed. Sanskrit contains elements not found in the Greek and Roman alphabets, such as retroflex consonants. And it is clear that Aryans could be enemies of each other, and the group seen as those already in India, "Dashyas," could become part of the ruling elite. Most scholars now hold that there was an early mix of all groups. "R. S. Sharma has shown that in later Vedic times *sudras* constituted a small servile class of defeated and dispossessed Aryans and non-Aryans employed in domestic labour" (Jaiswal 1998, 70).

It should be noted that Indo-European (Aryan) and Dravidian are both terms of language, not race. But today there is considerable belief in the race theory among ordinary people. In spite of Ambedkar's insistence that all Indians were of one race, many Untouchable groups believe they were once "Lords of the Earth," dispossessed when the Aryans conquered India. But where did Untouchables come from? Ambedkar, their chief leader, thought they had been Buddhists, condemned to live outside the village when Hinduism became totally dominant, probably in the fourth century CE. Jha (1975) denies this theory, although he too finds that the development of Untouchable castes led to a solid hierarchical system in the fourth century. The classic texts mention a low-born Chandala whose work was in cremation grounds and as a village guard, and this seems to be the prototype of the Untouchable, but the idea of groups with lower status than the Shudra is a later development (Jha 1975, 14–31; Zelliot 1988, 169–171). The term *avarna,* without varna, was used, or *panchama,* the "fifth," and later *asprishya* ("not to be touched"), and those considered Untouchable were not only cremation ground workers—as was the prototype Chandala—but also the removers of human waste and those who worked with leather. The name of the Untouchable caste of drummers (and of course the drum had a leather surface, leatherwork being considered highly polluting) in the south, the Parayan, has come into English as "pariah" to mean someone (or a dog) despised and rejected by others.

No one has provided a theory that totally explains the caste system as it exists in India today. The classical theory found in the Laws of Manu clearly was never based on actual observation, nor were the harsh punishments recommended for crossing caste boundaries probably ever enforced by any specific kingdom, but the theory should be noted: Unsuitable marriages between caste groups produced new and inferior castes. The theory probably evolved to protect the purity of upper-class women, but it may be responsible for one of the basic rules of each jati—endogamy, marriage only within the group.

The Nature of Caste

Two books have caused much rethinking of the nature of caste and its recent history. The most thorough (and controversial) theory of caste published recently is that of Louis Dumont, whose *Homo Hierarchicus: The Caste System and Its Implications* was first published in French in 1966. As the title indicates, Dumont sees the caste system as totally hierarchical, with the concepts of purity and pollution determining the place of a caste in the hierarchy. Critics of Dumont have accused him of seeing caste from a Brahminical point of view, of ignoring historical factors, of setting aside the king-Brahmin interaction with the power of the king at times dominant, of leaving "little or no room . . . for agency in [his] structural universe" (Parish 1996, 77), of not recognizing the links between economic and political power and caste. Nevertheless, he has caused much rethinking of the importance of polluting factors and the nature of hierarchy today.

Among those whose theories challenge or contrast Dumont are Declan Quigley (1993), who argues for tension between the forces of kingship and the forces of kinship, which, combined, create order in society. He builds his theory, with some criticism, on one of the earliest of scholarly theories, that of A. M. Hocart (1950). Dumont and some of his critics, as well as major scholars of Indian society, including G. W. Ghurye, McKim Marriott, T. N. Madan, and Andre Beteille, are represented well in Dipankar Gupta's *Social Stratification* (1993).

Another book causing quite a bit of current discussion is *Castes of Mind: Colonialism and the Making of Modern India* (2001), by Nicholas Dirks. Dirks also considers kingship as a factor that challenges any easy domination by Brahmins, and he brings to the fore the certainty that caste became far more rigid in the colonial period due to the British need to categorize and control their subjects. The argument that the British solidified caste structure in their attempt to understand (and rule) India is compelling. The Census, begun in 1871, soon listed and arranged in hierarchical order the castes of the various areas. Castes dissatisfied with their ranking would appeal to the Census bureau, just as in earlier days a caste that felt its rights had been challenged would appeal to the local ruler. Most important, the *Castes and Tribes* volumes began to appear somewhat late in the nineteenth century. These were monumental surveys of all the castes in a language area or a unit of the British government such as the province of Bombay, which included an area from Sind in the north to part of Mysore (Karnataka) in the south. The work of describing all the castes and tribes of Bombay was discussed in 1885 and the project entrusted to R. E. Enthoven, superintendent of ethnography. Among those determining the project was H. H. Risley, whose *People of India* (1908) presented a comprehensive categorization of Indian peoples into seven races and racial combinations.

The *Castes and Tribes* volumes discussed in detail the origin of caste; racial influence; influence of occupation and religion; birth, marriage, and death ceremonies; endogamous units; and so on for each of thousands of castes. Although they did not rank castes in each area, they made very clear whether or not the caste was Brahmin or a tribe (outside the caste system and often not Hindu), and their relationship to other castes on the basis of food exchange and the taking of water. Eleven of the studies were reprinted in the 1970s by Cosmo Publications in Delhi. The material in the *Castes and Tribes* volumes seems to be the basis for a new publication of the "Peoples of India," a project begun in 1985 that identified, located, and studied 4,635 communities. Much has been added by the 600 scholars who participated in the series. Volume 2 is on Scheduled Castes (the word for Untouchables in common use since the British government prepared a schedule—or list—of castes deserving special places in government jobs and political structures in 1935) (Singh 1993). The *Gazetteers* were also produced in the colonial period; these delineated caste structure as well as geology, history, and so on, and have also been reprinted in the current era. The British certainly did not "create caste," but they most probably solidified the nature of the various castes and made the hierarchical structure more rigid.

A. L. Basham's monumental *The Wonder That Was India* (1954), used as a text for many introductory courses in Indian history, stresses the development of caste through thousands of years, with castes rising and falling in the social scale, and old castes dying out and new ones entering the system. The myth of the Chitpavan Brahmin, whose prototype bones were found on the coast of the Arabian Sea, seems to indicate the integration of a foreign group into the caste system. Certainly other examples from Maharashtra indicate a less-than-rigid system when it comes to warfare and power. In the course of the eighteenth century the Maratha empire broke into five pieces: three, Nagpur, Gwalior, and Baroda, were headed by Marathas, but the Brahmin *Peshwa* (prime minister) still ruled from Pune, and the important state of Indore was guided by a Holkar of the lowly shepherd caste of Dhangars.

Among the many other theories that challenge any easy definition of a static hierarchy or an always rigid system are those of Gloria Raheja (1988), who argues for the centrality of a dominant caste in any village, a theory first developed by M. N. Srinivas (2002). Srinivas's Sanskritization theory (2002), the emulation of Brahminical or Kshatriya mores, eventually enabling higher status, has also been very influential. Milton Singer (1973) has shown that traditional occupations could change, and both he and Suzanne and Lloyd Rudolph (1967) have produced extensive work on the modernizing of the Indian tradition.

There has been some scholarship on the structure of caste as it exists outside the Indian subcontinent. Best known is Gerald Berreman's work in the 1960s and 1970s, which argued that race in the United States and caste in India could be profitably compared. In a chapter entitled "Berreman Revisited: Caste and the Comparative Method," Ursula Sharma comments that Berreman's comparisons "encourage us to think about general interactional processes through which domination is achieved and resistance expressed" (Sharma 1994, 73). The clearest comparison of those in the lowest strata in another country is that to the Burakumin, the leather workers and butchers of Japan (Hane 1982). The Burakumin leadership of Japan is in touch now with India's Dalit (ex-Untouchable) leadership.

The Critics and Reformers of Caste

Throughout the ages, individuals and sects have challenged the right and justice of caste. The Buddha admitted anyone into the order of monks, and those monks did not practice untouchability, as indicated by a story of a monk taking water from the hand of a Chandala, a polluting individual. The Jain religion contained no special social message in its austere doctrine but was egalitarian, as was Buddhism. Jainism has continued in India as a religion that has no castes within it but is now very much like a jati, considered on a par with Hindu merchant castes. The Baul singers of Bengal seem to be without caste identity, and the Nath aesthetics have no interest in caste. The Mahanubhavs, a fourteenth-century unorthodox sect in Maharashtra, totally rejected caste. But the Mahanubhavs were pushed out of the mainstream of Maharashtrian life because of their radical attitudes and are not active as reformers today.

The philosophers and poets of the bhakti movement, which swept through India from south to north in the premodern period, practiced devotional religion rather than ritual. Many were outspoken critics of caste. They admitted all castes and women to their circles of saints and poets. The philosopher Ramananda is said to have inspired the Untouchable bhakta Ravidas and the Muslim-Hindu Kabir, both bhakti poets very much against the idea of caste hierarchy. Kabir in his direct and unorthodox way put it in these words:

> It's a heavy confusion.
> Veda, Koran, holiness, hell, woman, man,
>   a clay pot shot with air and sperm . . .
> When the pot falls apart, what do you call it?

Numskull! You've missed the point.
It's all one skin and bone, one piss and shit,
    one blood, one meat.
From one drop, a universe.
    Whose Brahmin? Who's Shudra? (Hess and Singh 1983, 67)

The poetry and legends of Ravidas make clear that in the bhakti religion there was equality, at least on a spiritual plane. He speaks of the high born coming to him in recognition of his worth, and this is an observation from several other sources, so it probably is true. Ravidas himself puts it this way:

I belong to the Chamar caste
And men of my caste still carry carcasses on
    the outskirts of Banaras.
But now, before me,
    even the Brahmin chief falls prostrate
Because Ravidas, Thy slave,
    has taken refuge in Thy Name. (Upadhyaya 1992, 32)

Others also acknowledged the high place Ravidas had earned among all men. Guru Ramdas (sixteenth century) praises Ravidas in this way:

Ravidas the Chamar praised God,
    and every moment sang the praises of the Old God.
Though of fallen jati he became exalted
    and all four castes came and fell at his feet.
    (Callewaert 1992, 11)

In Maharashtra, the Untouchable poet of the fourteenth century, Chokhamela, and his family could not enter the temple but were part of a circle of devotees who accepted them as devout equals, and four hundred of their poems have been preserved through the ages. Chokhamela accepted his karma, which makes him no longer a hero to today's Untouchables who deny karma as the determiner of caste, but he did cry out against ideas of pollution, saying that all were polluted by birth and death: "O Lord, who is pure?" (Zelliot

2001). The bhakti movement was, in terms of spiritual life and the inner circle, inclusive of all castes and of women. From the thirteenth through the seventeenth centuries, poets from some forty different castes emerged in the Marathi-speaking area. Brahmins did not dominate, although two of the most important saints were Brahmins. Dnyanadeo, whose commentary on the Bhagavad Gita (the *Dnyaneshwari*) is revered by most Maharashtrians, was a Deshastha Brahmin, son of a man who was outcasted for returning to family life from a period as a renouncer. Eknath, also a Deshastha Brahmin, produced the next most important document, a commentary on the Bhagavata Purana known as the *Eknathi Bhagavat*. He also, however, wrote drama-poems as if he were an Untouchable Mahar, a Kaikai (wandering fortune teller), a prostitute, a Mahanubhav, a passing Muslim, allowing each of these to tell of the glory of bhakti. Most of the other poet-saints were Shudras, including the most beloved poet of all, Tukaram.

The songs of all the saints, including those of Chokhamela, are sung on the annual pilgrimage to Pandharpur, which all the devout bhaktas, and a good many others, take in an unusually joyous spirit. Each poet-saints' *padukhas* (symbols of footprints) are carried by a group of devotees in a *dindi,* and there are a number of such dindis in each *palkhi,* a procession that begins from some saints' birthplace or place of *samadhi* (religious death) and winds its way to Pandharpur. Untouchables have their own dindis for their own poet-saints. The pilgrimage seems to breathe equality in the spiritual realm, but even here there are caste divisions. Irawati Karve, a Chitpavan Brahmin scholar, wrote movingly of her participation in the palkhi from Alandi, the place of Dnyanadeo's samadhi. She was lovingly accepted in a dindi of both Brahmins and Marathas, but she wrote sorrowfully of the permanent caste divisions that appeared in the cooking of the food and the eating arrangements:

> Every day I regretted the fact that one and the same *dindi* was divided into these two sections. All the people were clean, and they ate their food only after taking a bath. Then why this separateness? Was all this walking together, singing together, and reciting the poetry of the saints together directed only towards union in the other world while retaining separateness in this world? This question was in my mind

all the time. In the same way I had become friendly with the Brahmin group, the Maratha women had also taken me to their hearts. As I could not bring the groups together, I joined now one group and now the other, trying to construct a bridge—at least as far as I was concerned. After I had taken my meal with them, I felt that they were more friendly. Many of them walked alongside of me, held my hand, and told me many things about their life. Toward the end, they called me "Tai," meaning "Sister." A few of them said, "Mark you, Tai, we shall visit you in Pune." And then one young girl said, "But will you behave with us then as you are behaving now?" It was a simple question, but it touched me to the quick. We have been living near each other thousands of years, but they are still not of us and we are not of them. (Karve 1988, 153)

In Karnataka, the twelfth-century poet Basavanna went beyond poetry and encouraged the parents of a Brahmin and Untouchable couple to let them marry. Chaos and death followed, but the gesture has remained as testimony to his profound belief in equality. The radical anticaste beliefs of Basavanna, however, and his fellow poet-saints, did not carry over into the sect that arose later from that early devotion, the Lingayats. They now form a caste with Brahmin ritual specialists and no longer have an egalitarian attitude.

These examples from the bhakti movement indicate that although there clearly was equality on a spiritual plane, and some of the poets, both Untouchable and Brahmin, condemned caste, no specific social movement for an egalitarian society arose from the bhaktas. The names of Chokhamela, Ravidas, Tiruppan Alvar, and Nandanar, however, can be used to evoke pride among those of their castes who encourage self-respect or are attempting change.

In the nineteenth century in Maharashtra, Jotirao Phule (1827–1890) was a non-Brahmin reformer from the Mali (gardener) caste, an educator and writer whose fierce criticism of Brahminism and efforts to educate women and Untouchables are remembered vividly today. He founded the Satya Shodak Samaj ("truth-seeking society"), which attempted to create rational humanistic religion and in its day had tremendous effect. The non-Brahmin movement itself became political, tended to lose interest in social equality involving the lowest castes, and in the era of democracy brought political power to the Marathas and middle-level castes.

In the Punjab in 1875 the Arya Samaj reform movement was begun by Dayanand Saraswati (1824–1883), a Brahmin who rejected the caste system and stressed a revived and reformed Hinduism based on the Vedas, with varna status given according to merit and character. A large and important educational system resulted, but the Arya Samaj did not become casteless. Other reform organizations, the Brahmo Samaj of Bengal and the Prarthana Samaj of Bombay, produced reformers but no lasting attempt to destroy the caste system and no lasting universal brotherhood. Suvira Jaiswal's words seem to be true: "Hinduism has infinite capacity to tolerate any kind of theology as long as its caste structure remains unharmed" (Jaiswal 1998, 236).

The great caste reformers of the twentieth century were E. V. Ramasami, B. R. Ambedkar, and Mahatma Gandhi. Ramasami (1879–1973) began his Self-Respect Movement in 1925 (Geetha 2003), decrying "God, caste and Brahminism as a triple chain of bondage" (Padma Rao 1998, 123) and creating a proud sense of "Dravidianism," as opposed to the "Aryan" north. Dravidian is a language term used for the four south Indian languages, but it has come to be a racial term in the mind of many. Although Ramasami spent some time as a member of the Indian National Congress party and supported Gandhi, he eventually left to build a political alternative that culminated in Dravidian political parties, several of which dominate Tamil Nadu today. Ramasami also knew Dr. Ambedkar, and translated his strong statement *The Annihilation of Caste* into Tamil.

B. R. Ambedkar (1891–1956) continues to be the most important reform figure India's Untouchables have known. Born in the Mahar caste of the Marathi-speaking area, he became, with the help of non-Brahmin princes, the holder of doctorates from Columbia University and London and a barrister. He used this remarkable education to speak to every political, educational, and economic issue, winning representation in government bodies and offices for Untouchables. He also created a higher educational system and many social and political institutions. He disputed with Gandhi because he thought political rights and legal protection were more important and productive than Gandhi's belief in "change of heart" on the part of higher-caste Hindus, and he believed a separate electorate was the only way Untouchables could have true political representation. Gandhi opposed this special system for Untouchables in a "fast unto death" in 1932, and from that point on, there was enmity between Ambedkar and the Indian National Congress. But in the first flush of enthusiasm for equality as India progressed toward independence, Ambedkar was named chair of the drafting committee of the Indian Constitution and became the law minister in India's first independent cabinet. In the end he rejected Hinduism and initiated a Buddhist conversion movement that continues today. As a symbol of Dalit pride and assertion, he is even more important now than he was during his lifetime.

Gandhi's stance on caste included great compassion for Untouchables, whom he called "Harijans"—people of God, a name politicized Untouchables like Ambedkar rejected. He brought an Untouchable family into his first ashrama and in his later years urged inter-caste marriages, but he upheld the virtues of the varna system and devoted his energies to change through convincing the higher castes to eliminate their prejudices against Untouchables. Gandhi himself had gone against the rules of his jati (the Modh Banias, a Vaishya group) by going over the forbidden seas to England to study law and was outcasted by that caste. He was already married, however, and this is important because marriage is within the caste and someone outcasted cannot find a partner. Gandhi's life was lived in an all-India atmosphere, so the outcasting made little difference to him or others and has been largely forgotten. His quarrel with Ambedkar over separate electorates, however, is still remembered.

Caste in the Contemporary Period

The latest effort to deal with all the changes of the modern period is the lucidly written and comprehensive book by Susan Bayly, which is based on history but also includes a study of various theories, caste in everyday life, and "caste wars and the mandate of violence" (Bayly 1999, 342). It concludes with the swearing in of K. R.

Narayanan in 1997 as the first Dalit to become president of India, an event of historic importance made even more so by his active and courageous presidency. The ascendancy of Narayanan may be related to the political importance of Dalit castes now, and that importance in electoral numbers is probably the most important change of the times, but there are other changes.

New caste clusters have been formed both in the premodern and modern periods. An example of the modern period amalgamation is in the absorption of the lower-class peasant farmers known as Kunbis into the large Maratha caste. Premodern formations can be represented by the Kayasthas, groups which entered Mughal service beginning in the sixteenth century as administrators, learning Persian and relating to Muslim rule as Brahmins, the traditional administrators, were more reluctant to do. The Kayasthas claimed Kshatriya status, however, not Brahmin. Another group known all over India as a caste are the Marwaris, people from a trading background in the area known as Marwar in Rajasthan, who have migrated all over India for trade, money lending, and business. They claim Vaishya status.

Caste relationships are most apparent in India's villages, where over 70 percent of people live. The *jajmani* system, whereby the serving castes through generations worked with "their" own *jajman* (overlord), was important in the north. However, in Maharashtra, the serving castes worked for the entire village at the direction of the headman, or *patil,* in a system called *balutedari,* and there were traditionally twelve *balutedars,* including Untouchable Mahars and Brahmin Joshi (astrologers), who received *balut,* a share of the harvest. In both forms of organization, payment was generally in grain and in kind, and especially in the *jajmani* system it involved quite a bit of interdependence. As cash economies began to come into play and transportation from village to city became easier, both systems broke down, although most villages still retain a number of castes filling certain functions.

The kinship and marriage systems in villages have not been affected very much by modernity. In northern India, strict rules of endogamy mean that a couple related more closely than seven generations cannot be married, and never a couple from the same village. In the south and Maharashtra, cross-cousin marriages—for example, a son with his mother's brother's daughter—are allowed and favored, and the couple can come from the same village. In both systems, marriages are arranged and the kinship group is an essential social unit, coming together for weddings and funerals and at times acting as a form of social protection. Marriages in the urban setting are also usually arranged, and marriages and funerals can bring together today even far-flung members of the larger family.

Caste has responded to modernity in a number of ways. One way, probably practiced through the ages, M. N. Srinivas termed "Sanskritization," which is to adopt the practices of higher castes in the hope of raising status. An example of this method, successfully combined with economic factors, is that of the Shanars of Tamil Nadu, who, based on the wealth they could extract from their ownership of coconut trees and the toddy tapping that was their profession, and aided by Protestant Christian mission schools and the development of coffee plantations that provided employment, rose to higher status and claimed the name of Nadar (Hardgrave 1969). Another response is in caste organizations, a response still apparent when a group of related jatis is challenged. Voting as a block has given large groups of jatis political clout; whether this strengthens caste or encourages more egalitarian sharing of power is a matter of current debate.

Change from Sanskritization to radical religious and political efforts has been documented in Agra. Owen Lynch's 1969 study of the Jatavs of Agra remains the classic work on the efforts of an Untouchable caste to claim high status as Kshatriyas. The Jatavs in the 1920s claimed to be Yadavs and hence Kshatriya, a claim their occupation of work with leather made difficult to sustain. Myths of loss of status undergirded this attempt, but in the end the Jatavs became committed to the Ambedkar movement and were, as such, the first group in the north to follow his political and religious path. They converted almost en masse in the initial 1956 conversion to Buddhism and have become more powerful in Agra politics through great effort.

The two greatest changes today are in the realms of politics and "affirmative action," the Indian reservation system in government establishments and political representation. Dr. Ambedkar began the first of his three political parties in 1937 with some success, but the current party established in his last year, the Republican Party, is factionalized and powerful only in a few local areas. In the south, several parties have recently arisen, one taking the name of the earlier Maharashtrian militant movement, the Dalit Panthers. The most successful is the Bahujan Samaj Party (BSP), "the party of the majority of the people," established by Kanshi Ram, an Untouchable Sikh. Its most remarkable victory is in India's largest state, Uttar Pradesh, which has been ruled for three periods by a Chamar woman, Mayawati, whose BSP success rests on a highly politicized caste of Chamars as well as on her extraordinary political skills (Jaffrelot 2003; Pai 2002).

The most far-ranging change in modern times affecting caste, and even its structure, is the reservation system. There has been in place since 1935 nationally (and even longer in the south) a system of reservations for the bottom layers of society that allowed representation on a quota system in all government bodies and in government employment and government-aided educational institutions. Castes and tribes that met certain criteria of discrimination were placed on a list or schedule in the government reorganization of 1935, and so "Scheduled Castes" and "Scheduled Tribes" became the names used for Untouchables and Adivasis, or Tribals. Although the quotas at the highest levels of officialdom have never been completely filled, the system has created a large number of educated Scheduled Castes, now known as Dalits, many of whom hold important government positions. The reservation system is comprehensive both for government jobs and in government-aided educational institutions, both for students and teachers, and has produced a critical mass of educated Dalits who, in turn, have founded educational institutions, literary movements, and self-help organizations. Dalit groups are currently demanding that the reservation system, or "affirmative action," be extended to the private sector.

A rather passive group of Scheduled Castes and Scheduled Tribes representatives, elected to government bodies by a majority of voters, has been less successful in creating change. The political representatives do allow a certain amount of connection with government benefits for the Scheduled Caste and Tribe members, but few representatives speak out in ways that might annoy the majority of voters who elect them.

In 1990 the reservation system underwent a massive change. Prime Minister V. P. Singh of the Janata Party implemented an earlier report from the Mandal Commission on the need to extend reservations to other "backward castes" numbering 3,743. In the Indian Constitution, reservations were limited to 50 percent of the positions in government, and because the Scheduled Tribes and Scheduled Castes together were eligible for 22 percent, that left 27 percent that could be alloted to over 50 percent of the population, castes that were socially and/or economically backward. Even though this left 50 percent of the government positions in the hands of the 15 or so percent of the three upper castes, there was a frenzied backlash. Young men, chiefly Brahmin, protested by immolating themselves, and perhaps as many as sixty died. The controversy rages on, although without such extreme protests. "Mandalisation" is a phrase much used nowadays, but studies of its total impact have yet to be made. Together with the rise of the political parties, the Mandal Commission report is the most important development in contemporary politics.

The reservation system, the continuing stimulus of the figure of Ambedkar, and the politicization of the lower classes have all encouraged Dalits to claim rights and dignity. But the other side of the dynamic of this movement is that when Dalits claim land in defiance of caste Hindus, use wells or ponds closed to them, begin a relationship with an upper-caste woman, or in other words cross the invisible line that keeps them in their place, there is violence, especially in the rural areas (Narula 1999).

Many Indians will tell you that caste is illegal in India. Unfortunately, this is like saying "race is illegal." What is illegal in India is discrimination. The "Fundamental Rights" section of the Constitution of India lists the following provisions:

> 15 (1) The State shall not discriminate against any citizens on grounds only of religion, race, caste, sex, place of birth or any of them.

(2) No citizen shall, on grounds only of religion, race, caste, sex, place of birth or any of them, be subject to any disability, liability, restriction or condition with regard to—

(1) access to shops, public restaurants, hotels and places of public entertainment: or

(2) the use of wells, tanks, bathing ghats, roads and places of public resort maintained wholly or party out of State funds or dedicated to the use of the general public.

Article 17 is very clear:

"Untouchability" is abolished and its practice in any form is forbidden. The enforcement of any disability arising out of "Untouchability" shall be an offense punishable in accordance with law.

At the 2001 World Conference against Racism held in Durban, South Africa, Dalit representatives pled for the inclusion of Untouchables as descent-based groups akin to race groups and subject to discrimination as such. The government of India denied their claim.

A sophisticated and very honest editorial by Narendra Pani and Shiv Viswanathan on the current state of castes in India appeared on February 22, 2003, in the *Times of India*.

Does caste still call the shots in modern India?
Yes. Caste is as local as you want, as global as you can get.

If you drop your ideological spectacles, your secularist contact lenses and stop swinging on the indifference curve of right and left, your vision clears and it is apparent that caste lives and calls the shots.

Caste is continually reinventing itself. Caste is to-day what caste does. It is best understood not as an old orientalist code but a new instrumentalist grammar that shifts from context to context.

Caste has shifted its original axis from a horizontal perspective to a wider vertical amalgamation. It is part community, part association, even cadre.

We have today castes functioning as vote banks, creating the original yellow pages as caste directories, providing caste associations for urban migrations and services. Caste is as local as you want, as global as you can get. Between its rigidity and its plasticity, caste creates a civil society of welfare in a state without security nets.

It is the diversity of castes still performing different functions that sustains our diversity in ritual and botanical life.

It creates new civil societies of competence and relief allowing victims to recover from disasters. In fact NGOs [nongovernmental organizations] have a lot to learn from caste if they wish to transcend it.

Caste today can be understood in terms of two metaphors—the organism and the virus. An organism lives in symbiosis with the host or the environment. A virus destroys it.

Caste as organism provides symbiotic spaces in the city and the Diaspora. But as virus it can be lethal providing an edge of violence to the future.

Caste threatens the discourse of citizenship but as a Mandalist discourse it has provided the dynamics of middle caste electoral politics. Mandalism redefines the worldview of Indian democracy, opening possibilities and yet truncating democracy into horizontal segments.

But while caste is protean for the middle castes, it is procrustean for the Dalits. As vote banks Dalits have entered politics in a big way yet Dalit politics is a reminder for the limits of casteism. It is a reminder that democracy creates a cheat code in terms of caste, truncating democratic politics in the very act of opening it.

Caste eventually is a grammar of symbolic violence terrorising vulnerable groups in segments. Its moral indifference and its technological illiteracy are caught in the figure of the scavenger. The presence of scavenger ensures that caste narratives can never deodorise themselves.

Casteism binds the moral imagination, rendering democracy a ritual of hypocrisy. It is this Janus edge of caste that turns the celebration of its inventiveness into a wall. Castes hide this often by operating through clichés. In fact a cliché sums it all. 'Caste is dying but long live casteism.' In this, lies the pity. (*Source:* Times of India, *reprinted with permission*)

BIBLIOGRAPHY

Ambedkar, B. R. *The Annihilation of Caste.* Bombay: Privately printed, 1936.
———. *Dr. Babasaheb Ambedkar: Writings and Speeches.* 18 vols. Edited by
    Vasant Moon. Bombay: Department of Education, Government of
    Maharashtra, 1979.
Basham, A. L. *The Wonder That Was India.* New York: Grove Press, 1954.
Bayly, Susan. *Caste, Society, and Politics in India from the Eighteenth Century to
    the Modern Age.* Vol. IV, 3 in the New Cambridge History of India series.
    Cambridge: Cambridge University Press, 1999.
Callewaert, Winand M., and Peter G. Friedlander. *The Life and Works of
    Raidas.* New Delhi: Manohar Publishers and Distributors, 1992.
Dangle, Arjun, ed. *Poisoned Bread: Translations from Modern Marathi Dalit
    Literature.* Hyderabad: Orient Longman, 1992.
Dirks, Nicholas. *Castes of Mind: Colonialism and the Making of Modern India.*
    Princeton: Princeton University Press, 2001.
Dumont, Louis. *Homo Hierarchicus: The Caste System and Its Implications.*
    Translated by Mark Sainsbury, Louis Dumont, and Basia Gulati. Rev.
    English ed. Chicago: University of Chicago, 1980.
Dutt, N. K. *Origin and Growth of Caste in India.* Vol. 1, 2nd ed. Calcutta:
    Mukhopadhyaya, 1968. First edition published in 1931.
Geetha, V. "Anti-Caste Radicalism in Tamil Nadu: Remembered Moments
    from a Receding Past," in *Dalit International Newsletter* 8, 2 (June 2003):
    1, 9–11.
Gupta, Dipankar, ed. *Social Stratification.* Oxford in India Readings in
    Sociology and Social Anthropology. Delhi: Oxford University Press,
    1993.
Hane, Mikiso. *Peasants, Rebels, and Outcastes: The Underside of Modern Japan.*
    New York: Pantheon, 1982.
Hardgrave, Robert L., Jr. *The Nadars of Tamilnad.* Berkeley: University of
    California Press, 1969.
Hess, Linda, and Shukdev Singh, trans. *The Bijak of Kabir.* San Francisco:
    North Point Press, 1983.
Hocart, A. M. *Caste.* London: Methuen and Company, 1950.
Jaffrelot, Christophe. *India's Silent Revolution: The Rise of the Low Castes in
    North Indian Politics.* London: Hurst and Company, 2003.
Jaiswal, Suvira. *Caste: Origin, Function, and Dimensions of Change.* New
    Delhi: Manohar, 1998.
Jha, Vivekanand. "Stages in the History of Untouchables," in *Indian
    History Review* 2, 1 (1975): 14–31.

Karve, Irawati. "On the Road," in Eleanor Zelliot and Maxine Berntsen (eds.), *The Experience of Hinduism*. Albany: State University of New York Press, 1988. First published in English in the *Journal of Asian Studies* 22, 1 (1962): 13–29.

Keer, Dhananjay. *Dr. Ambedkar: Life and Mission*. 2nd ed. Bombay: Popular Prakashan, 1992.

Khare, Ravindra S. *The Changing Brahmans: Associations and Elites among the Kanya Kubjas of North India*. Chicago: University of Chicago, 1970.

Klass, Morton. *Caste: The Emergence of the South Asian Social System*. Philadelphia: Institute for the Study of Human Issues, 1980.

Kolenda, Pauline. *Caste in Contemporary India: Beyond Organic Solidarity*. Prospect Heights, Ill.: Waveland Press, 1978.

Lynch, Owen M. *The Politics of Untouchability: Social Mobility and Social Change in a City of India*. New York: Columbia University Press, 1969.

Marriott, Kim, and Ronald Inden. "Social Stratification: Caste," in *Encyclopedia Britannica*, 15th ed., vol. 27 (1985): 348–356.

Moon, Vasant. *Growing Up Untouchable*. Translated from the Marathi by Gail Omvedt. Lantham, Md.: Rowman and Littlefield, 2001.

Narula, Smita. *Broken People: Caste Violence against India's Untouchables*. New York: Human Rights Watch, 1999.

Olivelle, Patrick, trans. and ed. *Dharmasutras: The Law Codes of Ancient India*. Oxford: Oxford University Press, 1999.

Padma Rao, Katti. *Caste and Alternative Culture*. Translated by D. Anjaneyulu. Chennai: Gurukul Lutheran Theological College, 1998.

Pai, Sudha. *Dalit Assertion and the Unfinished Democratic Revolution: The Bahujan Samaj Party in Uttar Pradesh*. New Delhi: Sage Publications, 2002.

Parish, Steven M. *Hierarchy and Its Discontents: Culture and the Politics of Consciousness in Caste Society*. Philadelphia: University of Pennsylvania Press, 1996.

Quigley, Declan. *The Interpretation of Caste*. Oxford Studies in Social and Cultural Anthropology. Oxford: Clarendon Press, 1993.

Raheja, Gloria. *The Poison in the Gift: Ritual, Prestation, and the Dominant Caste in a North Indian Village*. Chicago: University of Chicago Press, 1988.

Risley, H. H. *The People of India*. Calcutta: Thacker, Spink, and Company, 1908.

Rudolph, L. T., and S. H. Rudolph. *The Modernity of Tradition: Political Developments in India*. Chicago: University of Chicago Press, 1969.

Sharma, Ursula. "Berreman Revisited: Caste and the Comparative
    Method," in Mary Searle-Chatterjee and Ursula Sharma (eds.),
    Contextualising Caste. Oxford: Blackwell Publishers, 1994: 72–91.

Singer, Milton, ed. *Entrepreneurship and Modernization of Occupational
    Cultures in South Asia*. Durham, N.C.: Duke University Program of
    Comparative Studies in Southern Asia, Monograph 12, 1973.

Singh, K. S., ed. *The Scheduled Castes*. Vol. 2. of The People of India series.
    Delhi: Anthropological Survey of India, Oxford University Press, 1993.

Srinivas, M. N., ed. *Caste: Its Twentieth Century Avatar*. New Delhi: Viking by
    Penguin Books, 1996.

———. *Collected Essays*. New Delhi: Oxford University Press, 2002.

Upadhyaya, K. N. *Guru Ravidas: Life and Teachings*. Punjab: Radha Soami
    Satsang Beas, 1982.

Valmiki. *The Ramayana of Valmiki*. London: Christian Literature Society,
    1896.

Zelliot, Eleanor. "Untouchability," in Ainslee Embree (ed.), *Encyclopedia of
    Asian History*. New York: Charles Scribners' Sons, 1988: 169–171.

———. "Chitpavan Brahmin," in Paul Hockings (ed.), *Encyclopedia of
    World Cultures*, vol. 3: *South Asia*. Boston: G. K. Hall, 1992: 68–71.

———. *From Untouchable to Dalit: Essays on the Ambedkar Movement*. 3rd ed.
    New Delhi: Manohar, 2001.

Two Indian women, dressed in colorful saris, attend a festival celebration.
COREL

Chapter Nine

Voices of Dissent

Gender and Changing Social Values in Hinduism

Kalpana Kannabiran

The issue of women's location and roles within Hinduism is complex and has been the subject of both debate and resistance for several centuries. The debates, which began with a juxtaposition of textual/ orthodox traditions against oral/devotional/heterodox traditions, gradually drew in other strains as well, such as the articulations of Hindu society created by early scholars of Hinduism and by reformers, nationalists, and leaders of groups such as the Self-Respect Movement. During the colonial period, these articulations were virtually all writing about women by men. Women's writing, however, stands in stark contrast to that of men across this entire period.

The textual/orthodox traditions are elaborated in the Hindu dharma literature as part of a tradition of universal law for the Hindus. Placing the Brahmin male at the center of the social universe, it contains an elaboration of the caste system that is prescriptive: Brahmin, Kshatriya, Vaishya, Shudra. Of these, the first three were the twice-born, "clean" castes, the men of which are entitled to initiation into Hinduism. A fifth order, the Untouchables, slaves who performed "menial chores" (cleansing villages, washing clothes, in general engaged directly in production and connected closely to organic life), was included later. The panchamas ("fifth"), or "Untouchable" castes, have for centuries been ghettoized in separate colonies, enslaved to the other four varnas in perpetual bondage. An additional implication for women of these castes is sexual slavery. The word *asprishya* (literally "untouchable") was first used in the *Vishnusmriti,* which prescribes death for any member of these castes who deliberately touches a member of a higher caste. However, this proscription on physical contact did not extend to sexual relations between upper-caste men and Untouchable women, sexual labor being part of the physical labor provided by slave women and appropriated by the upper-caste owner/master.

With few exceptions, the caste system is patrilineal and patrilocal. Despite wide variation in the practice of the caste system, formal education remained the preserve of the Brahmin male. Endogamy (specifically the absolute proscription on upper-caste women engaging in marital or other physical relationship with lower-caste men), ritual purity, commensality, and slavery defined the caste system. Within this framework, women and slaves figure as subjects, women by nature fickle and unchaste, whose sexuality, bodies, and minds must be reined in by the "dharma," the Laws of Manu epitomizing this view (Kannabiran 2000, 142–144).

At the other end of the discourse on women's position in Hinduism are the traditions of the heterodox sects and devotional movements such as the bhakti movement that allowed women to transcend the physical constraints imposed on them by institutions of caste, marriage, and female seclusion. Mirabai, Avvaiyar, Bahinabai, and Lal Dhed are examples of women who challenged the notions of subservient wifehood and conjugality central to the practice of orthodox Hinduism. Their pursuit of a larger devotion meant they would inhabit a public space and not be subject to normal restrictions of caste or patriarchy. This struggle was far from easy and met with often violent opposition from the conservatives, but they survived in their own lifetime and through their work for posterity. These women and others like them opened a whole new world to women of their times and later—a world they were free to inhabit on their own terms.

Whether in bhakti or orthodox Hinduism, gender is central to the construction of religious identity. On the face of it, the family seems to be at the base, the pivotal institution around which spin the intricacies of gender. We could extend Connell's assertion that "gender relations are present in all types of institutions" (Connell 2002, 30), to say that gender structures institutions, memory, and historical experience itself. Gender gets institutionalized in the everyday practices of living, but the process of institutionalization it-self.is neither fixed nor linear. In this process, though identities are mapped on women's bodies, the contours shift constantly, amoeba-like, with shifts in meaning hidden by similarity in form and nomenclature; or, as in the case of widow remarriage, apparently opposing practices signaling conformity to the same patriarchal norms. The fixity of terms over a period of a century, or the exis-tence of contrary practices at the same moment in history, there-fore tends to mask or distort the changes in values and systems of belief, and often the changes in the constitution of the nation itself, if the processes of change are not subjected to a complex, nuanced reading.

This chapter will explore some continuing, persistent themes of gender in Hindu society. What are the key themes, the constants, in the proliferation of concerns about women? And what does this tell us about the specific ways in which Hinduism is structured by patri-archy? Women's experience in Hinduism was problematized during the colonial period of the late nineteenth and early twentieth cen-turies. Practices of female infanticide, sati (widow immolation), en-forced widowhood (the prohibition of remarriage for widowed women), child marriage (prepubescent marriage, especially for girls, wherein girls were married by age six), pardah-pativrata (seclusion-chastity), restitution of conjugal rights, and marital rape were central to the debates on the position of women within Hin-duism. Today these themes continue to be central, despite an inter-vening period of reform, resistance, and prohibition through legis-lation.

Current engagements with the constraints that Hinduism im-poses on women and analyses of change therefore must draw semi-nally from the past in order to inscribe a new future. Tarabai Shinde was a key architect of the transition to a new womanhood in a predominantly Hindu caste-ridden society. Writing in fury over the conviction to death (later reduced to transportation to a penal settlement outside the state) of a young widow for the murder of her infant, Shinde wrote in 1882, "God brought this amazing universe into being, and he it was also who created men and women both. So is it true that only women's bodies are home to all kinds of wicked vices? Or have men got just the same faults as we find in women?" (Shinde [1882] 1994, 75).

Debates on social reform in the nineteenth century revolved around women. There were several inflections in these debates. Whereas Shinde marks a moment in the process of genealogy formation of a new womanhood, two other voices provide an interesting contrast in terms of intent and understanding. In the 1920s, Katherine Mayo, the American author of *Mother India,* launched a polemical attack against Indian self rule, arguing centrally that the sexual depravity of the Hindu was at the root of India's problems, drawing on the realities of child marriage, sati, the *devadasi* system (dedicating young women and girls to temples, literally by marrying them to the deity), untouchability, and so on, that were also the preoccupation of Indian reformers. Although in many ways Shinde was more scathing in her critique, Mayo's portrayal of Indian society in the early twentieth century created a storm.

> In the great orthodox Hindu majority, the girl looks for motherhood nine months after reaching puberty—or anywhere between the ages of fourteen and eight. . . . She is also completely unlettered, her stock of knowledge comprising only of the ritual of worship of household idols, the rites of placation of the wrath of deities and evil spirits, and the detailed ceremony of the service of her husband, who is ritualistically her personal god.
>
> As to the husband, he may be a child scarcely older than herself or he may be a widower of fifty, when first he requires of her his conjugal rights. . . .
>
> The infant . . . must look to his child mother for care. Ignorant of the laws of hygiene, guided only by the most primitive superstitions, she has no helpers in her task. . . . Because of her place in the social system, child-bearing and matters of procreation are the woman's one interest in life, her one subject of conversation, be her caste high or low. Therefore, the child growing up in the home learns,

from earliest grasp of word and act to dwell upon sex relations.
(Mayo [1927] 1998, 83–84)

Mapping the responses of Indian women (the examples she takes
are primarily Hindu women) and of reformers on their behalf to
the tumultuous changes of the early twentieth century, Margaret
Cousins, in stark contrast to Mayo, wrote of Marwari girls riding on
horseback in a procession of Marwari women on their way to an
Anti Pardah Women's Conference in 1941; women workers of the
cotton mills in Madras Presidency meeting to demand a ban on
polygamy; an office bearer of the All India Women's Conference
persisting in her public duties a fortnight after the death of her husband, the only signifier of widowhood being the absence of the
puttu (sacred vermilion mark worn by Hindu men and unmarried
and married Hindu girls/women, prohibited for widows) on her
forehead; a Brahmin woman conducting afternoon classes for
ladies in adult literacy; the talented daughter of an active social reformer being withdrawn from school and married off "to the consternation of all around"; a Brahmin woman who could in her
child's and her own interests go through legal divorce proceedings
when the marriage broke down because the marriage had also been
registered (under secular law in addition to the religious ceremony); 700 women—Hindus, Muslims, Christians, Parsees, Brahmins, and non-Brahmins—dining together in a school courtyard in
Bangalore, "self-released from inter-dining restrictions of community or caste"; and women participating in the Noncooperation
Movement after convincing their husbands of their commitment to
the cause of freedom (Cousins 1947, 116–130).

Cousins was a friend of India closely associated with both the nationalist movement and the Indian women's movement in the early
twentieth century (Volga et al. 2001). Mayo supported colonial rule
and was widely perceived as someone who undermined the cause of
freedom. Despite differences in politics, Cousins and Mayo represented two significant voices of modernity in that era, drawing on
frameworks of rationality and progress of the European Enlightenment. Modernity was both "coeval with the idea of progress" and
"the promise of development," with imperialist and nationalists es-

pousing its cause (Chakrabarty 2002, xix). Whereas Cousins drew upon the moment of transition to the modern in her writing on Indian women, Mayo focused on realities prior to that moment—although even while she was writing, the transition had already begun, as Tarabai Shinde's writing clearly demonstrates. Predictably, therefore, Mayo's *Mother India* created a storm (Sinha 1998). There were those who condemned Mayo's writing as totally motivated and false, others who felt reform was necessary if for no other reason than to deny Mayo and her ilk of reason for writing about India in derogatory fashion, and yet others who felt that everything Mayo said was absolutely true of orthodox Brahminism, which had to be dismantled if a more egalitarian order with democratic gender values was to emerge. However, though many narratives of Hinduism in the colonial period focus on men's efforts at social and religious reform, Shinde and other authors show that there was a growing subculture of resistance that was fashioned and nurtured by women themselves, rarely spoken about, but radical and spontaneous (O'Hanlon 1994, 53–59), subcultures that were invisible to Mayo's imperialist eye and to Cousins' nationalist eye.

Hindu Women's Lives

The debate on the position of Hindu women is a debate about the lifetimes of Hindu women, with all their twists and turns. Quite naturally, this debate must begin with the birth of the female infant, moving along the lifetime, plotting the significant moments. What is immediately striking when we look at women's lifetimes in the course of the past century or more, Hindu women particularly, is the fact that these moments are defined far more in terms of negation than as an affirmation of life; of pain, deprivation, and even death rather than survival and blossoming: birth, marriage, widowhood, and death—all stages cradled in religious belief and fervor—carrying the symbols of devaluation and discrimination where women are concerned.

As the first moment in a lifetime, then, female infanticide is irreplaceable (as also its contemporary avatara, female feticide). "The census of 1870," Pandita Ramabai wrote, "revealed the curious fact that 300 children were stolen in one year by wolves from within the city of Umritzar, all the children being girls," eliciting from her the ironic comment that "even the wild animals are so intelligent and of such refined taste that they mock at British law, and almost always steal girls to satisfy their hunger" (Chakravarti 1989, 69). Research into practices of female infanticide has shown that in Gujarat, for instance, for a hundred years beginning in the late nineteenth century not a single female child was born in the royal house of the raja of Porbandar. Reviewing research on female infanticide in contemporary India, Harriss-White, reiterating Amartya Sen, observes that the declining sex ratio since the turn of the century points to the fact that the missing women are a social product. Agnihotri's painstaking documentation of district-level data on sex ratio differences in the five-to-nine age group leads him to map a Bermuda Triangle of twenty-four districts in north India where the sex ratio of children averages 774 girls to 1,000 boys (Harriss-White 1999). Research from the southern state of Tamil Nadu shows that two-thirds of female infant deaths and 40 percent of female neonatal deaths are due to "social causes." More recent work on sex-selective abortion points to the abortion of five million female fetuses after sex determination tests during pregnancy, taking the practice of "gender cleansing" to the more affluent sections of the Indian population as well. Though deteriorating life chances for female infants is not a peculiarly Indian phenomenon—indeed, it is reflected in several patriarchal societies across the world—and though the correlation between religion and infanticide has not been established to date (Harriss-White 1999), the demographic spread of infanticide does point to regions and castes that are predominantly Hindu—both in contemporary India and in the colonial period. If rhetoric is any indication, arguments against this practice, from Pandita Ramabai to women's rights activists today, squarely address the relations between culture/custom and human rights—demanding a new, safe cultural space for female children and, I would argue, a more equitable religious/customary ethic.

In the case of Hindu society under colonialism, the relationship between British penal law and Hindu customary law was repeatedly invoked to inscribe variously the notions of individual rights, barbarism, and immorality on the one side, and the superiority of

British jurisprudence over native law on the other. One of the first rules set down on the relation been custom and the written text of law was in 1868 in *Collector of Madura* v. *Mootoo Ramalinga,* where it was held that custom could override the written text of law if its antiquity was proven. In addition, the legitimacy of a custom also hinged on whether it militated against public policy and on the primacy of public law over private law. Yet at a practical level in several cases there was a reinforcement of native law against demands by women for change, arguing that acquiescing to demands for change would constitute interference with Hindu religion (Kannabiran 1995, WS 59–WS 69). In 1887, Rukmabai, an educated girl from the carpenter caste, refused to live with her uneducated, consumptive husband, challenging the validity of infant marriage and asserting her right to repudiate it in adulthood. She was threatened with imprisonment under Act XV of 1877 for nonrestitution of conjugal rights (Chakravarti 1989, 73–74; Sarkar 2001, 194). Resisting the use of force, Rukmabai interrogated the twin forces of religious orthodoxy and colonialism. Commenting wryly on the decision to force her to live with her husband, she wrote to Pandita Ramabai, "The learned and civilized judges . . .are determined to enforce, in this enlightened age, the inhuman laws enacted in barbaric times, four thousand years ago. . . . There is no hope for women in India, whether they be under Hindu rule or British rule. . . . The hard hearted mothers-in-law will now be greatly strengthened and will induce their sons to sue the wives in British courts since they are now fully assured that under no circumstances can the British government act adversely to the Hindu Law" (Chakravarti 1989, 74).

Rukmabai was not alone in questioning the permanence of unions contracted without the consent of women. Tarabai Shinde wrote in 1882,

> What does *stridharma* [women's dharma] really mean? It means always obeying orders from your husband and doing everything he wants. He can kick you and swear at you, keep his whores, get drunk, gamble with dice and bawl he's lost all his money, steal, commit murder, be treacherous, slander people, rob peoples' treasures or squeeze them for bribes. He can do all this, but when he comes

home, stridharma means women are meant to think, "Oh, Who's this coming now but our little lord Krishna, who's just stolen the milk-maids' curds and milk" . . . then smile at him and offer their devotion, stand ready at his service as if he was Paramatma himself. But how can people go on believing this idea of stridharma once they have begun to think about what's good and bad? They'd change their ideas straightaway, won't they? (Shinde [1882] 1994, 79–80)

In a context where the Hindu wife, her chastity and absolute monogamy were imbued with mystical qualities, repositioning con-jugality in this manner was far from easy.

The matter of Hindu marriage then was twisted and knotted. There were some resolutions that women forced, through their ac-tions and their writing, in their own individual and collective inter-est; there were others that the community forced in defense of reli-gious and cultural integrity against the state—but even the latter resolution was a gendered prescription that ultimately came to rest on women's bodies like the ubiquitous *thali* (neck ornament—sa-cred symbol of marriage with man or god) worn by women as a sym-bol of monogamous chastity.

Women and Marriage

In 1890, Phulmani, a girl ten or eleven years old, died of marital rape in Bengal. Marital rape was not (and still is not) a criminal of-fence (Law Commission of India 2000, 3.1.2.1). Phulmani was above the statutory age of ten, so legally she could not be raped by her husband, because intercourse within marriage was by definition consensual. Although pre-pubertal marriages were the norm in Hindu society, there was some debate over whether pre-pubertal co-habitation was customary. The votaries of Hindu tradition argued that the age of cohabitation could not be pushed beyond ten years under any circumstances because normally in Bengal, menarche set in between ten and twelve years, and raising the age over ten would constitute an interference with custom. Reformers, however, of which medical reformers formed a considerable section, cam-paigned vociferously for raising the age of consent from ten to twelve years, bringing out long lists of cases where child wives had been grievously hurt or killed because of rape, and nonconsenting infant wives battered (Sarkar 2001, 210).

Haimabati Sen, born in 1866, widowed in 1876, traveled through the pain of a pre-pubertal marriage with a debauched husband and widowhood as a child, searching for release through education, remarriage, and reform. She found that none of these really offered any space for her spirit, having to fight every inch of her journey until she finally set up practice as a doctor and wrote her memoirs, which provide a gripping account of what it meant to be a Hindu woman in the late nineteenth and early twentieth centuries. Describing her marriage, she wrote: "The groom was a Deputy Magistrate in Jessore and his brother was the police inspector of Khulna. The prospective bridegroom was kulin-kayastha by caste and forty-five years old. He had lost two wives and was now planning a third marriage. . . . This was the groom everyone approved of. . . . I was nine years and six months at the time" (Forbes and Raychaudhuri 2000, 69–70).

And of her widowhood:

> Shame on you, Hindu society, great is your glory! A girl of ten will have to pay for the marriage of an old man of fifty. I bow a thousand times at the feet of parents who would in this way turn a daughter's life into a desert. In no other country does one find either such a society or such conduct. Such oppression of women is possible only in India; in no other country are such customs in vogue. I was but a mere child and I had already relieved my parents of all their responsibilities for me and become a slave dependent for my sustenance on my husband's elder brothers. I had to learn to accept the fact that at this tender age I would be a slave to other people's whims for a handful of rice. (Forbes and Raychaudhuri 2000, 98)

Two issues intersect in these cases: child/infant marriage, and violence in the conjugal home. Almost a century later, there still was no specific legal protection for women against violence within the home. In 1983 and 1986 India's Criminal Acts were amended to deal with cruelty to wives, dowry harassment, and "dowry deaths," using the experience of Hindu women in marriage as the norm to institute protections for all women in marriage (Agnes 1992). More than a decade later, Amnesty International continues to urge the fixing of responsibility on the state to institute these protections, shifting the customary norm of a specific form of domestic violence—"dowry deaths"—out of the community and into a secular, democratic space (Amnesty International 2000, 10).

Women as Symbols

Rukmabai and Haimabati articulated for thousands of women of their time the connections between nation and family in terms of the need for the state to redress grievances of women in the family vis-à-vis husbands especially, but also community (the extended family). In stark contrast are assertions that mirror either exactly or in milder form Bankimchandra's eulogy of sati at the end of the nineteenth century. Bankimchandra Chattopadhyaya (1838–1894) was a Bengali Brahmin with a Western education who served in the British government for thirty-three years. A prolific writer, he drew on classical literature, Western philosophy, and Hindu philosophies in his writing on Indian (Bengali) society and culture. During the era of Hindu nationalism in the late nineteenth century, Bankim's writing focused on the Hindu way of life and the Hindu nation carving out a new identity for the Hindu woman, one based on her individualism and free spirit, a utopian construction based on the ideals of freedom from colonial rule where the woman and the nation constantly mirrored each other, which he juxtaposed to oppressive domesticity/colonial subjugation (Sarkar 2001, 135–162). Ironically, however, this construction of the new womanhood by Bankimchandra romanticized the nation-as-woman/woman-as-nation rhetoric, thus actively putting women beyond the pale of justice and the law: "I can see the funeral pyre burning, the chaste wife sitting at the heart of the blazing flames, clasping the feet of her husband lovingly to her breasts. Slowly the fire spreads, destroying one part of her body and entering another. Her face is joyful. . . . The flames burn higher, life departs and the body is burnt to ashes. . . . When I think that only some time back our women could die like this, then new hope rises up in me, then I have faith that we, too, have the seeds of greatness within us. Women of Bengal: You are the true jewels of this country" (Sarkar 2001, 203).

Just as the body of the chaste Hindu woman was sacred, so also were the symbols of chastity and conjugality that adorned that body. The virtue of chastity reified in the embodiments of that chastity: the wife and the thali were two such objects. The thali was the knotted cord that marked off and separated the chaste conjugal body (the wife) from the pure, virginal, preconjugal one and the inauspicious postconjugal one (the widow). By containing and defining the auspicious state of marriage, the thali bears for Hindus particularly in south India the weight of culture that must be protected from any defilement. In 1932 a Mr. Dodwell, a subdivisional magistrate in Tellicherry in Madras Presidency, made one Mrs. Prabhu remove her thali in lieu of a fine. Although the government immediately issued an apology that was published in the government communique, members of the council did not feel the matter ended there. They wondered whether it was a mere error of judgment or an act of willful perversity: If the issue had been between an Indian magistrate and a European lady, rather than Mr. Dodwell and Mrs. Prabhu, would the reparations demanded be more severe? Alleging racial discrimination in this case, one member wanted to know whether the government realized that the thali was not a toy to be handled by everyone. Another wondered whether "the Government approve[d] of the conduct of the said Magistrate in so ordering the *removal of a wearing apparel* of an Indian lady." When representatives of government in a meek attempt to defend the action said that the Criminal Procedure Code did not explicitly prevent the seizure of the thali, they were immediately asked how, after ten long years of service in this country, the magistrate was still not aware of the sanctity of the thali as a symbol (4 MLC 1932, 1012Q; emphasis added).

As a response to incidents in the nineteenth century, the Indian Penal Code specifically made sati (immolation of a woman on the funeral pyre of her husband) a criminal offense punishable by the law. On September 4, 1987, Roop Kanwar, a Rajput woman, was burnt to death on her husband's pyre in the village of Deorala in the northwestern state of Rajasthan. Not only did Roop Kanwar die on her husband's pyre (there are accounts of her reluctance and her attempt to jump off the burning pyre), she was glorified and worshiped publicly in the region. The Penal Code was found to be inadequate, and a new state law was passed, but the perpetrators enjoyed impunity and the active support of the state. This marked a watershed in the increasing stridency of Hindu nationalism in the country, with sati once more becoming a somber marker of Hindu heritage. The public immolation of a woman with the active participation of the entire village and the celebration of her "martyrdom" for months and years afterward, and the inability of the government to act effectively under the plea that it was a case of religious rights that made interference of any sort undesirable, eerily repeats the debates of the colonial era and reveals the changing values in Hinduism, where the "true Hindu spirit" is seen as coming to rest on the public (forced) deaths of women (Kishwar 1999, 55–70).

The continuities between nineteenth-century eulogists and contemporary protagonists obliterates the difficult struggles for change, particularly for the abolition of sati and enforced widowhood. Invocations of "tradition" today must rest on a moral amnesia of women's struggles against tradition in the immediate past and the hard-won gains of those struggles. They must also rest on the slide back from the woman citizen to woman subject/object, communally owned and controlled. Whereas the earlier debate on sati took place in a larger context of the absence of education for women and the widespread acceptance of practices like infant marriage, sati today coexists with a 40 percent female literacy rate and 70 percent male literacy rate in Roop Kanwar's village of Deorala. Yet accounts of Kanwar's immolation skirted secular frameworks and eulogized her chastity (Dhagamwar 1992, 288). Although the law against sati (past and present) makes the insidious distinction between voluntary and involuntary sati, that women like Roop Kanwar are in fact held in custody in their conjugal homes, and that the Penal Code explicitly bans the taking of one's own life, complicates the assumption of impunity that goes with sati even today. The only resolution, therefore, is possible through an assertion of tradition and the blurring of the critical distinction between a secular and a religious state. Both this assertion of tradition and the plea of helplessness by the state become possible through an essentialization of the attributes of particular classes/castes of women, valor and chastity becoming natural attributes of ascribed status. In stratification systems that are descent based, like caste, then, attributes of gender adhere to those of caste and are transmitted along with attributes of caste, so that as caste gets reconfigured and meanings shift as do contours, gender too gets reconfigured. And this entire process is intimately linked to the politics of religion in the wider society: "Though Rajput women formally inhabit the realm of high civilization, both their valour and wifely fidelity in acts of *jauhar* [collective suicide by women to avoid capture and dishonour by the enemy] or in plans of *sati* are enacted not as culture but as nature— as the untaught emanation of racial essence which inheres in rajput blood. . . . In a patriarchal inflection . . . the bond of Hindu indissoluble marriage is given its ideological frontier in the ideology of '*sati*' while its practical culmination is found in the immolation of women!" (Sangari 2001, 76).

Traditions of sati are peculiar to some regions and castes in the country. Extreme forms of discrimination against widows are more common and evenly spread across the country. Prem Chowdhry's research on widow remarriage (*karewa*) among the Jats (a caste group) of Haryana points to the fact that remarriage by itself does not necessarily offer a solution for women, because it could exist in areas where women's physical and reproductive labor is an asset that must regenerate, within a larger patriarchal, misogynist culture, so that widow remarriage becomes a matter not of individual will but of community control over women's labor (Chowdhry 1989, 302–336).

The constitution of patriarchy therefore has been neither uniform nor homogenous across caste and region. The upper castes (especially "twice-born" castes) asserted the permanence of marriage for women and enforced absolute monogamy (permitting women to marry only once in a lifetime), but elsewhere in the caste hierarchy women could be forced to remarry during their reproductive years, and elsewhere still, as in Kerala, the law of patrilineal primogeniture could support a system of matrilineal hypergamous polyandry among the non-Brahmin Nayars, with Nayar women taking Namboodiri partners. In general, in consonance with a ranked or graded social order was a system of "graded patriarchies" (Chakravarti 2002, 167).

Hindu women in the late nineteenth and early twentieth centuries were generally extremely vulnerable in the face of religious orthodoxy and caste bigotry, and neither wealth nor high caste status—nor even lack of caste privilege—mitigated their suffering as women. This led women such as Haimabati to strike a shrill new note of resistance and change. The genealogy of changing values within Hinduism begins with those resistances.

Women's Resistance

An early critique of Hinduism, specifically centered on the position of women in Hindu society—denoted by Aryan religion and Brahminism—was developed by Jotiba (Jotirao) Phule in Maharashtra. Writing on "the most delicate subject of enforced widowhood upon Brahmin women," Phule says:

> The partial Aryan institution inconsiderately allows polygamy to males, which causes them to fall into new habits of wickedness. When his lust is satisfied with his legal wives, he for novelty's sake haunts the houses of public women. . . . In old age in order to obliterate the stigma upon his character, the shameless fellow becomes a religious man and hires public harlots to dance and sing in the temples with a view to venerate the stone idols, for his own satisfaction. After the death of this wicked man, his young and beautiful wife is not allowed by the same Aryan institution to remarry. She is stripped of her ornaments; she is forcibly shaved by her near relatives; she is not fed well; she is not properly clothed; she is not allowed to join pleasure parties, marriages or religious ceremonies. In fact she is bereaved of all the worldly enjoyments, nay she is considered lower than a culprit or a mean beast. (Phule [1884] 2002, 195)

In upper-caste Hindu society, the state of being married (*sumangali*) is the most auspicious state for women. Women's social life and ritual obligations were tied to their wifehood, and men could only fulfill their social and ritual obligations in their role as householders. However, Hindu women in most parts of India were allowed to marry only once in their lifetime while there was no such restriction on men. In addition, norms of chastity dictated that women were best married before the onset of puberty (even in the case of the matrilineal Nayars of Kerala), often to men in their thirties or forties. In several regions this requirement was prescriptive with families that had unmarried girls who had attained puberty being excommunicated from their caste. Widowhood, particularly during childhood, sometimes without consummation of marriage, was commonplace. Living in a state of social death, widows were required to wear either white or ochre clothes, no ornaments, and a tonsured head, and they ate only the barest of food. The campaign for widow remarriage thus hit at the base of Hindu family ideology.

The first widow remarriage in the southern Indian region of Andhra was performed in the year 1881 (Ramakrishna 1983, 119). If remarriage itself was resistance, there were other strategies that women developed as well—refusing to wear the traditional white clothes of the widow (Veeresalingam 1984a, 123), refusing the traditional practice of tonsure for widows, marrying across caste (Veeresalingam 1984b, 242), conducting marriages without Brahmins, starting shelters for pregnant widows (thus recognizing sexual abuse in the family) and homes for their children, and assisting births. In all this, they risked and braved social ostracism (Ramakrishna 1983, 122, n166).

The other side of the norm of enforced widowhood, especially in western and southern India, was the devadasi system, the practice of dedicating young women and girls to temples, literally by marrying them to the deity, making them sexually available to the priesthood and landed classes of appropriate caste. Because these women were married to the deity, they could never be widowed; thus they were known as *nityasumangali* ("eternal wife," one who can never be widowed). They played a ritual role in marriages because it was believed that a bride blessed by a devadasi would not be widowed. In the early twentieth century, the devadasi system (and also Nayar polyandry) was condemned by the social reform movement as a degenerate system that encouraged sexual promiscuity and legalized prostitution. The crisis that came to a head over the devadasi system was one of gender and power. The fact that devadasis were the only women who legitimately occupied public spaces in Hindu society, their inheritance of property down the female line, the fact that devadasi women from the upper castes were the only women who had access to education and learning at a time when these were proscribed for other Hindu women, and that the earliest and finest performing artists and poets came from this class meant that it was only through the elimination of gendered class privilege that ordinary married Hindu women could lay claim to these privileges; indeed, it was the only way they could lay claim to the public space. There were then several women from within the community who resisted this reform, asserting their position and questioning the wisdom of reform as well as its politics. Several of them saw it as a conspiracy by men of their community to appropriate resources and property that was traditionally denied to them. The absence of property transmission to men, argued abolitionists, made the men "drones and parasites." An important objective of reform was the restoration of men of this community to their rightful place as head of the domestic unit. The traditional proscription on devadasi women cohabiting with men of their community was seen as an emasculation of the men (Kannabiran 1992, 1995). Religion and women's place in Hinduism was central to this entire debate because the devadasi practice was an important part of institutionalized Hinduism.

The major part of the debate however, concerned immoral sexuality, a recurrent concern in the debates around social reform: "[T]hese lewd women, who make public traffic of their charms, are consecrated in a special manner to the worship of the divinities of India. . . . [T]heir singing . . . is almost always confined to obscene verses describing some licentious episode in the history of their gods"(Dubois [1906] 1989, 585). "The dasi herself is a recognised prostitute. The result is that a depraved woman . . . is allowed to tempt God's bhaktas [devotees] away from the path of morality, by her dancing and singing, even at the time they are praying to overcome temptation" (Anjaneyulu 1924).

The most significant positions on devadasi abolition were taken by Muvalur Ramamirthammal and Bangalore Nagarathnamma, both women from the community of devadasis. Ramamirthammal was an ardent reformer who wrote a novel to propagate reform, apart from personally campaigning to stop the practice of temple dedication in the 1920s and 1930s, who saw the system as exploiting women in the name of religion (Ramamirthammal [1936] 2003). Nagarathnamma was a reputed musician, dancer, and scholar of the performing arts who resisted every attempt to denigrate the women of the devadasi community and resisted reform because she read a larger agenda of dispossession of women in the agenda of reform. Apart from resurrecting classics like *Radhika Santvanamu* by Muddupalani, a sixteenth-century courtesan, and putting in place the annual Tyagaraja music festival at Thiruvayyaru, which celebrates the life and work of the famous saint-poet Tyagaraja, Nagarathnamma defended devadasis from charges of sexual promiscuity and adultery: "For a woman who has once been married to a man before the sacred fire to then go to another husband is adultery, but a *vesya* [prostitute] can never be called an adultress" (Nagarathnamma 1948, 4).

Ramamirthammal's critique of Brahminical Hinduism, in contrast, saw caste differences, untouchability, enforced widowhood, and prostitution as the creation of religion and God (both terms by implication Aryan and Brahmin). "If Brahma was such a great god with a sense of equality then he would have made man and woman equal partners. Is it right for him to tie the knot between a sixty-year-old man and a six-year-old girl? If that was all right then he should have also married a sixty-year-old woman to a six-year-old boy. That would have been justice" (Ramamirthammal [1936] 2003). Both these arguments were powerful signifiers of change within and around Hinduism.

Women as creators, reproducers, and propagators of a new social order demonstrated a commitment that was of a completely different order from the commitment of those who traditionally occupy hegemonic positions in intellectual history. The anonymous women from different strata who came forward to offer support to women, and those who fashioned everyday resistance to cultures of oppression and dependence in the face of stiff opposition from the orthodoxy and faced possible ostracism, were women without whom there would be no intellectual history of reform. While Jotiba Phule organized a strike of barbers in Pune to protest against the custom of tonsuring widows, Singaram, a Tamil Brahmin child widow in Nellore, demanded a piece of land from the men of her family if she must undergo tonsure, so that she could pay the barber without having to stand at their door for those few cents every month. The demand for tonsure was immediately withdrawn.

Though men like Periyar and Jotiba Phule demonstrated a rare sensibility, in general, women's engagement with reform was substantively different from that of men. More critical than the work of reformers was the fact that women survivors, through living out their lives, fashioned an intellectual and social life that belonged really to a new era. The same is the case with women who were active in social reform, particularly wives of noted reformers, whose work has often become blurred in constructions of "modern" conjugality—the ideal wife being one who is enlightened and supportive of her husband in his social mission (Volga et. al. 2001).

Unlike peasants and workers, who could function as "objects of investigation" without providing a "methodological advance or fuller understanding of the historical process"(K. N. Panikkar 1995, 62), women "subjects" of reform, particularly widows, had to display an active agency in order for the ideology of reform to take shape and acquire meaning. Although it is true, for instance, that the debates on widow remarriage occupied a position of universality on the reform agenda across regions as fundamental to women's emancipation, the radicalism of widow remarriage unequivocally rests in the act of the widow in remarrying, an act that in itself constitutes the production of intellectual history, and represents the ultimate methodological advance in the creation of that history. Intellectuals such as Kandukuri Rajyalakshmi, Muvalur Ramamirthammal, Haimabati Sen, Savitribai Phule, Tarabai Shinde, Pandita Ramabai, and Rukmabai reproduce the agency and radicalism of the women-widows, devadasis, and child-wives (by definition nonconsenting) through their praxis, which includes but transcends debate.

The Self-Respect Movement

A discussion of changing gender values within Hinduism would be incomplete without a consideration of the ways in which the Self-Respect Movement, which was essentially a resistance to Brahminical Hinduism, imagined a new womanhood and a new world built around mutuality where women would be equal to men. E. V. Ramasami, the architect of the Self-Respect Movement launched in 1925 in Tamil Nadu, mapped a non-Brahmin worldview by standing the caste system on its head. The new social order could emerge only through a radical transformation of structures of feeling and material conditions.

Constructions of masculinity and femininity are central to the social order. Transformation therefore must dislodge these constructions somewhat both rhetorically and in practice, resulting in shifts in perception and, ideally, an inversion of constructions of gender within various traditions. Speaking of the Vedic period, which is constructed as the archetypal patriarchal normative order in a monolithic Hinduism, Sitambaranar, Ramasami's biographer, writes that even within the Vedic schema women were superior to men, masculinity itself defined not in opposition to femininity but in essentially feminine terms. Qualities of courage, fearlessness, beauty, education, fame, and victory, essentially traits of the ideal man, are always described in terms of Lakshmi, a goddess (Sitambaranar 1929).

Ramasami's treatment of the question of masculinity is, however, distinctive. In an article titled "Masculinity Must Be Destroyed," Ramasami observed that the term *masculinity* itself degraded women because it was built on the assumption that courage and freedom inhered in the man, with its obverse femininity implying subservience. The very existence of the norm therefore ensured that men and women would constitute themselves within its parameters. Despite constraints that women face, they had to begin reconstituting themselves as equal partners with men instead of remaining as dependent subjects (Geetha and Rajadurai 1998, 389). Penn-ina-nallar, echoing Tarabai Shinde, draws up a balance sheet for men and women, wherein levels of social tolerance of behavior were starkly different for women and for men, the plight of widows did not in the slightest measure reflect the situation of widowers, and culture and custom only further entrenched women's subjugation. The solution to this situation, proposed by most Self-Respecters, was equality in marriage—and marriages based on love and comradeship—for oppression of women within the home, particularly in the conjugal relationship, was seen as the core problem. Self-Respect marriages therefore became an important message bearer—with the eschewing of Sanskrit incantations, Brahmin priests and ritual, and the introduction of explicit consent from the bride and the groom and the encouragement of intercaste marriages (Geetha and Rajadurai 1998, 379–382).

This change and the new emphasis on mutuality was part of a larger critique of Hindu religion. Geetha and Rajadurai identify five major elements in the Self-Respect critique of Hindu religion: the critique of the Brahmin priest and brahminism as ideology; a rationalist and subversive critique of the Vedas, Itihasas (histories), and Puranas; a criticism of religion as worldview; a critique of religious doctrine; and, finally, a critique of religious practices, rituals, and festivals.

Atheism, which constituted the core of Self-Respect ideology with respect to faith, was "redefined and re-signified to reflect the critical and iconoclastic tenor of the Self-Respect movement, [so as to emerge] as a creative mode of engagement with the problems of faith in a society ruled by caste"(Geetha and Rajadurai 1998, 308). However, the critique of Brahminism did not come from non-Brahmins alone, but from Brahmin women as well, who identified completely with the Self-Respect critique, bringing to mind Jotiba Phule's inclusion of *all* women in the category *shudratishudra* (the castes ranked lowest in the caste system: peasant cultivators, laborers, serfs, and artisans) because orthodox Hinduism did not make a distinction between women and the shudratishudras. Instead of separating jati from varna, Phule spoke of the caste system as consisting of a two-varna structure rather than the traditional four-varna structure. The Brahmins and the Shudratishudras formed the two poles, and all women, irrespective of caste, were placed in the latter category, following the Laws of Manu, which viewed all women as shudra or dasa. Resonating this view is the following testimony of a Brahmin woman in the mid-twentieth century:

> Self-Respect activists involved in various social reforms hold the Brahmins responsible for the oppressed and enslaved state of other peoples. . . . The Brahmins, you see, also oppress their own kind. . . . I am a Brahmin woman, the only daughter of my parents. . . . When I turned thirteen, my parents declared that it was unseemly for a grown girl to set foot outside the home. Since then, I have lived in-

side these four walls like a caged bird. After I came of age, my parents tried to perform my *ritushanti* [ritual consummation of prepubertal marriage]. The event never happened. . . . My life has been laid waste. . . . My plight . . . is worse than a widow's. (Kamalakshi [1930] 2003, 28–30)

Women and Caste

The disease of untouchability has spread far and wide among our people. The *adi-dravidas* [panchamas, dalits, ex-"untouchable" castes] are the worst hit. . . . As for adi-dravida women, they are forbidden from wearing a blouse. They cannot use brass utensils or pots. They are not permitted to wear gold jewels. Such are the cruel prohibitions they are forced to endure! Hesitant to face strange men without her upper cloth or blouse, a sister who has to step out of her house might sometimes dare to cover herself with the *mundanai* [end of sari used to cover the breasts]. At once, the upper castes will set their servants on her. She will be beaten soundly for daring to act contrary to custom. . . . Women, they say, are soft-hearted and kind. But just look at the humiliation our women heap on an adi-dravida woman. . . . Many women believe that it is a sin to give an adi-dravida water when they are fasting or on *amavasai* nights. Strange, is it not, that people can claim to be fasting for *punyam*, even as they refuse water to the thirsty. (Maragathavalliyar [1930] 2003, 57–59)

This passage foregrounds the critical relationship between caste and gender, one that continues to be articulated today in the context of Dalit mobilization. Dalit women were required to leave their breasts uncovered and fought long and hard to be able to wear a blouse and cover their breasts with the upper end of the sari, the mundanai, both signs of upper-caste privilege. Caste hierarchies are welded to definitions of masculinity and power based on gender and generation and are enforced through the systematic use of violence. And women are passive bearers of tradition and honor of the caste (Kannabiran and Kannabiran 2001, 55–67).

Articulations of caste by the Dalit Panther movement in Maharashtra and elsewhere in India since 1972 illustrate the intermeshing of gender with caste, although the connections are not explicitly theorized. Dalit writing in general presents a worldview that defines social location in terms of centrality in production processes (Ilaiah 1996).

Dalit literature also articulates the playing out of nationality and citizenship on the bodies of women that already bear inscriptions of caste, by juxtaposing, for instance, the fine of fifty rupees (approximately US$1) for molesting a Dalit woman against the fine of three hundred rupees for disrespect to the national flag. This echoes the concerns of Pandita Ramabai, who in the late nineteenth century drew a parallel between English rule in India and the rule of high-caste men over low castes and women throughout the ages.

The National Federation of Dalit Women, formed in 1995, brings together the various perspectives in Dalit assertion and resistance, encapsulating a history of two hundred years. The federation interrogates upper-caste, Brahminical hegemonies in inter-caste relations (particularly the antagonistic, often violent relations between upper castes and Dalit women, in a climate of increasing right-wing nationalism) and Dalit patriarchies from within. The federation's mandate brings into sharp focus current debates on the place of Dalit women in quotidian politics: Should they have a quota within the quota earmarked for reserved categories, or should they have a quota within the quota reserved for women? That they have a right to both is rarely admitted (Kannabiran 2000, 142–144).

> Dalit Women in India . . . have been beaten and otherwise abused at wells and in other public spaces. These assaults often occur as these women pursue their gendered responsibilities of acquiring water in a context in which their putative untouchability renders them vulnerable to violence from higher caste members if they are perceived to have transgressed their corporeal boundaries. Although this violence is most readily framed as simply anti-caste discrimination, it is actually intersectional: the women must therefore negotiate a complex set of circumstances in which a gendered set of responsibilities positions them to absorb the consequences of caste discrimination in the public sphere. (National Federation of Dalit Women 2000)

The NGO Declaration on Gender and Racism at the World Conference Against Racism asserted that Dalit and minority women faced targeted violence from state actors, powerful members of the dominant Hindu community and dominant castes, and drew a clear connection between racism, religious fundamentalism, and caste. The declaration represents a major shift in the understanding of Hinduism and caste at the level of mobilization, a shift effected yet again by women, like the critique of Hinduism in colonial India:

> [T]his distinct manisfestation of racism—in the form of exclusion, forced segregation and targeting through systematic violence—has been legitimized in the Indian context, through the ideology of *hindutva* [a Hindu state] that is an authoritarian and discriminatory ideology and has seriously eroded the operation and functioning of the Indian State, the Indian Constitution and its secular egalitarian character. . . .
>
> [I]n practice, caste based discrimination, aggressive communalism and marginalisation of the indigenous people have meant the denial of the freedom to live without fear, threat and intimidation, the denial of equality before the law, organized ghettoisation and hate preaching in educational texts. (National Federation of Dalit Women 2001)

The themes of coercion, force and violence in marriage, sati, and sexual slavery based on caste recur. The language of abduction, disrobing, and rape as fundamentalist constructions of masculinity and femininity acquire a new belligerence in the era of state-sponsored right-wing Hindu nationalism, especially during the 1990s. These constructions of gender, far from being empowering or representing positive values, undermine the dignity and integrity of entire classes of persons in fundamental ways, a trend that the declaration above captures. This process harks back to the origins of Hinduism, the root causes of its conflict with other religious groups traced back several hundred years, and the "essence" of the "original" Hindu tradition increasingly constructed as something that has been corrupted and must be resurrected. The authoritative definition of the "authentic" tradition or the "invention of tradition," to use Hobsbawm's term, is a product of power, so that any argument for resistance to tradition evokes a hegemonic defense of culture against the "corrupt modern." And women are trapped in webs of modernity and tradition today as they were a century ago, although the rhetorical and political frameworks are radically different (Hobsbawm and Ranger 1983; Chakrabarty 2002).

Genealogies are indispensable to the present. The construction of the genealogy of Indian/Hindu women's rights has been an intrinsic part of projects as wide ranging as Indology/Orientalism, nationalism, the Self-Respect Movement, feminism, and secularism.

Conclusions

We will now look briefly at the validity of claims of a "homogenous, authentic Hindu tradition," with specific reference to the construction of womanhood and femininity.

"Hinduism looks on Woman as the Shakti of Shiva, the Power behind the Throne, the equal Half of that Half-Lord-Half-Lady which constitutes the One, 'Ardhanareshwara'" (Cousins 1941, 12). Any discussion of the woman question has, in India, from colonial times harked back to a golden age when women were equal, and also to the women scholars of ancient time as being the foremothers of contemporary movements for women's rights, particularly the rights of Hindu women. Orientalist and Indological studies in the eighteenth and nineteenth centuries, which originated in the commercial and political interests of the British East India Company, rapidly expanded from the study of history and customs to more encompassing work on Sanskrit and Hindu philosophy, the German Indologist Max Muller being a central figure in this larger project. Clarisse Bader's *Women in Ancient India,* for instance, argues that Western civilization had much to learn from ancient Indian civilizations, particularly with respect to its emphasis on spirituality, abnegation, renunciation, and asceticism, and also the Aryan woman's devotion to the family. For her, sati was an example of this spiritual courage. Indology, however, made two simultaneous sets of juxtapositions—between Western and Indian civilizations and between ancient and contemporary India, with ancient India providing the ideal in both cases. With respect to the West and nineteenth-century Indian society, Bader argued that the decline of Vedic society demonstrated the "physical and moral degradation the most gifted people could fall, once it exchanged the yoke of duty for that of passion"(Chakravarti 1989, 44–45). This teleological view of Indian history was shared by several Indian campaigners for women's rights in the process of inscribing new values for women that fused the modern with the "traditional"—a hazy, mythic ancient tradition, of which there was no written record, one invented to be *modern* in ethic. Muthulakshmi Reddi, for example, held a firm belief in a glorious Hindu past in which the devadasis who served in temples were pure and chaste like the vestal virgins of ancient Greece. Her explorations revealed to her that devadasis were originally a band of pure virgin ascetics attached to temples. They were believed to have lived a holy life, wearing only the simplest clothes and subsisting on the food given to them by the temples (Reddi 1940). Her argument reiterated earlier such arguments that "in times of yore, women who were disgusted or satiated with family life devoted themselves to the service of God, in the temples; they engaged themselves in cleaning the temple and decorating its walls. . . . These had plaited hair, wore *kashayam* [ochre robes], and lived upon the small ration given them out of the cooked rice offered to God, so as to keep body and soul together. In short they lived like ascetics. They prayed and danced in deep devotion to God, and centred their whole thought on Him and Him alone. But alas! . . . They are now so many living monuments of debauchery and vice" (Ramachandram 1900, 2).

The integrity of the Hindu nation had to be safeguarded against onslaughts from the Christian evangelical efforts to counter the system through proselytization. Reddi's aim was to rescue Hindu society from the clutches of blind superstition and obscurantism, which, she believed, could only spell its doom: "[Prostitution] is a question that vitally concerns the dignity and status of every woman in India, inasmuch as it is a stigma on the whole womanhood, and a blot on Hindu civilisation"(Reddi n.d., 533–539).

Feminist historiography, on the other end, has resurrected little-known writing by women from ancient to modern times, in an effort to build a genealogical archive for feminist praxis today, an archive that is radically different in politics, intent, and content from the Indological-nationalist archive. The bhakti movement, for instance, provided women in medieval India a rare space outside of the family to carve out a women's worldview. By definition this involved an interrogation of patriarchal norms of the primacy of submission, domesticity, conjugality, and wifely devotion over religious faith for women (Tharu and Lalita 1991). It also involved the reinterpretation of literary work by women, the construction of a feminist genre that spoke against the grain of mainstream ideologies (Volga et al. 2001).

The other part of the project of reinscription has consisted of an exploration of the question of myth and tradition and their interpretation of women's position, an effort that has asserted the historicity and materiality of *tradition* as also its diversity, against universalizing and homogenizing essentially fundamentalist interpretations of Hindu belief and religion. Romila Thapar has argued persuasively that traditions are constantly invented, in the very process of being handed down from one generation to another, and that legends have been interpreted in widely varying ways, making the declaration of "authentic" tradition deeply political. Thapar argues that "the way in which present day society picks up a tradition is determined by present day attitudes to women"(Thapar 1987, 3). Although there are several versions of the Ramayana story, the only versions that are picked up for projection in film and television are the Tulsidas and Valmiki versions, both of which present a valorizing of a patriarchal Kshatriya tradition; the Tulsidas version especially makes extremely disparaging comments about a woman's nature. Drawing further on the concentration of the Tulsi epic on godhead, Thapar points out that "roughly in the period before the early centuries AD . . . the hero became the incarnation of the deity. . . . [Whereas] in the Greek epics gods participate with the heroes . . . in the Indian epics, at a certain point in the process of their being rewritten, the heroes became the incarnations of the gods" (Thapar 1987, 6).

A secular text by this process of rewriting gets transformed into a sacred text, central to Hinduism and the Hindu religious identity. The folk variants of the Ramayana reflect the social structure of that area, its ethnic relations, and its belief structures—and each of these versions contains a different depiction of Rama, Sita, and Ravana, not all projecting Ravana as a villainous demon or Sita as the meek, submissive wife. For both men and women in Hindu society, Uma Chakravarti argues, the ideal woman has been traditionally personified by Sita, who is portrayed in the Ramayana as the "quintessence of wifely devotion" (Chakravarti 1983, 68–75). And yet, she argues, this homogenizing is not true to the many versions of the Ramayana that predate Valmiki's Ramayana. Chakravarti posits that several versions of the Ravana myth were not originally connected to the Rama story. The Valmiki Ramayana brings together the Rama legend and the Ravana myth, Chakravarti argues, "to create a major epic with the emphasis on masculine heroism, valour and honour in the person of Rama and of feminine self sacrifice, virtue, fidelity and chastity in the person of Sita . . . [T]he text was a potent instrument for propagating the twin notions that women are the property of men and that sexual fidelity for women was life's major virtue" (Chakravarti 1983, 71). This text also represents a later stage in the development of marriage, with the patriarchal monogamous family being firmly entrenched.

The development of the Sita myth, however, according to Chakravarti, suggests that successive versions only added to the theme of ideal marriage and female fidelity and chastity, reinforcing a patriarchal stereotype of the ideal woman. The fire ordeal, the line Sita must not cross if she is to be safe, and even her ultimate return to the earth resonate the only two options available to women in a patriarchal society: conformity or death (Chakravarti 1983).

With Rama today being the hegemonic center of a larger political debate, Thapar's assessment of Sita is refreshing: "Sita is a very interesting figure. She is not an ordinary Kshatriya woman. She is born out of a furrow. So there is something unusual about her. One cannot be sure whether she will accept the mores and behave as a Kshatriya woman should, or whether she will be in some way nonconformist. And, ultimately, after all the trials and tribulations, she, in a way, goes back to mother earth. She says, in a way . . . 'I am different. I was born of the earth. I have been through all this and have proved myself. But now I go back where I belong. I don't belong to you'"(Thapar 1987, 6).

The seclusion of women is yet another concern, because Hindu society does practice an active separation and segregation of

women. Though the question of spatial boundaries is often explained away as a reaction to fear of abduction by Muslims and is
generally traced to the tenth century CE, cultures of seclusion were
prevalent in India long before this. In the period of the Rig Veda,
when land was not yet a source of economic and political power
and the economy was predominantly pastoral, the family and
women were central to pastoral production units, managing dairy-
ing while men went out to war. *Duhita,* the word used for daughters,
literally meant "one who milks the cows." The Aryan woman was
called the *grihapatni,* the equal partner of the head of the household, the *grihapati.* This early association of women with the household, however, Chakravarti argues, became the core of the Hindu
ideal, without its larger context. The disintegration of the pastoral
economy and the centrality of women to it led to a metamorphosis
of the grihapatni into a *pativrata,* or the chaste wife. This change
also had to do with settled agriculture and land as a source of power
and with the entrenchment of patrilineality. The Sita ideal in the
Valmiki and Tulsidas Ramayanas particularly represented the crystallization of the pativrata and also the segregation and control of
women (Chakravarti 1986). In this entire process the family is the
locus of interest and of emotion.

The representation of mythic characters has always been a matter
of political strategy. Often, the representation has relocated the
characters from realms of myth and legend into history. A common
way of doing this, particularly in the recent past, has been to forge a
brotherhood of the faith-deepening lines of exclusion. Jotiba Phule
shows us another way of representing myth, historicizing pain and
physical hurt in the process. On the story of Parashurama, whose
mission was to decimate the Kshatriyas, Phule writes:

> He not only killed several kshatriya men but also snatched from the
> arms of their orphaned wives their innocent infants and mercilessly
> sent them to a cruel death. . . . When he heard of widowed, pregnant
> and helpless kshatriya women, desperately running away to save the
> lives of their unborn babies, he chased them like a hunter and cap-
> tured them. . . . Womenfolk are not used to running. Besides, most
> of them belonged to families of good descent and never had occa-

sion to cross even the thresholds of their houses. . . . [T]hey must
have tripped and fallen and dashed against the boulders on the way
or the rocky mountain by the sides of the roads and bled profusely
throughout the several wounds caused by the fall on their arms, foreheads, knees and ankles. . . . Their mouths must have been parched
dry in the burning sun and because of the lack of water and constant
running, they must have felt sick. Their mouths must have frothed
with fear and the tiny lives inside their bellies must have rolled frantically, causing them unendurable, acute pains. They must have
prayed desperately for the earth to open up and swallow them so that
they could escape from this merciless pursuit. . . . How many terror
stricken women must have embraced death! How many women must
have fallen at his feet and begged Parashuram for mercy. . . . The
ruthless tyrant butchered babies in front of their mothers . . . some
of them must have perished with grief, and some of them must have
gone raving mad. . . . But we should never hope to get this account
from the brahmans. (Phule [1873] 2002, 41–43)

In imagining and giving voice to women's pain, Jotiba Phule was
in fact inverting the dominant narrative of the period, which centered on and was confined to assertions and contestations of tradition, where neither women's bodies nor their lived experience were
relevant. Especially when speaking of the "high caste" woman, the
assumption of the capacity to bear extreme and grievous physical
hurt sublimated women and elevated them to the level of divinity,
described and defined of course by men. Inscribing the experience
of pain of women in a myth or legend immediately foregrounds the
high-caste woman's experience of pain as a consequence of that
same tradition in the here and now. Through the writing of pain,
Jotiba Phule dislodges in a very powerful way the normative structure of gender and caste in traditional Hinduism. This reconfigura-
tion is relevant even today, when the sublimation of pain is a strategic device to deny women rights (to life and dignity, importantly) in
the name of tradition.

Take, for instance, this rendition of Draupadi's pain in the current context of war (Draupadi was the wife of the five Pandava
princes of the Mahabharata):

I am Draupadi
My throat holds the poison of humiliation
I am Draupadi, the sorrowful
grieving the death of my sons
I Draupadi, stake for a husband's dice
My princely husbands' royal gifts
Beginning with a public disrobing
Moving through shame abduction humiliation
In a world filled with Kichakas Dusasanas and Saindavas
What were the gains of this war
Save the destruction of brothers, sons, friends?
The bleeding hearts of
Gandhari, Bhanumathi, Kunti and Subhadra?
The unending grief of bereaved mothers?
—VOLGA 2000

The dislodging of stories of patriarchal power, both through the writing of histories of diversity and pluralism and through the devalorization of that power by inscribing the stories of pain and hurt at the center of mythic traditions, creates new possibilities for reinscribing values of equality and justice (especially with respect to gender and caste) in those traditions, both in practice and pedagogically. The central attempt in this chapter has been to map the complex and difficult process of this reinscription of positive gender values in relation to Hinduism in the Indian subcontinent over the past century.

BIBLIOGRAPHY

Agnes, Flavia. "Protecting Women against Violence? Review of a Decade of Legislation, 1980–1989." *Economic and Political Weekly* (April 25, 1992): WS 19–WS 33.
Amnesty International. "Respect, Protect, Fulfil—Women's Human Rights: State Responsibility for Abuses by 'Non-State Actors.'" London, September 2000.
Anjaneyulu, S. "Presidential Address to the Andhradesa Kalavanthula Social Conference." *Muthulakshmi Reddi Papers*. Subject File 12. Nehru Memorial Museum and Library. New Delhi. 1924.

Chakrabarty, Dipesh. *Habitations of Modernity: Essays in the Wake of Subaltern Studies.* Delhi: Permanent Black, 2002.

Chakravarti, Uma. "Development of the Sita Myth: A Case Study of Women in Myth and Literature," in *Samya Shakti* 1,1 (1983): 68–75.

———. "Pativrata: The Ideological 'Purdah' of a Hindu Woman," in *Seminar* 318 (1986): 17–21.

———. "Whatever Happened to the Vedic Dasi? Orientalism, Nationalism, and a Script for the Past," in Kumkum Sangari and Sudesh Vaid (eds.), *Recasting Women: Essays in Colonial History.* New Delhi: Kali for Women, 1989: 27–87.

———. "Exploring a 'No-Conflict' Zone: Interest, Emotion, and the Family in Early India," in *Studies in History* 18, 2 (2002): 165–187.

Chowdhry, Prem. "Customs in a Peasant Economy: Women in Colonial Haryana," in Kumkum Sangari and Sudesh Vaid (eds.), *Recasting Women: Essays in Colonial History.* New Delhi: Kali for Women, 1989: 302–336.

Connell, R. W. "Gender Regimes and Gender Order," in *The Polity Reader in Gender Studies.* Indian reprint. New Delhi: Polity Press, 2002: 29–40.

Cousins, Margaret E. *Indian Womanhood Today.* Allahabad: Kitabistan, 1947.

Deshpande, G. P., ed. *Selected Writings of Jotirao Phule.* New Delhi: LeftWord Books, 2002.

Dhagamwar, Vasudha. *Law, Power, and Justice: The Protection of Personal Rights in the Indian Penal Code.* New Delhi: Sage, 1992.

Dubois, Abbe. *Hindu Manners, Customs, and Ceremonies.* Edited and translated by H. K. Beauchamp. Delhi: Oxford University Press, 1989 [1906].

Forbes, Geraldine, and Tapan Raychaudhuri, eds. *The Memoirs of Dr. Haimabati Sen: From Child Widow to Lady Doctor.* New Delhi: Roli Books, 2000.

Foucault, Michel. *Power/Knowledge: Selected Interviews and Other Writings, 1972–1977.* Edited by Colin Gordon. New York: Pantheon Books, 1977.

Geetha, V., and S. V. Rajadurai. *Toward a Non-Brahmin Millennium: From Lyothee Thass to Periyar.* Calcutta: Samya, 1998.

Harriss-White, Barbara. "Gender Cleansing: The Paradox of Development and Deteriorating Female Life Chances in Tamil Nadu," in Rajeswari Sunder Rajan (ed.), *Signposts: Gender Issues in Post-Independence India.* New Delhi: Kali for Women, 1999: 124–153.

Hobsbawm, Eric, and Terence Ranger, eds. *The Invention of Tradition.* Cambridge: Cambridge University Press, 1983.

Ilaiah, Kancha. *Why I Am Not a Hindu.* Calcutta: Samya, Kancha, 2001.

Kamalakshi, Miss and Mrs. "What Is in Store for Us?" in K. Srilata (ed. and trans.), *The Other Half of the Coconut.* New Delhi: Kali for Women, 2003: 28–30.

Kannabiran, Kalpana. "Judiciary, Social Reform, and Debate on 'Religious Prostitution' in Colonial India," in *Economic and Political Weekly* 30, 43 (October 1995): WS 59–WS 69.

———. "Caste," in *Routledge International Encyclopedia of Women.* Vol 1. New York and London: Routledge, 2000: 142–144.

Kannabiran, Kalpana, and Vasanth Kannabiran. *De-Eroticizing Assault: Essays on Modesty, Honour, and Power.* Calcutta: Stree, 2001.

Kannabiran, Vasanth, and Kalpana Kannabiran. "The Frying Pan or the Fire? Endangered Identities, Gendered Institutions, and Women's Survival," in Tanika Sarkar and Urvashi Butalia (eds.), *Women and the Hindu Right: A Collection of Essays.* New Delhi: Kali for Women, 1995: 121–135.

Kishwar, Madhu. *Off the Beaten Track: Rethinking Gender Justice for Indian Women.* New Delhi: Oxford University Press, 1999.

Law Commission of India. Review of Rape Laws. 172nd report, March 2000.

Mani, Lata. "Contentious Traditions: The Debate on Sati in Colonial India," in Kumkum Sangari and Sudesh Vaid (eds.), *Recasting Women: Essays in Colonial History.* New Delhi: Kali for Women, 1989: 88–126.

Maragathavalliyar, Mu. "The Sufferings of the Adi-dravidas," in K. Srilata (ed. and trans.), *The Other Half of the Coconut.* New Delhi: Kali for Women, 2003: 57–59.

Mayo, Katherine. *Selections from "Mother India."* Edited and introduced by Mrinalini Sinha. New Delhi: Kali for Women, 1998 [1927].

Nagarathnamma, Bangalore. "Preface," in *Radhika Santvanamu* by Muddupalani. Madras: Vavilla Ramasastrulu and Sons, 1948.

National Federation of Dalit Women. *Background Paper for the Expert Meeting on the Gender-Related Aspects of Race Discrimination* (November 21–24, 2000), Zagreb, Croatia.

———. *NGO Declaration on Gender and Racism, Racial Discrimination, Xenophobia, and Related Intolerance* (August 28–September 7, 2001), Durban, World Conference Against Racism.

O'Hanlon, Rosalind. *A Comparison between Women and Men: Tarabai Shinde and the Critique of Gender Relations in Colonial India.* New Delhi: Oxford University Press, 1994.

Panikkar, K. N. *Culture, Ideology, Hegemony: Intellectuals and Social Consciousness in Colonial India.* New Delhi: Tulika, 1995.

Phule, Jotirao. "Slavery," in G. P. Deshpande (ed.), *Selected Writings of Jotirao Phule*. New Delhi: LeftWord Books, 2002 [1873]: 25–46.

———. "Opinion from Jotteerao Govindrao Phulay on Note No. II, by Mr. B. M. Malabari on Enforced Widowhood" in G. P. Deshpande (ed.), *Selected Writings of Jotirao Phule*. New Delhi: LeftWord Books, 2002 [1884]: 195–197.

Proceedings of the Fourth Legislative Council of the Governor of Madras, March 12, 1932.

Ramachandram, M. *The Devadasi*. Conjeevaram: S. K. B. Press, 1900.

Ramakrishna, V. *Social Reform in Andhra (1848–1919)*. New Delhi: Vikas, 1983.

Ramamirthammal, Muvalur A. "Web of Deceit," in Kalpana Kannabiran and Vasanth Kannabiran (eds.), *Web of Deceit: Muvalur Ramamirthammal and Devadasi Reform in Colonial India*. New Delhi: Kali for Women, 2003 [1936].

Reddi, Muthulakshmi. "Kudikars in Dewaswoms," *Muthulakshmi Reddi Papers*. Subject File 11, 3 (17.3.40). Nehru Memorial Museum and Library. New Delhi. 1940.

———. "A Paper against Dedication of Girls to Temples," *Muthulakshmi Reddi Papers*. Subject File 11, 3: 533–539. Nehru Memorial Museum and Library. New Delhi. n.d.

Sangari, Kumkum. *Politics of the Possible: Essays on Gender, History, Narratives, Colonial English*. New Delhi: Tulika, 2001.

Sangari, Kumkum, and Sudesh Vaid, eds. *Recasting Women: Essays in Colonial History*. New Delhi: Kali for Women, 1989.

Sarkar, Tanika. *Hindu Wife, Hindu Nation: Community, Religion, and Cultural Nationalism*. New Delhi: Permanent Black, 2001.

Shinde, Tarabai. "A Comparison between Women and Men: An Essay to Show Who's Really Wicked and Immoral, Women or Men?" in Rosalind O'Hanlon, *A Comparison between Women and Men: Tarabai Shinde and the Critique of Gender Relations in Colonial India*. New Delhi: Oxford University Press, 1994 [1882]: 73–134.

Sidambaranar, Sami. "Penn Makkal Perumai." *Kudi Arasu* 5, 28 (October 27, 1929).

Sinha, Mrinalini. "Editor's Introduction," in Katherine Mayo, *Selections from "Mother India."* Edited and introduced by Mrinalini Sinha. New Delhi: Kali for Women, 1998: 1–61.

Srilata, K., ed. and trans. *The Other Half of the Coconut: Women Writing Self-Respect History*. New Delhi: Kali for Women, 2003.

Talwar, Vir Bharat. "Feminist Consciousness in Women's Journals in Hindi, 1910–1920," in Kumkum Sangari and Sudesh Vaid (eds.),

Recasting Women: Essays in Colonial History. New Delhi: Kali for Women, 1989: 204–232.

Thapar, Romila. "Traditions Versus Misconceptions." *Manushi* 42–43 (1987): 2–14.

Tharu, Susie, and K. Lalita, eds. *Women Writing in India: 600 BC to the Present.* New York: Feminist Press, 1991.

Veeresalingam, Kandukuri. *Rachanalu,* vols. 1–2. Hyderabad: Visalandhra Publications, 1984.

Volga. *War and Peace.* Translated by Vasanth Kannabiran. Secunderabad: Asmita, 2000.

Volga, Vasanth Kannabiran, and Kalpana Kannabiran. *Mahilavaranam/Womanscape.* Secunderabad: Asmita, 2001.

Chapter Ten

Hinduism in Independent India

Fundamentalism and Secularism

ROBERT J. STEPHENS

When the British left India in 1947, two new nations were created. The partition of the Indian subcontinent and the resulting migration of people from one nation to the other brought horrific communal violence. Since then, Pakistan has struggled to define itself as an Islamic republic. In contrast, India chose to define itself as a secular republic. Nonetheless, with a population that is over 80 percent Hindu, but which also includes the world's second-largest Muslim population, the role of religion in politics and public life in India has been at the forefront, and conflicts amongst religious groups have continued in many areas.

Some Indian leaders have stressed the value of creating a secular society in which all religions are treated equally. Advocates of the secular stance often highlight India's long tradition of nurturing a variety of religions as well as what they understand to be the tolerant nature of Hinduism. Another strand of thinking, however, often known as Hindu fundamentalism, argues that with a Hindu majority, India should be a Hindu nation. Questions about the role of Hinduism and other religions in the nation of India remain a central feature of Indian public discourse. Even the question of how to study and understand the role of religion in India generates debate, as suggested in this quote from the Indian novelist Shashi Tharoor:

> But it's not enough to hail composite religiosity, to applaud complacently the syncretism of Hindu-Muslim relations in India. Of course we have to keep reminding people that tolerance is also a tradition in India, that communal crossovers are as common as communal clashes. But we mustn't abdicate the field of religious conflict to the chauvinists on both sides. What we need . . . are nonsectarian histories of sectarian strife. (Tharoor 2001, 64)

Tharoor calls for "non-sectarian histories of sectarian strife" at least in part because he is aware that not all interested parties are convinced that such "non-sectarian" historical writing is possible—especially when it involves the value-laden categories of "fundamentalism," "secularism," or "Hinduism." Careful attention to such issues as point of view, the definitions we use, the categories we impose, and the historical context—both our own and that of those we study—are necessary considerations of the scholar's quest. We must keep in mind our own attitudes toward fundamentalism and secularism and strive for fairness in our assessments and judgments. In this chapter, significant attention will be placed upon the issue of definitions. This is important because one finds that when discussing such powerfully charged concepts as "fundamentalism" and "secularism," a plethora of competing and often-contradictory definitions already exist. Given the various uses (and misuses) of these terms, it is necessary to point out the *primacy of context* for determining meaning. The label *fundamentalist,* for instance, nearly always carries a pejorative connotation, whereas *secularist* may be used to connote either approval or disapproval, depending upon context. In this chapter, however, fundamentalism and secularism will be used descriptively as a way to understand certain developments in "Hinduism."

The subjects addressed in this chapter, "Hinduism," "fundamentalism," and "secularism" are all recently developed conceptual categories that, in theory, help us to understand Hinduism in the modern period. They are ways of categorizing certain beliefs and behaviors—reactions to modernity—that we call "fundamentalism"

and "secularism" among persons who identify as, and who are identified by others as, Hindus. Fundamentalism and secularism function within the context of ethnic identities and nation-states—a
context that has become increasingly central to the modern age.
Fundamentalism and secularism in independent India are emblem-
atic of opposite reactions to modernity, and as such, they must be
understood within the context of a heightened religious concern
with nationalism.

Although certain "family resemblances" can be detected among
fundamentalists and secularists worldwide, a distinguishing feature
of South Asian fundamentalism lies in the acute presence of ethnic,
sociopolitical, and nationalistic concerns. This is not to say, however
(as some critics of Hindu fundamentalism have), that fundamentalists in South Asia are merely politicians who make use of religious
tropes to further their cause and amass public support. Rather, if
one defines the study of religion as a study of that which concerns
people ultimately or the study of what people have considered to be
of ultimate importance, then one can argue that nationalistic and
political concerns have been raised to a level of ultimacy among
Hindu fundamentalists in India.

"Fundamentalism" and "secularism" have recently become popular categories, and as a result some people currently use these terms
rather loosely. One should remain attentive to how these words are
used by considering the issue of who is applying the label and who
is being labeled—who gains, who loses. That persons employ the
terms *fundamentalism* and *secularism* is often secondary to *when* and
how they use these words. For example, when a candidate for political office in India praises the "secular" virtues of the Constitution,
he or she may be lauding the fundamental right "freely to profess,
practice and propagate religion" found in Article 25(1). Equally
possible, he or she may intend to point up the Hindu spirit of tolerance toward all religions that some claim is enshrined in the Indian
Constitution. Alternatively, the candidate may merely appreciate
what he or she construes to be the equal treatment of religions by
the state or the careful noninvolvement with religions on the part
of the state. In contrast, the "secular virtues" favored by the candidate may refer to the direct involvement with religion by the government in terms of reserved seats and "affirmative action" quotas

in educational or political institutions based upon caste status and religious affiliation. Succinctly put, "secularism in India is a multivocal word: what it means depends upon who uses the word and in what context" (Madan 1997, 235).

From the Fundamentals to "Fundamentalisms"

As a category for classifying social phenomena, "fundamentalism" has been dramatically expanded in recent decades in academic and popular literature alike. Originally, the term referred to a specific movement among late nineteenth-century Protestant evangelicals in the eastern United States. Currently the term is no longer used only in reference to certain Christian groups. The first fundamentalists now serve as a symbolic point of reference for a new semantic classification, namely the category of "fundamentalism" (Frykenberg 1988, 22).

How then does one get from the original meaning of "fundamentalism" as a particular type of nineteenth-century North American Protestant biblical literalism, to a discussion of "fundamentalisms" among Muslims, Hindus, or Sikhs in modern India or elsewhere in the world? Or, perhaps more important, how does the category "fundamentalism" add to our knowledge of "Hinduism"? Bruce Lawrence addresses this issue in his article "From Fundamentalism to Fundamentalisms: A Religious Ideology in Multiple Forms," in which he responds to the criticism that the concept is both "too embracing and too restrictive" and simultaneously demonizes and homogenizes its referents (Lawrence 1998, 89). Because "no one has devised a better term to refer to a phenomenon that all agree constitutes part of the current period in world history," Lawrence retains the category without apologies. He delineates three basic types of fundamentalism (with a fourth mixed category) as a way of adding nuance to the discussion: (1) literalist, such as North American Protestant biblical literalists; (2) terrorist, such as certain Muslim fundamentalists; (3) political activist, such as nonviolent Jewish Zionists; and (4) political activist/terrorist, such as certain Sikh fundamentalists who betray both violent and nonviolent tendencies. Lawrence's rubric shows that the terms *fundamentalist* and *terrorist* should not be taken conterminously. Despite this, "fundamentalism" and "terrorism" are often equated in mass media discussions of the subject.

In his book *The Arya Samaj as a Fundamentalist Movement*, J. E. Llewellyn argues that in addition to presenting a value-neutral definition of fundamentalism, scholars have a responsibility to study fundamentalism cross-culturally as a means of rescuing the word from the imprecise way that it is often used in mass media. Llewellyn's value-neutral definition serves as an answer to William Shepard, who argues that the term *fundamentalist* "in journalistic and academic writing has such a strongly pejorative connotation that its use should not be extended to other cultures by scholars who aspire to objectivity" (Llewellyn 1993, 6). By employing value-neutral definitions, scholars can thereby bring a level of precision and sophistication to the discussion, which is generally lacking in popular treatments of fundamentalism.

In their multi-volume work on fundamentalisms in the modern world, R. Scott Appleby and Martin Marty have proposed the following working definition of *fundamentalism:* Fundamentalisms are reactionary; they engage in selective retrieval of the essences of the faith. They are exclusive and separatist; they are absolutists in determining who the enemies are, and in this regard they are authoritarian. Above all, fundamentalists see themselves as militants. Fundamentalists "fight back" against "some challenge or threat to their core identity." They "fight for" a constantly reinforced worldview; they "fight with" certain resources at their disposal, such as "real or presumed pasts," "actual or imagined ideal original conditions," and selective doctrinal fundamentals. They "fight against others," both those inside their community of faith (perceived in many cases as the more dangerous enemy) and those outside of the fold. Finally, fundamentalists "fight under God" or on behalf of "some transcendent reference"—they are the sole representatives of righteousness in the world (Marty and Appleby 1991, ix-x).

Robert Frykenberg further identifies five foundational features and three functional features for accounting for fundamentalism in South Asia. Above all, fundamentalism in South Asia must be understood as an extreme religious reaction to modernism. This reaction tends to be conservative, separatist, and radical. South Asian fundamentalists possess "the Truth" in the form of a central doctrine or set of doctrines; this is the metaphysical system grounded in ultimate reality that informs their ideology or their "text." The Truth is intimately related to "the messenger," or the "one who embodies or personifies the Truth and is the original person who conveyed it." Fundamentalists view the world in terms of a community of insiders versus outsiders. They share a common destiny or teleological hope in the form of a utopian future, which belongs solely to insiders. They stand opposed to evil whether it is in the form of pollution, corruption, aberrant behavior, or social or political danger; threats come from both insiders and outsiders. In addition to these "foundational features," fundamentalists in South Asia tend to display certain "functional features": Fundamentalists tend to experience a "radical conversion," or a complete and drastic reaction against evil. The group functions by means of "revivalism," or "a strategy for restoring vitality to what has become moribund," and by observing a strict separatism or exclusivity (Frykenberg 1994, 596).

Though it is not necessary for our purposes to compare and contrast the differences between North American Protestant fundamentalists and South Asian—or more specifically, Hindu—fundamentalists, the following observation may prove helpful. North American Protestant fundamentalists historically may have found themselves in a nation that to their thinking had strayed from its spiritual moorings. Thus in organizing and maintaining a fundamentalist Christian subculture, their concern lay primarily in the area of social and religious reform, not the political realm. Hindu fundamentalists presently, in contrast, may find themselves in a modern Indian state that is seemingly suffused with competing cultures and ethnic and religious identities. Consequently, their interests do not lie in establishing a fundamentalist Hindu subculture. Rather, a major concern lies in establishing a national identity for all of India in the here-and-now. Missing is the familiar Protestant Christian affirmation found in many hymns that "this world is not my home." The evidence would seem to indicate that fundamentalism in India is intimately related to the quest for political power and autonomy in a way that it has not been historically, but perhaps is presently, for North American Protestant fundamentalists.

Early Hindu Fundamentalism:
The Arya Samaj

With this background on the origins of the term *fundamentalism* and how the term has been expanded in recent scholarly discourse, we are now ready to proceed to specific examples of fundamentalist beliefs and behaviors among certain persons who identify as Hindus. Many scholars agree that a fountainhead event in the history of Hindu fundamentalism was the formation of the Arya Samaj in Bombay in 1875. The founder of the Arya Samaj, Swami Dayanand Saraswati, was one of the first openly to defend "Hinduism" as he understood it, against the "modernist" critiques of the Christian missionaries of his day.

The reaction of Dayanand and the Arya Samaj to the religious pluralism of late-nineteenth-century India resembles the response of other fundamentalists when confronted with religious competition. Dayanand formed the Arya Samaj in the hope of fostering a society to defend and to propagate ancient "Vedic" values. He appropriated certain modernizing critiques of social justice in his reconstruction of the Aryan past. As a result, "it is the fundamentals from the normative Vedic period which the Arya Samaj defends" (Llewellyn 1993, 94). The historical construction of a pristine, mythic past is a common project undertaken in fundamentalist movements. In his defense of "fundamentals from the normative Vedic period," Dayanand preached passionately on the justice of traditional karma theory in the face of Christian polemics (Coward 1987, 47).

Swami Dayanand Saraswati was born in 1824 to a Brahmin family in Gujarat (Jones 1995a, 27). His early life, as it has been piously reconstructed by several biographers, was spent studying Sanskrit grammar and memorizing religious hymns and commentaries. Like his reputedly strict father, Dayanand was raised a devotee of Shiva. As per the Laws of Manu, he was invested with the sacred thread at the age of eight and henceforth began his life as a *Brahmachari,* or a student of the sacred lore. It is during this period that Dayanand is said to have witnessed the desecration of a Shiva shrine by a lowly rodent and was bewildered at the god's lack of power (or refusal) to defend his own shrine. He fled his home at the age of twenty-one

(or twenty-two) to avoid an unwanted marriage and eventually became a *sannyasi,* or renouncer, and was given the name Dayanand.

After some years spent with the blind guru Virajananda,
Dayanand's concerns shifted from personal salvation to the reform
of what he saw as the numerous "corrupted religions and sects prevailing in India." Making use of his studies of Sanskrit grammar,
Dayanand sought to restore true Vedic heritage as he found it in
the four Vedas. His underlying assumption was that all truth is
Vedic truth. In other words, whatever is true has been revealed in
the Vedas, a term that itself connotes true knowledge.

To posit that Dayanand found scientific, political, and social
knowledge, in addition to "religious" knowledge, in the Vedas is to
misunderstand his program. For Dayanand, knowledge is holistic,
unanimous, and universal. The various discursive "types" of knowledge are not what is discovered in the Vedas, but rather *knowledge itself,* and it is for this reason that all persons should endeavor to
"know the meaning of the Veda." Any reconstruction of Dayanand's
views must take into account his understanding of the unanimity
and universality of "Vedic" knowledge (Madan 1997, 217).

The emergence of the Arya Samaj in the Punjab toward the end
of the nineteenth century marks a watershed in the development of
Hindu fundamentalism. Dayanand's "Back to Veda" battle cry
demonstrates the fundamentalist tendency toward both scriptural-
ization and the desire to return to an ostensible golden age in the
distant past. The reaction to the modernism of the day exhibited by
Dayanand and the Arya Samaj led them to defend the "Truth" of
Vedic justice staunchly. A major component of this defensive strategy included the formation of large-scale *shuddhi* ("purification")
campaigns, particularly after Dayanand's death. Dayanand's glorifi-
cation of scripture provided the impetus for his defense of Vedic
culture and led ultimately to the shuddhi movements, some of
which are still active today (Thapar 1997, 62). Shuddhi rites assert
the ritual reconversion into the Hindu fold of typically low-caste
persons who had previously converted to Christianity or Islam.
Precedents for religious conversion movements may be traced as far
back as the Buddha (circa sixth century BCE) in Indian history;
however, never before had there been a call for reconversion. The

Arya Samaj's conversion movements gave rise to a new kind of Hinduism—a single, newly reified religion—born out of conflict with what followers saw as "militantly aggressive forms of Christianity and Islam, if not later also against radical forms of secularism and modernism" (Frykenberg 1994, 601).

Modern Hindu Fundamentalism:
The "Hindutva" Family

With the rise of politically oriented organizations (even if clandestine), notions of Indian or Hindu culture have become more important than the quest for a definitive Hindu scripture. Vinayak Damodar Savarkar, a political prisoner of the British Raj in 1923, wrote *Hindutva: Who Is a Hindu?* Savarkar's creation of the neologism *Hindutva* (literally "Hindu-ness") belies the desire to concretize and solidify a distinctive group, like Dayanand's noble "Aryas," from among an otherwise amorphous composite of persons. His definition of Hindutva, or the essence of what it means to be a "Hindu," bears quoting at length:

> A Hindu . . . is he who looks upon the land that extends from Sindhu to Sindhu—from the Indus to the Seas—as the land of his forefathers—his Fatherland (*Pitribhu*), who inherits the blood of that race whose first discernible source could be traced to the Vedic Saptasindhus, and which on its onward march, assimilating much that was incorporated and ennobling much that was assimilated, has come to be known as the Hindu people, who has inherited and claims as his own the culture of that race as expressed chiefly in their common classical language Sanskrit, and represented by a common history, a common literature, art and architecture, law and jurisprudence, rites and rituals, ceremonies and sacraments, fairs and festivals; and who, above all, addresses this land, this Sindhusthan, as his Holyland (*Punyabhu*), and the land of his prophets and seers, of his godmen and gurus, the land of piety and pilgrimage. These are the essentials of Hindutva—a common nation (*Rashtra*), a common race (*jati*), and a common civilization (*Sanskriti*). (Savarkar 1989, 116)

The religion of "Hinduism" for Savarkar was only one part of the broader concept of Hindutva. Savarkar had room enough under the broad rubric of Hindutva for other indigenous groups who looked upon India in some sense as a holy land, such as the Jains, Buddhists, Sikhs, and even the more recently emerging Arya Samajis and Sanatana Dharmis. Jews, Christians, Muslims, and to some extent, Parsis (descendants of Persian Zoroastrians), were necessarily to be excluded from the nation (if not the country) precisely because their "Holy lands" were located elsewhere on alien soil. "Savarkar's momentous declaration—'a coherent and powerful pattern of concepts'—has in recent years acquired the undisputed status of the manifesto of Hindu fundamentalism, which is totalitarian in relation to those forcibly grouped together as We Hindus, and exclusivist towards those stigmatized as the spiritually alienated 'Others'" (Madan 1997, 220). The fusion of the concepts of nationhood with language and territory had far-reaching implications in India's quest for independence (Dalmia and von Stietencron 1995, 19).

The Rashtriya Swayamsevak Sangh

In consonance with Savarkar's concept of Hindutva, Keshav Baliram Hedgewar founded the Rashtriya Swayamsevak Sangh (RSS) in Nagpur with "Maharashtrian Brahmins in 1925 on the day commemorating Rama's slaying of Ravana" (Lutgendorf 1995, 274). This "National Organization of Volunteers" was formed for the protection of "national religion and culture." Among the first recruits to the new movement were Brahmins concerned with the welfare of the Hindu nation (*rashtriya*) in light of the rising political mobilization of the Muslim community and the escalating conflict between Brahmin and non-Brahmin Hindu communities. Since its inception, the National Organization of Volunteers has emphasized ideological instruction coupled with physical exercises as a method of "character building."

The early RSS claimed that the group merely sought the advancement of a national Hindu culture and was not politically motivated. But because the RSS was linked to Mahatma Gandhi's assassination in 1948, the Indian government placed a ban upon the organization that was not to be lifted until the group produced a written constitution. In its 1949 constitution, the RSS describes its objectives as follows: "To eradicate differences among Hindus; to make them realize the greatness of their past; to inculcate in them a spirit of self-sacrifice and selfless devotion to Hindu society as a whole; to build up an organized and well-disciplined corporate life; and to bring about the regeneration of Hindu society" (cited in Madan 1997, 221, n17).

Before his death in 1940, Hedgewar named M. S. Golwalkar as his replacement. Under his leadership, the RSS expanded its influence north and east from Maharashtra. Though the RSS maintained a strategy of noninvolvement in overt political activity, its leaders' keen interest in power was still centered on the "Five Unities" of the ancient Hindu nation: geography, race, religion, culture, and language. Only two years before assuming leadership of the RSS, Golwalkar wrote:

> The non-Hindu people in Hindustan must either adopt the Hindu culture and language, must learn to respect and revere Hindu religion, must entertain no idea but the glorification of the Hindu nation, i.e., they must not only give up their attitude of intolerance and ingratitude towards this land and its age-long traditions, but must also cultivate the positive attitude of love and devotion instead; in one word they must cease to be foreigners or may stay in the country wholly subordinated to the Hindu nation claiming nothing, deserving no privileges, far less any preferential treatment, not even citizen's rights. (cited in Madan 1997, 223)

Here one sees again the equation of nationality (*rashtriya*) with Hindutva. To deny that one is Hindu is tantamount to denying that one is Indian. This sentiment finds wider acceptance in the political parties and social organizations that have coalesced around RSS ideology. In RSS literature, political parties like the historical Hindu Mahasabha (no longer in existence), the Jana Sangh, and the Bharatiya Janata Party (BJP) and "nonpolitical," "civic" organizations such as the Vishva Hindu Parishad (VHP) and the Shiv Sena ("Shiva's Army") are referred to as "the Hindutva family" (*Sangha parivara*). For this family of organizations, "Hindu" is coterminous with membership in the Hindu nation of the Indian Motherland. As Golwalkar indicates above, those foreigners or non-Hindu Indians who cannot get with this program may remain in India at their own peril, "deserving no privileges . . . not even citizen's rights."

Golwalkar's theory of history goes beyond merely equating Hinduness with Indianness. For him, "Hindu" is the name applied to the greatest civilization the earth has ever known:

> The origins of our people, the date from which we have been living here as a civilized entity, is unknown to the scholars of history. . . . We existed when there was no necessity for any name. We were the good, the enlightened people. We were the people who knew about the laws of nature and the laws of the Spirit. We built a great civilization, a great culture, and a unique social order. We had brought into life almost everything that was beneficial to man. Then the rest of mankind were just bipeds and so no distinctive name was given to us. . . . The name "Hindu," derived from the river Sindhu, has been associated with us in our history and tradition for so long that it has now become our universally accepted and adored name. (cited in Embree 1994, 630)

The Hindu Mahasabha, one of the earliest members of the Sangha parivara family of organizations, was founded as a political party in 1913 to counter the rising threat of the Muslim League. A group of upper-caste Hindu men in search of greater social and economic autonomy, the Hindu Mahasabha jockeyed for political power against the Muslim League in the dying days of the British Raj. The Jana Sangh, another family member, was founded in Delhi in 1951, merged into the Janata Party in 1977, and then in 1980 was reformed into an independent political party called the Indian People's Party, or Bharatiya Janata Party (BJP). As political parties, the Jana Sangh, and later the BJP, stressed Hindu national identity. They showed a keen distrust of the long-ruling Congress Party, arguing that it consistently exhibited "favoritism" toward the largest minority population, the Muslims (roughly 12 percent of the Indian population). A. B. Vajpayee, prime minister of India as this book went to press, was a founding member of the BJP. L. K. Advani, Indian home minister and former president of the Vishva

Hindu Parishad (VHP), was recently nominated by Vajpayee to the Office of Deputy Prime Minister. Advani presented himself as the god Rama in a 1991 cross-country religious parade, or *Rath Yatra* (a "royal procession" led by a Volkswagen van decorated to resemble the chariot of the god Rama upon his triumphant return to Ayodhya). A modern version of this scene was fresh on the minds of millions because it had only recently been portrayed in the immensely popular 1987 Doordarshan television serial production of the Ramayana.

The Vishva Hindu Parishad

Although the Sangha parivara has toned down its elitist rhetoric somewhat since the days of Hedgewar and Golwalkar, three concerns may be detected that serve to connect the early Hindu fundamentalists with their modern offspring. First, fundamentalists of the Sangha parivara have opposed religious conversion to nonindigenous religious traditions. Second, they have been active in promoting anti–cow slaughter legislation. Third, they continue to promote the teaching of "Hindu culture" as "Indian culture" by means of celebrating the "pure" (that is, "Sanskritized") Hindi language and insisting that Hindi be continually emphasized as the official, national language.

As "founding father" of the Sangha parivara, the RSS sponsored a national organization to carry out its cultural agenda at the popular level. Founded in Bombay in 1964 on the god Krishna's birthday, the "World Hindu Council," or Vishva Hindu Parishad (VHP), was created to "protect, develop and spread Hindu values." The VHP's 1982 pamphlet entitled *Message and Activities* lists the following objectives:

(1) To take steps to arouse consciousness, to consolidate and strengthen the Hindu Society. (2) To protect, develop and spread the Hindu values of life—ethical and spiritual. (3) To welcome back all who had gone out of the Hindu fold and to rehabilitate them as part and parcel of the Universal Hindu Society. (5) [*sic*] To render social services to humanity at large. It has initiated Welfare Projects

for the 170 million down trodden brethren, who have been suffering
for centuries. These projects include schools, hospitals, libraries, etc.
(6) Vishva Hindu Parishad, the World Organization of six hundred
million at present residing in eighty countries, aspires to revitalize
the eternal Hindu society by rearranging the code of conduct of our
age old Dharma to meet the needs of the changed times. (7) To
eradicate the concept of untouchability from the Hindu Society.
(cited in van der Veer 1994b, 653–654)

Since its inception, the VHP has sought to recover low-caste and
untouchable persons who have converted to "non-indigenous"
faiths. In 1966 the VHP held a meeting in Allahabad that sought to
"re-admit into the Hindu fold those who had been converted to
other faiths no matter how many generations before." They used
the Hindi term *paravartan* ("turning around," "coming home," or
"reversion") to connote returning to one's "original" or ancestral
faith as part of their belief that "all true Indians see themselves as
Hindus" (Embree 1994, 638). The VHP is not the first to engage in
such activities. Precedents for ritual reconversion back into the
Hindu fold (as distinguished from rituals to readmit one into a
caste) may be traced as far back as the Muslim period, and there
was a resurgence of reconversions with Dayanand and the early
Punjabi shuddhi campaigns.

In addition to its active resistance to "non-indigenous" religious
conversion, the VHP has sought to ban cow slaughter. The issue of
cow slaughter has been viewed as symptomatic of the "invader's
presence," especially the Muslim community in India. In Golwalkar's rhetoric, cow protection is envisioned as an important
Hindu responsibility alongside the need to shore up and unify the
apparently schismatic tendencies within "Hindu culture" itself. On
the subject of cow slaughter Golwalkar writes: "It began with the
coming of the foreign invaders. In order to reduce the population
to slavery, they thought that the best way was to stamp out every ves-
tige of self-respect in Hindus. They took to various types of barbarism such as conversion, demolishing our temples and . . . cow-
slaughter" (cited in Embree 1994, 639). That the Qur'an
prescribes the slaughter of a cow as one possible means for celebrating the end of the fast of Ramadan during the feast of Bakr Id

only served to deepen Golwalkar's convictions regarding the barbarity of the Muslim religion.

Finally, there remains the issue of the Hindi language. India has always been a land of diverse ethnic and linguistic groups. Schedule 8 of the Constitution of India currently lists some eighteen officially recognized, regional language groupings. In addition to the major languages enumerated in the Constitution there are over one thousand local dialects. How, then, did the Hindi language, of north-central Indian provenance, come to be singled out as the official language of the Republic of India? For many Hindus in eighteenth and nineteenth century north-central India, the Hindi language functioned as a "symbolic instrument for fighting colonialism and English." In the quest for national self-identity that was an integral part of the struggle for independence, "the development of Hindi as the medium of modern education was the major function that Hindu revivalist forces assigned to themselves" (Kumar 1993, 537). During the colonial period, the British administration used Urdu as the official court language. (Hindi and Urdu share the same grammatical structure and much basic vocabulary; Urdu uses more words derived from Persian and Arabic whereas Hindi uses more words derived from Sanskrit.) The Urdu language (written in a modified version of the Persian script) was adopted by the British because it was in use in the Muslim courts when the British arrived on the subcontinent. Up to the early twentieth century, school textbooks were often written in Urdu or in Hindustani, a form of mixed Hindi/Urdu available in Devanagari or in Persian script. The rise of certain north Indian, self-consciously "Hindu" Hindi literati in the 1920s and 1930s ushered in a trend toward the exclusion of words from Urdu and Arabic as "non-Indian."

The Hindi literati's cultural agenda led to the formation of Hindi departments in schools and universities, Hindi syllabuses, and Hindi anthologies that often excluded the major Urdu poets of the nineteenth and twentieth centuries. The Hindi-speaking "Hindu nation" was envisioned in terms of the "religion, cultural norms, language and dress of pre-Mughal [pre-Muslim] India." Children were taught the poem "Matribhoomi" ("Mother Country") in which the poet declares, "One who has no thought for one's own language, nor has a knowledge of one's own community [jati] and religion; one who feels no pride for his country—such a person is dead though he lives" (Kumar 1993, 543).

In the 1940s, Mahatma Gandhi pled for the retention of Hindustani, the old Hindi/Urdu mixed language, as a means of unifying a country drifting ever closer to partition. He sought to unite Hindus and Muslims into a single Indian nation with Hindustani as the officially recognized language. Members of the Constituent Assembly, including Nehru and the Muslim leader Azad, favored Hindustani as well. The Congress Party, however, favored what many called "pure" (that is, "Sanskritized") Hindi. Article 343 of the Constitution, enacted in 1950, declares "Hindi in the Devanagari script" to be the "official language of the Union," with 1965 as the targeted year for the official changeover from English to Hindi. However, after strong opposition from non-Hindi speaking areas, the Official Languages Act of 1963 permitted the use of English for official purposes for an indefinite period. Despite this concession, the south of India in particular—as an area whose mother tongues derive from the Dravidian language family rather than the Sanskritic family—has generally opposed (sometimes violently) the imposition of Hindi as the official language of the union.

The Ramajanmabhumi Mandir/ Babri Masjid Controversy

The Sangha parivara organizations have complained that Congress Party governments at local and national levels have placated minority communities such as Muslims at the expense of Hindu culture. There is perhaps no better example of this issue than the events surrounding the Babri Masjid in the northern Indian city of Ayodhya. Hindu fundamentalists asserted that the Babri Masjid, or "mosque of Babar," had been built upon the ruins of a temple honoring the birthplace of Rama (Rama-janma-bhumi mandir). For the Sangha parivara, this was yet another example of Hindu honor desecrated at the hands of Muslim "invaders."

On December 6, 1992, said to be the day of the righteous king Rama's birth, two hundred thousand *kara sevakas* ("those who lend

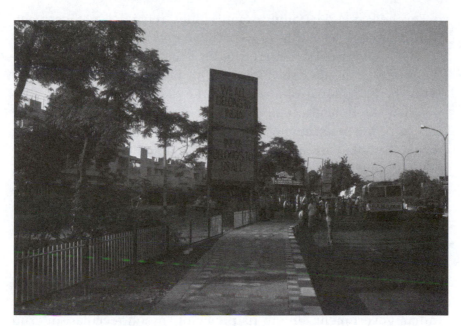

Billboard in New Delhi.
ROBIN RINEHART

a hand," that is, a mobilized mass of Hindu fundamentalists) systematically attacked and destroyed the Babri Masjid, in some instances tearing away bricks by hand, and announced plans to build
an elaborate temple dedicated to Rama where the mosque had
stood.

The Muslim mosque, and the ruins of the temple believed to be
beneath it, proved an excellent symbol around which to rally certain militant Hindus of the Sangha parivara. For the VHP in particular, the mosque signified a violated Hindu community that had
been emasculated by Muslim invaders instead of rightfully defending or reclaiming what was its own. That the masjid had been allowed to replace Rama's temple all these centuries only provided
further evidence of the Indian government's pampering of minorities, which Sangha parivara literature craftily described as the government's interference in the form of "pseudo-secularism." The
sense of Hindu emasculation was captured in the VHP's nationwide
publicity campaigns (Lutgendorf 1995, 276).

For the RSS and its family organizations, religion is not just a personal matter, as secularists argue. The temple/mosque issue, for instance, is construed not merely as an issue of local, sectarian conflict but as a broader social issue with far-reaching implications. What the Sangha parivara rejects is the definition of religion proposed by the Indian secular state, which necessarily identifies some aspects of life as existing outside of the realm of the religious. But for the Sangha parivara, religion plays a ubiquitous role in public life. The government-enforced "pseudo-secularism," they point out, does not restrict itself to private matters, so why should Hindu culture and religion remain quietly sequestered while the Indian state supports minorities, especially the Muslim "enemy"? In this context, the figure of Rama functioned as a powerful metaphor for Hindutva in a number of ways. First, Rama's temple became a symbol of a violated Hindu community. The mosque signified an abused Hindu nation humiliated by a "pampered" Muslim minority. The Indian government, due to its policy of "pseudo-secularism" run amuck, lacked the gumption to respond adequately to Hindu subjugation. This fundamentalist rhetoric eventually gave rise to an inquiry into what was called the "systematic destruction of Hindu places of worship." The BJP called in archaeologists to verify that Muslim invaders had systematically and purposively sought out the holiest Hindu temples to tear down and replace with Muslim mosques. Others, however, oppose the Hindu fundamentalists' view by claiming that there never really was a temple of Rama under the Babri Masjid.

Rama himself became a metaphor for the "essential Hindu-ness of Indian culture" (Hansen 1999, 174). The great antiquity of Rama as a paramount god, champion of the Hindus, was dramatized in fundamentalist rhetoric. Rama also became a metaphor for the "catholicity of traditional forms of Hindu devotion and piety" (Hansen 1999, 176). Although previously "Hindu culture" may have lacked a clearly defined center and an overall sense of unity and cohesion, proponents of Hindutva now had a universal symbol around which to rally in the form of the Ramajanmabhumi movement. Finally, Rama was employed in order to demonize the Muslim "other." Rama was depicted as the guardian of the Hindu order against the once geographical and now internal enemy. As during the struggle for independence, Indian Muslims were again saddled with having greater loyalties to a worldwide Muslim community than to the nation of India.

The final repercussions of the violent communal conflict over the Babri Masjid in Ayodhya have yet to be seen. Surely Ayodhya provides a glimpse into one type of fundamentalist ideology in action, that is, what Bruce Lawrence would identify in his rubric as "political activist/terrorist" fundamentalism. In India, this type of activism is frequently referred to as "communalism" or "communal violence"— "a euphemism that conceals the fact that in nearly all the most brutal episodes the victims were overwhelmingly Muslim" (Lutgendorf 1995, 277). For politically active fundamentalists, whether in India or Israel, a major threat comes in the form of the secularist critique of their totalizing religious worldviews. Secularism, an ideology that posits a distinction between the realm of the religious and the realm of the political, is the topic to which we turn next.

Secularism in Modern India

If fundamentalism is a highly contested category, secularism is no less so. The term *secularism* is employed by a variety of persons in a variety of ways, and like the category "fundamentalism," "secularism" is a newly developed ideology with roots in the modern world. A *secular state,* as this term is used in the Indian juridical context, may be minimally defined as a nontheocratic, noncommunal state that seeks to embody equality for all citizens regardless of religious affiliation.

Though the coining of the term *secularism* itself is a rather recent phenomenon, the process of secularization can be traced somewhat further back in Western history. The first fruits of the secularization process can be seen in Europe with the Protestant Reformation and the subsequent rise of nation-states that sought to establish governments outside the jurisdiction of religious authorities. The term came into usage in the 1800s when "a British reformer, George Jacob Holyoake (1817–1906), propounded secularism as a doctrine which meant that 'morality should be based solely in regard to the well-being of mankind in the present life to the exclusion of all considerations drawn from belief in God or in a future state'" (De 1994, 11).

Peter Berger proposes a brief definition of the process whereby societies become increasingly secular: "By secularization we mean the process by which sectors of society and culture are removed from the domination of religious institutions and symbols" (Berger 1967, 107). Likewise, Berger lists several "carriers" of the secularization process: the spread of Western civilization, the rise of communism, modern nationalism, and the modern economic process, or the "dynamic of industrial capitalism." One result of the process of secularization in the modern world, states Berger, is that "probably for the first time in history, the religious legitimations of the world have lost their plausibility not only for a few intellectuals and other marginal individuals but for broad masses of entire societies" (Berger 1967, 124–125). How then has secularism confronted traditional religious legitimizations in the Indian context? Is there a one-to-one correspondence between Western models of secularism and Indian secularism? In the introduction to his work on religion and law in India, J. D. M. Derrett argues that "nothing will actually emerge in fact which is inconsistent with the ancient and traditional values, and these are consistent with 'secularism' in a wholly unique, Indian, sense" (Derrett 1968, 31). In other words, if this is, in fact, the case, then we should expect that the type of secularism to emerge in India will be unique to the Indian context. Western models of secularism will be helpful for India only to the extent that they are consonant with traditional Indian values widely accepted among the citizenry.

Secularism has become a word much brandished about in the modern Indian political context. Derrett notes that virtually everything in the Hindu past has been called "secular": "'Secularism' being in favor, naturally all Hindu culture, including the Vedas, are said to be 'secular'" (Derrett 1968, 516 n2). Such a loose characterization of the category of "secular," however, is not helpful for our purposes. If everything may be said to be "secular" in Hindu culture, then nothing may be said to be so; for secularism would no longer serve as a useful category descriptive of anything in particular.

A necessary question is whether and to what extent secularity fits the Indian context. T. N. Madan answers unequivocally that secularism has failed in India because it is "an alien cultural ideology" (Madan 1987, 757). The "borrowed idea" of secularism has failed to render meaningful the Indian historical experience. Madan states that "the only way secularism in South Asia, understood as inter-religious understanding, may succeed would be for us to take both religion and secularism seriously and not reject the former as superstition and reduce the latter to a mask for communalism or mere expediency" (Madan 1987, 757).

Secularism and Personal Laws

A major issue for secularists in India involves the use of traditional religious laws, based upon religious community (that is, Hindu personal law, Muslim personal law, and the like), versus the Constitution's directive principle to establish a "uniform civil code" equally applicable to all regardless of religious affiliation. This "uniform civil code" is intended to replace the personal laws (governing marriage, divorce, maintenance, and property rights) associated with the various religious communities. The reform of personal, religious laws among the various communities in India has raised a question regarding the cross-cultural applicability of the "secular versus religious" paradigm. Derrett writes: "the concept of 'secular' versus 'religious' may be valid in the West, but comes up against unexpected difficulties in India, where the two main religious communities profess, if they profess any religion, a religion which does not consider worldly or practical questions to be distinct from religion" (Derrett 1968, 31). Another way of understanding this issue is to ask if we may clearly distinguish, so as to isolate for purposes of legislation, secular matters apart from religious matters for believers in religio-cultural traditions, such as Hinduism and Islam, which propound worldviews in which religion and law are not separate categories.

One must look further back in history in order to address adequately the unique situation of secularism in Indian history. The classical law or dharma texts of India, such as the Laws of Manu, indicate that the righteous Hindu king is to rule in accordance with dharma, or the Hindu moral order. Muslim rulers of the

Mughal empire likewise enforced *shari'ah* (Islamic law or the accepted Islamic precedents) upon their Muslim subjects while they attempted, in many cases, to uphold local dharma for their Hindu populations (Engineer 1998, 189–190). The Western notion of secularism, as in Thomas Jefferson's "wall of separation" between church and state, caught on in India only among a small section of urban, Western-educated elites around the time of independence.

A tension between traditional concepts of rulership and law and modern secular approaches is evident in the Constitution itself (Baird 1999, 189). Robert Baird has pointed out the conflict between the governmental values of the secular Constitution and several "axiomatic values" of traditional Indian origin. The notion of "justice" in the Constitution assumes that justice is to be carried out in the present lifetime. Traditional Indian notions of justice, conversely, often take into consideration the roles of karma, rebirth, and caste within the framework of multiple lives. Likewise, the modern, secular notions of universal human equality and the equal rights of citizens reverse traditional Indian understandings of purity, pollution, class, and caste (Baird 1998, 342).

Nehruvian Secularism

Jawaharlal Nehru, India's first prime minister (1947–1964), serves as an excellent example of secularism at work in India. Nehru sought to minimize the role of religion in Indian political life. Though he was a close associate of Mahatma Gandhi, his view of secularism clearly differed from his somewhat older contemporary. Gandhi's view of secularism was based upon his religious conviction that all religions are in some sense "true." Gandhi claimed to have had "equal regard for all faiths and creeds"—"for me, all the principle religions are equal in the sense that they are all true" (Gandhi 1962, 4). He regarded it a "sacred duty" to know the religious views of others: "If we are to respect other's religions as we would have them respect our own, a friendly study of the world's religions is a sacred duty" (Gandhi 1962, 15). The role of secular government,

Pandit Jawaharlal Nehru is garlanded by members of the Indian Socialist Congress upon his arrival in London, UK, October 1935.

HULTON-DEUTSCH COLLECTION/CORBIS

then, was to treat all religions equally or to have equal regard for all faiths within its jurisdiction (*sarva dharma samabhava*). For Gandhi, this was the religious goal of the secular state.

Nehru concurred with Gandhi's call for the equal treatment of all religions, but for quite different reasons. For Nehru, all citizens were to be treated equally regardless of religious affiliation—not because all religions are true—but because this approach maximizes human freedom. During the framing of the Indian Constitution in January 1948, Nehru declared, "India will be a land of many faiths, equally honored and respected but of one national outlook" (Nanda 1998, 108). The view of secularism adopted by Nehru was rational, modern, and particularly suited to the Indian situation (Baird 1991, 135).

Nehru wrote of Gandhi's role in the independence movement in his 1941 autobiography entitled *Toward Freedom:*

> Gandhiji was continually laying stress on the religious and spiritual side of the movement. His religion was not dogmatic, but it did mean a definitely religious outlook on life, and the whole movement was strongly influenced by this and took on a revivalist character so far as the masses were concerned. . . . [S]ome of Gandhiji's phrases sometimes jarred upon me—thus his frequent reference to *Rama Raj* as a golden age which was to return. But I was powerless to intervene, and I consoled myself with the thought that Gandhiji used words because they were well known and understood by the masses. He had an amazing knack of reaching the heart of the people. (cited in Stoler-Miller 1991, 786)

Here we see that Nehru's insistence upon a secular India is just as pragmatic as it is ideological; to the extent that Gandhi's methods were effective, they were necessary. Nehru once quipped that his greatest difficulty as prime minister of independent India was "creating a just state by just means . . . perhaps, too, creating a secular state in a religious country" (Nanda 1998, 113). Though not endorsing Gandhi's religious message, Nehru was nonetheless willing to deploy Gandhi's methods to further his ultimate goal of nation building.

Radhakrishnan's View of Secularism

Sarvepalli Radhakrishnan, the president of India during the end of Nehru's term as prime minister and after (1962–1967), played the traditional role of *rajaguru* (that is, the spiritual adviser to the king) in Prime Minister Nehru's cabinet. Radhakrishnan, perhaps better known as a preeminent philosopher and theologian than as a political figure or statesman, like Gandhi understood secularism to consist of an acceptance of religion rather than its rejection. In discussing Radhakrishnan's view of secularism, Robert Minor indicates that "secular" and "religious" do not function as separate categories in Radhakrishnan's thought (Minor 1987, 121). For Radhakrishnan, India's secular Constitution is not irreligious or antireligious but actually affirms "the religion of the spirit." Radhakrishnan went even further than the traditional designation of secularism as the view that all religions are of the same nature; for him, the state is to function as the protector of all religions. This required that the secular state curtail evangelistic tendencies toward religious conversion. As Minor points out, a view of secularism that seeks to discourage religious conversion out of hand yet claims to protect equally *all* religions seems somewhat problematic (Minor 1987, 122).

Radhakrishnan's protectionist stance toward religious conversion may be contrasted with an alternate view of secularism in India. Described as the noninvolvement with religion on the part of the state, this view stems from the colonial British apprehension with becoming overly involved in the religious affairs of the colonized. The view of secularism as the noninvolvement of government in religious affairs, some claim, comes closest to the view of individual rights espoused in the Fundamental Rights section of the Indian Constitution. The notion of a secular state, as it may be gleaned from the Constitution itself, states Saral Jhingran, is such that "governmental dealings with citizens and other inhabitants must be independent of their religious identities." The Indian secular state must "boldly dissociate itself from any compromise with communalism of any brand whatsoever." What this means for Jhingran is "a total, unconditional rejection of the category of religious community for socio-political dialogue or action. Loyalty to separate communities has been the greatest hindrance to national integration and development of a secular approach" (Jhingran 1995, 235). Thus, by the state's theoretical blindness to the issue of a citizen's religious affiliation, the state may claim noninvolvement in the religious sphere.

Religious Conversion and the Constitutional Religious Model

D. E. Smith argues that despite the Constitution's explicit recognition of the right to propagate religion, it is precisely the issue of religious conversion that challenges the secular state's noninvolvement policy most assiduously. Both the legislative and the judicial branches of the Indian government have taken decisive steps "to discourage conversions from Hinduism and to reinforce the religious status quo." In Smith's view, "It cannot be denied that in India freedom of expression is rather consistently subordinated to the requirements of maintaining public order" (Smith 1963, 192). The constitutional role of the state in the reform of "Hinduism" likewise calls into question the possibility of a "noninvolvement of the state" approach to secularism.

Robert Baird has argued that the "Constitutional Religious Model" (that is, a modern, secular, egalitarian approach to law in which the "content of justice is based on equality") is one result of India's quest for secularism. This model, a view of reality that takes into consideration only the present lifetime for determining justice, has replaced traditional religious views of law and society among certain legal and political elites in independent India. But it is important to recognize that this model also furthers the state's goal of promoting "positive" religious change by eradicating certain elitist practices associated with traditional Hinduism. For example, the Constitution outlaws discrimination based upon caste status or religious affiliation, even though discrimination based upon caste is a traditional feature of Hinduism. This model, which prioritizes a concept of justice based upon the value of equality above traditional hierarchical views of justice, inherently subordinates religious freedom, at certain points, to the higher goal of social reform.

The Constitutional Religious Model consistently favors social reform over traditional religious expressions. Article 17 of the Constitution abolishes untouchability. Article 16(4) "provides for the possible reservation of positions for persons in backward classes." As a category, "backward classes" was added to the Constitution in 1951 to refer to members of traditionally disenfranchised and socially and educationally impaired caste groups and tribes. Article 15(4) prohibits discrimination on the basis of caste and states that "nothing shall prevent the State from making any special provision for the advancement of any socially and educationally backward classes of citizens or for the Scheduled Castes and the Scheduled Tribes." In several key decisions, the Supreme Court of India has lifted the ban on temple entry for low-caste and Untouchable persons. On the basis of its reading of the "equality of all persons" sought after in the Constitution, the Court has sought "to throw open temples to all classes of Hindus," even opening temples for those low-caste and Untouchable persons whose "polluting" presence had previously excluded them from temple worship.

Despite fundamentalist accusations that the government is engaging in "pseudo-secularism"—a kind of "reverse discrimination" in the form of the ongoing "liberalization" of social norms—the Indian judiciary, at least, does not seem currently inclined to desist. Fundamentalist critiques of this type of Indian secularism center on the fact that freedom of religion is denied to traditional observers of caste hierarchy. This "pseudo-secularism," they claim, espouses a new, modern religious goal, that of social equality. Here the critic's point must be conceded. Although freedom and equality are both important goals of the Indian secular state, when in conflict, preference has been given repeatedly to the value of equality.

Conclusion

Fundamentalism and secularism are two major Indian responses to modernity. Speculation as to the future success or failure of fundamentalism and secularism in India abounds, but it remains to be seen how "Hinduism" will be affected by the ongoing interaction between fundamentalist and secularist approaches to its interpretation. Calls are frequently made to divorce religion from politics in India as a solution to the subcontinent's social ills. Dhirendra Vajpeyi writes: "God must be liberated in India from the Babri Masjid, Ramajanmabhumi, and the politics of paradise eschewed in favor of a culturally and ethnically plural yet politically united, secular, and modern India" (Vajpeyi 2001, 7). Echoing the voice of Nehru some forty years earlier, Vajpeyi's call for a separation between the realm of the religious and the realm of the secular seems theoretically possible among the educated elite but unlikely to happen "on the ground" in India.

Taking a different tack, John Carroll reminds us that in India, "it is a secular state that is the goal, rather than a secular society" (Carroll 2001, 28). D. E. Smith asserted nearly forty years ago that India has an excellent chance of becoming a secular state—nowhere in Smith's claim, however, is there a notion of India becoming a secular *society*. The distinction is an important one. The 1976 addition to the Preamble of the Indian Constitution identifies India as a "secular state." As we have seen, however, the concept of a "secular state" remains multivalent and contested. Few would argue that the goal of the Indian secular state is to secularize its citizenry. Rather, the manner in which the state governs and interacts with its citizens is to be secular. Fundamentalists and secularists alike anxiously ply for advantage as India continues to seek clarity regarding what precisely the relationship between a secular state and its populace entails.

BIBLIOGRAPHY

Baird, Robert D. *Essays in the History of Religions.* New York: Peter Lang, 1991.
———. "Traditional Values, Governmental Values, and Religious Conflict in Contemporary India," in *Brigham Young University Law Review* 2 (1998): 337–356.
———. "Expansion and Constriction of Religion: The Paradox of the Indian Secular State," in John McLaren and Harold Coward (eds.), *Religious Conscience, the State, and the Law.* Albany: State University of New York Press, 1999: 189–205.
Baird, Robert D., ed. *Religion and Law in Independent India.* Delhi: Manohar, 1993.

————. *Religion in Modern India.* 3rd ed. Delhi: Manohar, 1995.

Berger, Peter L. *The Sacred Canopy: Elements of a Sociological Theory of Religion.* New York: Anchor, 1967.

Carroll, John J. "In the Shadow of Ayodhya: Secularism in India," in A. Sharma (ed.), *Hinduism and Secularism after Ayodhya.* New York: Palgrave, 2001: 25–39.

Coward, Harold G. "The Response of the Arya Samaj," in Harold G. Coward (ed.), *Modern Indian Responses to Religious Pluralism.* Albany: State University of New York Press, 1987: 39–64.

Coward, Harold G., ed. *Modern Indian Responses to Religious Pluralism.* Albany: State University of New York Press, 1987.

De, Amalendu. "Religious Fundamentalism and Secularism in Indian Historical Context," in *Communalism in Contemporary India.* Calcutta: University of Burdwan, 1994: 72–132.

Derrett, J. D. M. *Religion, Law, and the State in India.* New York: Free Press, 1968.

Doniger, Wendy, with Brian K. Smith, trans. *The Laws of Manu.* New York: Penguin, 1991.

Embree, Ainslie T. *Utopias in Conflict: Religion and Nationalism in Modern India.* Berkeley: University of California Press, 1990.

————. "The Function of the Rashtriya Swayamsevak Sangh: To Define the Hindu Nation," in M. E. Marty and R. S. Appleby (eds.), *Accounting for Fundamentalisms: The Dynamic Character of Movements.* Chicago: University of Chicago Press, 1994: 617–652.

Engineer, Ashgar A. "Secularism in India—Theory and Practice," in Ashgar A. Engineer (ed.), *State Secularism and Religion—Western and Indian Experience.* Delhi: Ajanta, 1998: 189–206.

Frykenberg, Robert E. "Fundamentalism and Revivalism in South Asia," in J. W. Bjorkman (ed.), *Fundamentalism, Revivalists, and Violence in South Asia.* New Delhi: Manohar, 1988: 20–39.

————. "Accounting for Fundamentalisms in South Asia: Ideologies and Institutions in Historical Perspective," in M. E. Marty and R. S. Appleby (eds.), *Accounting for Fundamentalisms: The Dynamic Character of Movements.* Chicago: University of Chicago Press, 1994: 591–616.

————. "The Emergence of Modern 'Hinduism' as a Concept and as an Institution: A Reappraisal with Special Reference to South India," in G. D. Sontheimer and H. Kulke (eds.), *Hinduism Reconsidered.* New Delhi: Manohar, 1997: 82–107.

Gandhi, Mohandas K. *All Religions Are True.* Bombay: Pearl Publications, 1962.

Golwalkar, M. S. *We or Our Nationhood Defined.* Nagpur: Bharat Prakashan, 1938.

Hansen, Thomas B. *The Saffron Wave: Democracy and Hindu Nationalism in Modern India.* Princeton: Princeton University Press, 1999.

Jhingran, Saral. *Secularism in India.* New Delhi: Har-Anand, 1995.

Jones, Kenneth W. "The Arya Samaj in British India, 1875–1947," in R. D. Baird (ed.), *Religion in Modern India.* New Delhi: Manohar, 1995: 26–54.

———. "Politicized Hinduism: The Ideology and Program of the Hindu Mahasabha," in R. D. Baird (ed.), *Religion in Modern India.* New Delhi: Manohar, 1995: 241–273.

Jordens, J. T. F. "Gandhi and Religious Pluralism," in H. G. Coward (ed.), *Modern Indian Responses to Religious Pluralism.* Albany: State University of New York Press, 1987: 3–18.

Juergensmeyer, Mark. "The Debate over Hindutva: 'Fundamentalism' and Religious Nationalism in India." *Religion* 26 (April 1996): 129–136.

Kumar, Krishna. "Hindu Revivalism and Education in North-Central India," in M. E. Marty and R. S. Appleby (eds.), *Fundamentalisms and Society.* Chicago: University of Chicago Press, 1993: 536–557.

Lawrence, Bruce B. "From Fundamentalism to Fundamentalisms: A Religious Ideology in Multiple Forms," in Paul Heelas (ed.), *Religion, Modernity, and Postmodernity.* Oxford: Blackwell, 1998: 88–101.

Llewellyn, J. E. *The Arya Samaj as a Fundamentalist Movement: A Study in Comparative Fundamentalism.* New Delhi: Manohar, 1993.

Lochtefeld, James G. "New Wine, Old Skins: The *Sangh Parivar* and the Transformation of Hinduism." *Religion* 26 (1996): 101–118.

Lutgendorf, Philip. "Interpreting *Ramraj:* Reflections on the Ramayana, Bhakti, and Hindu Nationalism," in D. N. Lorenzen (ed.), *Bhakti Religion in North India: Community Identity and Political Action.* Albany: State University of New York Press, 1995: 253–287.

Madan, T. N. "Secularism in Its Place." *Journal of Asian Studies* 46, 4 (November 1987): 747–760.

———. *Modern Myths, Locked Minds: Secularism and Fundamentalism in India.* Delhi: Oxford University Press, 1997.

Marty, Martin E., and R. Scott Appleby, eds. *The Fundamentalism Project.* 5 vols. Chicago: University of Chicago Press, 1991–1995.

Minor, Robert N. *Radhakrishnan: A Religious Biography.* Albany: State University of New York Press, 1987.

Nanda, B. R. *Jawaharlal Nehru: Rebel and Statesman.* Delhi: Oxford University Press, 1998.

Patwardhan, Anand. *In the Name of God.* Produced and directed by Anand

Patwardhan. Commentary by Apurva Yagnik. 97 min. New York: First Run/Icarus Films, 1992. Videocassette.

Saraswati, Dayanand. *The Light of Truth: An English Translation of the Satyarth Prakash*. Translated from the Hindi by Durga Prasad. New Delhi: Jan Gyan Prakashan, 1970.

Savarkar, V. D. *Hindutva: Who Is a Hindu?* New Delhi: Bharatiya Sahitya Sadan, 1923 [reprinted 1989].

Smith, Brian K. "Re-envisioning Hinduism and Evaluating the Hindutva Movement." *Religion* 26 (1996): 119–128.

Smith, Donald E. *India as a Secular State*. Princeton: Princeton University Press, 1963.

Stoler-Miller, Barbara. "Presidential Address: Contending Narratives— The Political Life of the Indian Epics." *Journal of Asian Studies* 50, 4 (November 1991): 783–792.

Tambiah, Stanley J. "Presidential Address: Reflections on Communal Violence in South Asia." *Journal of Asian Studies* 49, 4 (November 1990): 741–760.

Thapar, Romila. "Syndicated Hinduism," in G. D. Sontheimer and H. Kulke (eds.), *Hinduism Reconsidered*. Delhi: Manohar, 1997: 54–81.

Vajpeyi, Dhirendra K. "The Politics of Paradise: Islam, Identity, and Politics in India," in A. Sharma (ed.), *Hinduism and Secularism after Ayodhya*. New York: Palgrave, 2001: 57–77.

Van der Veer, Peter. "Hindu Nationalism and the Discourse of Modernity: The Vishva Hindu Parishad," in M. E. Marty and R. S. Appleby (eds.), *Accounting for Fundamentalisms: The Dynamic Character of Movements*. Chicago: University of Chicago Press, 1994: 653–668.

———. *Religious Nationalism: Hindus and Muslims in India*. Berkeley: University of California, 1994.

Chapter Eleven

The Environment and Environmental Movements in Hinduism

GEORGE JAMES

India contains more biological diversity than perhaps any other land mass of similar size in the world. With only 2 percent of the world's land area, India possesses around 5 percent of the world's living organisms. Its diverse environments stretch from the peaks of the world's highest mountain range, the Himalayas, to the tropical coastal estuaries of Kerala, and from the world's richest rain forests in the northeast region to the deserts of Rajasthan, with a multitude of bioregions between. India is also a country of enormous cultural and religious diversity. Many of the religious and cultural traditions of India have supported strategies of resource use that have helped sustain India's biological diversity, and the ways of life that have depended upon it over a vast period of time.

India is also a country in which colossal environmental damage has been done and continues to occur. According to unofficial estimates, three thousand square miles of India's forests are cut down every year. Depletion of native forests has led to soil erosion causing floods and landslides that devastate villages and farmlands. Without adequate forest cover, monsoonal rains carry off valuable topsoil, depleting the land of nutrients. Overuse of chemical fertilizers is further depleting soil fertility. Over one-third of India's land area has now been classed as unproductive. Half of India's energy consumption is devoted to cooking. But with steadily diminishing forest resources, women in villages are required to walk ever further to bring back firewood sufficient for domestic needs. The uncontrolled exploitation of groundwater has resulted in an alarming drop in the water table and the seepage of ocean water into groundwater sources, leading to a scarcity of drinking water. Forms of livelihood that depend upon the bounty of nature, such as fishing, sheep-rearing, and basket weaving, are being abandoned in many parts of India. People who once subsisted upon these professions are joining the surging wave of ecological refugees moving to the cities in search of employment.

Between the years 1951 and 1981 the population of Calcutta (now called Kolkata) and Hyderabad doubled. In the same period, that of Bombay (now Mumbai), Madras (now Chennai), and Ahmedabad tripled, and that of Delhi and Bangalore quadrupled. These cities have seen acute shortages of water and other resources. A third of the urban population of India has no access to sanitary facilities of any kind. When the Yamuna River enters the city of Delhi its water contains about 7,500 coliform organisms per 100 milliliters. As it proceeds south from the city on its way toward Vrindavan, the mythical birthplace of Krishna, the coliform count is 24 million per 100 milliliters. Seventy percent of all the fresh water available in India is polluted, and its use accounts for the continuous epidemic of diarrhea that takes the lives of over a million children every year. With the proliferation of transportation by diesel and petrol vehicles, sulfur dioxide and particulate matter in these cities far exceeds the limits set by the World Health Organization. Dangerous levels of pesticide residues are being recorded in foodstuffs, and in animal and human tissues.

Today the pressure of human activity upon India's forests and land threatens many of the 15,000 plant species and the 75,000 animal species found in India. A flourishing illegal trade in wildlife products including tiger bones and skins, many exported to China for traditional medicines, poses a further threat to India's biodiversity. These conditions have laid an especially heavy burden upon

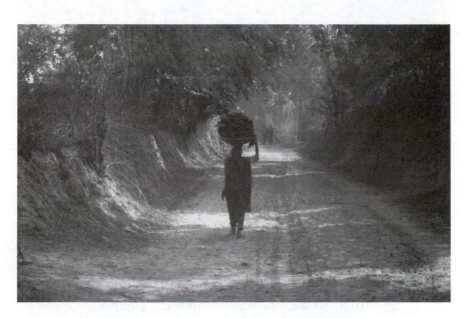

Woman carrying cow dung cakes used for cooking fuel.
ROBIN RINEHART

pastoral nomads and the tribal peoples of India, who have often been required to relinquish their habitat, heritage, and history to make way for projects to preserve biodiversity or for the construction of hydroelectric power projects to feed the energy needs of the burgeoning cities.

In 1962, the publication of the book *Silent Spring* by Rachel Carson brought widespread American public attention, perhaps for the first time, to the extent of ecological damage wrought by human intervention in nature. Interest in the preservation of nature, however, goes back to an appreciation of natural beauty sparked in large measure by the Romantic Movement of the nineteenth century in Europe and the United States. It is perhaps a paradox, then, that the Romantic philosophy of writers like Emerson and Thoreau was inspired by their encounter with some of the first philosophical and religious writings of India available in the West. Emerson's exploration of some of the sacred writings of India led him to reject the Western notion of deity as a Supreme Being that stands over nature, and the acceptance of divinity in nature itself. This led him eventually to the view that nature ought to be protected not for what it can provide for human beings but for its own intrinsic worth.

In this chapter we will first examine the understanding of India that has been a part of the development of contemporary environmental philosophy in the West. Second, we will examine some of the most pervasive attitudes and values concerning nature that are preserved in the Hindu religious tradition. Third, we will examine some of the differences between the environmental movements known in Western Europe and the United States, and those that are found in India. Finally, we will examine some of the movements for the preservation, protection, and restoration of nature in India that have been most effective in recent years.

India in Western Environmental Thought

In the 1960s the growing awareness of the global environmental crisis, and an awareness that Western ways of thinking had not provided a solution, provoked renewed interest in the religious ideas of non-Western civilizations, and in the religions of India in particular. In 1967 in an essay entitled "The Historical Roots of Our Environmental Crisis," the renowned environmental historian Lynn White argued that the environmental crisis was rooted in attitudes deeply embedded in Western religious traditions. The idea that human beings were created uniquely in the image of God, that God had given human beings dominion over the created order, and that God had created the world for the use of human beings had fostered attitudes hostile to the environment. This, White wrote, was an anthropocentric, or man-centered, religion. In some non-Western religions he found an attitude toward nature completely opposite that of the West. Other scholars joined White and affirmed that in non-Western traditions, nature is not the inert and spiritless product of a craftsman like God who stands above it. Rather, it is the very essence of divinity, to be adored, venerated, and cared for. Hinduism, with its doctrine of the divine spirit that pervades all of reality, its teaching of reincarnation that makes a family of all living species, and its doctrine of noninjury to all living things, seemed to provide an attractive alternative to the Western preoccupation with humanity as a special creation whose sense of privilege seemed to have put nature out of balance.

Not all writers concerned with the environment were so enthusiastic about Indian religious thought. Some were reluctant to forsake the religious and intellectual history of Western civilization for the ways of thinking very different from their own. The Australian philosopher John Passmore argued that the doctrine of the sacredness of nature and the claim that all living things are entitled to protection is fundamentally flawed. He held that the more reasonable teaching of stewardship toward nature is the unique product of Western religious and philosophical traditions.

Writing that draws such a stark contrast between non-Western traditions like that of India and the traditions of the West reflects the influence of what has been called Orientalist discourse. In such writing that is concerned with the environment, the traditions of India are seen either as (1) an ancient ecological wisdom that provides an alternative to modern exploitative Western attitudes toward nature, or (2) a primitive and irrational response to contemporary environmental problems. More recent research recognizes that neither of these views is accurate. Unlike the predominant religious traditions of the West, the Hindu religious tradition does not have a single doctrinal viewpoint. It is a living tradition in which differing viewpoints concerning the divine, nature, and the destiny of the human person have been negotiated over an enormous period of time. The Hindu religious tradition has not just one but a great variety of views and attitudes toward nature.

Nature in the Hindu Religious Tradition

A strong interest in nature is evident from the very earliest sources of Indian culture. Among the remains of the Indus Valley civilization, small, mostly square steatite seals (measuring one to three inches across) depict trees, water, and goddess figures, standing in close relation with one another. Some of them seem to depict the earth as a mother giving birth to a tree, along with scenes composed of animals, trees, and human beings, usually interpreted as revealing the common rhythm in human, animal, and vegetative life. The relationship of trees, water, and the goddess, found in the remains of the Indus Valley civilization, bears a striking resemblance to later Hindu images of the Ganges River as a goddess pictured beneath a tree.

In the Rig Veda, the earliest literary source of the Hindu religious tradition, hymns of praise and adoration are directed to a number of the phenomena of nature depicted as deities. Indra is the seasonal monsoon rain, pictured as a colossal male figure destroying the demon who is holding back the waters from the thirsty land. Surya is the sun, the Maruts are the storm spirits, and Apas is the waters. Prithvi is the Earth, praised as sustaining the world and all that dwells upon her:

> *You truly bear, Prithvi,*
> *The burden of the mountains' weight;*
> *With might, O you of many streams,*
> *You quicken, potent one, the soil.*
> *With garlands of speech our songs of praise*
> *Resound to thee, far spreading one,*
> *Who sends forth the swelling cloud,*
> *O bright one, like propelling speed;*
> *Who steadfast, holds with might*
> *The forest trees upon the ground,*
> *When from the lightening of your cloud,*
> *The rainfloods of the sky pour down*
>
> RIG VEDA 5:84
> AUTHOR'S TRANSLATION

The Rig Veda and other ancient Veda collections also lavish praise on such rivers as the Yamuna, the Saraswati, the Indus, and the Ganges. Indian religious traditions regard all rivers as sacred, and on the banks of such rivers we still find ancient temples in which a deep piety toward the river is expressed. In the Vedas we also find the origin of the idea of the universe as an organic whole, an idea that is developed more thoroughly in later Indian philosophy. In one of the hymns of the Rig Veda, the origin of the universe is depicted as the sacrifice of a colossal anthropomorphic deity, in which all of the elements of the natural world are related: "The moon was born from his spirit, from his eye was born the sun, from his mouth Indra and Agni, from his breath wind was born. From his navel arose the middle sky, from his head the heaven originated, from his feet the earth, the quarters from his ear. Thus did they fashion the worlds" (Rig Veda 10:90, author's translation).

Many scholars have observed that the universe is understood here as a living organism in which every part is related to the life of the whole. Later there develops the idea that all of life is sacred because all living beings reflect the one divine reality from which all of life has come, and the ethical injunction against injury to living things.

In the Upanishads, philosophical supplements to the Vedic hymns, the attitude of admiration for the natural world is retained. But here, alongside of that admiration a new understanding of nature is expressed. The result is that the overall attitude toward nature in the Upanishads is less consistent than it is in the hymns of the Rig Veda and other Vedic collections. There are over two hundred Upanishads, often portrayed as dialogues between a teacher and a student of sacred knowledge. Their subject matter centers upon such topics as the ultimate ground and source of the visible world; the nature of the true self, or atman, that resides within the depths of the human person and all other living creatures; the condition of embodied self in the visible world; and the path that leads to knowledge that liberates the embodied self from its condition of bondage and rebirth in the visible world, called *samsara*.

Despite the great variety of figures and analogies employed to express the insights of the Upanishads, their attitude toward the natural world can be gathered together in terms of two diverging tendencies. On the one hand the natural world and all that it contains, all that has being at all, is nothing other than brahman, the ultimate reality. Sometimes phenomena of nature are presented as analogies upon which to recognize the true relationship of the visible world to its ultimate but not evident ground. As birds resort to a tree for a resting place, so does everything resort to that supreme self (*Prashna Upanishad*). As herbs rise upon the earth, as hairs of the head and body arise upon the body, so from the imperishable does everything here arise. As sparks from a well-blazing fire, so from the imperishable manifold beings are produced (*Mundaka Upanishad*). From this viewpoint the world of nature is supremely valuable because it is the visible manifestation of the ultimate divine reality. On the other hand, some passages emphasize that though the supreme self dwells in all things, it is also other than all things, the unseen seer, the unheard hearer, the unthought thinker. In some places this reality is to be sought not in the outer world, but by means of reflection upon the depths of the inner self. And though the Upanishads do not all agree upon a single method for the pursuit of the knowledge of this ultimate reality, many of the most influential of the Upanishads recommend a method that entails the renunciation of the material world, seen now as a provisional and transitory reality. There is, for this reason, a tendency in some of the Upanishads to minimize the importance of the material world and enjoyments available within the human body, in which the embodied soul is condemned to repeated lives. It is perhaps in the *Maitri Upanishad* (I: 3–4) that this attitude toward the material world is most forcefully expressed: "in this ill-smelling, unsubstantial body, which is a conglomerate of bone, skin, muscle, marrow, flesh, semen, blood, mucus, tears, rheum, feces, urine, wind, bile, and phlegm, what is the good of the enjoyment of desires? . . . In this sort of cycle of existence (samsara) what is the good of the enjoyment of desires, when after a man has fed on them there is seen repeatedly his return to this earth? . . . In this cycle of existence I am like a frog in a waterless well" (Hume 1971, 413–414).

Later Hindu tradition sought to mediate between these opposing tendencies by articulating four ends, or purposes, to human existence (purusharthas). They consist of the pursuit of (1) kama, or sensuous and aesthetic pleasure, (2) dharma, or the demands of moral life, (3) artha, or political and economic well-being, and (4) moksha, or release, the final and spiritual end that culminates in liberation from the cycle of rebirth. For later Hinduism as well, a man's life is understood to be laid out in terms of four stages: that of the student, the householder, the forest dweller, and the renouncer. Although the pursuit of pleasure as well as economic and political gain is always mitigated by considerations of morality (dharma), and though the final goal of liberation remains on the horizon of every stage of earthly life, the four ends of life are not seen to be of equal relevance to all the stages of life. The life of the householder consists largely of the pursuit of the pleasures and responsibilities of raising children and of material and economic welfare for family and society. When such responsibilities are fulfilled, this stage is followed by that of withdrawal from material and economic life. Then at the stage of renunciation, a stage but rarely put into practice, the most relevant pursuit is the mastery of those religious texts that focus upon final end of release (moksha) from the cycle of rebirth. It is at this last stage of life that all privileges and responsibilities associated with material and economic life come finally to an end.

Although support for the care of nature can be found even in those texts that recommend renunciation of the visible world, it is in the dharma texts and texts concerning *artha*, or economic and political well-being, that the most explicit guidance concerning the treatment of the natural world can be found. One of the most important sources for the understanding of economic and political value is the *Artha Shastra* (ca. fourth century BCE), attributed to Kautilya, a minister to the first ruler of the Mauryan empire. For Kautilya, artha is not limited to what we today would associate with economics and politics. What he calls *Artha Shastra* is an account of the views of the ancient teachers concerning the acquisition and maintenance of the earth. The earth, however, means both the material source of the life and welfare of the community *and* the society that is dependent upon it. It is Kautilya's view that a large part of the responsibility for maintenance of the earth falls upon government. Kautilya believes that a competent monarchy is the form of government most likely to protect the weak from the strong and maintain the welfare of the people. For this to work, much depends upon the character and competence of the sovereign.

As guardian of the social and ecological order, the sovereign understands, supports, and enforces all duties (dharmas) distributed among the various classes (varnas) and stages of life (ashramas) into which the society is divided. He also supports the duties that pertain to all persons regardless of their social class or stage in life: nonviolence, truthfulness, purity, compassion, and forgiveness.

Much of what we today would call agricultural administration, disaster management, and environmental policy falls, in Kautilya's view, within the purview of the king. When appropriate, the king is expected to undertake agrarian reforms, establish policies for the proper maintenance of pastures and forests, and enforce laws that protect the environment. The attention of this ancient authority to matters of environmental concern is indicated by specific fines for such offenses as disposing of dust on roads; urinating or defecating near a well, pond, or temple; and inappropriately disposing of a dead animal. A striking example of Kautilya's concern for forest resources is the specific schedule of sanctions he imposes upon those who destroy trees, groves, or forests. Here he recommends fines of varying severity corresponding to the damage done. For the cutting off of the tender sprouts of fruit trees, flowering trees, or shade trees in parks near a city he recommends a fine of six *panas*. For the cutting of the minor branches of such trees the fine is twelve panas, and for the cutting of the large branches of such trees, the fine is twenty-four panas. For the cutting of the trunk of such trees the fine is forty-eight to ninety-six panas, and for the felling of such trees the fine is two hundred to five hundred panas. And for trees that mark boundaries or are worshiped, the sanctions are doubled. Though it is difficult to determine what a pana would be worth today, it is significant that offenses resulting in damage to forest resources were taken seriously enough to require the imposition of fines. Moreover, the fact that the gradations of the fines increase geometrically with the size of the damaged branches strongly suggests that trees were objects of value. And the fact that damage to a tree that has religious significance has especially severe penalties indicates not only that trees were objects of worship, but that provisions of law supported the worship of trees.

Another ancient Hindu legal document is the Laws of Manu. Widely considered the most authoritative of the ancient treatments of dharma, or duty, it states specifically that impure substances like urine, feces, and spit, and anything that contains blood or poison, are never to be disposed of in water.

Though ancient legal writings take specific measures for the protection of nature, attitudes toward nature are also reflected in the great literary narratives of the tradition, the Mahabharata and the Ramayana, as well as the Puranas. It was in the great forests of India that Rama and Sita spent the years of their exile from Ayodhya, and it was with the help of the forest animals, especially the monkeys, that Rama succeeded in the rescue of Sita from the demon Ravana. It was in the forest that the five sons of Pandu spent their exile in the years that led up to the great battle that was the climax of the Mahabharata. In the Bhagavad Gita, Krishna as the Supreme Lord of the universe proclaims: "I am the taste in the waters . . . the light of the sun and moon. I am the pure fragrance in earth and brightness in fire. I am the life in all beings" (Bhagavad Gita 7:8–9).

The Bhagavata Purana tells the story of the birth and childhood of Krishna as he grows up in the twelve forests of Vrindavan on the banks of the Yamuna River. The forest is the context of the stories of his miraculous childhood pranks, his play with the *gopis*, or cowherd girls, of his village, and the story of his love for Radha. The forests are the context of the many stories in which his teachings are set.

In the Matsya Purana (composed between the fifth to tenth century CE), the goddess Parvati plants an ashoka tree and cares for it. As the tree prospers and the other deities and sages observe her attention to this tree, they begin to question her. They point out that people desire children and feel they have been successful in life when they have seen them grow up and become the parents of another generation. Parvati replies that a person who digs a well in a place where water is scarce lives in heaven for as many years as there are drops of water in the well. And she states that a large reservoir is worth ten wells, and that one son is like ten reservoirs. She goes on to say, however, that one tree is equal to ten sons. "This," she says, "is my standard." The same Purana describes a festival for the planting of trees, indicating that in the context in which the Puranas were originally written, the planting of trees was an activity that had strong religious support. Another document of the period, the *Vishnu Dharmamottara*, states that one who plants a single tree will never fall into hell.

In many of the narratives in the Puranas, animals are often symbols of the deities. They are the *vahanas*, or vehicles, and therefore the representatives of the gods. They are also featured in the narratives in which the stories of the gods are told: The bull is the vahana of Shiva, the cow is the vahana of Krishna, the elephant of Indra, the peacock of Parvati. Often a particular animal gains religious sig-

Decorated image of Nandi the bull, Shiva's vahana.
ROBIN RINEHART

nificance because of its significance in the narrative. The monkey, among the most ubiquitous of Indian fauna, is the living representation of Hanuman, the monkey god who rendered assistance to Rama when his wife, the goddess Sita, was abducted by Ravana. Today these animals appear prominently in Indian religious life.

We observed earlier that as compared with the Rig Veda and other Vedic collections, the attitude toward nature in the Upanishads was more ambivalent. This ambivalence is closely related to the quest in the Upanishads for liberation from the cycle of rebirth, what becomes in later Hinduism the final purpose of human existence. In the philosophical traditions that are based upon the Upanishads, this ambivalence emerges again. Contemporary with many of the narratives that extol the value and virtue of nature, India has produced philosophers and philosophical texts that tended to look upon the visible world and its engaging variety with suspicion. One of the most influential of the philosophers of India is a man named Shankara. Although he lived a mere thirty-two years sometime during the eighth or ninth centuries of the Common Era, he became the principal exponent of a school of Indian philosophy known as *unqualified nondualism* (Advaita Vedanta), what Western scholars have sometimes called *monism*. On the basis of the Upanishads and other ancient texts, Shankara developed the view that in truth there is but one reality. It is known in the Upanishads as brahman, the ultimate. He held that the world that is experienced in everyday life as a world of infinite diversity is the world of mere appearance. Though he did not argue that the visible world is an illusion, he maintained that it is not reality, either. The visible world, for Shankara, is an appearance of the ultimate reality under the conditions of ignorance, the condition of the self that is embodied in temporal existence. Because Shankara was committed to the goal of moksha and recommended this goal to his followers, he encouraged them to place as little value as possible upon the world of appearance. He argued that one should cultivate an attitude of indifference to the visible world and direct one's affection toward the ultimate within, the true reality beyond appearance. Some of the passages in which Shankara expresses these views are clearly intended to evoke an attitude of disgust for the present natural world. It is described as a terrible ocean infested with monsters.

Selves trapped in this world go from birth to birth without peace. Like worms caught in a river, they are swept from one whirlpool to the next. The person who would follow the teachings of Shankara and his followers should be possessed of the desire to escape the round of death and rebirth in the present world. Such a person is expected to be celibate and to renounce all attachment to the visible material world.

Some argue that Shankara's understanding of the visible world encourages an attitude of indifference to environmental problems. Some have even attributed the deplorable condition of the environment in India to the influence of such thinking. Although it is true that we are unlikely to find any sense of communion with nature or an understanding of nature as having intrinsic worth in the writings of Shankara or his followers in the Advaita Vedanta tradition, it does not follow that this school of thought is completely at odds with environmental concerns. In the first place, though the Hindu tradition fully acknowledges the importance of Shankara's thought, we have already seen that it did not commend his lifestyle as the social norm, and it seems unreasonable to assume that Shankara did. "Let the wise one," he says, "strive after freedom." Whereas Shankara renounced the world at a young age, the most influential of the dharma texts consider renunciation and the pursuit of moksha to be the goal of the last of the stages of life. Thus, as we saw above, though moksha remains the ultimate goal of life, the penultimate goals of material and economic well-being are governed by considerations of dharma that pertain to mundane conditions in the visible world. Second, though Shankara and his followers frequently spoke disparagingly of the visible world, their purpose is clearly to oppose *attachment* to the material world. It is attachment that feeds ignorance of the true reality and leads to continuous rebirth. Third, having renounced the natural world, the follower of Shankara has radically reduced his desire to exploit the earth's resources, or to consume the products generated from its exploitation. The life of the renouncer, though appearing to despise the visible world, is a life in which consumption has been radically reduced. The earthly life of the renouncer is one of self-control, nonviolence, simplicity, and frugality, with the lowest possible environmental impact. Finally, as we shall see, it is precisely in the renunciation of worldly ambition that some leaders of environmental movements have achieved the moral authority to address abuses of power that profit from the exploitation and destruction of environments upon which the powerless and disenfranchised depend.

Although Shankara's influence was significant, his attitude concerning the visible world, and therefore the natural world, was not the only viewpoint of the time. Another influential philosopher of medieval India was Ramanuja (eleventh century CE), an exponent of what came to be known as qualified nondualism. Like Shankara, he believed that reality is one, that brahman is the only reality. But whereas Shankara argued that reality was pure identity without difference, Ramanuja held that reality was the *unity* of the differences within the visible world, including individual souls and the objects that constitute the empirical world. Under the conditions of bondage and ignorance we fail to see this unity, but with the achievement of true insight this unity can be realized. For Ramanuja the natural world is not simply an appearance to be dispelled by the higher knowledge of the One. Rather, the sentient and nonsentient matter that forms the universe is the body of God. Just as the individual soul pervades the individual physical body, so does Vishnu, or God, pervade all souls and the entire natural world. Ramanuja's viewpoint is supported by those passages in the Vedas that describe the physical world as pervaded by the presence of divinity, and by the image in the Bhagavad Gita and the Bhagavata Purana of the universe as the body of Krishna as ultimate reality incarnate. Ramanuja encouraged renunciation of material attachments as the practical path to liberation, but he also recognized virtue and devotion to God as the legitimate means to recognition of the presence of God in the natural world.

Gandhi on the Environment

At the end of the nineteenth century and the beginning of the twentieth century, religious thinkers in India came fully to recognize the centrality of the natural world in the principle sources of the Hindu religious tradition. The works of Swami Vivekananda (1862–1902) inspired a movement for ecological restoration that will interest us later in this chapter, and the teachings of Aurobindo (1872–1950) inspired the founding of a community near Pondicherry in southern India called Auroville, in which ecological restoration and progress toward sustainability have been central concerns. Among these figures, the thought of Mahatma Gandhi is of special significance. His thought has had a visible impact upon some of the most celebrated of contemporary environmental movements in India.

Born the son of the chief minister of a small princely state in what is today the Indian state of Gujarat, Mohandas K. (Mahatma) Gandhi was sent to England in his late teens to be educated in the field of law. Following his promise to his mother to remain a vegetarian, he found himself in the company of a circle of friends who were interested in the philosophical traditions of India, and he read, for the first time, the Bhagavad Gita as well as the Bible and the Qur'an. On his return to India he accepted the offer of legal work in Natal in South Africa. Here he encountered abysmal prejudice toward the Indian community and quickly became involved in the struggle of Indians in South Africa for civil rights. During his years in South Africa, Gandhi rejected the image of an upwardly mobile English lawyer to recover the ideals and values he had found in the Hindu religious tradition. Though he insisted that he was a practical man without interest in metaphysics or philosophical speculation, an analysis of the central features of his thought reveals a strong environmental ethic grounded in the religious thought of India.

Some recent studies of Gandhi's views concerning the environment suggest that his personal life and political vision reflected the influence of yoga, the ancient philosophical science of control of the body and mind that leads finally to the union of the human soul with the Ultimate Reality. In 1915, when Gandhi returned to India, his rise to political influence placed him at the center of the independence movement. His vision for India entailed both the independence of India from foreign control and the economic liberation of India's people. "Real home-rule," he said. "is self-rule, or self-control."

As it was developed in classical Indian thought, the practice of yoga consisted of eight stages of discipline. The first two stages, known as the five *yamas*, or abstentions, and the five *niyamas*, or injunctions, are the ethical foundation upon which the higher disciplines of posture, breath control, withdrawal of the senses, fixing of attention, contemplation, and concentration all depend. Exponents of yoga hold that without them, further yogic practice is useless, and that if one proceeds no further, they constitute in themselves a firm grounding for ethical action in the world. Each of these steps had a critical place in Gandhi's life and thought. By appropriating them, he was recovering his cultural roots.

The centerpiece of Gandhi's philosophy is the first of the *yamas*, called *a-himsa*, or noninjury. Gandhi is widely recognized for having transformed the idea of noninjury from a personal code of behavior to a social, economic, and political force. Yet because he applied this doctrine to the entire world, it also had profound environmental significance. "It is an arrogant assumption," he said, "to say that human beings are lords and masters of the lower creatures." For Gandhi, the human being is not the master but the trustee of the lower animal kingdom. He argued, in fact, that a society could be judged on the way it treats its animals. Gandhi's practice of noninjury, however, cannot be fully understood apart from his commitment to truth, the second of the *yamas* of the philosophy of yoga. Whereas most theologians would accept that God is truth, Gandhi took the decisive step of affirming that truth is God. The implication is that commitment to God can never be used to stand in the way of truth or justify the repudiation or suppression of truth, and it can never justify violence. Gandhi spoke frequently of truth and nonviolence as being two sides of the same coin. Violence can never establish truth, and truth can never rely upon violence. Because his method of social and political change was based upon truth, he called it *satyagraha*, or persevering in the truth without recourse to violence of any kind. As we shall see, this method for bringing about social and political change has been the characteristic feature of movements for the protection of India's environment.

The third of the *yamas*, called *asteya*, means abstention from stealing or the misappropriation of the possessions of others. When asked whether an independent India would achieve the standard of living of Britain, Gandhi replied that it took half the resources of the planet to achieve the prosperity that Britain enjoys. He then rhetorically inquired, "How many planets will a country like India require?" (Khoshoo 1995, 33). On another occasion he pointed out that the economic imperialism of a tiny island kingdom was keeping the world in chains. He suggested that if India were to follow Britain's example of industrial development and economic exploitation, "it would strip the world bare like locusts" (Gandhi 1999, 412–413). These views have supported movements against forms of development that have degraded the environments of the many for the benefit of the few.

Gandhi stated that when fully and properly understood, the fourth of the *yamas*, called *brahmacharya*, "means search for Brahma," or God. In the classical context the student of sacred knowledge was expected to remain unmarried and celibate in order to devote full attention to study and discipline. For Gandhi it signified "control of all the senses at all times and all places in thought, word, and deed." In addition to sexual restraint, it also embraces restraint of diet, emotions, and speech. It precludes violence, hate, anger, and any deviation from truth. Being without desire, it creates stability of mind, leading to thoughtful and sound judgment. Brahmacharya is closely related to the last of the *yamas*, called *aparigraha*, the rejection of worldly possessions beyond one's requirements. For Gandhi this meant dispossessing the symbols of wealth and status to which he had become accustomed in his days as a student in England. He laid aside the wardrobe of a young English gentleman for a plain *dhoti*, the garment worn by common Hindu men. Beyond this he retained only those objects necessary for his life and work: spinning wheel, sandals, cap, staff, glasses, and a watch. "Man falls from the pursuit of the ideal of plain living and high thinking," he said, "the moment he wants to multiply his daily wants." Gandhi's future life would be a protest against the supposed needs of a consumer society and its unreasonable demands on the biosphere. His advice to the wealthy capitalists of his day was to undertake business with restraint so as not to exhaust the resources of the earth. "The earth," he said, "provides enough to satisfy every man's need, but not every man's greed."

The *yamas*, or restraints, of the philosophy of yoga are followed by five positive injunctions called the *niyamas*. They begin with *shaucha*, or cleanliness. In the ashramas that Gandhi founded in

South Africa and later in India, cleanliness was a paramount concern. Cleaning duties were distributed among all participants. Gandhi stated that "anyone who fouls the air by spitting about carelessly, throwing refuse and rubbish, or otherwise dirtying the ground, sins against man and nature. Man's body is the temple of God. Anyone who fouls the air that is to enter that temple desecrates it" (Gandhi 2000, 138). One of Gandhi's most celebrated achievements was the elevation of the class of persons responsible for the cleaning of Indian streets from the status of Untouchability to that of people of God, or Harijans. The second of the *niyamas* is *santosha*, or contentment. The person "who is discontented, however much he possesses, becomes a slave to his desires." Happiness, he said, "lies in contentment." Yet the life of truth and nonviolence must remain an empty dream, according to Gandhi, without the third of the *niyamas*, called *tapas*, meaning exertion toward self-purification. For Gandhi, fasting and prayer are the most powerful forms of tapas. "A genuine fast," he wrote, "cleanses the body, mind and soul. It crucifies the flesh and to that extent it sets the soul free." A sincere prayer, he wrote, "is an intense longing of the soul for its even greater purity." For Gandhi, prayer is as indispensable to the soul as is food for the material body. *Swadhyaya*, the examination of oneself in the light of sacred scriptures, is closely related to the last of the *niyamas*, called *Ishvara pranidhana*, or devotion to God. An examination of one's self in the light of sacred scriptures dislodges the human person from the understanding of one's self as the master of creation. It locates the person within the larger web of life and the duties and responsibilities of a thinking being. Devotion to God supports this self-understanding. Gandhi acknowledged that there are innumerable definitions of God because of His innumerable manifestations. For this reason he acknowledged the validity of the many images of God that the Hindu tradition has generated. Yet he pointed out that he worshiped God as truth alone. He also wrote that he had not found God but was seeking after Him. When he stated that he "worships God as truth alone," he pointed out that what he means by truth is not simply truthfulness in thought or assent to the relative truths of our experience but "the Absolute Truth, the Eternal Principle." He also stated that as human beings, we cannot know the Absolute Truth in itself.

Though he spoke of "faint glimpses of the Absolute truth," he held that we must constantly seek the approximations of truth that occur in daily life. "That relative truth," he said, "must, meanwhile, be my beacon, my shield and buckler." In his daily life the Bhagavad Gita was Gandhi's constant companion and guide. Its call to self-sacrifice and devotion to God engendered in him the conviction that nonviolence was not just an effective strategy for social change but an eternal quality of truth or reality itself.

In 1948 Gandhi stated that the Indian National Congress had won political freedom but that economic, social, and moral freedom was yet to be attained. For this his focus was upon rural and especially village development. He held that just as the whole of the universe is contained in the self, so the whole of India is contained in its villages; if the villages should perish, then India would perish as well. He argued that it is only in the simplicity of the village that India could fully realize truth and nonviolence. He explained that in the ideal village, people will not live in ignorance, darkness, or filth. Rather, free, intelligent, and independent women and men will dwell neither in luxury nor indolence. Gandhi conceived of the future of India as a republic of independent self-reliant villages. He thought of circles of villages working collaboratively with one another, with other circles of villages, and with cities that served as clearing facilities for their products. He believed that the self-reliant village would be the heart of a self-reliant and truly independent India (Khoshoo 1995).

The Role of the Forest
in Indian Religious Life

The understanding of nature embedded in Indian culture can be perceived in classical religious documents, in ancient legal documents, and in literary narratives. It can also be seen in the role of the veneration for the various features of the landscape that are not always preserved in documentary form. In various parts of India today, sacred groves are dedicated to a deity that is understood to reside within it. Such groves, sometimes fifty hectares in area, are ancient natural sanctuaries wherein living creatures and the vegetation of the area are protected. The removal of even dead wood or twigs from such areas was and remains religiously forbidden. In areas such as the Western Ghats, where sacred groves still flourish, they are the only remains of the forests that once flourished throughout the Indian subcontinent. Even when they were not designated as sacred groves, forests have had a significance for Indian culture that is absent in the dominant traditions of the West.

In ancient times villages were responsible for maintaining the forests in their region. Forests were the dwelling of the *rishis*, the mythical sages of the Vedas. They were also the dwelling of those teachers whose forest hermitages were set apart from the preoccupations of worldly life, a place pervaded by the sense of the presence of God. In ancient times, the shade of a tree was the proper place for a disciple to receive spiritual instruction from his guru. Even those philosophical traditions of India that have tended to minimize nature and seek salvation in liberation from every kind of earthly bondage are therefore themselves dependent upon a fundamental appreciation of nature that made the development of those philosophical traditions possible. From such places arose the profound literature that forms the background of the Upanishads, called the Aranyakas, the forest books. Near the places where the sages lived, no animal or tree was to be harmed. Even kings were forbidden from hunting in regions close to these dwellings. Today the tulsi plant retains a place of religious importance, and daily veneration of that plant is an honored tradition in Hindu homes all over India. The bilva tree is understood to be sacred to Shiva, as is the aswattha to Vishnu. The list of sacred plants is extensive. Whereas in Western philosophical and religious traditions nature is all but absent, India stands today at the end of a very long and considered tradition in which the importance of nature is recognized, celebrated, and valued.

Environmentalism in Two Different Keys

Recent scholarship that is occupied with environmental movements in India often distinguishes between the environmentalism of the First World and the environmentalism of the Third World, or the environmentalism of the rich and the environmentalism of the poor. A passing glance at the two reveals that their priorities are different. The environmentalism that has developed in Western industrialized countries and has roots in the Romantic appreciation of nature that blossomed in the nineteenth century has tended to support the preservation of nature and the protection of endangered species. Some environmental writers in the Third World see this environmentalism as the reflection of a mass consumer society, in which the enjoyment of nature is yet another leisure activity. Here nature is made accessible above all by the availability of the automobile, an artifact no longer restricted to the elite. The automobile (particularly the SUV) makes nature accessible as a reality refreshingly different from the city, the office, and the factory, from the stale routine of institutions and the dictates of the clock. India, in comparison to Western nations, is a country in which 70 percent of the population resides in villages, where the life and welfare depends upon local production of food, fiber, fertilizer, and fodder. Here environmental issues often center on conflicts over natural resource use, conflicts that are usually played out against a background of already severe ecological degradation: the depletion of forest resources, water resources, and land. Whereas Western environmentalism has tended to emphasize the intrinsic value of nature as opposed to its use for humankind, the environmentalism of the Third World has tended to focus on human needs, human rights, ethnicity, and distributive justice. The environmentalism of the West tends to oppose one interest group against another of roughly equal economic and political power, but the environmentalism of the Third World frequently opposes the interests of the rich and politically powerful against the poor and disenfranchised. There is also another difference. The environmentalism of the West has proceeded without a great deal of support from organized religion or from religious ideas, whereas Indian environmental movements have derived support and inspiration from religion. The understanding of the place of nature in human life and the strategies of protest against the exploitation of nature that such movements have deployed are deeply rooted in the Hindu religious tradition.

Some Third World writers have observed that though we can find striking examples of the environmentalism of the poor in the First

World (such as the movement in the United States for environmental justice for minorities disproportionately subject to the hazards of incinerators and toxic waste dumps), the predominant concerns of Western environmentalism have been with the health of the biosphere, the protection of the forests, oceans, and wilderness areas that cannot protect themselves. Third World environmentalism, in comparison, has been occupied with environmental problems arising from social, political, and economic inequities that exist in the face of scarcities that are the result of the inappropriate strategies or incompetent management of natural resources.

The *Chipko* Movement

In India the term *environmental movement* functions as an umbrella term that refers to a great many struggles, initiatives, and conflicts often over local resource use. The movements are diverse because they focus upon local issues in differing environmental regions. Yet because they often turn on issues that pit the interests of the most powerful against the least, they tend to have much in common. Leaders of a movement in one region are often able to lend support to those in others. The movement that has attracted perhaps the most international attention in recent years is called the *Chipko andolan*. *Chipko* is a Hindi word meaning "to hug," and the word *andolan* means "movement." The Chipko movement is so called because of its strategy of literally hugging the trees to save them from the ax. The Chipko andolan began in the town of Gopeshwar in the Indian state of Uttar Pradesh (now in the new state of Uttaranchal) as the response of local people to an assault upon their forest resources.

In early 1973, a cooperative organization concerned with generating local employment made a request to the Forest Department for an allotment of ash trees to make agricultural implements. The Forest Department refused the request but granted a request for ash trees to a company manufacturing sporting goods for the export market. A local organization, the Dashauli Gram Swarajya Sangh (DGSS, Society for Village Self-Rule), responded by organizing several meetings. The strategy that was finally implemented was to embrace the trees. A leading local activist named Chandi Prasad Bhatt said, "Let them know they will not fell a single tree without felling one of us first." To this plan the young members committed themselves with signatures in blood, and the Chipko movement was born.

The Chipko movement was not the first to use a strategy of this nature. In a famous incident in 1731 the Bishnois people, a desert-dwelling people in the Indian state of Rajasthan, in a similar action resisted the decision of the maharajah of Jodhpur to cut down their *khejri* trees to use in a lime kiln for a new royal palace. By their religious heritage the Bishnois were committed to the protection of all of nature, and to the khejri tree (*Prosopis cineraria*) in particular. This tree provided food and fodder, as well as building materials for fencing and other purposes. For the Bishnois the tree was sacred. On this occasion they embraced the trees in order to prevent the maharajah's workers from cutting them down. In the protest, 363 people were killed. The story of the martyrdom of the Bishnois people has become an important resource in the struggle of local people for control of their natural resource base. The Chipko movement identified with this effort, evoking not only historical precedent but the support of a religious perception of nature.

The place in which the Chipko movement received its name is also the place in which it achieved its first visible success. The agents of the company that had been allotted the timber were forced to depart without felling a single tree. In June of the same year, the Forest Department allotted trees to the same company in another location. Word of this scheme reached the DGSS, and a massive demonstration was organized. The company's agents returned to Gopeshwar complaining to the Forest Department that they were unable to take any of the trees they had been promised.

Much of the effectiveness of the Chipko movement arose from the role of religion in support of the cause. An incident concerning the protection of the trees of the Advani Forest is one of the most celebrated in the legacy of the Chipko movement. In October 1977, in the district headquarters in Narendranagar, the government auctioned 640 trees of the Advani Forest and 273 trees of the Salet Forest in the Hemvalghati region. On this occasion, the

Chipko leader Sunderlal Bahuguna undertook a fast at the town hall at Narendranagar and appealed to forest contractors and district authorities not to carry out their intended mission. The villagers declared that they would hug the trees in order to protect them. The contractors warned a group of village women that if their men entered the forest to hug the trees, they would be cut down along with the timber. In response, the women themselves took to the forests. Hundreds of women took a pledge to save the trees even at the cost of their own lives. The village women tied sacred chords, called *rakhis*, to the trees as a token of their bond of protection and for seven days guarded the forest while listening to recitations from the *Shrimad Bhagavatam*, a religious text that tells the stories of the earthly life of Krishna. The text included the story of the birth of Krishna in Mathura, and of his miraculous escape across the Yamuna River from the evil King Kamsa. They also included the stories of the sons of Kubera, who learned humility by being incarnated as trees, eventually liberated by Krishna; of Krishna's swallowing of a forest fire; and of Krishna's raising of Mount Govardhana to shelter people and cattle from a storm. The story of the demon Dhenuka, who was keeping Krishna and his childhood companions from the palmyra forest and from enjoying the fruits of the palmyra trees, was similarly retold. The village women celebrated the story of Krishna's defeat of Dhenuka and of his opening of the forest so that the local people could enjoy its fruit and their cattle could graze on the grass in the shade of the trees. It is not difficult to see how these women found support in these texts for their struggle to save the forests upon which the lives of their families depended.

It was also on this occasion that a forest officer made a speech to convince the women that the felling of trees was both profitable and scientifically viable. He ended his speech with what is now a famous proclamation: "You foolish village women! Do you know what the forest bears? Resin, timber, and foreign exchange!" To this remark the women replied in chorus with words that have become the most famous Chipko slogan: "What do the forests bear? Soil, water, and pure air! Soil, water, and pure air sustains the earth and all she bears."

The Movement against the Tehri Dam

Although the Chipko movement began as an effort to maintain the traditional right of peasants to their forest resources, it gradually expanded to embrace issues of wider ecological concern. In May 1978, Sunderlal Bahuguna, one of the most visible representatives of the Chipko andolan, took a pledge to devote himself to the protection of the Himalayan environment in all its aspects. He gradually came to hold that forest-based industries were not necessary to improve the economy of the people. Like Gandhi, he believed that a viable economy required self-sufficient rural communities living in a sustainable relationship with their natural surroundings. In 1981, with a small group of young people, he took this message to the people of the Himalayas in a *padyatra*, or foot march, of some three thousand miles through the Himalayan foothills from Srinagar in Kashmir to Kohima in Nagaland. The padyatra bears a striking resemblance to the tradition of the pilgrimage, a central feature of Indian religious life from ancient times. During the padyatra the participants depart from their homes for a limited period of time and encounter the forest as a threatened sacred space. The padyatra has remained one of the most effective strategies for the spread of the Chipko message.

Though Chipko activism succeeded in bringing a ban on the felling of trees in the Uttarakhand region of the Himalayas above 1,000 meters (about 3,275 feet) in elevation, commercial penetration has continued to endanger the region. It is perhaps in the struggle against the construction of the Tehri dam that the name of Sunderlal Bahuguna has come to be most widely known.

The earth and rockfill dam of 855 feet across the Bhagirathi River, the northernmost tributary of the Ganges, will be the fifth highest in the world, and the largest in Asia. It will flood 28 miles of the Bhagirathi Valley and 22 miles of the Bhilangana Valley, impounding 4.2 million cubic yards of water spread over a reservoir of 16 square miles. The dam will submerge the town of Tehri and twenty-three villages in the vicinity, and partly submerge an additional seventy-two villages. It will submerge nearly thirteen thousand acres of land, much of which has been productively farmed by local people for generations. Estimates of people to be displaced by

Ganges River in Hardwar.
ROBIN RINEHART

the project are uncertain, but range from 85,000 to 109,000 people. The benefits promised from the project include 2,400 megawatts of electric power transmitted to the state grid, 155 miles away, largely to power industry in such lowland cities as Allahabad and Kanpur. It is expected to irrigate some 667,000 acres of land in the Western districts of Uttar Pradesh and provide 500 cubic feet per second of drinking water to Delhi.

Among the objections to the dam is the fact that the site is located on a seismically active region. The Indian tectonic plate is pressing under the Eurasian plate at a rate of about two inches per year. The project is located only nine miles from the plate boundary. Possible failure of the dam presents a grave threat to lives and property downstream. Another objection is the unfair burden it imposes upon the local people. Bahuguna states that the valley upstream from the damsite is picturesque and productive. The scenic terraced fields sculpted over centuries are the legacy of a peaceful, hardworking people whose village culture will be consigned to the depths of a manmade sea. The town of Tehri, on the pilgrimage route to Gangotri, the source of the Ganges River, is the cradle of an ancient culture that has given birth to eminent poets, scholars, and artists. Though the project will bring electric power and other benefits to regions far away, it will leave local villages virtually in darkness and without the electric power to irrigate their own fields. In these objections it is not difficult to see an analogy to the grievance that was the catalyst for the Chipko movement in Gopeshwar. Just as ash trees were allotted to outside contractors to provide sporting goods for a distant market, the government here endorsed a project to provide hydroelectric power to distant Delhi and irrigation to the western districts of Uttar Pradesh. Just as the Forest Department denied forest resources for the needs of the local people of Gopeshwar, the government here imposed the burden of loss of heritage, history, and habitat upon the local people of Garhwal.

Bahuguna and other opponents of the Tehri dam found support for their cause in the Hindu religious tradition. Bahuguna writes of a legend about an ancient king named Bhagiratha who prayed to the goddess Ganga (the Ganges River) to come down from the heavens to wash off the sins of his forefathers. After much penance on his part she agreed to do so. But she warned the king that when she came down, she would have to be contained. "If I am not tied down," she said, "I will not be the life-giving source you expect me to be, but I will cause chaos and destruction on the earth." King Bhagiratha then searched for someone strong enough to restrain the tempestuous Ganga. He concluded that the only power sufficient for the task was that of the mighty Lord Shiva. He then fervently prayed for Shiva's help. Shiva eventually agreed, and Ganga descended into the matted locks of his hair, from which she comes forth as a life-giving stream to the northern plains of India.

In Hindu mythology, Shiva is identified with the Himalayas. Bahuguna states that the locks of Shiva are the natural forests of the Himalayas, which help contain the water in the soil and protect the land from floods. In these matted locks the waters of the Ganges River are entangled every year, making it a life-giving goddess by regulating its flow. Today, he says, the catchment area of the Bhagirathi River is a victim of the worst deforestation brought about by commercial forestry in India. The sacred locks of Shiva have been cut, turning the Ganges River into the destructive force against which the story warned. For Bahuguna, the construction of the Tehri dam is a further violation of the sacred Himalayan environment. Yet the sacredness of the Ganges cannot be separated from the equity in her distribution of the benefits she provides. Bahuguna states that when the Ganges flows in her natural course, she benefits all of the people, regardless of caste, creed, color, poverty, or wealth. When she is dammed she becomes the possession of the privileged and powerful, who then dispense her blessings on a partisan basis.

One of the most visible features of the role of religion in the challenge to the Tehri dam is the standing of Bahuguna as a prophetic voice against compromise with a new religion. He calls it the religion of economic growth. The engineers and the politicians who accommodate their ambition, he says, are the new class of priests; the dollar is the new God; and projects like the Tehri dam are the temples of the new and alien faith. With his long white beard, his frail body, and his simple homespun apparel, he looks the part, as one journalist expressed it, of a prophet warning of disaster. Though Bahuguna would readily be recognized as one of the most visible leaders of the Chipko movement, his own claim is that the real leadership of the movement has always been the women of the forest communities who have courageously defended the resources upon which their villages depend. He identifies himself simply as a messenger of the movement. Yet his renunciation of political ambition to commit himself to the welfare of the people of the hills, his repeated fasts, his arrests, and his endurance of maltreatment at the hands of police have only supported his moral authority. This dam, he says, is a project to realize a false hope based on a mistaken understanding of reality.

The *Appiko* Movement of Karnataka

Another movement in which the spirit of the Chipko movement remains alive today is known as the *Appiko* movement. The word *Appiko* means "embrace" or "hug" in Kannada, the language of the Indian state of Karnataka. Although the Appiko movement is a response to conditions peculiar to the ecological history of the hill regions of Karnataka, it was inspired by the Chipko movement and derived from the Chipko movement its name and its method of nonviolent resistance. The leader of the Appiko movement, Pandurang Hegde, worked with Sunderlal Bahuguna, and in 1981 participated in part of Bahuguna's famous foot march through the foothills of the Himalayas. After the Appiko movement was launched, Bahuguna accompanied Hegde and other Appiko activists in padyatras in the Western Ghats, the mountain range that stretches along a line parallel to the west coast of India, to create environmental awareness there.

In one of the hill districts of Karnataka, known today as Uttara Kannada, the people of a small village gathered in early spring every year in a thick forest known to them as Ammanavara Kadu, or Forest of the Goddess. Here they prepared food and offered their worship to the goddess. In April 1983 when the people went to worship and share food in this forest, they were shocked at what they saw. The Forest Department had permitted the felling of the trees of this forest for the use of a plywood factory, and what was left was a barren site. The youth of the village decided to organize the villagers against the felling of trees. In the neighboring village of Gubbigadde, a youth group was also considering measures to stop deforestation. They wrote letters to the Forest Department and the government ministers concerned. In response, the forest officials stated that the tree felling was being undertaken according to scientific principles and warned them not to interfere. The people responded by announcing their intention to launch a movement to protect the trees. At the time, Sunderlal Bahuguna was visiting Karnataka. In response to their invitation, he related the story of the Chipko struggle and the nonviolent method of hugging the trees to save them from the ax. The people took an oath to save their forest by embracing the trees.

That September, when the Forest Department began felling trees, they chose a forest some distance from either Salkani or Gubbigadde. But the news soon reached the two villages. Before dawn on September 8, 1983, some 160 people started out, despite rain and the menace of leeches, for the forest. Some of the axemen had already started into the forest, but the village people rushed to the first tree and embraced the trunk before the workers could strike the first blow. The resolve and dedication of the villagers impressed the forest workers. They agreed not to fell any trees until the Forest Department had consulted with the local people. That October, a similar movement was launched in the village of Hursi. Two months later, the state government sent the Forest Minister to the area. After discussions with local people and an examination of the affected areas, he agreed that tree felling was responsible for significant ecological damage. He assured the people that no further clear felling of natural forests would take place, that only dead and dry trees would be cut. Appiko activities soon began in Modagu, another hill district of Karnataka. In the Kodagu district, the government imposed a ban on the felling of trees. As the Appiko movement spread throughout the state, it began to engender a new ecological awareness.

The Appiko movement is committed to promoting the preservation of the remaining tropical forests of the Western Ghats. To do this its members are exerting pressure upon government agencies for a basic change in forest policy, from revenue-based management to ecology-based management. It is committed to the restoration of the natural forests of the Western Ghats by planting indigenous species that provide food, fodder, fuel, fertilizer, and fiber to local people. It also promotes the rational use of forest resources by educating local people to avoid harmful practices. Recently the Appiko movement has launched an initiative called the Kali Bachao Andolan (Save the Kali Movement) to protest the proposed seventh major hydroelectric dam on the Kali River in the Uttara Kannada district of the Western Ghats. The movement has also been actively protesting the pollution of the Kali River by effluents from paper mills in the region. To support its objectives the Appiko movement employs methods derived from the religious traditions of the people. During the padyatras, members of the Appiko movement perform works from the traditional folk theater of Karnataka, called *Yakshagana*, integrating traditional subject matter from the Mahabharata and the Ramayana with contemporary environmental themes. Special pujas also are undertaken in which the local people pledge themselves to the protection of the forest by nonviolent means.

The Swaraj Movement
of Maharashtra

We stated above that the environmentalism of the Third World frequently opposes the interests of the affluent and politically powerful against the poor and disenfranchised.

Not all environmental movements in India, however, have arisen from conflicts between the demands of local resource use and their exploitation by industry and business. In some cases the struggle has been against the force of apathy and resignation toward environmental conditions that governmental agencies have failed to address adequately. In the Indian state of Maharashtra there is a village that is the setting of one of the most successful programs of ecological, economic, and social restoration that has occurred in India in recent years.

Before 1975 the village of Ralegan Siddhi was stricken with poverty. Irrigation sources had dried up, agricultural production could not meet local needs, and drinking water was scarce. Lack of sanitation afflicted villagers with water-borne diseases. Infant mortality was high. Villagers borrowed heavily from lenders in neighboring villages. Unable to repay, their debts increased, leading to hopelessness and alcoholism. Alcohol consumption led to domestic violence. Crime was rampant. Living on degraded and unproductive land, the village of 1,500 was surviving on the sale of illegal alcohol to neighboring villages. Hardly 10 percent of the village children attended school. Religious life in the village had lost all meaning. Villagers had removed wooden parts of the temple to fuel the liquor stills.

A villager named Anna Hazare (1940–) grew up in a family whose fortune had dissipated as it responded to relentless economic pressures. When he came of age he joined the army, where he began to question the meaning of his existence. He had decided to end his life when in a bookstall in a railway station he encountered a short collection of the thoughts of the religious thinker and reformer Swami Vivekananda (1862–1902). Here for the first time he heard that life is meant for service to God through service to others. The insight transformed his life. On his retirement from the army in 1975 he returned to the village to put the thoughts of Vivekananda into practice.

His work began with the renovation of the village temple. Because he used his own retirement fund for the restoration of the temple, his work attracted the attention of villagers. The temple became his venue for teaching the ideas of Vivekananda and for the application of these ideas to community problems. His preaching of purity of mind, purity of action, and the value of self-sacrifice addressed the sense of hopelessness and apathy that had immobilized the village. Hazare's most influential teaching was that selfless work is worship. Impressed by his initiative, the people gradually began to contribute their labor to the project. As work progressed, Hazare brought singers and storytellers to the temple who supported his teachings with songs and stories from the religious tradition. Such meetings became the foundation for the *gram sabha*, or village assembly, that eventually became the principal decisionmaking body of the village.

By means of the organization of voluntary labor as service to God, the villagers undertook a watershed management plan to restore irrigation and agriculture and provide drinking water for the village. During the process, the temple became the focus of the restoration effort. It was at a meeting in the temple that the villagers collectively resolved to close the liquor dens and impose a ban on alcohol consumption in the village. Because the decision of the village had been made in the temple, it had the force of a religious commitment. The restoration of the moral fabric of the community brought results. With cooperation among the members of the village, the watershed system proved successful. Replenished groundwater supply made water available to irrigate fields, and eventually brought drinking water to a faucet in every household. The village now exports more agricultural products than it imported in the days before the restoration began.

The village collectively authorized the five principles that have been credited with the continued social and economic development in the village: (1) A ban on alcohol production and consumption has helped mend the frayed social fabric of society. (2) A ban on the free grazing of livestock has helped restore the grass cover of the hills, preventing runoff and erosion. (3) A ban on tree felling has saved the green cover of the village. (4) Family planning, restricting families to three children (usually by means of vasectomy), has helped reduce pressure on the environment. And (5) *shramdan*, or voluntary labor for community welfare, has enabled the village to address environmental, economic, and educational needs. Through voluntary labor the village constructed a school building that was furnished with local materials. Today 80 to 90 percent of the young people of Ralegan Siddhi complete the tenth standard exam.

Following the thoughts of Vivekananda, Anna Hazare holds that nothing has fractured Indian society more than the caste system and the practice of untouchability. With Hazare's leadership, social barriers grounded in caste distinctions have been removed. Once a year the community celebrates the birthday of the village by honoring the eldest male and the eldest female villager as well as new brides who have come to the village. New clothes are made and presented to every infant born over the year, and students who have been successful in education or have completed other achievements are honored.

The success of Ralegan Siddhi is now being replicated in other villages in Maharashtra and beyond. With the support of the government of Maharashtra, three hundred villages have been designated for the implementation of programs similar to that of Ralegan Siddhi. Villages are selected on the basis of their willingness to implement the five principles employed at Ralegan Siddhi and their willingness to arrive at decisions collectively through a gram sabha. Young people selected from these villages undergo training at Ralegan Siddhi in various aspects of rural development to provide leadership for similar programs in their own villages. Hazare challenges them with the analogy of the grain of wheat that has to sacrifice itself to give birth to a swaying field of grain.

Concern for Nature in
Contemporary Religious Renewal

In addition to movements specifically committed to the preservation, protection, and restoration of nature, some of the most striking forms of environmental action have come from movements for religious renewal. Because nature occupies a central role in the Hindu religious tradition, it is hard to imagine a genuine renewal of commitment to Hindu religious values in which the condition of India's environment is left out of account. An especially interesting movement to examine in this light is one centering on the teachings of the Rev. Pandurang Shastri Athavale (1920–2003), known as Swadhyaya. Over the past five decades, Athavale, known to his followers as Dada, or Dadaji, meaning elder brother, has been teaching from a center in Mumbai (formerly Bombay). As we saw in our discussion of Gandhi, the term *swadhyaya* refers to the recitation of sacred texts for one's individual spiritual benefit. For the adherents of the movement by this name, it has the more literal connotation of the examination or study of oneself. Based on ancient Indian religious texts, and the Bhagavad Gita in particular, Swadhyaya invites one to recognize the divinity within oneself and within all persons. This recognition engenders self-respect, esteem for others, and grateful devotion to God. Swadhyaya teaches that God dwells in every person, and that all persons are spiritual brothers and sisters in the family of God. The Swadhyaya community has been spreading this message through devotional tours that Athavale initiated in 1957. Adherents visit villages, proceeding from hut to hut, to share Dadaji's insights from the Bhagavad Gita and other ancient texts. Without a hierarchy and without any paid workers, Swadhyaya has spread to roughly 100,000 villages in India. Athavale accepts no funding from any outside source. In a way reminiscent of Anna Hazare, he teaches that labor can be an act of devotion, and he recommends the offering of one's time, talent, and expertise, for one day a month, as devotion (bhakti) to God. Such devotion has supported a variety of experiments in farming, forestry, fishing, water resource management, sanitation, education, and other areas that have directly improved the lives of as many as twenty million people. Athavale endorses neither fundamentalism nor politics, but teaches that devotion is a social force that can effectively address any human problem.

Athavale's objective is the recovery of the insights and values of India's cultural heritage. In 1979, he initiated a phase of the restoration of India's classical heritage that addressed the depletion of forest cover. He pointed out that the ancient sages saw trees as the dwelling of the Lord who pervades the universe. Athavale established what he called Tree Temples to cultivate the perception of trees as the dwelling and image of divinity. The Tree Temple is without walls, doors, pillars, or artistic embellishments, but for those who offer their devotion here, it is a sacred space. Those who maintain these temples are not called workers, but priests or *pujaris.* People from various villages within a region spend twenty-four hours at a time as priests of the temple of trees. Participants who come from differing castes and classes of society work effectively together. They visit, sing hymns, and eat together, breaking down traditional barriers between sectors of society. By the year 2000, twenty-four tree temples had been established. Many others are planned, and the idea of the tree temple is at various stages of implementation in thousands of villages across India.

Another initiative for the restoration of forests centers on a temple in the pilgrimage center of Tirumala-Tirupati, in the Indian state of Andhra Pradesh. The procedure of worship, or puja, at Hindu temples all over India entails the giving of gifts to the deity, the blessing of those gifts by the officiating priest, and the sharing of those gifts with the deity in the form of prasada, or blessing, that is given back to the worshiper to be consumed. Gifts to the deity include such fruits as bananas and coconuts, as well as flowers, and sweets that are sometimes made within the temple complex. The Venkateswara temple at Tirumala-Tirupati produces and sells in the region of 100,000 *laddus*, a small, ball-shaped sweet confection, per day. Like many in India, this temple standing at an elevation of 3,000 feet in the Venkata hills was once surrounded by rich forests. That region is now the victim of severe deforestation. To call attention to the original setting of the temple and to address the crisis of deforestation, the temple has initiated a program called the *Vriksha Prasada,* or tree blessing. In addition to the kitchen that produces an enormous number of confections for temple consumption, the temple has now established a productive nursery that grows seeds from a variety of indigenous trees and plants. The saplings are appropriate for a variety of soil conditions around the country. In the course of worship the priests now distribute young tree saplings as prasada and encourage the pilgrims to take them home and plant them there. In planting and caring for such trees, the pilgrims cultivate a living symbol of the temple and its holiness in their very midst. In addition, temple officials encourage benefactors to make donations for the purchase and planting of trees. Because of the fame and prestige of the temple, such sponsorships have proven attractive and have resulted in the planting of over two million trees in the plains and hill regions of India.

Conclusion

The examples of environmental movements discussed here are a mere sampling of the many and varied expressions of environmental concern to be found in India today. Clearly India has produced initiatives supported by traditional religious ideas and practices and supported by influential religious authorities that have addressed a variety of ecological concerns. From their encounter with the sources of their religious traditions, local people have found guidance and inspiration to attend to what seemed insurmountable environmental problems. Some argue, however, that as impressive as they are, these movements remain mostly grassroots activities of local interest and influence, and that they have had little impact on the state of India's environment as a whole, and that such movements have proven ineffective against the economic and political interests that support a vision of development inimical to the needs of the local people. Though protest continues, the Tehri dam, which will undoubtedly destroy the homeland and village culture of so many thousands, is moving relentlessly toward completion. Likewise, the Narmada River Development Project that will displace many more thousands is making similar progress. Like the Tehri dam, the Narmada project has also long been the object of a struggle for which Gandhi's method of nonviolent resistance has provided inspiration and vision. The question arises whether such movements can realistically invite optimism concerning the ecological future of India. We close with one more story of ecological restoration, this time at the earthly birthplace of Krishna, and one more story from the Bhagavata Purana.

In our discussion of the Chipko movement we referred to a recitation from the Srimad Bhagavatam that was undertaken while the village women were guarding a local forest. The text that treats the earthly life of Krishna also describes the landscape in which he was born and spent his youth. In that narrative, Krishna expresses deep admiration for the picturesque forests of Vrindavan, with their trees laden with flowers and fruits. The text describes clear lakes with water that relieves all fatigue, and sweet flavored breezes that refresh the body and mind. The text lavishes praise on the scenic Yamuna River that flows through the region and that plays a central role in the stories of Krishna's early life. The present town of Vrindavan, with a population of just twenty thousand, eighty miles downstream from Delhi on the Yamuna River, is the destination of over two million pilgrims every year. For the devotee of Krishna, the Srimad Bhagavatam is the most beloved of all the ancient texts, and the land it describes is so sacred that devotees wear markings on their foreheads taken from the ground on which Krishna walked. Devotees walk the eleven kilometer (6.8 mile) *parikrama*, or pilgrimage path, that encircles the sacred town, and desire to bathe in the sacred Yamuna River that cleans away their sins. Today, however, deforestation has devastated this sacred landscape, and industrial runoff and sewage has made the sacred river unfit for drinking or bathing. Two-thirds of Delhi's water is taken from the Yamuna River, and most of its sewage is returned untreated to the same river. Many of the sacred groves associated with the childhood of Krishna have completely disappeared, and raw sewage flows over parts of a parikrama now strewn with rubbish.

In 1991 a group of devotees undertook an initiative to address this environmental disaster. With community involvement and a grant from the World Wide Fund for Nature (WWF), they organized a program to begin to restore the land to Krishna. Their purpose was to demonstrate the environmental traditions of cleanliness, simple living, and respect for nature at one of the most widely recognized sacred places in India. To do this they undertook a program to educate the pilgrims about the destruction of Vrindavan and similar environmental problems, showing how the ecological values embedded in the Hindu tradition relate to these conditions. They established a nursery where they have grown ten thousand trees and shrubs of local origin, and begun to raise public consciousness about environmental problems by means of publications and outreach programs to local schools. Their initial program included the clearing of rubbish from the pilgrimage path and the planting of two thousand trees and shrubs along a two-kilometer (1.24 mile) stretch of the parikrama. Eventually this program is to encompass the entire path. They have also begun to deal with the problem of sanitation by addressing the living conditions of the local sweepers and by encouraging public recognition of their work.

Much of the inspiration for this work has come from the Srimad Bhagavatam itself. The text tells the story of a venomous serpent named Kaliya who intruded upon the waters of the Yamuna River to make it his home. He poisoned its waters, killing the trees on the riverbank. Birds could not fly over the river without being overcome with its toxic fumes. Krishna's friends, the cowherds, inadvertently drank from the river and fell unconscious. Moved with concern over this ecological disaster, Krishna dived into the poisoned waters and wrestled with the serpent. After an enormous struggle, he prevailed against the serpent and danced on its many heads. When Kaliya was evicted, the purity of the water was restored, and the trees received new life. Krishna revived his fallen companions, and together they celebrated his triumph. The story has special significance today because the Yamuna River is poisoned again. Today the poison comes from industrial runoff and sewage from the city of Delhi, and from the town of Vrindavan itself. For those engaged in the ecological restoration of Vrindavan and of India, Krishna remains an inspiration and a powerful symbol of hope.

BIBLIOGRAPHY

Agarwal, Anil, Ravi Chopra, and Kalpana Sharma, eds. *State of India's Environment: The First Citizen's Report*. New Delhi: Centre for Science and Environment, 1982.

Chapple, Christopher K., and Mary E. Tucker, eds. *Hinduism and Ecology: The Intersection of Earth, Sky, and Water*. Cambridge: Harvard University Press, 2000.

Guha, Ramachandra, and Juan Martinez-Alier. *Varieties of*

Environmentalism: Essays North and South. New Delhi: Oxford University Press, 1998.

Hume, R. E. *The Thirteen Principal Upanishads.* London: Oxford University Press, 1971.

James, George A., ed. *Ethical Perspectives on Environmental Issues in India.* New Delhi: APH Publications, 1999.

Khoshoo, T. N. *Mahatma Gandhi: An Apostle of Applied Human Ecology.* New Delhi: Tata Energy Research Institute, 1995.

Nelson, Lance E., ed. *Purifying the Earthly Body of God: Religion and Ecology in Hindu India.* Albany: State University of New York Press, 1998.

Prime, Ranchor. *Hinduism and Ecology: Seeds of Truth.* New York: Cassell, 1992.

Chapter Twelve

Global Hinduism
The Hindu Diaspora

ANANTANAND RAMBACHAN

Although the majority of Hindus continue to reside in India, the historical influence of Hinduism extended to Southeast Asia and to places such as Bali, Java, and Cambodia. Brahmin priests, at the invitation of local rulers, visited these lands and established aspects of the Hindu tradition. The continuing popularity of the Ramayana in Thailand (where it is known as the *Ramakien*) is a legacy of such early contacts and settlements. The past two centuries, however, saw large-scale migration of Hindus from India to other lands. This migration occurred in two major periods (Vertovec 2000).

The first occurred under colonialism during the nineteenth and early twentieth centuries when, under indenture contracts, Indians migrated to Guyana, Surinam, Trinidad, Jamaica, Mauritius, South Africa, East Africa, and Fiji, as well as to Burma and Malaysia. These were some of the earliest places where the Hindu tradition established itself outside of India and where it still thrives. The second period, occurring after World War II, witnessed migration especially to the Western world. Beginning with small numbers of students and businessmen migrating to Britain, this accelerated in the 1960s to include also the United States, Canada, and Australia. During the 1970s there was also movement of skilled Indian labor to the Gulf states, as well as the movement between diasporic countries. Such diaspora-to-diaspora movements include the migration of Hindus from the Caribbean to Britain, Canada, and the United States; Surinamese Hindus to the Netherlands; and Hindu Fijians to New Zealand. Vertovec estimates the world Hindu population to number around 768 million and puts the number outside of South Asia to be approximately 12.3 million (Vertovec 2000, 14).

Disaporic Hinduism reflects the original plurality of the tradition as well as the innovations and adaptations made as it transplanted itself to new settings. Hindus took with them local and regional traditions as well as practices specific to caste and family. These traditions did not remain static and were, in turn, transformed by the new challenges and influences.

Because discussing the history and development of Hinduism in each diaspora location would be an ungainly task, this chapter will focus on several examples, namely Trinidad, North America, Europe, and South Africa. It will conclude with broader reflections on the character of diasporic Hinduism, its challenges, and its contributions to the larger tradition.

Trinidad

The Genoese sea captain Christopher Columbus, in quest of the riches of Asia, was firmly convinced that the way to the East was by way of the West. Hoping to beat the Portuguese in the race for the East, the Spanish monarchy agreed to provide support for his venture, and on August 3, 1492, Columbus set sail from Palos. About two months later, with his crew on the verge of mutiny, Columbus sighted the island of San Salvador in the Bahamas. He explored the northern coast of Cuba and founded a settlement at Hispaniola (modern Haiti). Convinced that he had reached the East, Columbus wrote back with great enthusiasm to the Spanish rulers of islands that promised "as much gold as their highnesses may need, spice, and cotton and mastic and aloes-wood and a thousand other things of value." He named the islands "las Yndias" (the Indies). In 1502 he added "Occidentales" to make them the West Indies. Columbus made three subsequent voyages to these islands during the years 1493–1502.

Christopher Columbus died in dishonorable circumstances, firmly convinced that he had found a route to the East. He had not reached the East by sailing westwards, but in one of those intriguing paradoxes of history, the East was later to establish itself in the West. In an unusual way, his dream was realized.

On July 31, 1498, during his third voyage, Columbus reached the island of Trinidad, situated just off the northeastern coast of Venezuela. The native population, the Caribs and Arawaks, were part of the large family of people known as Amerindians who inhabited the Americas. Even though Columbus claimed the island in the name of the Spanish crown in 1498, it was not until one hundred years later that the Spanish established their first successful settlement. The evidence of Spanish colonization can be found still in many place names, such as the towns of Port of Spain and San Fernando, and in the musical traditions and festivals of Trinidad. The native Amerindian population was virtually exterminated by forced labor and European diseases, and by the time the British took the island in 1802, there were few natives left. Today, only traces of a native population can be found.

In the eighteenth century, considerable numbers of French planters came to Trinidad, and there has also been a French influence in the shaping of the island's life and history. Africans from West Africa were brought in as slaves to work on the sugar plantations from as early as the seventeenth century, and they constituted the basic population, along with the British, until 1838, when slavery was abolished.

The abolition of slavery meant the virtual collapse of the plantation economy on which the economic life of the island was based. Africans refused to work on the sugar plantations, preferring instead to become small independent farmers. Harsh measures to induce them back to the land included laws against squatting and heavy taxes on land and buildings not connected with sugar cultivation. These efforts, however, proved futile. The harsh memories of slavery and its association with sugar cultivation were not easy to erase. The planters in most of the colonies, especially Guyana, Trinidad, and Jamaica, where labor problems were desperate, looked elsewhere for workers. They turned to immigrants to provide a plentiful source of cheap labor. Portuguese and Chinese immigrants were tried, but they soon drifted into business or private cultivation as soon as, or even before, their contracts expired.

In 1837 John Gladstone, the owner of two plantations in Guyana, applied to the secretary of state for the colonies for permission to import workers from India. In 1838, 396 Indian workers arrived. The scheme was considered a success in Guyana, but investigation by the Anti-Slavery Society revealed that many of the immigrants had succumbed to diseases, some had been flogged and unjustly imprisoned, and others had not been paid promised wages. In 1839, the Indian government suspended immigration to the West Indies while conditions were being investigated. The need, however, was great, and immigration resumed officially in 1844, lasting until 1917. The end came as a consequence of agitation on the part of Indian nationalists who attacked the whole policy of emigration because they were disturbed by the conditions of workers in Fiji and Natal. In 1916, the Indian Legislative Council passed the Abolition of Indenture Act, and in 1918 the secretary of state for India refused to reopen emigration under indenture. In roughly eighty years, 548,000 Indians emigrated to the West Indies under the official scheme. Of these, the majority went to Guyana (239,000) and Trinidad (143,939). The port of embarkation was Calcutta (Madras and Bombay were occasionally used), and the majority of Indians came from the districts of the United Provinces and Bihar. Although various north Indian dialects were brought to Trinidad, Bhojpuri was the dominant one, and it is still spoken by many elderly members of Trinidad's Indian community.

The reasons for emigration were many. In several instances, force was employed and misleading information was provided by recruiting agents. Some migrated out of a love for adventure, and others were fleeing the hands of British law for their involvement in the 1857 uprising. In the main, however, emigrants were seeking escape from the effects of frequent famines in the provinces of Agra, Oudh, and Bihar.

Indian immigrants to the West Indies came under a system of indentureship. The labor contracts were generally for a period of five years in the case of males, and three years for females. At the end of this period, the immigrant could reindenture himself, return to India, or take up some independent occupation. A significant proportion of these immigrants chose to return home to India after completing the conditions of their contracts. In all, 75,547, or 31.62 percent, of those who migrated returned from Guyana, and 33,294, or 23.13 percent, of the migrants eventually returned from Trinidad. The important statistic is that 71 percent of those who made the arduous journey around the Cape of Good Hope and across the Atlantic Ocean chose to make their permanent homes in the Caribbean. At the present time, Hindus comprise 23.8 percent of the population of Trinidad and number approximately 300,000.

In an environment that was alien and prejudiced against the persistence of Indian cultural traditions, the Hindu immigrants sought to reestablish the basic elements of their religion and way of life. There is evidence that by the 1860s, Hindu temples were built, and festivals such as Shivaratri, Holi, Ramlila, and Divali were celebrated in the early twentieth century. Though Hindu traditions are continuously subject to challenge and change, these have survived with remarkable persistence during the past 150 years (see LaGuerre 1974; Klass 1961; Vertovec 1992).

One of the important reasons for the survival and persistence of the Hindu tradition in Trinidad is the fact that immigrants brought with them texts such as the Ramayana, Bhagavata Purana, and the Bhagavad Gita. Among the early Indian settlers in Trinidad were also members of the Brahmin caste, the traditional repositories of sacred learning and ritual. These religious specialists, while also working on the sugar plantations, played a vital role in the continuity of Hindu traditions in Trinidad.

The most popular scriptural text for the Hindu community in Trinidad is the *Ramacharitmanas* of the poet Tulsidasa (sixteenth century CE). Even though most of the Hindus in Trinidad today are not fluent in Hindi, the text continues to be widely read and expounded. The recitation is usually done in Hindi, but the commentary and exposition are almost always in English. During any week of the year, expositions of the text occur in various locations throughout the island, and these are usually publicized in the local newspapers. These sessions last from a week to nine days and are held in temples or in Hindu homes. Elaborate preparations are made for these readings, which are usually very well attended. There are also regular but smaller gatherings for the study of the

Ramayana, called *Ramayana satsangas,* when people gather in temples or homes for recitation and discussion. Hindus in Trinidad still look to this text as a source of moral values and religious instruction. Many important family events and life-cycle rituals are celebrated and marked by recitations of the Ramayana. It is quite common for the text to be read on the occasion of a birthday or wedding anniversary as well as in homes as a source of consolation when a family member dies. Musical recordings of the Ramayana by popular Hindi singers are extremely popular and are regularly broadcast on radio stations.

In Trinidad, the Hindu home continues to be the center of religious life. Most of the life-cycle rituals (*samskaras*) connected with birth, initiation, marriage, and death take place in Hindu homes. Each home continues to have a room or part of a room set aside as an altar. Here, icons of Hindu deities are kept, and worship takes place on a daily basis. The most popular domestic ritual is the performance of puja. This is an elaborate ritual of worship performed annually, semi-annually, or to mark important family events and occasions. Elaborate preparations are usually made for this formal worship ceremony, and members of the extended family, friends, and neighbors are invited. The wife or husband (or sometimes both) is led through the various procedures of the ritual by the family priest, who is referred to locally as a pandit. The deity that is the focus of the puja is usually the family's chosen God-form, or *ishtadeva*. Among the popular personal deities venerated in Trinidad are the incarnations of Vishnu such as Rama and Krishna, along with Durga, Shiva, and Hanuman. The goddess Kali is not a popular figure of worship, but there are several communities in various parts of the island where her worship continues. Many Hindu families still elaborately perform each year the puja of Satyanarayana (Vishnu), a popular worship practice in north Indian states like Bihar and Uttar Pradesh. Traditional stories that reinforce the value of faith in this particular deity are usually read in Hindi and translated in English. It is customary for Hindus in Trinidad to hoist a small triangular flag in front of their homes after the performance of puja. Particular colors are indicative of specific deities, and Hindu homes in this multireligious community can be distinguished by the presence of these religious emblems.

Members of the local Arya Samaj, a reform movement launched by Swami Dayanand Saraswati (1824–1883) in 1875 in Bombay and emphasizing the centrality of the Vedas, substitute the Vedic fire ritual for the puja. This is referred to locally as the *havan* and is the central domestic ritual for families affiliated with this movement.

The visibility of Hinduism in Trinidad is primarily through numerous public festivals. The preeminent among these is Divali (festival of lights), which is usually celebrated in October and November. In Trinidad, Divali primarily commemorates the triumphant return of Rama with his wife, Sita, and brother, Lakshmana, to the city of Ayodhya after his long exile and his defeat of the evil king Ravana. Divali is celebrated on a lavish scale in Trindad and is the occasion for a national public holiday. Newspapers publish special supplements focusing on the festival and broadly on Hinduism, and the television and radio stations broadcast appropriate music, messages, and information throughout the day. Public celebrations, sometimes in the weeks leading up to the festival, are held at various venues in the island. In recent years, the major public celebration occurs in central Trinidad, at Divali Nagar, on lands donated by the government to a major local organization, the National Council for Indian Culture. During the week leading to the festival, Hindus and non-Hindus in the thousands converge at this venue for a nightly feast of Indian song, music, dance, food, and educational displays. Local businesses set up display booths, and charitable organizations make their services available. Almost every school and college in Trinidad has its own celebration.

Although the celebration of Divali has, in recent years, developed a public aspect, it still retains its character as a family-centered festival. Homes are washed and painted and illuminated on the night of Divali with numerous earthen lamps, sometimes arranged in intricate patterns. For Hindus in Trinidad, the festival is essentially religious in character. Most Hindus will abstain from intoxicants and meat in the days leading up to the celebration, and it is customary for families to worship God in the form of Lakshmi, the goddess of wealth and prosperity. Gifts, cards, and food are shared with friends and neighbors, and, increasingly, many non-Hindus illumine their homes and share Indian meals with Hindu friends.

Another festival that is widely celebrated in Trinidad is Holi, a traditional spring festival. Its popularity has been growing over the years, and its observance at public venues often includes a parade of bands, the sprinkling of red liquid or powder, and the singing of traditional songs to the accompaniment of drums and cymbals. Other festivals include the birth anniversaries of the incarnations of Rama (March–April) and Krishna (August), the night of Shiva (February), and a ritual sea-bath during Kartika, the eighth lunar month of the Hindu calendar. Outdoor dramas enacting the story of the Ramayana have a long history in Trinidad, and the public interest in this drama has not wavered. During October, thousands of Hindus gather each night at several established venues to witness the story of Rama's birth, marriage, and exile, the abduction of Sita, the defeat of Ravana, and Rama's triumphant return to Ayodhya. Camps at both ends of the field represent the respective abodes of Rama and Ravana, and the story unfolds while narrators recite the Ramayana of Tulsidasa. The festival ends with the burning of a large effigy of Ravana.

The largest Hindu organization in Trinidad is the Sanatan Dharma Maha Sabha, founded in 1949 by a legendary businessman named Bhadase Sagan Marajh. Under his leadership, the Maha Sabha in the 1950s launched a vigorous primary school building program in agricultural areas and ensured the availability of a basic education for many Hindus, especially girls, who did not have access to the schools that were administered by Christian missionary organizations. The operation of its schools, which now include forty-three primary and five secondary institutions, still remains an important focus of the activity of this group. Though the medium of education is English, and students are prepared for a national high school entrance examination, these schools also offer basic exposure to Hindu religion and culture and participate in competitive Hindu cultural programs where prizes are awarded for song, music, dance, dramatic performances, and knowledge of Hinduism. In addition to its educational concerns, the majority of Hindu temples in Trinidad are affiliated with the Maha Sabha, and it is also the organization with which the majority of Hindu priests in Trinidad identify.

The Arya Samaj movement was established in the early twentieth century through the work of Vedic missionaries. Like the Maha Sabha, this organization has also made significant contributions to primary education in Trinidad, and many of its schools have attained prominence for excellence and success in national examinations. Many of its doctrinal views were different from those championed by the Maha Sabha, and the relationship between the two organizations has been occasionally contentious. In recent years, however, relationships have been cordial, but the Arya Samaj has also grown weaker due to declining membership and participation. It retains a visible presence largely through its educational institutions.

The Sathya Sai movement, established in the mid-1970s, is one of the more vigorous new bodies. Its various centers, now scattered throughout the island, sponsor regular worship meetings (satsangas) consisting of devotional songs and chants and lectures on the life and teachings of Sathya Sai Baba (1926–). In addition to participation in satsangas, members engage in service-oriented activities of various kinds. Many of the more recent Hindu or Hindu-based organizations have established branches in Trinidad, such as the International Society for Krishna Consciousness (ISKCON), Transcendental Meditation (TM), the Brahmakumaris, and the Chinmaya Mission.

After a century and a half of existence outside of India, Hinduism in Trinidad continues to thrive with remarkable persistence. Its historical ability to adapt and to assimilate under changing conditions has clearly served it well in this new environment. Traditional temple architecture has been modified for purposes of congregational worship and lectures, while preserving the nature of the temple as a place for personal worship. Congregational worship, on the whole, has become a prominent feature of Hindu life in Trinidad, and temples throughout the island conduct regular services on Sunday mornings to reflect the pattern of work and leisure in the West. Though Sanskrit and Hindi remain the liturgical languages, they are increasingly used along with English translations, and the medium of religious instruction is English. Caste is a minimal feature in the everyday life of Hindus in Trinidad. The major Hindu organization, the Sanatan Dharma Maha Sabha, is still a vigorous defender of the orthodox ideal that priests must be Brahmin by birth, but there are other groups that do not insist on this requirement and instead emphasize aptitude. The Arya Samaj broke new ground in Trinidad with the appointment of a woman to serve as one of its priests. Caste issues sometimes become important in decisions concerning marriage, but with less frequency. The Hindu experience in Trinidad points to the future promise of a Hindu tradition without the hierarchy and burdens of caste.

North America

The year 1965 marked a turning point in the history of Hinduism in the United States. The Immigration Act of 1965, initiated by President John F. Kennedy and signed into law by President Lyndon B. Johnson at a ceremony at the foot of the Statue of Liberty, eliminated national origins quotas and made it possible for significant numbers of Asians and other non-Europeans to take the first steps to becoming citizens of the United States.

Prior to 1965, it is estimated that Indian immigrants to the United States numbered less than 15,000. Many of these were farmers from the Punjab who settled first in British Columbia, Canada, in the late nineteenth and early twentieth centuries. Some of these then migrated south into the states of Washington, Oregon, and California. In 1923, the United States Supreme Court ruled that Hindus could not be citizens of the United States. "Hindu," as Diana Eck points out, was interpreted as a racial and not a religious category (Eck 1993, 34–36; Mann, Numrich, and Williams 2001, 64–66). The case that resulted in this ruling involved an application for United States citizenship by Bhagat Singh Thind, a Sikh settled in Canada. The court argued that Hindus were not "free white persons" under the law and, therefore, not entitled to citizenship. A federal law of 1790 permitted only white immigrants to become naturalized citizens. The Immigration Act of 1924 established a national origins quota system that excluded Indians, along with immigrants from China, Korea, and Japan, from entering the United States.

Although the Immigration Act of 1965 was restrictive in the sense that it gave priority to immigrants with professional skills, the influx of Indian immigrants to the United States was significant. The 1980 census listed 387, 223 "Asian Indians" as permanent residents. In the 1990 census, this number had climbed to around 1.7 million. The estimated Hindu population in the United States is now 930,000 (Vertovec 2000, 14). As a consequence of the restrictive immigration policy, they constitute a distinct group, "with a higher proportion of educated and skilled individuals than Indian populations elsewhere in the world" (Mann, Numrich, and Williams 2001, 67). They are concentrated largely in the metropolitan areas of New York, New Jersey, Illinois, Texas, and California, although there are few urban areas without a Hindu presence. It is estimated that approximately 40 percent of Indian immigrants in the United States come from Gujarat, and about 20 percent from the Punjab. Following these are immigrants from the Hindi-speaking states of northern and central India, Tamils, Telugus, Keralites, and Bengalis (Coward, Hinnells, and Williams 2000, 213–217).

Though the arrival of Indian immigrants to the United States after the passage of the Immigration Act of 1965 significantly hastened the establishment of Hinduism in the country, these were not the first to cultivate the seeds of Hinduism on American soil. The credit for this must go to the New England Transcendentalists and, in particular, to Ralph Waldo Emerson and Henry David Thoreau. They encountered Hinduism through sacred texts such as the Bhagavad Gita and the Upanishads and were attracted to Hinduism's nonexclusive character and its vision of a single reality underlying all phenomena. The writings of Emerson and Thoreau created a climate of interest and familiarity with strands of Hindu thought for Swami Vivekananda, who arrived in the United States in 1893 to speak at the World's Parliament of Religions, held in conjunction with the Chicago World's Fair. Vivekananda's impact at the parliament was memorable, and this was followed by two years of intense lecturing along the eastern and western coasts of the United States and also in cities such as Minneapolis, Des Moines, Detroit, and Memphis. He established branches of the country's first Hindu organization, the Vedanta Society, in New York (1894) and San Francisco (1899).

As noted elsewhere in this book, the term *Vedanta* literally means "the end of the Vedas" and refers to the collection of dialogues constituting the Upanishads, the last sections of the Vedas. Philosophically, the Vedanta Societies subscribe to the interpretation of the Upanishads developed by ninth-century theologian Shankara, and as expounded by Vivekananda and his teacher, Ramakrishna. There are twelve Vedanta Society centers in the United States. The American headquarters is located in Los Angeles, but the Ramakrishna Mission in Calcutta, India, is responsible for the overall supervision. The head of each center is traditionally a renouncer and though most of these are Indians, there are now ordained American men and women active in these communities. The philosophical approach of the Vedanta society has made it attractive to the educated middle class, and programs also include many traditional features of Hinduism such as puja, *bhajans* (devotional singing), and the celebration of various festivals. The distinctive lineage of the organization is also affirmed through birthday celebrations for significant persons such as Ramakrishna; his spouse, Sarada Devi; and Vivekananda. The Vedanta Press, located in Hollywood, California, is an important source for translations of Hindu texts and for expository material on Hinduism (see Eck 2001, 101–103).

Vivekananda's death at the early age of thirty-nine did not allow him to consolidate personally the work initiated in the United States. Paramahamsa Yogananda, who arrived in 1920 to attend the Unitarian-sponsored International Congress of Religious Liberals, became the first Hindu teacher to reside permanently in the United States. In 1925, Yogananda established the Yogananda Satsang; this eventually became the Self-Realization Fellowship, with headquarters in Los Angeles. Yogananda sought to build bridges between religion and science by contending that the claims of religion can be verified by experience and by offering the method of Kriya Yoga as a technique "for attaining direct personal experience of God." The Self-Realization Fellowship also seeks to "reveal the complete harmony and basic oneness of original Christianity as taught by Jesus Christ and original Yoga as taught by Bhagavan Krishna," and to "unite science and religion through realization of their underlying principles" (Paramahansa Yogananda 1990, 573).

Yogananda was a tireless and creative worker, and until the 1960s, the Self-Realization Fellowship was one of the most extensive and popular Hindu-based organizations in the United States. He developed a mail-order self-study course on yoga that enabled people throughout the world to study his teachings, and his *Autobiography of a Yogi* continues to be inspiring reading for those interested in the practice of yoga. Though there are now only a dozen Self-Realization Fellowship centers in the United States, affiliated groups continue to function in almost every major U.S. city. Many members are attracted by the attempt to integrate Hinduism and Christianity and to explain yoga through the terminology of Western psychology.

Until the mid-1960s, the dominant public forms of Hinduism in the United States were the traditions of advaita and yoga. This changed, however, with the arrival in New York in 1965 of Swami A. C. Bhaktivedanta Prabhupada, who launched the International Society for Krishna Consciousness (ISKCON). Bhaktivedanta belonged to the Vaishnava traditon, inspired by the writings of the eleventh-century theologian Ramanuja and by the teaching of the sixteenth-century Bengali saint Chaitanya. The tradition emphasizes devotion, or bhakti, to Krishna, regarded as the supreme incarnation of Vishnu. The aim of life is complete surrender and service to God, and one of the essential practices of discipleship is the chanting (*kirtan*) of the *maha-mantra* (great verse), "Hare Krishna Hare Krishna Krishna Krishna Hare Hare/Hare Rama Hare Rama Rama Rama Hare Hare." During the 1960s and 1970s, ISKCON members were visible on the streets of American cities, chanting this mantra and distributing devotional literature. ISKCON introduced a distinctive form of Hinduism to the American religious landscape that had hitherto existed only on the soil of India. Bhaktivedanta was a prolific writer, translator, and commentator, and his works continue to be published and distributed by the Bhaktivedanta Book Trust.

The temple-centered practices of Hinduism were also introduced to the United States by ISKCON, and these temples were among the few available for early Hindu immigrants, with ISKCON members serving as priest and teachers for the immigrants and their children. The traditions of bhakti continue today in the over sixty temples affiliated with the ISKCON movement. Following the theology of Ramanuja, the image is seen as a unique incarnation of God and is the recipient of daily ritual offerings such as food, flowers, perfume, and light. In many cities, ISKCON temples have successfully bridged the gap between American disciples of Krishna and Hindu devotees.

The puritanical lifestyle of the movement and its unabashedly Hindu character limited membership, and the death of the founder in 1977 also resulted in a decline in its growth and influence. The movement has been adversely affected by internal divisions, allegations of child abuse, defections, and criminal charges against certain leaders. ISKCON continues, however, to be a part of the American Hindu landscape, and many of its temples in cities such as Chicago and Dallas are vital centers of Hinduism.

One of the most popular and successful forms of "export Hinduism" in the United States is Transcendental Meditation (TM), launched by Maharishi Mahesh Yogi through the Spiritual Regeneration Foundation in 1959. A college-based organization, the Students International Meditation Society (SIMS), grew rapidly during the 1960s, but the movement's popularity was bolstered when members of the Beatles turned to the Maharishi for wisdom and instruction. Today, TM centers continue to function in almost every major American city, and the organization has a university in Fairfield, Iowa—Maharishi International University—offering both undergraduate and postgraduate programs in various disciplines within the framework of the Maharishi's philosophy. TM also has a political party, the Natural Law Party, which supports candidates at both state and federal levels.

At the center of TM practice is the traditional Hindu discipline of *japa,* or mantra-repetition. This is the method offered for the attainment of ultimate reality or pure being. TM practitioners, who pay for a course of training, are expected to dedicate twenty minutes twice a day to this practice. TM, although deeply influenced by Hindu thought and practice, does not emphasize its Hindu roots. It does not represent itself as a religion, but as a technique for the development of creative intelligence, reducing stress, and achieving health. This, along with the fact that it does not require significant lifestyle changes and is relatively easy to practice, helps to explain its success and popularity. Its continuity with the methods of Vivekananda and Yogananda may be seen in its efforts to demonstrate that its outcomes are scientifically verifiable. TM publications regularly cite studies in various medical journals as validating its claims, although critics have argued that such benefits may be gained through alternative relaxation techniques and not specifically meditation.

Other enduring forms of export of missionary Hinduism include the Integral Yoga Institute, established by Swami Satchidananda in rural Virginia in 1966, and the Siddha Yoga Dham of America (SYD), founded in 1974 by Swami Muktananda, a disciple of the Indian guru Bhagavan Sri Nityananda. Siddha Yoga belongs to the wider tradition of Kashmir Shaivism and is based on a belief in the ability of the *siddha* (the spiritually realized teacher) to awaken the spiritual energy of the disciple at the time of initiation (*shaktipat*). Before his death in 1982, Muktananda chose two Indian disciples as his successors, Swami Nityananda and his sister Gurumayi Chidvilasananda. Nityananda resigned amidst controversy in 1986, and his sister became the effective spiritual head of the movement. She teaches and initiates disciples at the various centers and ashramas affiliated with the movement.

Whereas the impact of some Indian gurus, such as Bhagwan Shree Rajneesh (the Rajneesh Meditation Center) and Guru Maharaj Ji (Divine Light Mission), has been short-lived, other teachers and movements continue to thrive. Among these are the Divine Life Society, the Sivananada Yoga Vedanta Center, and the International School of Yoga and Vedanta. Today, however, the primary energies of the Hindu tradition in the United States are to be found in institutions and movements associated with the immigrants who have, since 1965, made the United States their home. The vitality of these energies is best evident in the establishment of Hindu temples all across the United States.

The construction of a temple is one of the most important ways in which Hindus express their identity with a new place and their concern for the future of the tradition. It is a statement that the community now understands itself to be a permanent part of the religious landscape of the United States. The construction of a temple is simultaneously the forging of a new community. The complex tasks that are involved invite the community into cooperative activity and forges new bonds. The temple often becomes the center of the group's identity. The Harvard-based Pluralism Project lists 706 Hindu temples and centers in the United States. While many communities adapted existing buildings to serve their needs, at least thirty temples have been constructed during the past two decades (Eck 2000, 222). Among the earliest in the United States were the Sri Venkateswara Temple in Pittsburgh (1977) and the Ganesha Temple in Flushing, New York (1977) (Narayanan 1992). These were soon followed by temples in Albany, Detroit, Chicago, Los Angeles, Nashville, Lanham (Md.), Flint (Mich.), and Minneapolis (see http://www.pluralism.org/directory/). Many of these temples replicate the sacred geography of India, providing a familiar space and experience for Hindu immigrants and fostering an identification with their adopted homeland. The Sri Venkateswara Temple in Pittsburgh, for example, replicates the famous temple of Sri Venkateswara at Tirupati, in Andhra Pradesh. Sri Venkateshwara temples have also been constructed in Malibu Hills (Calif.), Milwaukee (Wisc.) and Du Page County (Ill.). Other temples that duplicate sacred spaces in India include the Sri Meenakshi Temple (Houston), associated with a temple of the same name in Madurai, Tamil Nadu; the Divya Dham Temple (Queens, N.Y.), replicating the famous Vaishno Devi Temple in Jammu; Barsana Dham (Austin, Tex.) named after the hometown of Krishna's beloved consort Radha; and the Paschimakasi Sri Viswanatha Temple (Flint) named for the city of Kashi in Varanasi.

Although Hindu temples in the United States serve many of the more traditional worship requirements of the community, the multiple uses of the temple also reflect changing needs. Traditionally, the Hindu home is the center of religious life and worship and the place where religious practices and values are absorbed by a new generation. Hindus are not required to go to temples and generally do so only on festival days in the Hindu calendar. Most Hindu homes in the United States continue to have shrines that are the focus of worship (puja) in the morning and/or evening. Hindu temples have not entirely displaced homes as the loci of religious activity in the United States, but temples are increasingly the location for domestic rituals and observances.

In addition to hosting major festivals such as Divali, Navaratri, and Holi, these U.S. temples are now the locations for traditionally domestic rituals such as pre- and postnatal ceremonies, weddings, anniversaries, and memorial services. Narayanan notes that "in Hin-

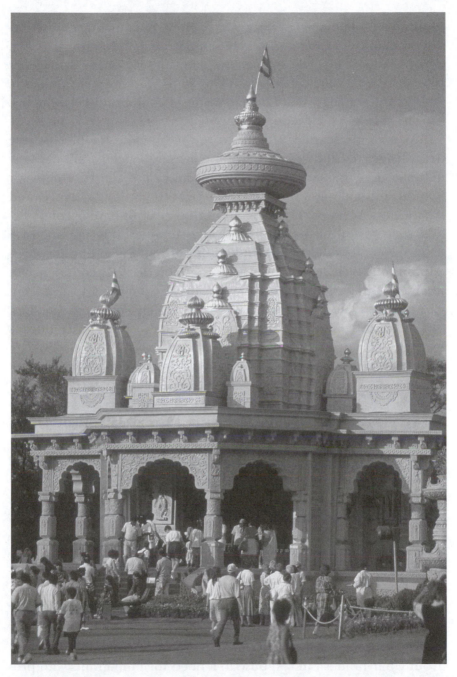

Crowds of visitors enter a temporary Hindu temple on the grounds of the Festival of India in Middlesex County, New Jersey.
KELLY-MOONEY PHOTOGRAPHY/CORBIS

duism as it is practiced in this country, there is a blurring of lines between domestic, community, and temple rituals" (Narayanan 1992, 170). Though this may appear to be an innovation, she notes the similarity with village celebrations in south India, where domestic and temple rituals take on the character of community celebrations. In village India, she notes, there are few private domestic rituals.

Increasingly, temples are replacing the home as the place where knowledge of Hinduism is transmitted to a new generation. Many temples now regularly offer programs and classes in Hinduism for Hindu youth along with training in yoga, Indian music dance, and languages. Weekend, holiday, and summer camps have become regular features in the annual life of many temples, offering intensive exposure to Hinduism and Indian culture and a setting in which Hindu youths can encounter each other and discover confidence in their Hindu identity. Hindu temples are also adapting to a new environment by adding new occasions for celebration and worship, such as high school graduations, and joining with fellow Americans in the celebration of Thanksgiving, Mother's Day, and the New Year. Temples in the United States, in other words, have also become centers where Indian culture is kept alive, celebrated, transmitted, and displayed with pride to American friends. The use of temples for religious, cultural, and social purposes is an important part of the strategy of keeping Hinduism alive in the United States.

The first Hindus to settle in Canada came from the Punjab early in the twentieth century (Coward and Botting 2001, 35–59; Coward 2000, 151–172). Although the total number of South Asians was quite small, they, along with Chinese and Japanese immigrants, were soon perceived as a threat by the small Anglo-Saxon community, and legal measures were soon instituted to curtail immigration. South Asians were required to purchase return tickets to their native countries, denied the right to vote, and barred from serving on juries, working in the public service, and in the professions of law and pharmacy. Immigration from South Asia was reduced to a trickle until the 1960s, when the first large group of Hindus arrived from Uttar Pradesh in response to a need for immigrants with professional training. During this same period, Hindus moved to Canada from former British colonies where they claimed discrimination after independence. Such places included East Africa, South

Africa, Fiji, Mauritius, Trinidad, and Guyana. They moved across the country, settling mainly in larger cities such as Toronto and Vancouver, with smaller concentrations in Montreal, Edmonton, Quebec, Ottawa, Calgary, and Winnipeg. The Hindu community in Canada is estimated to be over 120,000.

Hindu immigrants to Canada, like those in the United States, continued with the practice of the tradition in a domestic setting and occasionally joined with other families for worship and festivals. The need was soon felt, however, for temples, and diverse groups came together in the 1970s to begin construction. One of the earliest to be built was in the city of Vancouver by the Vishva Hindu Parishad. This is a multiuse facility, and the pattern has been duplicated in places such as Toronto, Calgary, Regina, Winnipeg, and Edmonton. Today, there are over fifty Hindu temples and organizations in Ontario, with most of these located in Toronto.

Because of the significant size of the Hindu community in Toronto (over 100,000), many of the temples cater to the religious needs of a specific ethno-linguistic group such as the Tamils and Gujaratis. The Ganesha Temple, for example, was founded by Tamil immigrants from Sri Lanka, South Africa, Singapore, and Malaysia and caters to the special traditions of this community and preserves the distinctive south Indian style of ritual and ceremony. Other temples, however, are more eclectic in tradition and congregation. One of the best examples of this is the Vishnu Mandir on Yonge Street, Toronto. Started very humbly in 1981 in a small house, by Hindu immigrants from Guyana and Trinidad, a new temple was constructed in 1984. Construction has continued over the years, and today, the temple has expanded to over thirty thousand square feet. Its ecumenical altar, like that of many new temples in Canada and the United States, offers images of all the major deities of the Hindu tradition. Under the leadership of Dr. Budhendra Doobay, the temple offers an eclectic mode of worship that attracts Hindus from many geographical backgrounds. Its congregational-style Sunday morning services are popular and well attended.

Another important expression of the Hindu tradition in Toronto is provided by the Arya Samaj, the organization founded by Swami Dayanand Saraswati (1824–1883) in 1875. The reforming zeal of the Arya Samaj and its offensive against Christian proselytization made it attractive to many overseas Hindus. Arya Samaj followers in Canada come mainly from the Caribbean and East Africa. They are part of a North American network with branches in over seventy cities.

Europe

The total number of Hindus in Europe is estimated to be around 700,000. Most of these are settled in Great Britain, with smaller concentrations in the Netherlands, Germany, and Portugal.

The Hindu community in the Netherlands, numbering about 70,000, traces its origin primarily to migration from Surinam during the mid-1970s, after the colony gained its independence. They brought an Indo-Caribbean expression of Hinduism, characterized by sharp divisions between the reformist Arya Samaj and the orthodox Sanatan Dharma practitioners. By 1991, the Arya Samaj had established twenty-six regional societies and three temples. The Sanatan Dharma, in comparison, had forty regional branches and sixteen temples. Tamil refugees from Sri Lanka, the International Society for Krishna Consciousness (ISKCON), and the Sri Sathya Sai Baba movement have added to the forms of Hinduism now available in the Netherlands.

Hindu professionals from India migrated to Germany in the 1950s, but their numbers were too small to establish places of worship and organizations. In the mid-1980s, however, about 40,000 Hindu Tamil refugees from Sri Lanka migrated to Germany. Today, Tamil Hindus are the largest group among Germany's 65,000 Hindus, giving the tradition a distinctively south Indian flavor. They maintain temples in subterrace flats and former industrial halls as places of worship and cultural centers where language and dance classes are available (Baumann 1998, 25–30).

The Hindu community in Portugal, consisting of around eight thousand, is made up almost entirely of Gujarati Hindus, most of whom are refugees from Mozambique. They are concentrated in Lisbon and have established temples in Lisbon, Porto, and Faro.

Although Hindus have settled in Great Britain since the nineteenth century, their number did not increase significantly until the

1950s and 1960s with the arrival of immigrants from the Caribbean and India who were attracted by post-war work opportunities. The Hindu population in Britain grew in the mid-1960s and early 1970s with the migration of educated middle-class Hindus from East Africa (Kenya, Zambia, Tanzania, Malawi, Uganda) (Vertovec 2000, 87–107; Knott 2000, 89–108). They came to Britain to escape the policies of "Africanization" implemented by many governments after independence. These policies, on the whole, sought to ensure that the commercial and professional sectors were controlled by indigenous black Africans. Hindus with British passports took the opportunity to migrate. In 1972, the expulsion of persons of Indian origin from Uganda also resulted in the arrival of tens of thousands of Hindus in Britain.

Today, the Hindu community in Britain is estimated to be over 400,000 and quite diverse. About 70 percent are of Gujarati ethnicity, followed by Punjabis (15 percent) and Hindus from other Indian states such as Bengal, Tamil Nadu, and Andhra Pradesh. The community also consists of Hindus who trace their origins to the Caribbean, Mauritius, Fiji, and Sri Lanka. The Gujaratis are not a homogenous group and are differentiated on the basis of regional origin, caste, and religious tradition.

In contrast to Sikh and Muslim immigrants, Hindus in Britain were rather late in the establishment of temples. As in other parts of the diaspora, religious activity was confined initially to the domestic sphere. Communal forms of worship developed as numbers increased, networks established, and confidence grew. Town halls and other public buildings were usually rented for major events and celebrations. The organizational ties that came into being through groups of families meeting in homes and gathering for the public festivals became the foundations for fund-raising and property acquisition in order to build temples. The first Hindu temple in England was built in Coventry in 1967; this was soon followed, in 1969, by the construction of temples in Leicester and London. Immigration from East Africa in the 1970s quickened the establishment of temples and temples sprung up in cities such as Leeds, Birmingham, and west London. The number of Hindu temples in Britain now is estimated to be over three hundred. As in the United States and Canada—and unlike in India—most of these are multiuse buildings providing religious services of various kinds, but also language classes, cultural activities, and meeting space for various community organizations. Though temples are, in principle, open to Hindus of all backgrounds, many in reality serve particular ethnic groups, castes, or subcastes. Examples of such temples include the Gujarati Prajapati Hindu Temple in Bradford; the Sri Murugan Temple in London, catering to Tamil Hindus; and the Indo-Caribbean Temple in south London. There are also broad-based eclectic temples seeking to bridge ethnic and sectarian boundaries.

In August 1995, Hindus celebrated the opening of the first traditional temple to be built in Britain. Constructed according to traditional design and specifications, the Sri Swaminarayan Temple has become both a center of worship and a tourist site. It is affiliated with the Swaminarayan Hindu Mission, a Gujarati movement led by a well-known guru, Pramukh Swami Maharaj. The Swaminarayan Hindu Mission is a part of the worldwide Bochasanwasi Akshar Purushottam Sanstha, a rapidly growing movement among the Hindu Gujarati diaspora in North America, Africa, and Great Britain (Williams 2001).

In addition to the traditional forms of Hinduism brought to Britain by Hindu immigrants, new religious movements, often originating in North America, have also taken roots. These include groups such as ISKCON, Transcendental Meditation, Siddha Yoga, and Sahaja Yoga, started by Mataji Nirmala Devi. Britain is also home to the Ramakrishna Mission, the reformist Arya Samaj, and movements centered on gurus such as Sri Sathya Sai Baba and Morari Bapu.

South Africa

Hindus migrated to South Africa in the mid-nineteenth and early twentieth centuries for the same reasons that they went to other parts of the British colonial empire: They were recruited under the system of indentureship to fill an agricultural labor vacuum created by the abolition of slavery. The first group of Indians, from the Madras province, arrived in 1860 in Natal and, by the time the system was abolished in 1911, a documented sum of 152,184 Indians had been transported to Natal. About 24 percent of these chose to return to India following their service. Others either reindentured themselves after completing the stipulated five years of service or took the option of freedom and moved into independent farming or other occupations. Indentured and freed laborers were joined by so-called free passenger Indians. Most of these were merchants with British passports of Gujarati origin.

Indentured laborers to South Africa embarked from two Indian ports. From the port of Madras came workers from the modern Indian states of Tamil Nadu and Andhra Pradesh, speaking Tamil and Telugu. From Calcutta came workers from Uttar Pradesh and Bihar, speaking Hindi. Smaller numbers came from Bengal and Madhya Pradesh. The contemporary Hindu community in South Africa consists of four predominant language groups: Tamils, Telugus, Hindis, and Gujaratis. The current Hindu population is estimated to be 685,000.

As in other parts of the diaspora, Hindus affirmed their sense of permanence and identity with South Africa by the construction of temples, an activity that continues to the present day. By the late nineteenth century, several temples were established in the Durban area. These soon became, as they still are today, centers of both cultural and religious activities (Kumar 2000). Along with the founding of temples, the establishment of Hinduism in South Africa received a significant boost in the early twentieth century through the work of various visiting teachers from India. Among these was Bhai Paramanand (1905), an Arya Samaj missionary who traveled throughout the Natal and Transvaal provinces spreading the teachings of the reform movement and strengthening its roots. He was followed by Swami Shankaranand (1908), who founded the Hindu Maha Sabha in 1912 and who was instrumental in having Divali declared a public holiday in 1910. Gandhi's presence in South Africa (1893–1914) is still recalled with great pride by Hindus. He is revered for his loyalty to Hinduism and his resistance to Christian conversion. Several Hindu temples have the statue of Gandhi within the complex.

Unlike the Caribbean, where the majority of Hindus trace their ancestry to north India, South Africa reflects the traditions of both north and south India. There are temples dedicated primarily to the major Hindu forms of God (Shiva, Vishnu, and Amman or Shakti), but temples on the whole seem to be more ecumenical in architecture and worship patterns. This may be the consequence of an early effort for unity and consensus in the Hindu community, as well as limited resources. Priests from the south Indian Shiva temples, many of whom come from Sri Lanka, are often recruited to serve in the Vishnu temples on major occasions. One of the important adaptations in South Africa, as well as in other parts of the diaspora, is the practice of regular temple worship on Sunday mornings. The origins of this go back to the experience of indentureship, when Sunday alone was labor-free and thus available for communal religious activity.

Although temples have a central role in the practice of Hinduism in South Africa, domestic rituals continue to be regularly performed. Marriage and death rituals are performed in homes, along with birth ceremonies. One of the most popular domestic ceremonies is the Satyanarayana Vrata Katha, centered on reading the narrative of Lord Satyanarayana, or Vishnu. It is done annually by some families or at more infrequent intervals. Worship of Hanuman, Rama's beloved servant in the Ramayana, is also extremely popular in South African Hindu homes.

The major Hindu festivals celebrated in South Africa reflect the traditions of both northern and southern India. Festivals such as Thai Pongal and Thai Pusam (Kavadi) enjoy great popularity among Hindus with south Indian origins. Mahashivaratri is celebrated by both communities; Ramanavami and Krishna Jayanti are more popular among north Indian groups and less so among the Tamils and Telugus. All Hindu groups in South Africa celebrate Divali, although the traditions differ among the various communities.

Neo-Hindu movements are a prominent feature of the South African religious landscape, providing Hindus with more philosophically oriented forms of the tradition. One of the earliest to become established is the Arya Samaj. Its origins in South Africa may be traced to the visit in 1905 of Bhai Paramanand. He was followed in 1908 by Swami Shankaranand, who introduced the Vedic fire ritual and then revived the celebration of Divali. Pandit Bhavani Dayal Sanyasi, a South African–born leader, continued the work of early pioneers by founding Hindi schools and popularizing ceremonies performed in accordance with Vedic custom. A seminal moment in the history of the Arya Samaj was the establishment in 1925 of the Arya Pratinidhi Sabha in Natal, which later became affiliated with its parent body, the Sarvadeshik Arya Pratinidhi Sabha in India.

Today, the activities of the Arya Samaj are focused on the dissemination of the teachings of its founder, Swami Dayanand Saraswati, the administration of schools, publications, social welfare activities, and the training of priests. It is one of the few Hindu organizations offering training for women who desire to serve as priests. Its social outreach, under the auspices of the Aryan Benevolent Home, caters to the needs of people of all backgrounds. Its work for orphans is funded by both state and private agencies.

The Divine Life Society in South Africa was established in 1949 by V. Srinivasen, after a visit to India where he met the Indian founder, Swami Sivananda. In 1956, Srinivasen returned to India and was initiated into monasticism by Swami Sivananda. He returned to South Africa, as Swami Sahajananda, establishing several branches and starting a printing press for the dissemination of Hindu religious literature. Swami Sahajananda continues to head the organization and to direct its activities.

The Divine Life Society is well known for social welfare programs serving the black communities in South Africa. These include educational training, medical relief, family planning, and food. The organization is also active domestically through the conduct of religious services (satsangas) at the homes of its members and those who receive its help.

Unlike the Arya Samaj, the Divine Life Society is ecumenical in its theology and mode of worship. Though leaning philosophically toward the Vedanta tradition of Shankara, it is accommodative of a wide variety of traditional Hindu belief and practice and makes no sharp distinctions between theistic and nontheistic views.

The Ramakrishna Centre was founded in 1946 by D. C. Naidoo, who was interested in the study of Indian philosophy and the teachings of Ramakrishna. He was initiated into the Ramakrishna Order of monks in India in 1949 as Swami Nischalananda and, after returning to South Africa in 1953, expanded the activities of the movement. In addition to disseminating religious teachings, Swami Nischalananda also gave attention to social welfare activities. Like the Divine Life Society, these include school feeding, medical relief, food distribution, and educational support.

Other active neo-Hindu groups in South Africa include the International Society for Krishna Consciousness (ISKCON) and the Sathya Sai Baba movement. In addition to temple worship, study groups, public chanting, and the dissemination of literature, ISKCON administers welfare programs including a "Food for Life" service that provides over ten thousand meals for people in the Durban area. The Sathya Sai Baba movement is one of the new groups to emerge on the South African scene. Centering on the person and teachings of Sathya Sai Baba (1926–), devotees gather regularly in over fifty-one centers to study his message, sing songs of praise, and engage in worship. Within the movement, Sathya Sai Baba is venerated as an incarnation (avatara) of God.

Conclusions

Although the traditions of Hinduism have been transported outside the borders of India since ancient times, particularly to South and Southeast Asia, the contemporary establishment of Hinduism outside of India is without historical precedent. The construction of a temple is a traditional and orthodox expression of Hindu faith, and temples have become the most visible signs of the contemporary establishment of Hinduism in the diaspora. They are usually read as signs of religious vitality and growth. In the case of the Hindu tradition, it must be remembered that the community, particularly in North America, is of recent origin, and almost all of these temples are constructed by immigrants who were born in India and who still retain strong family, linguistic, and cultural ties with the subcontinent. The future of Hinduism, however, will be determined by the descendants of these immigrants. The outward focus on temple construction often conceals the serious challenges faced by the Hindu tradition as it seeks to establish new roots and to ensure its transmission in a new context. The future of Hinduism in the West will depend upon and will be shaped by the ways in which it deals with the exigencies of its circumstances that are historically unique.

Historically, Hinduism has embraced both religion and culture, and the disentanglement of one from the other is quite difficult. It is significant that there is no Sanskrit equivalent for the word *religion,* and the term *dharma,* sometimes equated with religion, is far more inclusive. The detachment of religion and culture, however, is rapidly becoming a reality in the experience of a new generation of Hindus born in the Western world. The unity of religion and culture is being severed, and the traditionally pervasive influence of Hinduism is relegated to fewer areas of life. How will the Hindu tradition develop and thrive in a context in which it does not exert a pervasive cultural influence? What forms will it assume, and what would it mean to be a Hindu? Will it be limited to ritualistic practices in the home and temple? What will be its public character, if any? What will constitute the essential components of Hindu self-identity?

Though the number of Hindus in North America, for example, has been increasing, Hindus still constitute a small percentage of the total population of the United States and Canada. The preservation and transmission of religious values become increasingly difficult when these have to be done in a context where the norms of the dominant culture are different and, in some instances, in conflict with Hindu ideals. Although Hinduism has had the experience of living under alien political dominance for many centuries, it was never required before to cope with the challenges of being a minority in a non-Hindu-dominant context. Minorities wrestle, more than others, with issues of identity and carry a greater burden of self-explanation. The children of minorities often find themselves wanting the acceptance and approval of the majority community, and for this reason may be more willing to accept the values of this community, even when they contradict their own. Many Western societies still know very little about Hinduism, and many of the predominant images are negative.

The unity of religion and culture in India obviated the need for special agencies for the transmission of the Hindu tradition. It was correctly assumed that a child would receive the necessary religious exposure by the mere fact of growing up in a particular community. The conditions of life in modern Western societies, however, invalidate such an assumption. In a secular society of competing cultural and religious choices, the future of Hinduism can no longer be guaranteed by the fact of birth. The fact of birth will not be a sufficient reason for being a Hindu, and for the first time, increasing numbers of Hindus will be Hindus by choice and will have to be re-converted or converted to Hinduism. They will choose Hinduism from a variety of options available. Hinduism in the next millennium will be challenged to define itself with precision in relation to a variety of competing choices. Appeals on the basis of antiquity and the authority of tradition may not be very persuasive. Its challenges today are quite different from the Buddhist and Jain refutation of Vedic authority and a personal deity, and its responses will have to be appropriate. Its primary rivals today are those alternative worldviews that deny a transcendent character to human existence and those value systems that glorify greed and the economic systems based on it. Hinduism will not have a future in the diaspora unless it offers convincing arguments that demonstrate its ability to satisfy the universal human need for fulfillment in ways that are not ephemeral and that are both individually and communally meaningful.

Successful strategies and agencies will have to be developed to ensure transmission from one generation to another. The evolution of such methods may prove quite challenging, for a number of reasons, to the Hindu tradition. Doctrinal issues have been debated vigorously by Hindu philosophers and teachers throughout the ages, but it is accurate to say that in the transmission of the tradition, the emphasis historically has been on orthopraxis. In the Western world, influenced heavily by the Christian stress on orthodoxy, Hindus are increasingly challenged to articulate and transmit their tradition in a manner that places more emphasis on its doctrinal content and stance. Hinduism will be challenged into a more explicit and self-conscious reflection and articulation of its worldview. There is a rich tradition of intellectual debate and discussion in Hinduism and a concern for doctrinal clarity and definition evinced in the commentaries of theologians such as Shankara and Ramanuja. The recovery of this often-neglected tradition will serve Hinduism well in its advent into the future.

There may be many positive features in such a challenge and the response it elicits, but it is one for which history has left the Hindu tradition unprepared. The decentralization and lack of organization that have characterized Hinduism and that may be explicable in its Indian context may not be assets in its current reality. Still to be developed in the diaspora are credible theological institutions that offer a contextual education for Western-born Hindu teachers. Priests and teachers who serve in temples and who teach in communities are still imported, but they often lack sympathetic understanding of the conditions of life in the West and are unable to help Hindus, especially young men and women, interpret their tradition in a relevant way to their particular circumstances. The absence of such teachers drawn from local communities reinforces the division that exists between monks and laypersons. It also deprives the community of a potential body of committed teachers who have a background in the intellectual disciplines and critical methods of the West and who can bring these to bear creatively in their reflection on the Hindu tradition. The recruitment, training, and renewal of such teachers will be vital for the survival and growth of the Hindu tradition. Hindu communities and parents will have to encourage and support young men and women who evince interest and aptitude for the study and teaching of religion.

Hindu immigrants in North America are an extremely diverse group and reflect the regional, linguistic, and cultural diversity of the Indian subcontinent. Most of them are still fluent in their native languages, such as Gujarati, Bengali, Tamil, Telugu, and Marathi. In almost every major city one will find organizations representing particular linguistic and cultural interests. There are temples that have been built by specific communities and that, in ritual and worship, reflect the uniqueness of a particular region. Yet, in the United States and Canada, Hindus from a variety of cultural backgrounds coexist religiously in an unprecedented manner. They face the challenge of confronting their own differences along with the demands of life in the West, and the results may be significant for the future shape and evolution of the tradition.

Being a numerical minority with limited resources and distance from India geographically and temporally, combined with a new generation with tenuous ties to India linguistically and culturally, would seem to minimize the significance of previously important differences and lead to the search for commonness in belief and worship practices. The beliefs and practices that survive will address, in a more universal manner, the human condition; those that are inseparable from specific historical contexts will be left behind. Identifying and articulating the more relevant elements of the Hindu worldview should extend the appeal of Hinduism across the frontiers of ethnicity. Hinduism has the potential to become a significant choice for increasing numbers who do not have ancestral roots in the Indian subcontinent.

I do not predict or wish for the attenuation of the rich diversity of the Hindu tradition. There is an orientation in Hinduism to gloss over differences without reflecting on their significance, and this new historical context offers a valuable opportunity for considering these differences and searching for commonness. The future of Hinduism in the diaspora will be determined also by the way in which Hindus confront internal realities. I remember, for example, a recent meeting of Hindu scholars when many in the audience gasped audibly at the suggestion that English may replace Sanskrit as the liturgical language of Hinduism. The reaction was one of astonishment at the very thought of this possibility. Sanskrit is the language of divinity, and the success and meaningfulness of Vedic rituals depend upon the right intonation of words, or so many believe. The nature of such claims will be reevaluated by a new generation for whom the languages of India will only be a part of ancestral history.

The problems are admittedly complex and challenging, but there are promising signs of innovation and resilience in the diaspora. Many new temples in the West still have a regional character and following, but there are increasing numbers of new temples that serve the needs of Hindus of diverse regional and linguistic backgrounds and bring together Hindus from the Indian subcontinent and those from parts of the Caribbean and Africa. They share a common rootedness in the traditions of Hinduism, and this may eventually override the particularities of language and geography as these recede in the memory of a new generation. Temple architecture is already reflecting the need and emphasis on those forms of Hindu worship that have a more communal and collective character, and worship services now usually occur in large halls facing an altar on which images of the major Hindu deities are located. Most temples have regularly scheduled worship services, many on Sunday mornings, in which a communal worship service consisting of congregational singing, ritual, and a lecture are essential ingredients. It is clear that we will continue to see an emphasis on the more congregational forms of Hindu worship and the development of temple forms that will adapt to new community needs.

Lay participation in the management and liturgical life of Hindu temples is on the increase. The Hindu Society of Minnesota in the United States has managed a Hindu temple for almost two decades without a trained ritual specialist. There are always expressions of surprise when new visitors from India learn that they can enter the sanctum of the temple and make their own worshipful offerings. The lecture that is central to the Sunday satsanga is followed by an often lively exchange between the audience and the speaker. Annual Hindu camps for boys and girls have become a regular feature in many communities. These are usually run by lay people and offer an intensive exposure to basic elements of Hindu practice and belief.

Many traditional features of Hindu life and culture are undergoing rapid change in the diaspora. The significance of caste is being minimalized, as is the system of dowry. Children are also more actively involved in the selection of marriage partners. One of the fascinating developments of Hinduism in the future will be the ways in which developments in the diaspora influence the character or the Hindu tradition in the home country. The ease and frequency of travel and communications enhance the possibility of such influence. Diaspora Hindu communities will not merely be the recipients of developments and changes in India, but will become the sources and catalysts of innovation in India.

If the Hindu tradition responds creatively and resourcefully to the special challenges of existence in the Western world, it should emerge with a clearer sense of the distinctive elements of its own worldview; a better perspective on what the essential elements of that view are, and what its accidental features are; the ability to articulate its vision in terms that are relevant to the Western human context; and a readiness to engage in continuous self-critical reflection. A leaner Hindu tradition will be a more vigorous and enthusiastic partner with other religions in the common human quest for justice and peace.

BIBLIOGRAPHY

Baumann, Martin B. "The Hindu Presence in Europe and Implications for Interfaith Dialogue." *Hindu-Christian Studies Bulletin* 11 (1998): 25–30.

Coward, Harold. "Hinduism in Canada," in Harold Coward, John R. Hinnels, and Raymond Brady Williams (eds.), *The South Asian Religious Diaspora in Britain, Canada, and the United States.* Albany: State University of New York Press, 2000: 151–172.

Coward, Harold, and Heather Botting. "The Hindu Diaspora in Western Canada," in T. S. Rukmani (ed.), *Hindu Diaspora in Global Perspectives.* Delhi: Munshiram Manoharlal, 2001: 35–59.

Coward, Harold, John R. Hinnels, and Raymond Brady Williams, eds. *The South Asian Religious Diaspora in Britain, Canada, and the United States.* Albany: State University of New York Press, 2000.

Eck, Diana. *Encountering God: A Spiritual Journey from Bozeman to Banaras.* Boston: Beacon Press, 1993.

———. "Negotiating Hindu Identities in America," in Harold Coward, John R. Hinnels, and Raymond Brady Williams (eds.), *The South Asian Religious Diaspora in Britain, Canada, and the United States.* Albany: State University of New York Press, 2000.

———. *A New Religious America.* New York: HarperCollins, 2001.

Klass, M. *East Indians in Trinidad.* New York: Columbia University Press, 1961.

Knott, Kim. "Hinduism in Britain," in Harold Coward, John R. Hinnels, and Raymond Brady Williams (eds.), *The South Asian Religious Diaspora in Britain, Canada, and the United States.* Albany: State University of New York Press, 2000: 89–108.

La Guerre, John, ed. *Calcutta to Caroni: The East Indians of Trinidad.* St. Augustine: University of the West Indies, 1974.

Mann, Gurinder Singh, Paul David Numrich, and Raymond B. Williams, eds. *Buddhists, Hindus, and Sikhs in America.* New York: Oxford University Press, 2001.

Narayanan, Vasudha. "Creating the South Indian 'Hindu' Experience in the United States," in Raymond Brady Williams (ed.), *A Sacred Thread:*

Modern Transmission of Hindu Traditions in India and Abroad.
    Chambersburg: Anima Publications, 1992.
Paramahansa Yogananda. *Autobiography of a Yogi.* Los Angeles: Self
    Realization Fellowship, 1990.
Vertovec, Steven. *Hindu Trinidad: Religion, Ethnicity, and Socio-Economic
    Change.* Basingstoke: Macmillan, 1992.
————. *The Hindu Diaspora.* London: Routledge, 2000.
Williams, Raymond B. *An Introduction to Swaminarayan Hinduism.* New
    York: Cambridge University Press, 2001.
http://www.pluralism.org/directory/. Accessed March 1, 2003.

List of Contributors

William Harman is Professor of Religion at the University of Tennessee at Chattanooga.

Brian A. Hatcher is Professor of Religion at Illinois Wesleyan University.

George James is Associate Professor of Religion Studies at the University of North Texas.

Kalpana Kannabiran is Professor of Sociology, National Academy of Legal Studies and Research, University of Law, Hyderabad, and Founding Member, Asmita Resource Centre for Women, Secunderabad, India.

J. E. Llewellyn is Professor of Religious Studies at Southwest Missouri State University.

S. S. Rama Rao Pappu is Professor of Philosophy at Miami University of Ohio.

Anantanand Rambachan is Professor of Religion at St. Olaf University.

Robin Rinehart is Associate Professor of Religious Studies at Lafayette College.

A. Whitney Sanford is Associate Professor of Religious Studies at Iowa State University.

Robert J. Stephens is a Ph.D. candidate in Religious Studies at the University of Iowa and Instructor in the Department of Religion and Philosophy at the University of Northern Iowa.

Eleanor Zelliot is Professor Emerita of History at Carleton College.

Glossary and Pronunciation Guide

Terms are listed here first without diacritical marks, as they appear in the text. The transliterated form of the word with diacritical marks follows in parentheses and may be used as an aid in pronunciation using the guide below.

Guide to Pronunciation

a = as in butter. Typically not pronounced at the end of a word in most north Indian languages, e.g., Rama is pronounced Ram (rhymes with "Tom").

ā = as in father

ai = as in cat or kite

au = as in cause, or as in cow

c = as in chatter

ch = as in itchy

e = as in mason

g = as in gap

i = as in bitter

ī = as in machine

j = as in jug

o = as in road

ph = as in shepherd

ṛ = as in ripple

śṣ = sh

th = as in pothole (there is no sound in Indian languages equivalent to the **th** in *the*)

u = as in p**u**t

ū = as in r**u**le

v = as in **v**ary or **w**ary

A dot under a letter (*ṭ, ṭh, ḍ, ḍh, ṇ*) indicates a retroflex sound, which is made by placing the tip of the tongue against the roof of the mouth. In English, the letters **t** and **d** generally represent alveolar sounds, which are made by placing the tongue on the alveolar ridge behind the teeth. In Indian languages, these letters generally represent dental sounds, made by placing the tip of the tongue on the upper teeth.

Stress is usually placed on the penultimate (next to last) or antepenultimate (third from last) syllable in a word.

Glossary

Advaita Vedanta (*Advaita Vedānta*). Nondual Vedanta, especially associated with the philosopher Shankara.

Agni (*Agni*). God of fire in the Vedas.

ahimsa (*ahiṃsā*). Noninjury or nonviolence.

Alvar (*Ālvār*). Name given to Tamil Vaishnava saints.

Ambedkar, Dr. Bhim Rao (*Ambeḍkar, Bhīm Rāo*), 1891–1956. Untouchable religious and political leader from Maharashtra; led mass conversion of Untouchables to Buddhism in protest against caste discrimination.

Aranyaka (*Āraṇyaka*). "Forest-book"; texts appended to the Vedic samhitas.

arati (*āratī*). Circular movement of a light before an image of a deity or person as sign of respect or worship.

Arjuna (*Arjuna*). Main character in Bhagavad Gita; expert archer of the Pandava family.

artha (*artha*). Wealth, money; one of the four purusharthas.

Arya Samaj (*Ārya Samāj*). Society founded in 1875 by Swami Dayanand Saraswati with emphasis on the Vedas.

Aryan (*Āryan*). Pure or noble; term used by those who preserved Vedic tradition.

ashrama (*āśrama*). 1. stage in life. 2. hermitage, communal living space for practitioners of yoga.

Athavale, Pandurang Shastri, (*Āṭhavale, Pāṇḍuraṅg Śāstrī*), 1920–2003. Founder of the *Swadhyaya* Movement.

atman (*ātman*). Eternal spirit; soul, self.

avatara (*avatāra*). Incarnation of a deity.

Bhagavad Gita (*Bhagavad Gītā*). "Song of the Lord"; dialogue between Krishna and Arjuna in the Mahabharata.

bhajan (*bhajan*). Devotional song.

bhakti (*bhakti*). Devotion.

Bharata (*Bharata*). Character in the Ramayana; half-brother of Rama.

Brahma (*Brahmā*). God who is said to create the universe at the beginning of each cycle of the yugas.

brahman (*brahman*). The eternal, imperishable force underlying all reality.

Brahmin (*Brāhmaṇ*). The first of the four varnas.

Brahmo Samaj (*Brāhmo Samāj*). Organization founded in Calcutta by Rammohan Roy with emphasis on the Upanishads.

Congress, Congress Party. Organization founded in 1875; active in Indian nationalist movement; first ruling party of independent India.

dalit (*dalit*). "Oppressed"; term used for members of former Untouchable castes.

darshana (*darśana*). Sight, auspicious sight. Seeing and being seen by a deity or holy person.

Dasharatha (*Daśaratha*). Character in Ramayana; father of Rama.

Dashahara (*Daśaharā*). Festival celebrating defeat of the demon Ravana.

devadasi (*devadāsī*). Girl or woman dedicated to a temple.

dharma (*dharma*). Duty, religion, ethics, morality, etc.

Divali (*Divālī*). Festival of lights, also known as Dipavali (*Dīpāvalī*).

Dravidian. South Indian language family (Tamil, Telugu, Kannada, and Malayalam).

Durga *(Durgā)*. Goddess especially known for slaying demons.

Dvaita Vedanta *(Dvaita Vedānta)*. Dual Vedanta, associated with the philosopher Madhva.

Gandhi, Mohandas Karamchand *(Gāndhi, Mohandās Karamcand)*, 1869–1948. Important leader of Indian nationalist movement; developed philosophy of nonviolent resistance. Also known by the title "Mahatma" *(mahātma)*, or "great soul."

Ganesha *(Gaṇeśa)*. Hindu god with elephant head; known as an overcomer of obstacles.

gramadevam *(grāmadevam)*. Village deity.

guru *(guru)*. Teacher, spiritual preceptor.

Hanuman *(Hanumān)*. Monkey-god who assisted Rama in his battle against the demon Ravana.

harijan *(harijan)*. "People of god"; term Gandhi used to refer to Untouchables.

Hazare, Anna, 1940– . Maharashtrian villager who started the Swaraj Movement.

Hindutva *(Hindūtva)*. "Hindu-ness"; term coined by V. D. Savarkar.

Holi *(Holī)*. Festival in which colored water and powder are thrown.

Indology. Term used for study of Indian culture focusing on classical Sanskrit texts.

Indra *(Indra)*. Vedic god associated with thunder.

ishtadeva/ishtadevam *(iṣṭadevam)*. Chosen deity.

Jainism. Religion established in sixth century BCE India; especially associated with nonviolence.

jati *(jāti)*. Caste, subcaste.

jnana *(jñāna)*. Knowledge.

Kabir *(Kabīr)*. Fifteenth-century nirguna poet-saint.

Kaikeyi *(Kaikeyī)*. Character in Ramayana; Bharata's mother.

Kali *(Kālī)*. Fierce goddess known for slaying demons.

kama *(kāma)*. Desire, sensuality, lust; one of the four purusharthas.

Kama *(Kāma)*. God associated with love and desire.

karma *(karma)*. Act or action; acquired results of actions.

katha *(kathā)*. Story.

Kausalya *(Kausalyā)*. Character in Ramayana; Rama's mother.

Krishna *(Kṛṣṇa)*. Major Hindu god; incarnation of Vishnu, main character in Bhagavad Gita.

Kshatriya *(Kṣatriya)*. Second of the four varnas.

kuladeva/kuladevam *(kuladeva/kuladevam)*. Deity associated with a particular clan or lineage.

Lakshmana *(Lakṣmaṇa)*. Character in Ramayana; Rama's younger brother.

Lakshmi *(Lakṣmī)*. Goddess of wealth, spouse of Vishnu.

Laws of Manu *(Mānavadharmaśāstra, Manusmṛti)*. Important dharma text.

lila *(līlā)*. "Play"; theological term used for actions of gods.

linga *(liṅga)*. Column representing the god Shiva.

Mahabharata *(Mahābhārata)*. Major Hindu epic that includes the Bhagavad Gita.

mantra *(mantra)*. Phrase or formula, efficacious incantation.

moksha *(mokṣa)*. Release or liberation from samsara; also known as *mukti*.

naga *(nāga)*. Snake or serpent deity.

Nayanmar *(Nāyaṉmār)*. Name given to Tamil Shaiva saints.

Nehru, Jawaharlal *(Jawāharlāl Nehru)*, 1889–1964. First prime minister of India.

neo-Vedanta. Form of Vedanta developed by nineteenth-century thinkers such as Rammohan Roy.

nirguna *(nirguṇa)*. "Without qualities"; term for bhakti poets who believed greatness of God was beyond description.

Orientalism. Scholarship on Asia or the Orient, especially Western scholarship that exoticizes the Orient.

pandit *(paṇḍit)*. Scholar, learned person, pundit.

parda *(pardā)*. Practice of keeping women veiled and/or secluded, sometimes spelled *purdah*.

Parvati *(Pārvatī)*. Wife of Shiva.

pativrata *(pativratā)*. Faithful wife.

Practical Vedanta. Form of Vedanta developed in nineteenth century by Swami Vivekananda, advocating social reform.

prasada/prasadam *(prasāda/prasādam)*. Remnants of food that has been offered to a deity.

puja *(pūjā)*. Ritual worship.

Puranas *(Purāṇas)*. Sanskrit texts explicating mythology and other topics.

purushartha *(puruṣārtha)*. Human aims, of which there are traditionally four: artha, dharma, kama, and moksha.

Rama *(Rāma)*. Main character in the Ramayana.

Rama Raja *(Rāma Rāja)*. "Rule of Rama"; style of government advocated by some Hindu fundamentalists.

Ramajanmabhumi *(Rāmajanmabhūmi)*. Birthplace of Rama in Ayodhya.

Ramasami, E. V., 1873–1973. Founder of the Self-Respect Movement in south India.

Ramayana *(Rāmāyaṇa)*. Major Hindu epic attributed to the sage Valmiki.

Ramcharitmanas *(Rāmacaritamānas)*. "Lake of the acts of Rama"; Hindi telling of the Rama story composed by Tulsidasa.

Rammohan Roy *(Rāmmohan Rāy)*, c. 1774–1833. Founder of the Brahmo Samaj, often called the "father of modern India."

ras lila *(rās līlā)*. Drama depicting Krishna's dance with the cowherd girls of Vrindavan.

Rashtriya Swayamsevak Sangh *(Rāṣṭrīya Svayaṃsevak Sangha)*. "National Volunteer Organization"; paramilitary-style group founded in 1925.

Ravana *(Rāvaṇa)*. Character in the Ramayana; demon who kidnaps Sita.

rishi *(ṛṣi)*. Sage or poet; used especially for men understood to be those to whom the Vedas were revealed.

rita *(ṛta)*. Term used in Vedas for order, law, rule.

sadachara *(sadācāra)*. Virtuous conduct; standards established by virtuous persons.

sadharana dharma *(sādhāraṇa dharma)*. Duty encumbent upon all persons regardless of caste, sex, etc.

sadhu *(sādhu)*. Good, noble; term used for renouncers.

saguna *(saguṇa)*. "With qualities"; used for bhakti poets who believed attributes of God can be described.

samadhi *(samādhi)*. State of intense absorption or meditation; also sometimes used for tombs of renouncers.

samhita *(saṃhitā)*. Collection; used especially for the hymns of the Rig, Yajur, Sama, and Atharva Vedas.

sampradaya *(sampradāya)*. Community or sect.

samsara *(saṃsāra)*. Cycle of death and rebirth regulated by karma.

samskara *(saṃskāra)*. Life-cycle rite such as initiation, marriage.

sanatana dharma *(sanātana dharma)*. The eternal dharma; sometimes used as name of Hindu religion.

Sangha Parivara *(Sangha Parivāra)*. "Family of Organizations"; used for groups that promote values of Hindutva.

sannyasi *(sannyāsī)*. Renouncer, ascetic.

Sanskrit *(Saṃskṛta)*. "Perfected"; Indo-European language of many important Hindu texts.

Sarasvati *(Sarasvatī)*. Goddess of learning, music. Also name of a mythical river.

sat *(sat)*. Being, truth.

Sathya Sai Baba *(Satya Sāī Bābā)*, 1926– . Famous Indian saint renowned for ability to perform miracles.

sati *(satī)*. Good or virtuous woman; name for a wife who immolates herself on the funeral pyre of her husband; used for such practice; sometimes spelled *suttee*.

Sati *(Satī)*. Goddess who married Shiva after performing austerities.

satsanga *(satsaṅga)*. "Company of the good"; religious meetings or services.

satyagraha *(satyāgraha)*. "Grasping the truth"; Gandhi's strategy of nonviolent resistance.

Scheduled Castes. Term used in Constitution of India to designate castes of low/formerly Untouchable status.

Self-Respect Movement. Movement founded in 1925 by E. V. Ramasami emphasizing Dravidian culture over Brahminical traditions of north India.

seva *(sevā)*. "Service"; form of devotional worship.

Shaiva *(Śaiva)*. Related to Shiva; devotee of Shiva.

Shakta *(Śākta)*. Devotee of the goddess.

shakti *(śakti)*. Female creative energy or power.

Shambuka *(Śambūka)*. Character in Ramayana; Shudra who performed austerities and was killed by Rama.

Shankara *(Śaṅkara)*. Ca. ninth-century Advaita Vedanta philosopher.

Shitla *(Śītlā)*. Goddess of smallpox and pustular diseases.

Shiva *(Śiva)*. God especially associated with yoga and austerities.

Shivaratri *(Śivarātrī)*. Festival honoring the god Shiva.

Shri *(Śrī)*. Goddess of wealth; also known as Lakshmi.

shruti *(śruti)*. "That which is heard"; term used for Vedas.

shuddhi *(śuddhi)*. Purification; ritual used to reconvert Hindus who have converted to another religion.

Shudra *(Śūdra)*. The fourth varna.

siddha *(siddha)*. Perfected; term used for renouncers and practitioners of yoga who have acquired certain powers.

Sikhism. Religion established in sixteenth-century Punjab based on the teachings of ten gurus.

Sita *(Śītā)*. Main character in Ramayana; Rama's wife.

smriti *(smṛti)*. "That which is remembered"; term used for Sanskrit texts such as the epics and Puranas.

soma *(soma)*. Plant used in ritual and revered as a god in the Vedas.

stridharma *(strīdharma)*. The duties of women.

svabhava *(svabhāva)*. Character, nature, disposition.

swadeshi *(svadeśī)*. "Belonging to one's own country"; movement advocating Indian-made goods over foreign-produced goods.

Swadhyaya Movement *(Svādhyaya)*. Movement established by Pandurang Shastri Athavale that teaches that God dwells within everyone.

swami *(svāmī)*. "Master"; title given to renouncers.

Swami Dayanand Saraswati *(Svāmī Dayānanda Sarasvatī)*, 1824–1883. Founder of the Arya Samaj.

Swami Muktananda *(Svāmī Muktānanda)*, 1908–1982. Leader of Siddha Yoga movement.

Swami Prabhupada, A. C. Bhaktivedanta *(Svāmī Prabhupāda, A. C. Bhaktivedānta)*, 1896–1977. Founder of the International Society for Krishna Consciousness (whose followers are popularly known as Hare Krishnas).

Swami Vivekananda *(Svāmī Vivekānanda)*, 1863–1902. Disciple of Ramakrishna; Ramakrishna Mission leader; advocate of Practical Vedanta.

Swaraj Movement *(Svarāj)*. Ecological, economic, and social reform movement founded in Maharashtra by Anna Hazare.

Tagore, Rabindranath *(Ravīndranāth Ṭhakur)*. 1861–1941. Noted Bengali and English poet.

tantra *(tantra)*. Name of class of Sanskrit texts advocating particular ritual practices such as use of mantras and yoga for bodily purification and transformation.

tapas *(tapas)*. Heat; bodily mortification, penance.

Tija *(Tīja)*. Festival commemorating Parvati's departure from her parents' home to Shiva's as his bride.

tithi *(tithi)*. Lunar day.

twice-born *(dvija)*. Term for members of upper three varnas who undergo initiation ritual.

Untouchable. Term for members of castes below the four varnas, considered ritually impure and hence "untouchable" *(aspṛśya)*.

upanayana *(upanayana)*. Ritual of investiture with sacred thread signifying twice-born status.

Upanishad *(Upaniṣad)*. Class of texts appended to Vedas.

Vaishya *(Vaiśya)*. Third of the four varnas.

Valmiki *(Vālmīki)*. Sage to whom the Sanskrit Ramayana is attributed.

Varanasi *(Vārāṇasī)*. City in northern India through which Ganges River flows; important pilgrimage site, especially associated with Shiva. Also known as Benares, Banaras.

varna *(varṇa)*. Form, appearance, color; term designating the four caste groups of Brahmin, Kshatriya, Vaishya, and Shudra.

varnashramadharma *(varṇāśramadharma)*. Duties or rules pertaining to one's stage in life and varna.

Varuna *(Varuṇa)*. Vedic god guarding cosmic order.

Veda *(Veda)*. Knowledge; term applied to the samhitas, or Rig, Sama, Yajur, and Atharva Vedas, as well as the Brahmanas, Aranyakas, and Upanishads.

Vedanta *(Vedānta)*. The end or culmination of the Veda. Indian philosophical school.

vibhuti *(vibhūti)*. Sacred ash; used particularly by renouncers who are devotees of Shiva.

visheshadharma *(viśeṣadharma)*. Duties or rules pertaining to particular varnas and stages in life.

Vishishtadvaita Vedanta *(Viśiṣṭādvaita Vedānta)*. Qualified nondual Vedanta, especially associated with the philosopher Ramanuja.

Vishnu *(Viṣṇu)*. Major Hindu god associated with maintenance of cosmic order.

Vishva Hindu Parishad *(Viśva Hindū Pariṣad)*. "World Hindu Council"; organization seeking to promote and preserve Hindu values.

vrata *(vrata)*. Vow or pledge; religious observances undertaken most commonly by women for family welfare.

yoga *(yoga)*. Spiritual practice or discipline.

yogi *(yogī)*. Practitioner of yoga.

yuga *(yuga)*. Cosmic era (of which there are four in Hindu mythology).

Index